The Japan Christian Year-book Volume 24

THE

CHRISTIAN MOVEMENT

IN

JAPAN, KOREA & FORMOSA

A YEAR-BOOK OF CHRISTIAN WORK

TWENTY-FOURTH ISSUE

Editor:

A. OLTMANS

Associate Editors:

F. W. HECKELMAN   J. W. HASSELL

E. NEWLIN   C. B. OLDS

D. A. MacDONALD (Korea)

Statistician: D. S SPENCER

Published by

THE FEDERATION OF CHRISTIAN MISSIONS IN JAPAN

1926

Printed by

THE JAPAN TIMES & MAIL

Tokyo, Japan

58184
7-9-35

EMMANUEL

THE CHRISTIAN MOVEMENT IN JAPAN, KOREA AND FORMOSA

Is on Sale at the following places:

In Japan,

Kyo Bun Kwan, Ginza, Tokyo.

In Korea,

Christian Literature Society of Korea,

Chong-no, Seoul.

In China,

The Mission Book Company,

18 Peking Road, Shanghai.

In Great Britain,

Kegan Paul, Trench, Trubner & Co., Ltd.,

39 New Oxford Street, London, W.C.1.

In America,

Committee of Reference and Counsel,

25 Madison Avenue, New York City, New York

Price in Japan : Yen 3 00

FOREWORD

In this *twenty-fourth* issue of the "Christian Movement" a serious attempt has been made to take an inventory of the Christian Cause and of the Missionary Status in Japan. To this discussion large contributions have been made by Japanese leaders in the various departments of Christian work. It was thought of special importance to have their well thought-out opinions on these subjects, and these opinions have been given with all frankness and fairness, we believe.

The editorial committee regrets that, for obvious reasons, the material contributed had to be so strictly limited in each case to the amount allotted. This restriction has been disregarded, to a certain extent, in only one case, namely, that of the article contributed by Dr. Axling, and for the reason that it is in the nature of a symposium of Japanese opinions on the subject of *"The Present Place of the Missionary."*

Articles by Japanese contributors in English have been practically left unchanged. Those translated from the original Japanese have no doubt suffered more or less, unavoidably, by the translations.

A. OLTMANS.

N.B.—Except where otherwise indicated, the respective writers of the contributed articles are responsible for the views therein expressed. Editor.

TABLE OF CONTENTS

Title Page
Foreword
Table of Contents

JAPAN

GENERAL SUBJECT
" THE CHRISTIAN MOVEMENT IN JAPAN "

PART I.—THE PAST

PART II.—THE PRESENT

Page

FORMOSA

KOREA

PART I.—FOREIGN MISSION ORGANIZATIONS

JAPAN

PART I

THE PAST

CHAPTER I

REVIEW OF THE YEAR 1925

Rev. F. W. Heckelman, D.D

GENERAL

1. THE YEAR OF THE OX—1925—took precedence to that of the Rat—1924—a prophecy of steady upward movement in the total life of Japan—with the ringing of many Buddhist temple bells—108 times—in the City of Tokyo, a custom which has been observed for thirteen centuries. According to Buddhist teaching, there are 84,000 carnal desires in human nature. These are divided into 108 classes. So the bells are rung that many times to impress on the people that all things mortal are short lived.

In those first days after the earthquake there was an almost childlike, careless optimism. As time went on and affairs did not right themselves this gave way to a despair that at times partakes of sullenness and again approaches perilously close to desperation. On the other hand, there is much talk in this country of the national spirit and the invigoration of national thought. Frequently it comes from men who have not themselves thought what they are saying, who have confused national spirit with the more spectacular and more than its counterfeit or an artificial stimulant which, like a drug, may invigorate for the day but the effect of which is impermanent and ultimately detrimental.

The year did not end in a blaze of glory for the Empire of Japan, but it has brought a gift of great, albeit as yet unrecognized, worth. The field has been ploughed and harrowed and the seed is being sown for a rational conception derived from sound knowledge of Japan's place in the world, of how that place is to be achieved and then, fully as important or more so, of how it is to be retained. There is no just cause for the discouragement so prevalent in this country today. The conception based on fact rather than on fond illusion of the present and future Japan is the conception of a great nation and of one that will endure. The goal is to be attained not by the path of the sword or the caprice of luck; it is to be by earnest, conscientious, back-breaking work, than which there are few more glorious words in the language of any people.

II. THE IMPERIAL FAMILY

The outstanding event of the year was the Silver Wedding Anniversary of the Emperor and Empress, a celebration in which all classes joined in pledging allegiance and expressing affection. However as the illness of the Emperor is of a serious nature he was not able to attend any of the celebrations. This greatly disappointed the people, for. one could hear on all hands profound regrets expressed by a loyal people.

Japan's millions bowed and renewed their pledges of allegiance to the Throne, and there were celebrations everywhere throughout the Island Empire in commemoration of the Silver Wedding Anniversary of the Emperor and Empress. Messages of congratula-
ᴛⁱ ᵗ ⸱⸱ ⸱⸱ᵗ ᴴ ⸱⸱ ⸱ ᵗ⸱⸱ ᵈ ⸱⸱ʳ century

of wedded life together brought sincere expressions of friendship and respect from their friends and the friends of the nation throughout the world.

Thousands and hundreds of thousands of loyal subjects thronged into Tokyo and swarmed the main thoroughfares of the Capital. There was a carnival spirit which prevailed in the city as the ceremonies proceeded. At night there were electrical displays and picturesque lantern processions and bands played and along the tram lines floats appeared. The effect of all this was one of beauty and exotic appeal.

The festivities however brought joy, not only to the Imperial couple, but even to the prisoners whose hard life was made, if possible, brighter for a brief time; moreover many organizations for social service received Imperial gifts; and many loyal servants of the nation, and the aged, were remembered on the happy occasion with gifts and expressions of Imperial confidence and affection. Japan is fortunate in her Imperial family.

Another event significant to the nation was the birth of an Imperial Grand Daughter on December 6th. The reverberations of the guns merged into the sounds of bells and whistles and the shouting of Banzai which rose in the city on the reception of the joyful news. Even in the suburbs and distant places where the boom of the guns had not carried, the word was spread first by the radio and then by shouts of joy.

Early in the year—May—Prince Chichibu,— Second Imperial Son, left for England for two or three years of study. This departure is of great significance for the nation for it means that the nation is facing European civilization and progress fearlessly; and, too, contact with a civilization that has been so powerfully affected by Christianity, cannot help but influence for good the young life of Japan, which is so enthusiastic over the Prince, and for them he is a real hero; for they feel that he will voice the modern national leaders of present Japan.

In September Prince George of England visited Japan, thus offering additional occasion to cement the vital friendship between England and Japan. By visiting Japan and obtaining first hand impressions of a nation and people, friendship of major importance to both countries, and to the world will result.

The world tour of Prince and Princess Asaka is also of national significance. The sister of the Emperor and her husband won the praise of the American press for their democratic bearing. During their stay abroad, especially in America, they retained virtually none of their Court majesty, mixing democratically with all the people with whom they came in contact. In New York the Prince made four public addresses. This is all of significance for the new Japan.

III. The Government

The three outstanding problems of the Government under the leadership of Premier Kato, were, first, the House of Peers Issue; second, Manhood Suffrage; third, Public Finance Readjustment. All three problems created turbulent times for the government, and undoubtedly were the cause of undermining the health of the Premier, and perhaps had much to do with his untimely death. In announcing their policies for the year, especially as related to the above problems, both Premier Kato and Foreign Minister Shidehara spoke with moderation, and thus indicated their fitness as national leaders at a time of national perplexity. For, in addition to the three problems spoken of above, there was still the military group to be reckoned with, a group that seemed to think that the immigration question had raised a problem which could be settled only by some day resorting to arms. Undoubtedly Foreign Minister Shidehara had the in_____ ____ __ ____ ____ ____ said to his count_____ ____ ____ ____ ____ ____ powerful in strength, however rich in resources, can have its own way in the council of nations. History shows that all attempts made by any Power, in reliance upon strength and resources, to force its will upon the rest of the world, are doomed to grievous failure. The true and lasting interests of a nation can be secured only when they are in keeping with the rightful positions of other nations on a fair and equitable basis."

Baron Shidehara, unlike many of his countryman, really knows the American people. He knows them as neither angels nor devils, but as a people fundamentally moral and just, qualities which must inevitably guide their governmental policy over a period of time. He cherishes no illusions of a sudden repeal of the immigration law nor of executive interference with a legislative function, and tells his countrymen bluntly, frankly and, in truth, kindly, that the sole solution of the question lies in permitting these qualities to assert themselves in the United States, that "impetuous moods or impassioned utterances" are harmful to Japan.

THE HOUSE OF PEERS PROBLEM

At present its members number: Imperial Princes, 16; Princes and Marquises, 45; Counts, 20; Viscounts, 73; Barons, 73; members appointed by the Emperor 120; members elected from among the highest taxpayers, 47. The ordinance restricts the number of representatives of counts, viscounts and barons that it shall not surpass one-fifth of each rank, and the combined number of members nominated by the Emperor, both because of their merit and richness, can not surpass the combined number of all Peer members.

The natural result of this ordinance is that in the Upper House peers predominate, and that, owing to special electing methods allied small groups may wield i   that

own rank, which will naturally give the effect of a
real political party or faction with organization and
leaders. No fundamental change has been proposed
to this system since its proclamation except as regards
the increasing numbers of peers members on account
of the creation of new peers, especially after great
wars, and on several other occasions.

The Upper House is endowed with power almost
equal, or rather somewhat superior, to that of the
Lower House. In the first place, the Upper House
may revive any item in the Government's financial
budget which has been rejected or omitted by the
Lower House, albeit the Lower House has the right
to debate the budget first. In the second place, the
Ordinance which fixes the constitution of the Upper
House can be amended only with the consent of the
Upper House itself, while the amendments of the
organization of the Lower House are subject to the
discussion of both Houses. Undoubtedly such a system presented serious aspects for a growingly democratic country. The cry for Manhood Suffrage ac-
centuated it. Hence it was to be expected that even
some of the Peers should get their eyes opened. Here
is the opinion of one: Marquis Yoshichika Tokugawa:
"The reformation of the Upper House is one of the
most urgent problems at present. The nobles should
awaken from their long and idle slumber to set the
State on an adamant foundation. The people must
demand reform by the force of public opinion, hence
it is foolish to wait for the Upper House to reform
itself. As a practical plan I propose that both peers
and peeresses be eligible to election and be given the
franchise; the addition of members elected from
bodies from different trades; no annual allowance to
the members." · (

The task of the Kato Ministry, was made very
difficult not only by the attacks of the Peers, but also
by such public critics as Dr. Washio, who charged
the ministry without conviction, because of a "false

and desperate ally, the Seiyukai." At the height of
the fight against the Kato Ministry, Premier Kato
died.

Undoubtedly the Kato Ministry must be regarded
as one having accomplished much through, first,
giving public expression to the national feeling concerning an exclusive, and therefore out-of-date, arm
of the government; second, saving the nation from
economic disaster through 'luxury tariff" legislation,
and the encouragement of home industries; and, third,
through the universal manhood suffrage act.

INTERNATIONAL RELATIONS

I. JAPAN AND AMERICA

The outstanding problems of the year between
Japan and America centered around *the immigration
question; the problem of militarism;* and supposed
Anglo-Saxon Dominance. Perhaps the problem of dual
citizenship should also be included.

Without doubt the immigration law aggravated
all the problems of a vexing nature between the two
countries. And though there have been two voices
speaking, the general feeling seems to be that Japan
has been cut to the heart, and that there is a general
anti-American feeling throughout the country.

The visit of the American Squadron to Pacific
Waters was made the occasion of considerable outcry
by military propagandists, and the feelings of the
people were disturbed for some time.

However the general impression left upon one's mind
after a review of the situation during 1925 is distinctly
encouraging. At no time have so many prominent
and thoughtful men played important parts in Japanese-American relations. Zumoto told Americans that
her Diplomacy was unreliable; and writers like
Sawada Ken speak of America's Imperialism; and
Dr. K.

others speak of Anglo-Saxon dominance in Asia; but,
the more thoughtful men realize and speak of the
good part America is bound to play in the Pacific.
Count Soyejima returned from America enthusiastic
in his praise of the cordial spirit of the American
people; Mr. Y. Tsurumi, after a notable hearing in
America, says the United States is most friendly;
Mochizuki, though he fears the Powers will smother
Japan, insists Japan wishes only Peace in the Pacific.
It is true that some think Japanese control of Hawaii
will take place within ten years, as was voiced by
the *New York Tribune* and the *Washington Post.*
Nevertheless others give voice to the feeling that Japan
and America are *Brothers in Trust,* and no voices
have been more powerful in this sentiment than our
late Ambassador Bancroft and the most capable and
real representative of Japan, Matsudaira, Ambassador
of Japan to the United States.

The Pan-Pacific Conference too gave voice to a
saner expression of the common problems and their
solution. It is significant too that responsible leaders,
like Rear-Admiral Phelps and Ambassador Matsudaira,
speak out frankly about the impossibility of a conflict of arms between the two nations; and Lindsay
Russell's fourteen reasons why such a conflict is impossible would seem to be convincing to fair minds.
Whatever grounds there may be for suspicion, Japan
has perhaps more right to fear "the White Peril"
than America the "Yellow Peril," as was shown by
Bishop Welch. Perhaps T. Kagawa, Japan's great
Christian social worker, was right when he said that
America "utterly fails to understand Japan," for, he
says "not a single newspaper reports Japanese affairs
in a friendly spirit"; but the same must be said of
the Japanese press as touching American affairs.

Mr. Y. Tsurumi stated the case very well in speaking of *"the mysterious Oriental Mind"* by saying,
"J   does her
m   conclusion, namely

that what is needed is a mutual friendly approach and attempt at understanding.

Without question at the center of our relations is the Immigration Act. The question as Japan sees it is: will the United States in her dealing with Asia and Asiatics continue to make the Golden Rule her standard of action, as she has done in the past, and as she is doing with Europeans? The Japanese people insist that a great injustice has been done them in American discrimination on account of race. They say they could not complain if they had been put on a quota basis as have been European peoples. On both sides of the ocean the feeling seems to be however that a modification need not be looked for very soon; and gradually the feeling is growing in Japan that after all America has a real problem in trying to amalgamate widely different racial groups, and that perhaps immigration restriction was inevitable. It is realized too that while a persistent effort is being made, especially by the Christian forces of America, to modify the immigration law, that in Canada a strong exclusion movement is developing.

But, after all, the real feeling of the two nations is voiced in three important words, the first, from Foreign Minister, Shidehara: "There is no doubt that the same love of Justice that kindled American independence still continues to inspire the minds of the American people. The day will come when this fact will be fully demonstrated." The second word is from President Coolidge, which set forth eloquently America's national ideal: "America seeks no early empire built on blood and force. No ambition, no temptation lures her to the thought of foreign dominions. The legions she sends forth are armed not with the sword but with the cross." And we add a third word, almost the last word of Ambassador Bancroft: "My message to you and to all friends of Japan and America is: Have faith in Japan; have faith in the United States · · · · · · · · · · · · · · · · ·

them and trust them by their records. Judge and
trust each other by its fifty years of unbroken friendship and helpfulness."

II. JAPAN AND RUSSIA

The relations of Japan and Russia have been
necessarily formative. It has been a year of tension,
and some developments seem to portend future trouble.

The treaty between Russia and Japan excited wide
spread interest, especially in America. There are
two distinct phases of Russo-Japanese relations: the
economic and the political.

The economic phase overshadows the political
without doubt, although there may be expected an
outcry from the United States and from other quarters as to the possibility of a political rapprochement
between these two nations that will threaten the existing order.

The political aspect of the situation presents two
important questions. The first is, of course, the one
so greatly and so ignorantly discussed in Japan—
Communistic propaganda. Guarantees against the
spread of such propaganda are included in the agreement, guarantees which Russia may be expected to
observe in the same manner that she observes her
other pledges. But it is not the Communism of Russia
that the world needs to fear; it is the intense and
narrow nationalism of that nation, and against this
there are no guarantees. Through the recognition of
the validity of the Portsmouth treaty, the Soviet has
for the first time acknowledged the continuation of
an agreement made by the old Tsarist regime. Japan
may well consider this a feather in her cap.

The other political question that will receive attention is that of a possible close working together
of Japan and Russia, of the bogey that has been
sounded by some that one Japanese, especially since
the passage of the American Immigration law, of the

bogey of a Russo-Japanese-German combination in the Far East as arrayed against Anglo-Saxon-Japanese co-operation. To believe that Japan is considering such a course is to credit the Foreign Office with a lack of common sense which it in no wise deserves. How could any Power rely on present-day Russia as an ally? How could any Power believe that co-operation with the Soviet, even if absolutely assured, could obtain greater results than co-operation with Great Britain and the United States? Such a prophecy can be discounted without qualms.

Viscount Goto did much to bring about Russo-Japanese relations, for he feels strongly that amity between Japan and Russia is indispensable to the security and peace of the Orient, and the weal of the two contiguous nations.

It seems to be generally felt, as voiced by the *North China Daily News* that while Japan did not give away anything, that Russia did not get much advantage, unless she means to follow her old path of pressure upon Mongolia, Manchuria and China. For though the treaty specifies a cessation of Bolshevist propaganda, E. A. Welsh, in the *Washington Star*, shows that such promises are an illusion, for the virus of Bolshevism has been injected into the thought of nations, and is likely to be followed up.

Voices, pro and con, are heard from different world centers: Moscow professes faith in Japan's moves; Austin, in the *Empire Review*, London, views the treaty as anti-British, and says Japan desires Anglo-Saxon defeat. *The Washington Post* thinks the pact will end the open door policy.

Count Soyejima thinks that the Soviet and not America is the country whose interests conflict with those of Japan, and prophesies war with Russia within ten years. The same idea is voiced by H. K. Norton in a lecture at the University of Chicago. And, Viscount Goto seems to have changed his mind about Russ   the old policy in Mongolia, Manchuria, and China, and seems to think that conflict may come again. Others look forward to a large trade boom, but that this contest has in it the seeds of war, for both nations seem engaged in the titanic struggle to control the richest possessions of North China. Philip Kerby in the *China Press,* and the *Christian Science Monitor,* point out that the economic struggle in Manchuria is likely to develop into a military one. Manchuria is one of the danger spots of the world. It is far more likely that the future of Eastern Asia will be determined on the plains of that vast stretch of territory than on the waters of the Pacific Ocean, which is a fact of paramount interest not only to Japan and to Russia but equally so to those jingoists in the United States and elsewhere who are so fond of preaching about the coming of an American-Japanese war and of "discovering" a secret military alliance between Russia and Japan.

The problem is also aggravated by certain Japanese leaders who openly assert that Siberia and Manchuria are essential to Japan for her surplus population and for larger food supply. Hence Japanese are urged to migrate to these lands. Huge combines are being formed to exploit Siberia and Manchuria. It is therefore a problem fraught with danger.

It should be noted that while the treaty was hailed as a forward step, that Ambassador Kopp was received without demonstration upon his arrival in Tokyo, perhaps somewhat due to a reported interview in which he is reported as saying that the treaty was a mere scrap of paper. Undoubtedly at this writing Japan's faith in Russia is not very deep.

III. JAPAN AND CHINA

Foreign Minister Shidehara's speeches in February would e . . . indicate a . . . t Japanese in . . . attitude toward China, . . . that of some years ago.

The All-Asiatic Association of Japan, for example, has launched a campaign in China urging leading Chinese statesmen, business men and financiers, to form a similar organization in China to discuss problems of the Orient with particular reference to Occidental activities in Asia.

The Japanese Government's proposal for a cultural movement in China, and the appropriation of the Y.120,000,000 which China promised to pay for the return of the Shantung railway and salt concession, would indicate a changed front toward China.

It was to be expected that this gift was not specially welcomed by China, and that Japan's motives would be misunderstood; for China's anti-Japanese feeling having a rather long history will require a gradual change in character.

In fact strong anti-Japan moves were revived in China, perhaps inflamed by Russian propaganda, and boycotts appeared.

Another forward-looking step was Japan's attitude toward the Conference on Extraterritoriality, in which Japan seemed to take a decidedly favorable stand toward China, for, Hioki, Japan's chief delegate, pledged to do all in his power. And, Shidehara's stand as touching China seemed to indicate the announcement of a Monroe Doctrine for China, a new policy.

The Shanghai Folly overshadowed all good intentions for sometime, for it led to riots, strikes, anti-British and anti-Japanese violence. *The Tientsin Outbreak* too, interfered with Japan's relations to China.

Then the ominous military developments among the Chinese groups worried Japan and caused her to dispatch a rather large force into China. This greatly affected the feeling of China, especially the students, and no amount of official explanation in Japan, even by Shidehara, relieved the situation. Immediately Chin   ·   ·   ·   ·   ·   ·

Suspicion of Japan's motives was voiced in America; and Russian opinion warned aginst interference in Chinese affairs.

The attitude of the Powers toward China, in which Japan had a prominent part must be looked upon as fair and promising to China. There seemed to be a strong desire to meet China's wishes regarding extraterritoriality, taxes, and the courts; but China's internal confusion and lack of responsible, capable, leadership greatly hindered and delayed real accomplishments, and China's new day is still in the future.

IV. THE SITUATION IN KOREA

Viscount Saito, Governor General, says Korea likes Japanese rule; and that the ardor for independence has died out, and is replaced by outspoken loyalty to Japan.

On the other hand Hajime Hosoi, formerly in the office of the Government General of Korea, says that practically all Koreans are "red" these days; and, that there is a demand for suffrage, home rule, autonomy in local administration and independence; and, as these have been denied up to the present, that terroristic passions and radical thoughts thrill and encourage the Koreans.

Count Soyeshima would develop the distinctive Korean traits under the suzerainty of Japan, under Korean Home Rule. But, meanwhile, according to Korean and missionary voices Japanese exploitation and expropriation of Korean soil goes on at a rapid pace, spelling complete absorption by Japan.

There is no question but that Korea has prospered materially under the rule of Japan. Evidences of this prosperity are to be seen on every hand in the shape of improved living conditions, increased trade and sounder economic bases. There remains the question of whether this growth in material prosperity is sufficient · l   · .¹.   · .   · · · ·, · ·t for the

loss of independence.   Foreign observers in this country, as nearly disinterested but informed judges as
it is possible to obtain, are divided in their opinions.
Merchants and business men generally believe the
domination of Japan to be a good thing; missionaries
and teachers in the main deplore it.   It is an ethical
question in its essence, and therefore one difficult to
determine.

V.   THE PROBLEM OF ARMAMENTS

Sir Arthur Curtie says, "As a means of solving
the world's problems and removing international dis-
cord, war is a delusion and a lie."

The attitude of America and Japan toward this
problem seems very similar, though the voice calling
for disarmament and good-will seems strongest in
America.

The importance of "a disarmament of hatreds"
via the text-book route, as pointed out by Miss Sharp,
seems to have been an accepted suggestion.

That the race of armament is a futile one is
clearly shown by President Coolidge and by Shidehara,
both of whom hail any movement to check the mad
race of arms.

The bogey of Japan was brought to the fore again
in America by Admiral Fiske, and in Japan men like
General Oi bitterly attack any army reduction.

On the other hand Count Soyejima points out to
his countrymen the fact that armed peace is a prelude
to war.

Meanwhile Japan has a naval program for the
next five years of forty war craft, to cost Y.320,000,000;
and, the air force has had great impetus.   Pybus, a
British writer, says Japan does not dare to disarm;
and Sir Herbert Russell sees Japan getting ready for
another conflict.   On the other hand Japan has finish-
ed her naval scrapping program in good faith.

The visit of the American fleet to Australian waters
created much conflicting comment.   President Coolidge
interpreted the purpose of the cruise as merely a

friendly gesture to Australia; and Secretary Wilbur insisted there was no ulterior motive in naval exer- cises in Hawaiian waters.

The *London Times* carried an article insisting that the maneuvers were propaganda to produce results favorable to the advocates of a larger navy.

Underhill of Massachusetts, and Britten of Illinois, urged that Hawaii be made a second "Heligoland" and "Gibraltar" in the Pacific. Meanwhile the problem of arms has been made more difficult by placing long guns on the Pacific coast; the putting through of a National Defence Day in America, and, the establish- ment of a Naval Base at Singapore by Great Britain. In the wake of these movements, Hector Bywater urges another Disarmament Conference.

THE NATIONAL SITUATION

I. FINANCE: THE BUDGET

In spite of the after-effects of the terrible earth- quake disaster and economic depression, Japan's cre- dit abroad is good. The head of the Bank of Japan, Mr. Ichiki, speaks optimistically of the financial future of the nation. Finance Minister Hamaguchi sees the nation on the road to rehabilitation.

The budget adopted for the year is Y.1,598,235,000, carrying Y.199,833,000 for the Army; Y.239,028,000 for the Navy and Y.123,593,000 for education.

The financial year varied from hopeful optimism, to financial panic, as voiced by Yukio Ozaki. In the middle of the summer, the crash which Ozaki pre- dicted, came in the failure of the Takata Company, which affected leading banks and foreign firms, and other business houses failed.

These crashes were followed by the flotation of large loans abroad: The Daido firm for $15,000,000 in A... T... T... ... ... $15,000,000 in America and England; and, the Ujikawa Hydro-Electric Company for $15,000,000 in America.

The question which confronts the nation is whether this easy money may not greatly menace the nation in the near future; another question is whether the people of Japan have learned the lesson of hard work and thrift; and the danger from over-military expenditures.

II. JAPAN'S ECONOMIC SITUATION

The year began with predictions for a prosperous year by Dr. Dan, Baron Shijo, and by the Director of the Mitsui firm.

Nevertheless Governor Ichiki of the Bank of Japan, pointed out that an adverse trade balance must result, as is shown by the fall of the yen. Others are asking, How can Japan earn her own living, because of the diminishing returns? What will Japan eat with an increasing population and decreasing food? The cry of the farmer especially is an ominous one for Japan, for while much strength is focused upon industry the fate of the farmer seems to be neglected.

Some urge *the frugal life* upon a people whose standard of living is all too low now; and the cost of living shows an increase of 20% over pre-earthquake days.

It is however pointed out that Japan could better her situation at once by a careful use of her abundant labor upon abundant raw material close at hand.

III. THE SOCIAL SITUATION

Japan's social unrest, politically, economically, socially, and in thought, seems to be taken rather seriously by the Government and the press. Various causes are assigned, among them a blind super-patriotism from above; over-militarization; the classing of all as radicals, socialists, or breeders of "dangerous thought" who do not conform to the pattern cut out by conservative national·leaders. There seems to be a strong feeling by careful observers of the social problem, that the factors which underly the prevailing unrest, in town, country, and university, arise largely from the nation's industrialization, and the dependence of the nation upon the army and navy as the bulwark against this unrest, instead of a liberalizing cultural and social movement.

Dr. Fukasaki, in speaking of Japan's deterioration, lays the blame upon four causes: individualism, materialism, naturalism, and mechanicalism.

Dr. Washio says, Japan's family system is gone industrially and politically and is now passing morally. In sizing up Japan today he seems to think that discipline is impossible, the people skeptical, irresponsible, hopeless and licentious.

A crime wave has been sweeping over some parts of the nation, and there is noted moral laxity in business affairs.

On the other hand, an attempt at a Fascisti movement ended in failure; and, though radicalism and "the dangerous thought" movements seem to be gaining ground, there seems to be no immediate fear of national disorder, and confidence can be placed in Japanese stamina.

In the wake of manhood suffrage it is felt by many that the working classes should be given political education.

The traffic in women is considered "a national stain" by Dr. Kanasugi; and the attitude of prominent national leaders would seem to indicate that there has been considerable awakening of conscience upon this national shame.

The Prohibition Movement has had much attention, and here too there seems to be a more serious consideration of a national menace.

A certain type of liberalism having made inroads upon the moral life of the nation, government steps have been taken to control dancing halls, and strict control is exercised over all public gatherings.

It remains to be seen whether the government's appeal to Bushido as the social remedy will win over the moral force of the Christian movement.

IV. LABOR

While 15,000 of the Japanese men and women, who are the laborers and factory workers being created by the industrialization and Westernization of Japan, paraded the streets of the capital singing the Song of Labor and joining with their fellow-workers throughout the world in the celebration of May Day, another group of Japanese who are clinging desperately and fanatically to the customs and culture of pre-Meiji Japan, assembled to form the Toka-kai (Flowers of Yedo Association), the object of which is to perpetuate the spirit of old Yedo, the ancient name of Tokyo, and to oppose the inroads of Western civilization.

Labor has been making a political try; but the proposed proletarian party came to grief at the hands of the government as soon as it was born. This failure led the left wing to purge itself of communism. The influence that has brought this about has come from within labor itself—a significant fact. There seems to be some hope now of a proletarian party under suffrage; but a feeling seems to be coming over labor and capital that they are not necessarily in conflict.

In the meanwhile the trade union movement is growing. The farmers and laborers are more and more working together; and, women's labor unions are being formed.

What influence the Soviet labor visitors had upon Japanese labor cannot be even guessed, for these visitors were so hedged about by the Japanese police that they left in disgust. On the whole the impression of Japanese labor is a
sense,

Unemployment and decreased wage income developed into serious proportions during the year, for the number of unemployed in Tokyo alone ran into thousands, not to speak of similar conditions in outlying cities.

V.   Suffrage

One of the most significant steps ever taken by Japan is the manhood suffrage law, the fruit of 37 years of struggle.

There are many indications now that the very men who have accomplished this are frightened and appalled at which they have done.   The 3,000,000 voters of Japan were a rather definite mass, a group which could be guaged with considerable accuracy, but now there have been added to them some 9,000,000 or 10,000,000 who are a political enigma.   It is small wonder that the men whose business it is to manipulate the popular will to suit their own ends stand aghast.

The changes that are destined to come in the political field are recognized, but there is no authentic interpretation of them.

It would be a serious error, however, to conclude that the franchise is the unfailing panacea for all ills. The ballot is but an instrument, and as it is used wisely or indiscretely the nation will profit or will suffer.   It is capable of doing as great harm as ever was done by militarism, but the vital difference is that it is also capable of doing more good than is possible by military methods.   It is questionable whether Japan is ready for universal manhood suffrage, but the fact is that she now has it.   Of all the comment on the question, the most significant is the recognition of the necessity of training in citizenship for the millions of newly enfranchised men.

VI.   The Radical Control Bill

In this bill the government has undoubtedly committed itself to a measure fraught with future danger.

The folly of police-directed thinking seems not to be appreciated by the leaders who fostered this bill. The prohibition of studying social science, except as allowed by the government, must in the end prove a measure which will breed radicalism and revolt. The Youth of the Nation are charged with socialistic tendencies and as not worthy of confidence and national loyalty. Wild demonstrations against the bill have taken place; but the pent-up wrath of thousands of thoughtful youth is a force to be reckoned with in the future.

VII. Military Training in the Schools

In forcing military training upon youth in the schools, Japan has exposed herself to another dangerous step.

The opponents of universal military training for all school boys from 12 years upward have not done as much for their cause as have the military authorities themselves through their own blunders. The War Office and the Ministry of Education have consistently insisted that the primary purposes of the autocratically imposed measure were to provide physical training and, even more important they assert, "spiritual training," or intensification of loyalty and patriotism.

In the meantime, the deep opposition to the militarization of Japan's school generation is smouldering beneath the surface, where it will continue to grow until it gains strength to break through official restrictions. Exactly what will happen then can not be foreseen. The whole problem is far greater in magnitude than the question of whether or not there is to be military training in the schools of Japan. It is the present and most active phase of the only-continued struggle between feudal and modern ideas, between extreme conservatism and—what? That is up to the conservatives to determine. As they chart their course, so will the reaction come. They are offered the choice of su   to   or to radicalism

VIII.　The Educational Situation

Without doubt Japan's educational system is excellent, and there is a real effort being made by the educational leaders to make it efficient and up-to-date.

There seem to be two main currents of thought as to education: one, as sponsored by Education Minister Okada, which would close the doors of schools as tightly as possible to popular demand, and subject those who are admitted to rigid beaurocratic discipline.

Another ideal would have the gap between the schools and business bridged; and there seems to be a wide-spread feeling among scholars that the utmost freedom should be allowed in educational pursuits.

Mention should be made of the opening of the Municipal University which is specializing in socialogy and general subjects having to do with society.

A gift of Y.4,000,000 by J. D. Rockefeller, Jr., to the Imperial University to assist in the rehabilitation of the library which was destroyed by the great earthquake fire, is a significant gesture from America, and was accepted as the gift of a civilized and friendly people. The bequest of Y.5,000 to the Imperial Academy to encourage physics and astronomy is another significant friendly link. And the establishment of scholarships which will make possible the interchange of students between Japan and America is of the utmost importance in the cultivation of mutual understanding and appreciation.

While ample facilities for higher education are still wanting, strenuous efforts are being made to give the youth of Japan ample training for life and service.

There is great cause for thanksgiving over the rapid recovery in the Tokyo-Yokohama area where really fine schools have replaced those destroyed by the earthquake, Aoyama Gakuin alone spending more than Y.1,000,000 for three magnificent concrete three story buildings.

IX. The Religious Situation

The Christian Movement in Japan, during the year, has made conspicuous progress in a most extended evangelistic campaign; in the complete self-support assumed by the Japan Methodist Church; in the merger of the Kyo Bun Kwan with the Christian Literature Society, which is to issue in a seven story building and increased service on the Ginza; in the expanded building program of the Y.M.C.A.; and the rebuilding of important centers, such as the Misaki Tabernacle.

Of much significance was Dr. Mott's visitation and conference. Dr. Mott mentioned a number of points calling for major emphasis on the part of all who have at heart the ushering in of a better day: "We must all recognize that our best days lie in the future. We must take long and wide views. At all costs a policy of drift must be avoided. The world will never drift into a state of peace and goodwill, nor can the world remain static. We must concentrate on the conquest of five age-long enemies of mankind— ignorance, poverty, disease, strife and sin. Wherever else we fail, we must not leave any stone unturned to capture the youth. Pure and undefiled religion is of supreme importance at such a moment in the life of mankind."

Of significance is the far-reaching campaign of education on doctrines of Buddhism in Japan. At a gathering of 500 leaders, international celebration of Buddha's birthday was advocated, and propagation of Buddhism throughout the world.

Tai Shui, Lord Abbot of Tahn Temple in China, insisted that Buddhism included the Christian religion; that the platform of Buddhism was a world-platform; moreover that the Buddhist program included the salvation of all nations.

The Christian forces were bereft of several prominent leaders, among which were: the Rev. M. Uemura, who

Vice-President of Kwansei Gakuin; and Madam Yajima, internationally known social worker.

An estimate of the situation of the Christian Movement for 1925 leaves upon one the impression that the roots of Christianity have spread out in all directions; that the philosophy of Christianity has gripped the thought; the spirit of Christianity has gripped the heart; and that the faith of Japanese Christians is rooted in a true loyalty to the Person of Christ; moreover that this faith and loyalty will issue in rapid self-propagation, and in complete self-support at an early date. The leadership of the church has passed from the hands of the missionary to capable Japanese Christian leadership.

CHAPTER II

THE PLACE OF THE MISSIONARY
IN THE BEGINNING

Rev. Otis Cary, D.D.

Pioneer missionaries, if they are to be successful, must be opportunists. Though they may set out with theories about the way in which their work ought to be conducted, they find that in practice they must be largely governed by conditions of which they had little previous knowledge; conditions that may, as was the case in Japan, be rapidly changing. Well will it be for them if they are quick to understand their new environment and skilful in using to the best advantage whatever opportunities open before them.

The place that the individual missionary can occupy does not, however, depend solely on what he finds in his new field of labor, but in large part on what he himself brings thither in his own character and talents. The cause of missions in Japan was very fortunate (if that is the right word to use) in its early representatives. If we look over the list of those that in the first fifteen or twenty years after the opening of the country came to it as heralds of the Gospel, we cannot fail to recognize that a large proportion of them were men of unusual ability, possessed of qualities such as enabled them to set high standards for us who came later, even though as time went on we, as did they, modified some of their methods as changing conditions made advisable.

In

had to take was evident. For a while they were
watchful waiters. It was plainly seen that considerable time must elapse ere there could be the public
proclamation of a religion whose very name was hated.
Though they may "also serve who wait," mere waiting
is a trying experience for earnest men; but the first
missionaries were saved from some of its irksomeness
because from the very beginning a way of approach
to those whom they wished to reach lay before them.
Perhaps they would have held back if, before leaving
their native land, they had been invited to go to
Japan as teachers of English and told that they were
to open before men the old blue-covered Webster's
Spelling-book (strangely resurrected to new usefulness in Japan) instead of the Holy Scriptures; but
it soon became evident that the position of English
teacher was the first place for the missionary to take
and that in it he could really become a pedagogue
to lead men to Christ. We can now see a great
advantage that there was in this. Unlike what has
been true with missionaries in most countries, the
first close associations here were with men of the
educated classes, some of whom afterwards held influential official positions in which they showed favors
to their former teachers, while others became Christian ministers. Even before the coming of our missionaries, Chaplain Henry Wood of the United States
ship *Powhatan* had taught English in Nagasaki to
young men belonging to the Governor's staff and had
found that the occurrence in the reading-book of such
words as *church, pulpit, organ,* and *choir* opened the
way for speaking about Christian worship; and Dr.
McGowan of the Baptist Mission in Ningpo found
that the members of a similar class taught by him
were glad to receive copies of a Christian newspaper
printed in the Chinese language, though they had
refused to accept copies of the New Testament.

In Se... ... ... Dr. S. Wells Williams, who

had seen Chaplain Wood's class, wrote to Rev. Mr. Syle that the best way to begin mission work would be "to station a missionary at Nagasaki or Yedo whose object it shall be to teach English to the Japanese youths put under his charge, with the understanding that he shall have all the assistance he himself needs for learning their language." We know how this advice was followed and the great influence that was gained by Dr. Verbeck, the two Drs. Brown, Miss Mary Kidder, and others who in the early days began their missionary careers as teachers of English.

Another form of teaching was suggested in the letter of Dr. Williams. He recommended the sending of "a physician whose object will be to practice gratuitously among the people at large and educate a few pupils in medicine and surgery, if they can be obtained." The doubt implied in the last clause of this recommendation proved needless. The early medical missionaries were not only able to find young men desiring instruction, but many persons who had long practiced the Chinese system of medicine were eager to learn what they could by receiving formal instruction or by seeing how the missionary treated patients in whose behalf they had sought his advice. The number of physicians in some of the churches soon bore witness to the influence that the missionaries had gained over such men. Many persons too who were healed were made ready to hear what those who had helped them said about the great Physician who could bring spiritual health to their souls.

After a time the public teaching of Christianity became possible. At first, this in its various forms had to be done by the missionaries. They were the leaders of Bible classes, the superintendents and teachers in Sunday schools, and, however imperfect their knowledge of the Japanese language, they were the preachers and the ones who, with the aid of their teachers prepared tracts, translated portions of the

Scriptures, even wrote the hymns for the infant
church, and taught the Japanese how to sing these
hymns. They also held an important place as, by
preparing dictionaries and other language helps, they
made it easier for us who came after them to join
them in Christian work. Mention should also be made
of the great influence that was exerted, especially by
the missionary women, in the homes; for many Japanese have told how what they there learned concerning
the Christian idea of the family made them desirous
of further acquaintance with the religion that was
its source.

All were desirous of raising up as soon as possible from among the Japanese themselves those who
would take a part in making Christ known to their
people. As one missionary used to say, "If one of
these men has learned the A of the Christian alphabet,
he ought to teach it to his neighbors while he is
learning B; then to teach A and B while learning C;
and so on, advancing as fast as possible in both the
learning and the teaching." Because a large proportion of the early Christians were educated men, they
were soon able to take an active part in evangelizing
their countrymen. When the young men in Yokohama
who had studied in the English classes of the missionaries became Christians, they were eager to carry the
Gospel to others. In the early enthusiasm of the first
men joining the church in Kobe, eight of the nine
expressed a desire to be trained for preaching the
Gospel, and at their own costs they went to other
towns to tell what they had learned. The province
of some of the missionaries was now broadened as,
at first with small groups of young men and afterwards in special schools, they trained persons for the
Christian ministry.

The missionary ere long relinquished with joy
the place he had held as the only teacher of Christianity and gladly shared its duties with the Japanese

as his fellow-workers; in some things he and in some
things they taking the initiative, but each helping
the other.

As churches were organized the relation that the
missionaries held towards them varied according to
the different ecclesiastical policies that were represented. The convention of missionaries held in 1872
had indeed declared; "We will use our influence to
secure, as far as possible, identity of name and organization in the native churches in the formation of
which we may be called to assist, that name being
as catholic as the Church of Christ; and the organization being that wherein the government of each church
shall be by the ministry and eldership of the same,
with the concurrence of the brethren"; but some missions had not sent representatives to the convention,
and among those that did, the action taken was dif-
ferently interpreted so that ere long it was evident
that the churches were unlike in their organization
and methods. In most if not all points the churches
were patterned after those with which the missionaries instrumental in their gathering had been connected in their home lands. The place they held in
the new churches therefore presented much variety.
In some cases the creeds, conditions of membership,
and forms of worship were fixed by the rules or customs of the denominations to which the missions be-
longed. The missionaries could not approve of any
deviation from these. They themselves had recognized
official positions and more or less authority to decide
matters connected with the administration of the
churches' affairs. On the other hand the members
of some missions had no official position in the
churches. The most marked example of this is seen
in the mission of the American Board. For many
years none of its missionaries were even members of
Japanese churches. Although in rare cases one might
for a   '   ;   ·   ·   ,   ι ·   ι ι

church's services or serve in what resembled a pastoral
relation, this was regarded as a temporary expedient
to be set aside so soon as the church could find some
one of its own country to install as its pastor. When
the first of what were afterwards known as Kumiai
Churches was to be organized, a missionary helped
in the preparation of its creed and rules; but the
adoption of these rested with those that were to form
the new church. Though what the missionary suggested was accepted by this church and copied by
others, it could be rejected or changed as seemed advisable. The place of the American Board missionary
was that of an unofficial counsellor: the decision of
what a church should do resting with itself. When
the Kumiai Churches united in a national organization,
the missionaries of the American Board were invited
to attend its annual meetings as corresponding members, a position giving them no vote. It is evident that
with this polity of what may be termed high-Congre-
gationalism, the place of the missionaries, not only
in relations with the churches, but also in regard
to the various forms of work in which they engaged,
whether independently or in cooperation with the
Japanese, was very different from that held by members of the Episcopal missions. Between these extremes were other systems, such as those of the Method
ists and Presbyterians. However, with all of these
differences in theory and practice, all missionaries
desired to give to the Japanese so much of responsibility for the conduct of church affairs and the
carrying on of Christian work as they were thought
prepared to assume. Thus as the years went by,
although the place held by the missionary might in
its activities be much the same as before, it was less
prominent because of that to which the Japanese had
risen. In preaching, in the preparation of literature,
and in some other features of the work the foreigner
had to take a second ex place as compared with those

who used their own language and had such knowledge of the way to reach the hearts of the people as is not easily gained by persons of very different training and experiences from those whom they desire to influence.

It may have seemed at times as though the Japanese were too ready to push into places that they were not yet prepared to hold and that they pressed ideas of independence so far as to prevent them from receiving much of the help that missionaries were able to render. This was especially marked when the general reaction against Western influences gave rise to the ultra-nationalistic spirit. Christian ministers and evangelists, irritated by taunts that they were the servile lantern-bearers and sandal-carriers of foreigners, often tried to disprove the charge by speaking in derogatory terms of their former teachers. Articles in newspapers and magazines belittled the abilities of the missionaries and complained of the power they had to influence the churches by giving or withholding financial aid; even "little yellow-legged ducklings," as one writer styled young missionaries that had been only a short time in the country, being able by their votes in mission meeting to stand in the way of projects that the Japanese deemed important. Missionaries were less frequently invited to preach. Half in jest, half in earnest, they sometimes said among themselves that the only place left to them in the Sunday services was that of pronouncing the benediction. A few persons prominent in the churches gave broad hints that certain missionaries were *personae non gratae* and that they as well as most of their associates might as well leave the country. It was a trying time and a few persons, especially among recent comers to Japan, feeling that there would be little place for such usefulness as they desired, returned home. It may be that those who chose the little fo

ginning" should include this period; but since it does
not seem to be given a place in the general program,
it seemed well to make some mention of what happened at a time when mission policies were still in
an early state of formation. What occurred then did
much to determine what in later years was to be the
place of the missionary in Japan. This period passed
and more normal conditions prevailed; though there
could not be a return to those found at first. The
missionary of today cannot have the same kind of
leadership as that taken by his predecessors at the
beginning of their work; but he can rejoice that any
decrease in this respect is chiefly due to the increase
in numbers, devotion, and ability of his Japanese
fellow-workers. His right place will be found as he
goes forward with them shoulder to shoulder, yet
not regretful that the alignment is not kept perfectly
straight, if it be because their zeal and strength put
them somewhat ahead of himself.

CHAPTER III

THE BEGINNING OF THE JAPANESE CHURCH AS AN INSTITUTION

Prof. S. Yamamoto

It has been said that the "Timothy Church" in Osaka was the first Church organized in Japan. That, however, was a Church organized not by Japanese but by the foreign Mission of the American Episcopal Church. This was in 1871.

The first Japanese Church of modern times was the present "Kaigan" Church of the "Nihon Kirisuto Kyokwai," which was organized at Yokohama on March 10th, 1872. Its membership consisted of nine young men and two middle-aged men. There were at that time four more Japanese Christians at Kanagawa and Tokyo, but they were not members of said Church.

The predominant ideas in the minds of the Japanese Christians regarding a Church Organization were as follows:

To serve God, and by God's help to save Japan, both socially and individually, was their desire. Reading the accounts in the Book of Acts about the small circle of Christians at the beginning, they were very much impressed and believed that even though there might be here only such a small circle of believers, by uniting themselves in prayer and by the inspiration of the Holy Spirit they might be able to influence the people of Japan. These may seem to have be⸱⸱⸱⸱

themselves in the Salvation of Christ.

In regard to *one Christian Church for the whole of Japan,* they thought something like this:

Of course, as far as the spirit, and also the form, of the Christian Church are concerned, it ought to be *one.* For were not divisions in the Church severely censured in the Corinthian Epistle? The first Japanese Christians did not well know why there were divisions in the Churches of Europe and America, but thought there must be good reasons for it. That there should be quarrels because of theological differences seemed to them not only unbecoming but also caused them surprise. But even if for various historical reasons there were necessarily divisions in the Churches of the West, here in Japan, without such history, and in view of the need of spreading Christianity in the face of opposing Shinto and Buddhist forces, they were convinced that, beyond a fundamental statement of belief, they ought to sacrifice everything in order to unite all the believers into one Church. With this idea in mind they labored to adopt *a simple* creed in which they thought that both as to Church Government and as to belief, every Christian would be able to unite. The foreign missionaries then on the field also fully concurred with this idea and hence at the first Conference of Protestant missionaries. in September, 1872, they adopted the following:

"Whereas the Church of Christ is one in Him, and the diversities of denominations among Protestants are but accidents which, though not affecting the vital unity of believers, obscure the oneness of the Church in Christendom, and much more in pagan lands where the history of the divisions cannot be understood; and whereas we, as Protestant missionaries, desire to secure uniformity in our modes and methods of evangelization so as to avoid, as far as possible. the evil arising from marked differences; we therefore take the occasion of the opportunity offered by this

Convention to agree that we will use our influence to secure, as far as possible, identity of name and organization of the native Churches in the formation of which we may be called upon to assist; that *name* being as Catholic as the Church of Christ, and the *organization* being that wherein the government of each Church shall be by the ministry and eldership of the same, with the concurrence of the brethren."

As to *creed*, the thought was that creed was doubtless very important in Western countries, but in Japan, not having thus far any history nor any creedal disputes, there was no necessity for a minute and involved creed. This was the more emphasized in view of the attempt to have one united Church Organization. With this in mind they considered it important to have a simple creed in which all could join, and hence they adopted the creedal statements in the Nine Articles of the "Evangelical Alliance." There were some who took an opposing attitude in regard to the doctrines of original sin, fore-ordination and certain other doctrines then emphasized in the Presbyterian Church.

In the matter of *ecclesiastical relations between the Japanese Church and the Churches of the West,* they were not clearly conscious that there should be any difference between foreign and Japanese Churches as the Church of Christ is *one.* But the idea of the independence of the Japanese Church was clearly grasped by the earliest student members among the believers. At the same time, they thought that both foreigners and Japanese ought to be mutually helpful without any real separation between them.

Regarding *self-support,* many from the beginning realized that the Japanese Church ought to be independent not only ecclesiastically but also financially. Many of the early believers were young men who had received a "samurai" ("Bushi") training and who, from force of habit, considered it a disgrace to be assisted by othe   \ d. . ,. t ..   t′ , .   t· ·! ·! · ,t was no disgrace to receive financial help for the furtherance of the faith, naturally their inward feelings were that this was lacking in manliness. The more was this thought painful in the case of financial help received from foreign sources. Hence, in the early Church there were two ideas prevalent; the one, radical, insisting that no foreign financial support whatsoever should be received; the other, *modified* ("zen-shin-ka"), maintaining that the Church ought gradually to become self-supporting. At any rate, the question of independence became important from the start.

As to *the distinctive features of a Japanese Church,* it was at the time that Japan began to imitate the Western nations in every thing. They had begun to awaken to the fact that the Western nations were far advanced in the sciences and in general civilization and still more in the matter of Christianity and the Christian Church. Hence the Japanese Church was largely built upon the model of Western Churches. Perhaps the idea of *one* Church, without denominationalism, as favored by the earliest membership of the Church in Japan, might be called its "distinctive feature."

CHAPTER IV

EDUCATIONAL BEGINNINGS

Rev. T. H. Haden, D.D.

This paper will be confined for the most part to the first twenty years of Protestant Christian Missions in Japan. This will be divided into two parts:

1. From 1859, when the first missionaries arrived, to Feb. 19, 1873, when the edicts against Christianity were taken down—a time of preparation.

2. From 1873 to 1879—a time of realization.

The first problem for the early missionaries was to win the confidence of the government and people. Little could be done, except study the language, prepare grammars and dictionaries and do literary work, until confidence could be won.

But the young people wanted to learn English and other things that the missionaries could teach them, and this proved to be an effective point of contact. Even as early as 1862, Mrs. J. C. Hepburn had a class of five little boys in Kanagawa, and from time to time the missionaries had individuals or small groups come to their homes for the study of English, and occasionally of other things. Also, the governors or Kanagawa and Nagasaki established schools for the study of English, and invited the missionaries to teach in them. American text-books were imported, and the teachers were given a free hand in the use of them. The students would visit the homes of the teachers from time to time, and talk over many things in the established. The Government sent a dozen young men from Yedo (Tokyo) to Kanagawa to be taught English by one of the missionaries, and the Council of State in Yedo established a school, where English and French were to be taught to a hundred high-class young men, and the Protestant missionaries were invited to take charge of the English department.

It was not until 1869 that the first real missionary school was established. At that time, Rev. C. Carrothers (Am. Presby.) established a school for boys in Tokyo, and Mrs. Carrothers established one for girls. Both of these schools prospered, and became useful institutions by the end of this period.

In 1870, Miss Mary Kidder (afterwards Mrs. E. R. Miller (Am. Refmd.) began to teach two girls and a boy, that she took over from Mrs. Hepburn, in Yokohama. By the end of the year, she had given up the boy, and had six girls Governor Oye took an interest in her work, and she opened a school for girls, which had 22 pupils by the end of 1872.

In October, 1872, the American Mission Home was established at 212 Bluff, Yokohama, by Mrs. Mary Pruyn, Mrs. L. H. Pierson and Miss J. N. Crosby, who had been sent out in 1871, by the Woman's Union Missionary Society of America, to establish a boarding school for girls. While the preparations were being made for opening this school for girls, these ladies taught English to a group of young men, and through them gained access to the women and girls.

In the spring of 1872, the American Episcopalians opened a school for boys in the city of Osaka, which had 50 pupils by the end of 1873—which takes us over into the next period. Also, in the village of Ujino in Kobe, the American Board missionaries established a school in the latter part of 1872, which had 40 pupils. This continued during the winter.

We come now to the second period. On Feb. 19, 187?, the edicts against Christianity were removed, and the work soon began to show signs of new life.

At Nagasaki, the Rev. Henry Stout (Am. Refmd.) opened a school for boys in the latter part of 1872, and Mrs. Stout opened one for girls. The common English branches were taught in the schools, and the Bible at the Stout home. Thirty boys and fifty girls were soon in attendance. When the edicts were removed, it was decided to teach the Bible in the schools, and make them openly and boldly Christian. Intense opposition developed, and the schools had to be closed. However, many of the pupils begged that they be reopened, and this was done at the home of the missionaries. By the kind assistance of Captain Janes, of Kumamoto, a school house was built. There the schools were continued, a Sunday school was organized, converts were baptized, the first native prayer meeting in Nagasaki was held, and the gospel was first publicly preached in that part of the empire.

In 1875, the Rev. H. Maundrell (Ch. Mis. Soc.) arrived in Nagasaki, and soon began to train native evangelists.

On Dec. 1, 1879, Kwassui Jogakko (Meth. Epis.) was founded by Misses E. Russell and J. M. Gheer, who had been sent out for that purpose. The school was opened in a rented building, with one student By April, four more had entered. In June, 1880, the school moved to its own buildings, on its present site, and 43 girls moved with it to its new location.

It was not until Oct., 1881, that a permanent institution for boys and young men was established in Nagasaki. At that time Cobleigh Seminary (afterwards Chinzei Gakuin) (Meth. Ep.) was established, with 12 students, in academic, college and theological departments. The school closed the first year with an enrollment of 45.

The first Christian teachers in the schools

had been in Nagasaki and in the Kanagawa—Yokohama—Tokyo region for ten years before they began
to occupy this important section of the country.
Bishop C. M. Williams (Am. Epis.) moved to Osaka
in 1869, and was joined there by Rev. A. R. Morris
in 1871. Rev. D. C. Greene (Am. Bd). moved to Kobe
in Mch., 1870, and established the first mission station there. It has already been noted that a school
for boys was established in Osaka in 1872, and one
in Ujino, Kobe, which was continued for a short
time. Also, Dr. J. C. Berry (Am. Bd) had begun to
instruct a number of students at the Hiogo Hospital,
in materia medica, chemistry, physiology and anatomy. This was probably the first time in Japan
when anatomy was taught by the dissection of the
human body.

In 1874, Mrs. J. H. Quimby (Am. Epis.) began to
teach a class of little girls in Osaka. In Jan., 1875,
Miss Ellen Eddy (Am. Epis.) took over the care of
the children, rented a house, and opened a girls'
boarding school, known as "Light in Darkness
School." This was the beginning of Heian Kyoto
Jogakko (St. Agnes' Girls' High School), which was
later moved to Kyoto, and has occupied its present
site since Jan. 25, 1896.

In Nov., 1873, Miss Eliza Talcott and Miss J. E.
Dudley (Am. Bd.) began to teach a few boys and
girls in Kobe. A year later, their home Boards voted
to build and furnish a boarding school for girls in
Kobe, and provided $5,200, for that purpose. The
Japanese added $800, to this, bringing the total to
$6,000. With this money two acres of land were
bought, and a building was erected and opened Oct.
12, 1875, the school then having five boarders and
about 30 day pupils. This was the first school for
girls in Central Japan, and was the beginning of the
well known *Kobe College* for girls, which has done
so much for the womanhood of this part of Japan for

the past fifty years.

The Doshisha, Kyoto. Joseph Neesima, after ten years in America, had become profoundly convinced that one of the greatest needs of his native land was Christian schools of high grade. On Oct. 9, 1874, he made an urgent appeal to the American Board then in session for means with which to accomplish his purpose, with the result that $5,000, was immediately contributed. He returned to Japan in Dec., 1874, as an associate member of the American Board Mission, was warmly received by the missionaries, and Rev. J. D. Davis was appointed to be his associate in founding a high grade school.

Kobe was considered too unimportant a place for such a school; the governor of Osaka would not consent for it to be established there, if missionaries were to teach in it; so Kyoto was agreed upon as the best place. As Kyoto was outside of treaty limits, the only way to manage was for the school to be established in the name of a Japanese, and for the missionary teachers to be his "employees." This was agreed upon, and five and a half acres of land were bought, permits from the local and central governments secured. Mr Davis became the "employee" of Mr. Neesima and moved to Kyoto in Oct., 1875, and on Nov. 29, 1875, the Doshisha was formally opened, in an old rented building, with eight pupils, most of whom had been members of Mr. Davis' Training Class in Kobe. This number increased to about 30 during the winter. There were no appliances or curriculum—nothing but a few classes in English and simple mathematics. Three buildings were erected during the summer of 1876, on the land that had been bought, and on the 18th of September the Doshisha made its real beginning as an educational institution, with a definite curriculum, and 47 boarders and a few day pupils. About 30 of the boarders were fr   Cajt. .· ·. . · ¹ ¡ Ku ¡ ·· ti.·

famous "Kumamoto Band," who were transferred to Doshisha at this time, and had a great influence on its future history. This was the first Christian school of high grade in Japan. The Girls' Department of the Doshisha was begun by Miss Starkweather, in 1877, in her own house, with two boarders and three day pupils, but a large building was erected for it during the following year.

The Baikwa Jo Gakko was established in Osaka, in Jan., 1878, by two Congregational churches, of about 25 members each. It began with 15 pupils, and with a budget of $15. for rent, repairs and other expenses. It was the first school above primary grade in Osaka, and the first self-supporting Christian school in the country. The self-support was not absolute, however, as the American Board has from the first supplied one or more missionary teachers, and has sometimes helped otherwise.

The Poole Girls' School (Ch. Mis. Soc.), Osaka, was not opened until 1879, and the other important schools in Kobe and Osaka were all established later. and need not be considered in a paper on "Beginnings."

However, it may be well to call attention to the Woman's Evangelistic Training School (Am. Bd.), Kobe, which was opened in 1880, by Miss J. E. Dudley and Miss Martha Barrows. It was closed at the end of a year, for lack of teachers, and was not reopened until 1884. The Department for the Training of Bible Women at the American Mission Home in Yokohama was opened in 1881, and continued. Attention should also be called to the Glory Kindergaten and Training School, opened by Miss Annie L. Howe (Am. Bd.) in 1889. The first Christian Kindergarten in Japan was opened by the Presbyterians, in Kanazawa, in 1885, and the Glory Kindergarten, Kobe, seems to have been the second. But this Training School for training kinder gartners was the first in

Japan.

We come now to the *Tokyo—Yokohama* region for the period after the edicts were removed.

Ferris Seminary, Yokohama (Am. Refmd.). Attention has already been called to the work of Miss Mary Kidder, which began in 1870. The number of pupils in her school increased, and the girls began to clamor for a boarding school. After many discouragements, land was secured on the Bluff in Yokohama, money came for a building, Miss Emma C. Witbeck arrived from home to assist in the teaching, and the boarding school was formally opened on June 1, 1875, with 14 pupils, all of whom were old pupils of Miss Kidder's (the late Mrs. E. R. Miller). The name chosen was Ferris Seminary. The initial cost was $5,500. At the close of the year there were 18 pupils. The boarders paid $4, a month, and the day pupils $1. The school soon made a good name for itself, which it has kept to the present day.

Joshi Gakuin, Tokyo, (Presby.). On Jan. 5, 1874, Miss Mary C. Parke (now Mrs. David Thompson) and Miss Kate M. Youngman, who had been sent out from America to found a boarding school for girls in Tokyo, opened such a school at 6 B, Tsukiji, in a building erected for the purpose. This school was afterwards moved to No. 42, Tsukiji, and was known as Graham Seminary. In Sept., 1872, a school on the Ginza, which grew out of Mrs. Carrothers' school (1869), was united with Graham Seminary. In 1881, the Sakurai Girls' School, which was founded in 1876, by Mrs. Chika Sakurai, an old pupil of Miss Parke's, was bought by the Presbyterian Mission, more land was secured, new buildings were erected, and the school became large and prosperous. Thus the Presbyterian Mission had two girls' schools of the same grade in Tokyo. What could be more natural than to unite the two—Graham Seminary and Sakur   r is S , ）   ｌ   ꞏꞏ d well equipped institution? This was done after a few years, and Joshi Gakuin, Tokyo, was the result.

Aoyama Girls' School, Tokyo (Meth. Epis.), dates from Nov. 16, 1874, when Miss Dora E. Schoonmaker opened a school in the house of H. Okada, Azabu, Tokyo, with five pupils. On account of opposition, it moved five times in nine months, and finally landed in a Buddhist temple in Mita, Tokyo, where it kept company with the idols for fourteen months. Four of the pupils were baptized Apr. 9, 1876. The school was then called Kyusei (salvation) Jo Gakko. In Jan., 1877, it was moved to No. 10, Tsukiji, where it was completely burnt out in the great fire of Dec. 26, 1879. It moved to temporary quarters on Ginza, where it remained until Sept. 13, 1881, when it occupied its new buildings at No. 13, Tsukiji. Later, the school was divided, the lower grades remaining in Tsukiji, and the higher grades moving to a site adjoining Aoyama Gakuin.

The Surugadai Girls' School, Tokyo, (Am. Bapt.) was opened by Rev. James Hope Arthur, in 1874, on land owned by Mr. Arinori Mori, who had been Japanese minister to the U. S. As the site was outside of Tsukiji, Mr. Arthur had to have a Japanese "employer." Mr. Mori served as such until Mr. Arthur began to teach Christianity in the school, when the former immediately severed his connection with it. Then the troubles began. Miss Anna H. Kidder came in 1875, to help in the school, but there were many reverses. There were seven "employers" in succession, one of whom closed the school, to show his authority. Finally Miss Sowotome, an old pupil, became the "employer," and those troubles ceased, but there were plenty of others. The school finally moved to Tsukiji. At that time, there were only six pupils. It was not till July 29, 1885, that land was bought, buildings erected, and the school established at Surugadai, where it remained until 1921, when it was discontinued.

St. Paul's College (Rikkyo Daigaku), Tokyo, (Am. Epis.) was founded by Bishop C. M. Williams, in Feb., 1874, immediately after the American Episcopal Mission was established in Tokyo. Rev. C. T. Blanchet was put in charge and the school prospered until it was burnt out in 1876, when there was a great fire in Tsukiji. No other place could be found, so it was discontinued for two years, when it was reopened as a day school. At the time of the fire, there was 55 pupils, 46 of whom were boarders. In 1882, a school building was erected, and the boarding department was reopened. The Episcopal Divinity School was opened in 1878, by Rev. J. H. Quimby.

The Tokyo Union Theological School was founded in 1876, and was one of the results of the organization of the Nippon Kirisuto Itchi Kyokwai. Rev. J. L. Ammerman, Rev. William Imbrie and Rev. S. G. McLaren were the first professors, and Rev. G. F. Verbeck and Rev. David Thompson were lecturers. The students came from Dr. S. R. Brown's Theological Class at Yokohama (Am Refmd.), which began in 1871; from a class in Bible study under Rev. William Imbrie and Rev. David Thompson (Am. Presby.); one perhaps, from Mr. Carrothers' School; and a few from the Scotch Presbyterian Mission. There were about 25 of them, and K. Ibuka and M. Uemura were among them. The school found a permanent home at No. 17, Tsukiji. Dr. Brown's class (1874) was probably the first class of Protestant Theological students in Japan, as this school was the first Protestant Theological School in Japan. In 1886, this became the Theological Department of Meiji Gakuin.

The Academic Department of Meiji Gakuin originated in a small English school begun in Yokohama (Am. P........

kyo, in 1880, and was named Tsukiji College, with Mr. J. C. Ballagh as Principal; and an English school in Yokohama, under Dr. M. N. Wyckoff (Am. Refmd.), which was united two years later with Tsukiji College, the name being changed to Tokyo Union Eiwa Gakko. The following year, a Preparatory School was opened in Kanda, Tokyo. In 1886, all of these elements were united in a single institution, and Meiji Gakuin, as such, was founded.

Aoyama Gakuin, Tokyo, (Meth. Epis.) had its beginnings in a day school, opened in Tokyo, in 1878; and the Japan Conference Academy, which was opened in Yokohama, in 1879, as an Academy and Training School for evangelists. In Oct., 1882, these two schools were united in Tsukiji, Tokyo, and the whole was made into a boarding school. The Yokohama school took 63 students to the new institution, 11 of whom were studying for the ministry. In Nov., 1882, the present site of Aoyama Gakuin, consisting of about 25 acres, was purchased for $5,600-a gift from Dr. John F. Goucher, and the Tsukiji school was moved to this site in the fall of 1883.

This brings us to the end of the first twenty years of educational work. Strict limitation of space has made it necessary to omit many interesting and important details, and sometimes even specific mention of work that would otherwise have been considered, but it is hoped that a fair idea has been given of the beginnings of the educational work in Japan, as it has made such a large contribution to the Christian movement in this country.

CHAPTER V

FINANCIAL BEGINNINGS

.

Rev. G. W. Fulton, D.D.

Ten Japanese converts had been baptized in different parts of the country previous to organizing the first Christian church in Yokohama, March 10, 1872. Doubtless they were duly instructed in the matter of giving, judging from the practical character of the missionaries who were instrumental in leading them to Christ. But no data has come down to us as to what gifts were made, or how they were administered.

In the record of the organizing of the above mentioned first church in Japan, it is stated that both an elder and *deacon* were ordained, and the same is true of the church organized in Tokyo the following year. Deacons have to do with finances, so it may be taken for granted that the early Christians in Japan began at once making contributions toward the support of the work.

The first pastors of these churches were missionaries, whose salaries were provided by their respective Boards, but there were current expenses which would be borne by the Christians themselves. The converts were multiplying rapidly, as in the Yokohama church alone 166 communicants and 19 children had been received up to July, 1875, and a year later the total number of Christians in Japan had crossed the thousand mark. A paper read before the Osaka Conference in 1883 by Rev. G. W. Knox states that the conver'

a fair proportion of wealthy men, and suggests 25
sen per month as a minimum average contribution
per member.

In 1874 a Theological Class was started by Dr.
S. R. Brown in Yokohama, composed of a dozen or
more members, and within a year or two these young
men were being sent out to take charge of work that
had been established. Three candidates were ordained to the ministry in 1877, replacing the missionaries
as pastors of the churches, so that the expense of the
work gradually increased. Data is not at hand to
show how these first Japanese workers were support
ed, but presumably in whole or part by the Missions,
as in 1882, 56 ordained, and 81 unordained ministers
are reported, working in 146 congregations, of which
only 14 were self-supporting.

The salaries received by these early ministers
were very small., The instance of the Rev. Paul
Sawayama, who returned to Japan after four years
of study in America, and entered the pastorate of the
Naniwa Church in Osaka at a salary of seven yen
per month, is well known. Many other good men
worked for years with salaries not much beyond that.
Even in the late eighties, the writer recollects that
the ordinary salary paid to evangelists was 12 to
15 yen, and the pastors of churches received only a
little more.

Rents also were cheap, and a good substantial
building could be secured for one or two yen per
month, to serve as chapel or parsonage, and a rental
of four or five yen was looked upon as very high.
Wages were very low, a coolie or carpenter receiving
12 or 15 sen a day, while a maid servant was content with three yen a month, boarding herself. A
good-sized church lot was purchased on the main
street of Kanazawa, in the heart of the business section, for yen 31.20, and remains the site of the thriving
church to this day. Land for missionary residences
usually could be bought for less than a yen per tsubo,

and the large missionary houses erected in those early days cost about $2,000 gold.

Those facts are given because of their bearing on the financial problems confronting the Missions and the churches at the beginnings of the Christian work in this country. Looked at from the present high costs, the problems seem simple, but in reality they were no less difficult than they are today. Japan was poor, and it was just as hard, or possibly harder, for the Christians then to raise the meager sums needed for their work, as it is to raise the much larger sums required at present. And the Missions on their part were just as hard pressed to make ends meet as they are now.

The record states that monthly collections were taken up in all the churches from a very early period. These were probably monthly subscriptions paid privately to the treasurer of the church, and were used to pay the running expenses and such portion of the pastor's salary as they were responsible for. According to the writer's recollection, the weekly offering, as a part of Sabbath worship, did not come into vogue until much later. The Christians were afraid it would be misunderstood by outsiders, and might frighten away inquirers if the collection plate were passed around each Sabbath! Happily this fear has long since been dispelled in our Japanese churches.

While the Presbyterian and Reformed churches in and around Yokohama and Tokyo were the first to be established, and made commendable progress financially, the Kumiai churches established by the American Board Mission in western Japan, outstripped them in the matter of self-support at the beginning, and kept the lead for many years. At the time of the Osaka Missionary Conference in 1883, thirteen self-supporting Kumiai churches were reported out of a total of fourteen for the whole Christian body. The explanation of this as given at the Conference was the   . .' . '\'   , ' ..   d

and on the other the independent character of the
early pastors, who quickly gathered about them bodies
of believers able and willing to shoulder the financial
burdens.

In the matter of church property, the general
policy of the Missions was identical, that the Christians should provide for themselves. However there
were exceptions, as in the case of the Yokohama
(Kaigan) Church, whose building was erected at a
cost of $8,000 received from residents in the port,
Christians in Hawaii, and friends in America, the
building being used for many years as the place of
worship for Europeans and Americans gathered together as the Union Church. A member of the American Board Mission wrote in 1882: "Five of our
churches are provided with houses of worship, all
built without any aid from the Board, and all but
one entirely with native funds, except as members
of the Mission and others have made small private
contributions to aid in their erection. The value of
the church property is estimated at about 10,000 yen.
The Board makes no appropriation for church building." In the same year a member of the M. E. Mission
refers to "seven church edifices and nine parsonages"
as owned by the Mission, doubtless provided in accord with its usual policy of aiding generously in
property concerns.

At the end of the first decade of the church's
life in Japan (1882), it was able to report 14 self-
supporting churches, 43 receiving aid, 56 church
buildings, 5,092 full members, and contributions for
the last year amounting to yen 12,344. At the same
time work was being prosecuted in 146 stations by
137 Japanese ministers, including the above churches
and their pastors. No figures are immediately available to show the total cost of this work up to that
time, whether as affecting the churches or the Missions. But the calculation of Dr Verbeck near the
close of his own little History of Protestant Missions

in Japan is interesting. He there estimates the cost of the work in Missionary labor alone from 1859 to the end of 1882 at approximately $2,000,000 gold.

The financial outlay for the next decade of course was much more in proportion, as the missionary force and the Japanese force increased rapidly, and the scope of the work was much enlarged. But in this golden age of the missionary work in Japan the results were more than encouraging. There were now above five hundred native ministers at work in six hundred and fifty places, thirty three thousand Christians gathered into upwards of three hundred churches, of which seventy odd were entirely self-supporting. The Christians were now contributing at the rate of above sixty thousand yen a year.

Before the decade of the seventies, schools for boys and girls had been opened by the missionaries, and their number increased during the following years. These schools were not free, and a reasonable tuition was asked from the beginning. Rev. J. H. Ballagh was able to turn into the building fund of the Kaigan Church $559 received as tuition from students. Of the school which afterwards became Meiji Gakuin, it was written in 1882 that "the students' fees pay all expenses, the salaries of foreign professors excepted." By the end of the eighties' decade there were approximately 10,000 students of all grades in Christian schools, each of them paying their quota for the education being given them.

The question of the use of foreign money for the support of native work came to the front very early in the history of Christian missions in Japan. It was a matter of constant discussion, among missionaries, whether in their Mission meetings or larger gatherings for conference. There was not unanimity of opinion on the subject. The majority, apparently, felt that it was proper for the stronger churches of the West to help the weaker churches of the East financi⸺. But a⸺

such financial aid would be injurious to the real
spiritual life, as well as the progress of the native
church in its work of evangelization.

The Rev. H. H. Leavitt, missionary of the American
Board in the decade of the seventies, was prominent
among missionaries in advocating very radical self-
support, and the title of his paper read at the Osaka
Conference fully indicated the strength of his con-
victions: "Self-support in the Native Church: Should
Foreign Money be Used at all? I Answer: No!"
However, Mr. Leavitt's views did not become the
policy of his Mission, which followed the practice of
"using foreign money wherever it seemed to be expedient, stimulating the Japanese churches to take
over the financial responsibility as fast as possible."

The Cumberland Presbyterian Mission began its
work under a strong policy of self-support. Their
"basic idea was the responsibility of the native church
for the conversion of Japan. Mission funds were not
to be used in evangelistic work. No one was to be
aided with Mission funds without rendering to the
Mission an equivalent for the aid thus received. When
the Mission entered into union with the "United
Church" (Itchi Kyokwai) in 1889, it adapted its policy
to that of the other Missions in the interests of unity."

In the interesting discussions of this subject at
the Osaka Missionary Conference in 1883, it was apparent that all agreed on the importance of self-
support, but there was a difference of view on the
question of the use of foreign money. Five papers
on the general subject were read, three by missionaries and two by Japanese pastors, showing that the
topic easily held the leading place on the program.
Rev. G. W. Knox of the Presbyterian Mission declared
himself "a radical of the extreme left. He would
have no funds set apart for the support of the native
church," and then proceeded to read his paper on
the assigned topic, "Foreign Money being Used, How
shall the Native Church be led to Self-support?" The

Rev. G. M. Meacham, of the Mission of the Methodist Church of Canada, in his paper plead for the use of the golden mean in aiding Japanese churches, each case being dealt with on its own merits, but keeping constantly before the Christians the goal of self-support, as that which they are to attain at the earliest possible moment.

The whole subject was regarded as of such importance as to warrant its consideration by a special committee, whose report was later adopted. In substance it was that while pecuniary aid to the churches was not to be outlawed, the dependence upon foreign money was abnormal and dangerous. That the churches be exhorted to give regularly to the Lord, providing for their own support, and for the evangelization of their fellow countrymen. That no definite plan could be laid down for securing the desired end in view, but that missionaries should exert themselves to train pastors and believers in liberal and systematic giving, and in organizing new churches special effort should be made to bring the matter of self-support to a practical issue.

The subject of organized Home Missions was agitated by the Japanese Christians from an early date. Among the Presbyterian and Reformed churches, an independent Board consisting of three ministers and three elders was established in 1879. It received funds from the churches and carried on evangelistic work for four years. Following this, leading Japanese were invited to confer with the Missions regarding the operations of the latter in the evangelistic field. In 1886 a plan was adopted of financial cooperation and joint control, the Missions contributing three yen for each one yen raised by the churches, the whole work being administered by a joint committee. This was superseded in 1894 by a Home Mission Board, purely Japanese, and administering funds raised from the Japanese churches. This latter is still operative, and ha with a fund of 562 yen the first year, they have now a budget of above 23,000 yen, and are employing 16 .workers in 29 places.

Among the Kumiai churches, a Home Mission Society was organized at the end of 1877. The Mission cooperated with it from 1879 to 1895, planning its work under a joint committee. Originally the churches raised four-tenths of the total funds used, but in 1895 when the plan was abandoned the Mission was contributing three-fourths of the budget of approximately 2,500 yen. The Society continued its work independently, raising the first year something over 2,300 yen, and is carrying on a vigorous work today.

The other churches also formed their organizations for evangelism, which differ from the above in accord with their method of government, but agree in that they have gradually advanced in their independent activities. In each case the funds provided by the churches were small at the beginning, but have increased with the growth of the churches in financial strength.

A number of Missions began work in Japan at a later period, each of them having their financial beginnings, but a survey of which is beyond the limits of this article. As a general rule they have conformed to the policies and practices of the Missions already on the field when they arrived, and the newer churches have developed essentially along the same lines as the older ones.

PART II

THE PRESENT

___

CHAPTER VI

THE PRESENT PLACE OF THE MISSIONARY

___

(1) Rev. William Axling, D.D.

Missionary advance registers three distinct stages. In the pioneer stage the initiative comes entirely from without. In the second stage the indigenous church reaches self-consciousness and becomes a controling factor. In the final stage the missionary task itself becomes indigenous and the responsibility for its continuance passes over to forces native to the soil. In Japan we have more than arrived at the second stage. The reaction of the Japanese as to the missionary's place must therefore be determinative. This article presents a cross section of Japanese thinking on this vital question. Of twenty six leaders whose opinions were sought, twenty one responded.

It is significant that only one expresses doubt as to the need of missionaries. Even he however quickly modifies his doubt. Dr. H. Kozaki says, "the sending of missionaries to Japan is very expensive and the results are comparatively meager. There are exceptions however. We need those who can stand as specialists in special fields. We need men qualified to help us to organize and conduct a Christian Universit

welcome men who have won recognition as evangelistic campaigners. I also favor making missionaries pastors of Japanese churches." The remaining
twenty, representing almost every field of activity,
emphatically declare that Japan still needs missionaries. There is also a surprising unanimity of opinion as to fields which are open and the type of missionaries needed.

Evangelism in the Large

Dr. U. Kawaguchi says, "I believe there is a
special place for the missionary in direct religious
work. I feel that undue emphasis is being put on
activities that aim indirectly at Christianizing the
nation. The time arrived long ago when the missionary should venture forth in the directest kind of
evangelism in every section of society." Miss M.
Kawai finds a field, "in pioneer work in towns and
smaller cities where the people are neither too advanced nor too conservative, also among the families
of the upper classes."

Rev. K. Matsuno says, "the evangelization of Japan
is not simply a national question. It is a world question, because Japan's influence is going to be world
wide. There will always be need for exchange missionaries between Japan and other nations. Here
is a great opportunity for a life work for the finest
type of American and English youth. We must put
the urge into this appeal." Secretary K. Miyazaki
says, "Japan's position is strategic. When we consider the evangelization of Japan we must consider
it in its world relation. It stands between the East
and the West, a medium of communication of ideas.
Moreover you can not move the East unless you first
move Japan."

Rev. M. Kobayashi points to an overlooked field.
"We have forgotten the unevangelized commercial
centers. The merchants of Japan are practically un-

touched. This is true in every city and village. We Christians do not even know the terms in which they are thinking." Rev. S. Nukaga opens another field. "We need outstanding preachers, lecturers and other Christian workers to come from abroad for a definite piece of work. Moreover missionaries ought not to be simply guests of the Japanese church. They should become part and parcel of this indigenous organization. They ought to serve as assistant pastors and even become pastors. They should take other positions in the native church. In this way they would realize a new self-respect and find a great field."

Rev. S. Imamura says, "the missionaries' most important work from now on is to live among the non-Christians and interpret Christianity through their home, social and individual life." Prof. Bessho urges personal work. Bishop K. Uzaki feels that the day for pioneer evangelism has not passed. "Can it be said that Kyushu and the Hokkaido are sufficiently occupied? When we set 150,000 Protestant Christians off against a population of 60,000,000 do we not find places everywhere where missionaries can profitably invest their lives? The multitudes are still unreached. Listen to the call of rural Japan! The weak churches of this area need the missionary. Christian literature needs those possessing a unique gift for presenting the Gospel through the printed page."

Dr. K. Ibuka says, "Japanese Christianity is firmly planted. The larger denominations are self-supporting and self-propagating. Yet even though these should unite their forces, are they strong enough to Christianize the nation? Have they adequate men and means to evangelize the 36,000,000 of the rural districts? Decidedly no! The Japanese Mission Societies and the indigenous church are inadequate for the task. Here is a field not for any kind of a missionary but for the right man in the right place." Mr. H. Nagao says, "while the need of the city field is not as grea still present a challenging opportunity. However today, the Macedonian cry for missionaries comes from the youth of the rural districts. Here Japanese endeavor lacks both in quality and quantity."

THE EDUCATIONAL AND STUDENT FIELD

Practically every reply points to this open door. Prof. I. Abe of Waseda says, "every school or higher grade offers a good field for the missionary. The teaching of English furnishes a unique opportunity to bring the students of Japan under Christian influence." Dr. Y. Chiba says, "missionaries are needed who are qualified to lecture no social, scientific and philosophical questions from the Christian point of view." President Ishizaka says, "yes, by all means let us have missionaries for the educational and social fields."

President D. Ebina says, "the students' hearts and minds are open. They are internationally minded. They will listen to a Christian leader of any nation or race with a real message. Japan's students are facing today philosophical, social and political problems. We need Christian men able to help them in these fields. Students are intensely interested in Western music, vocal and instrumental. Anyone with the true spirit of music will find here a tremendous opportunity." Prof. R. Sawano suggests that, "the missionary can render a contribution in inaugurating and directing the work of religious education throughout the Empire."

The fact that four of Tokyo's universities alone enroll 33,000 students and that there are more students in the higher educational institutions of this one city than in the whole of the British Isles shows up the missionary opportunity in this area.

THE FIELD OF SOCIAL WELFARE

There is also unanimity of opinion that Japan's rapid expansion of industrial life and the less favored classes sound a clarion call for missionaries. Mr. D. Tagawa speaks of Christian settlement work as a crying need. Dr. Chiba mentions institutional church work. Miss Kawai says, "Japan's innumerable hot springs crowded with invalids and semi-invalids—a leisure class—are centers where the missionary can exert a wide influence." Prof. H. Takenaka feels that, the social service field in Japan is an increasing challenge to missionary endeavor." Prof. Sawano says, "that while the missionary is needed in the evangelistic field as an 'adviser,' in the field of social welfare he is needed as a 'pioneer' and a 'director of social service enterprises'."

Three million and more factory workers, 2,500,000 fishing folk, 100,000 sailors, 500,000 miners—multitudes of them women—62,000 people living like water rats on the canal boats of Tokyo and Osaka, over a million unemployed, one million "Shin-heimin," 850,000 victims of tuberculosis—with an annual death rate of 85,000, the poor crowded into semi-slums, the sickening slums packed with human wreckage! Who can face these facts and figures and not feel the urge to broadcast the Gospel of a finer and fuller life?

TYPE OF MISSIONARIES AND THEIR QUALIFICATIONS

All replies are emphatic that the "any-kind-of-missionary-will-do day has passed in Japan. There is such open-hearted expression that some apologize for their frankness. Bishop Uzaki says, "missionaries with genuine man-stuff, strong and well poised will win respect and confidence. They must have the evangelistic passion. They must sense the spirit of the Japanese and recognize that they are an understanding people. They must be friendly, sociable, cheerful and alive to the noxiousness of race prejudice. They must be kind, fair, broad-minded, tolerant and skilled in the art of bearing and forbearing. They must be willing failures equally with their Japanese colleagues. The Japanese are stepping into the places of leadership. This is an outstanding evidence of the success of missionary work in this land. As a tactful helper the missionary will still find a larger place and a large welcome."

Miss Kawai mentions, "adaptability, cheerfulness initiative, diligence and the spirit of the pioneer. They should have a high culture plus a deep spirituality. They must 'relearn' the meaning of the 'second mile.' Missionaries today are too practical. They do not venture beyond their own convenience." Prof. Bessho stresses, "strong faith, educational training and ability to appreciate Japanese nature and Japanese civiliza- tion. Too often missionaries fall short in intellectual training and in an understanding heart. They dif- ferentiate between Occidental and Oriental civilization and consider the latter inferior. Well educated Orien- tals of high birth and culture frequently feel that missionaries are not up to par intellectually or in personal qualities." President M. Ishizaka says, "a missionary should be a man of common sense, refined and a real specialist in his line." Mr. Tagawa says, "there is no place in Japan for missions or mission- aries which compete with the Japanese church. For those who are ready to co-operate there is a boundless field."

Mr. H. Nagao mentions, "the spirit of sacrifice, a tempered aggressiveness, understanding of, sympathy with, and respect for the place and worth of the Japanese. Highly trained but not a narrow specialist, able to lead in music, literary arts, sports and athle- tics. The reason the missionary field has narrowed is because the missionary's qualification has not kept step with the demand of Japan's knowledge-infatuated youth." Dr. Ibuka wants missionaries with, "a zeal for souls, those lacking this are not unknown. This is a prime requisite. Adaptable to environment, abili- ty to put himself in the place of those for whom he works, freedom from a sense of racial and cultural superiority—this does not mean blindness to faults or lack of courage to rebuke evil—and more patience than many young missionaries possess today." Prof. Sawano says, "the missionary in Japan today must be willing to stand on an equality with the Japanese. He should be willing to work not as a leader but as a co-worker, not as a supervisor but as an adviser." Dr. Kawaguchi lays down the acid test put forth by Jesus, "whosoever will be great among you, shall be your minister and whosoever of you will be the chiefest shall be servant of all."

CHAPTER VII

THE PRESENT PLACE OF THE MISSIONARY

(2) Rev. Chas. A. Logan, D.D.

"Preach the Gospel to every creature." The missionary is, first of all, a witness of the Risen Christ and a preacher of His Gospel. For this purpose he was sent out, and for this reason alone is the Church at home willing to support him. It is possible for him to preach through an interpreter, but he can not preach by proxy. Preaching by proxy means that one of the two is not preaching. He is not a listener but a preacher of the Gospel. If the Japanese preacher is able to do all the preaching in the church, let him go forward and make another one. Preaching is his crown, and he should let no man take his crown. All missionaries who are letting any thing crowd them out of preaching are making a regrettable mistake.

To the man who has a message of personal salvation and the Japanese language to express it, all Japan presents an open door. Missionaries who are determined to obey the command of the Risen Christ are finding places to preach every day. For outside of a few churches in the cities are hundreds of places where the Gospel has not yet been preached. He may go in his auto or walk, hang up a hymn, sing and teach it, and then deliver his message right there on the road-side or sea-side or mountain-side just like Jesus did. If there is a Christian family of good repute in the town, he may preferably make use of their home, and start a church in their house just as Pa.. ... ...

to other cities, but he will probably feel that he can not get around to all the towns before the Lord comes. There are too many of them.

For this reason some have gone into extensive tract distribution. There are others who think lightly of this method, but it is up to the critic to show a better way. Some have gone into Newspaper evangelism and are busy at it. Some have employed many Japanese preachers and are busy with them. If there is a church, he is welcome to deliver his message there. Most of the churches of Japan still welcome the missionary. Many of the independent churches continue to ask him to come and supply the pulpit once or twice a month. If he has worked it right, he is always welcomed as a preacher in the Mission churches. In the churches without a pastor, he is the Stated Supply. However he may do it, we always feel that the missionary is in his place as long as he is preaching the Gospel, and especially when he is preaching it where it has not been heard.

"BAPTIZING THEM"

Outside of a few churches in the large cities, the missionary is the only one to baptize. It would be far better for the Japanese preachers to do this. But the Japanese pastors who control the church at the present time are very reluctant about ordaining Japanese men to baptize, and they may be wise. The result is that there are very few Japanese who can baptize, and this leaves a large place for the missionary. I asked the pastor of the largest church in Nagoya, "If I should leave Nagoya and travel North, where could I get a Japanese preacher of your church to baptize me? At Matsumoto?" "No, there is no one there," he replied. "At Nagano," I asked. "No, there is none there." He did not name a place, but may be I could get baptized at Niigata. Then I asked him, "If I should travel West, where I could get baptized by a Japanese of your church?" At Gifu?" "No." "At

Ogaki?" "No." "At Maibara?" "No, you would have
to go to Kyoto." Now think of that! And all Japan
is just like that. Suppose there was no one but a
foreigner between New York and Rochester, or between Cincinnati and Chicago, or between Richmond
and Charlotte, who could baptize.

In the Island of Shikoku, by the coast road, it
is 136 miles from Tokushima to Kochi, and in all
that distance there is not a Japanese preacher who
can baptize a convert. It is 120 miles from Tokushima to Matsuyama, and in all those towns along
that road there is no one to baptize and receive a
convert into the church. The missionary has a big
place yet, too big. Some Missions are calling for new
missionaries to preach the word and to baptize.

Look at your map of Kyushu or Kwansai or
Kwanto or Hokkaido, and you will see that it is all
the same. Out of the large cities, there is no one to
baptize. And the Church has no plan for these places
out of the cities. It makes no appeal to its men to
take up the Cross and go out and preach the Gospel
where it has not been preached. It does not honor
a Japanese who will leave all and spend his life in
a small place where there is no hope of building a
self-supporting church. The honor and the right to
baptize is given to the man who stays in the city
where it is possible to make a large enough group to
form what is called a self-supporting church. But
Japan will not be evangelized until it honors its home
missionaries and clothes them with all the authority
of the Church.

"TEACHING THEM TO OBSERVE ALL THINGS

That is the place of the Missionary, teaching Bible
classes of all kinds, Men's, Women's, Young Men's,
Young Women's, Boys' and Girls', every day, at his
home, in the school, in the church, anywhere. This
is one

He knows the Bible. If he will, he can get splendid groups of people to come to his home to study it with him.

ADMINISTRATION

The Missionary in Japan need not waste time in the administration of the church. In a few of the older churches, he is not present in large numbers in the Church Councils, and there is danger of his going too far away from them. There is not much need of him, and he is glad to be free.

"MANY WOMEN WHICH MINISTERED UNTO HIM"

It is not fair to close this article without speaking of the place of the Lady Missionaries, native and foreign. Their work is what it has been from the beginning, only larger. They teach the Word in their homes, and churches, and Sunday Schools and factories. They visit the homes of Christians and enquirers, encouraging the disheartened, comforting the sick, always aiding in the upbuilding of the church.

They bear their own crosses for the Master with cheerful faces. One of them writes, "As far as my place is concerned, there are no Japanese workers here, so I have to take every part of the work." She is the Sunday School teacher, the pastor of the church and the lady missionary. She rode her bicycle 57 miles over the mountains of Japan, settled in a small town alone, because there was no man who would go, and has been doing it all alone ever since.

"Who follows in their train?"

CHAPTER VIII

THE PRESENT CHRISTIAN EDUCATIONAL SITUATION

(1) Male Education

Rev. D. B. Schneder, D.D., L.L.D.

That Christian education in Japan is carried on in an atmosphere of extraordinary eagerness for education is a fact too well known to need repetition. But the remarkable thing is that there are no signs of abatement in this eagerness. Earthquakes, floods, and business depression seem to make no difference. Japan is more keen and alert in its educational aspirations than ever.

Government education and all forms of public education are going on with vigor. Equipment is being amplified, teachers are being trained and methods improved at as rapid a rate as the economic condition of the country can possibly afford. Education is being more and more adapted to vocational and industrial needs. The five imperial universities are forging ahead and are getting to be well abreast with the best universities of the world. A comparatively new phenomenon is the recent decided increase of interest in scientific research. Half a dozen research institutes have been established quite recently, most of them financed privately by men of wealth.

Besides government and public education there is an increasing volume of private education. The greater of this is the enterprise has given a tremendous impetus to this class of educational work. Especially has the decision to grant full university standing to all private institutions that can qualify for the same, made a great change. The two foremost private universities, Waseda and Keio, now aggregate in their various courses and departments over 20,000 students. There are already 19 private universities, and all of them struggling toward further expansion and growth.

Christian education for boys and young men has been carried along on the tide of this educational eagerness and progressiveness, and to-day Christian schools everywhere are filled to over-flowing. Most of them are embarrassed by too many students, as they were years ago by too few. And these schools have also grown in equipment and scope. Two of them have acquired university recognition already, and two others are planning to apply for the same standing.

Alongside of Christian education Buddhist educational enterprise has also been growing. There are now four Buddhist institutions with full university standing. They are all thus far only "one department" universities, that is, they have only departments of literature, but the scope of their work is broad, with special emphasis on social subjects. Their students aggregate about 1,500. In addition there are the preparatory and other courses, and there are also six so-called universities, which however, have not yet obtained university recognition. Besides there are some twenty Buddhist schools of middle grade. All these aggregate about 11,000 more students. There is also a flourishing Shinto university, which furnishes many of the teachers of Japanese and Chinese for the schools of the country. The two Christian universities aggregate about 1,100 students of real university grade, and the total number of students of all Christian schools for young men is over 16,000, hence larger than the total number in Buddhist schools.

Taking these data into consideration it can safely be concluded that the situation of Christian education in Japan is hopeful. The fact that in spite of constant insufficiency of funds, lack of proper equipment, difficulty in securing and holding an efficient and devoted teaching force, these Christian schools have progressed, have won the confidence and even affection of the people, have influenced the religious thought and life of the nation profoundly, have built up loyal and virile alumni bodies that constitute a new factor in the situation, and have grown into the large and prosperous institutions of today, speaks much for the future prospects of this work. Such a force as Christian education has proven itself to be in Japan can not die. Moreover, there is one more feature of the situation that it is not unsafe to take into account at this stage in Japan's history. It is a certain attitude of expectation in reference to Christian education, which, if it can be met, will go far toward ensuring a large future for this form of Christian service. It is the expectation that possibly Christian education may hold the key to the solution of many of the moral, social and political problems that are now pressing upon the national life. Extreme radical ideas of all descriptions are penetrating into the thinking of the people at a disquieting rate. At the same time all effort to hold fast the nation to the old moorings is absolutely hopeless. What force can save society and the nation from drifting, who knows whither? Is not the constructive idealism of Christianity such a force,—a force that can furnish an anchorage at once satisfying to the liberal aspirations of the new day, and yet conservative of the stability of society? And is not Christian education the one agency that can instill this idealism into the youths of today? These are questions that seem to occupy consciously or unconsciously the minds of many, and certain it is that if Christian education has the t   t

of its future is assured. If the Christian schools can
manifest such sincerity and such earnestness along
this line that, instead of being looked upon as mere
instruments of religious propaganda, they come to
be regarded as the nation's foremost force to meet a
great need, then will they fulfil a mission unspeakably
appealing. There is a mighty challenge here.

However, in the presence of such a hopeful,
challenging future can Christian education measure
up? This is a great and serious question today.
Christian education is beset with many weaknesses
and handicaps. First, is the financial problem. The
annual budgets of the imperial universities run into
many millions of yen. How can the Christian institutions hope to put up anything at all comparable to
such figures? It is not a mistake for the present institutions to aspire to university standing. Unless
they do, there is not much of a future for them. Had
the union university proposed some years ago become
a reality, it would have been a vast advantage economically as well as strategically. But as that hope
was not realized, the next best thing is for the institutions now existing to develop to university grade.
A young man without a university training will have
less and less of a career ahead of him in the future.
But the financial problem is stupendous. Moreover,
government effort is systematized and coordinated,
while Christian effort is unorganized and divided. As
to educational method, the Christian institutions not
only make little of any distinct contribution of their
own, but often fall behind the government schools
in this respect. But most serious of all is the lack
of strong, united and devoted teaching staffs, that
give themselves wholly to the upbuilding of these
Christian institutions. To gather together groups of
persons who have the necessary educational qualifications and teaching skill, who are Christians not only
in name but in heart, who see the vision, and are
willing to cooperate with one another whole-heartedly

and sacrificially,—this is the hardest task in Christian education, and yet its future success and the fulfillment of its great mission depend upon this more than upon anything else. There are many noble men and women engaged in this work in Japan today, but they are far too few for the enlarging task. The main thing is that those who are responsible be not only forward-*looking* but forward-*moving*. In the midst of the rushing current of progress in this land, to stand still is to be left quickly in the rear. Constant and insistent progressiveness is needed. All friends of the work need to be awake.

And there are *conditions* to be met, and ways to be taken. Perhaps it can be said that the history of Christian education in Japan has been characterized by a wealth of ideas as to what should be done, and by much poverty in their realization. Nevertheless it may after all not be entirely profitless to restate again and again, as conditions change, various ideals as objectives of endeavor.

1. As to financial and moral resources, in addition to keeping before the foreign constituencies of this work the tremendous appeal of Japan, a new prospect is the phenomenon of a growing vision and sense of responsibility on the part of the alumni of the several institutions. As this interest is intelligently and systematically cultivated, and as especially the mission of these institutions is made clear to them in its newer and broader bearings, there is prospect of such increasing response from alumni bodies as will go far toward making the future safe and hopeful.

2. Although the handicaps to the achievement of high standards of discipline and educational efficiency are very great, the fight for these ideals must never be relaxed or given up. The military training recently introduced into the schools, so far as it is divested of its tendency to instill the spirit of militarism, is a distinct benefit to the Christian educational institu⋯   ⋯⋯⋯ ⋯⋯ ⋯⋯ ⋯ ⋯⋯ ⋯⋯ ⋯ ⋯⋯⋯⋯

of the Roman Catholic schools, are too lax in discipline. The dream of former times of the possibility of the Christian schools furnishing object lessons of superior educational method and efficiency has not been, and can not be, realized. But nevertheless the constant struggle for greater efficiency can not be given up without increasing loss of prestige, and of discredit to the Christian cause itself.

3. Probably the most urgent demand of the present situation is a fundamental and thorough-going revision of existing methods of realizing the Christian purpose of the institutions that bear the Christian name. Aided by past experience and with the flood of literature on religious education now pouring from the press, it should not be impossible to work out vastly better curricula of instruction in Christianity than now exist. Moreover, there is need of a re-study of the motivation of the Christian appeal. While the direct appeal to the religious sense must ever remain foremost and fundamental, yet closely connected with this appeal should be a much stronger appeal for the concrete realization in life of the new faith. School life together with its relations to the home offers a rich field for the practice of applied Christianity. That the securing of the finest kinds of personalities, properly qualified, as teachers of the religious and moral subjects is of supreme importance, would not require mention were it not for the fact that too often it seems to be taken for granted that anybody can teach the Bible or give the moral talks. Finally, a method of endeavor that can never be over-rated is that of group-work and personal contact outside of the class-room. It is not entirely true that "religion is not taught but caught," but neither is it entirely false, and perhaps the saying is truer in Japan than in some other countries. Certain it is that the young men of Japan are responsive to personal interest to a high degree. No kind of religious work in our

Christian institutions is so fruitful as this personal or group-work.

A matter that is worthy of much effort is the development and training of the Christian students in the several institutions. The Christian students ought to receive much attention outside of school hours. Be they many or few they should be led to feel together the challenge of the world's moral and spiritual needs. They should assiduously be brought into stimulating contact with Christ and His saving mission to humanity. This can be done in many ways,—in the dormitories, in the teachers' homes; through the school Y.M.C.A., the school church, students' clubs and other organizations. Moreover, it is very important to interest, through these same agencies, the Christian students in the Church and to train them for church membership and church activity. Perhaps the weakest point in the whole Christian movement in Japan is the weakness of the Church and of organized Christianity. This fact, instead of repelling Christian students, should be made to stand before them as a great challenge for service especially after entrance upon their life work. They have the intelligence, and they should have the training and the consecration to become leading workers in the churches wherever they go.

1. It is probable that both within the several schools, and much more outside, there is much lack of clearness as to the meaning of the "Christian purpose" of the Christian schools. Invariably and without hesitation it must ever be affirmed that the fundamental religious purpose of a Christian school is to lead individual students into the new life in Christ Jesus. Without that nothing else is of much avail. However, a second form which the Christian purpose should take is to impart Christian teaching as an integral part of an ideal education. Man educated only in rela

around him is only partially educated; to be ideally educated, he must be educated also in relation to God above him. But a third phase of the Christian purpose of the Christian institutions needs new and great emphasis. It is the fulfillment of the mission mentioned before, of instilling into the minds and hearts of youths the Christian idealism needed for the new day. The best that is in the hearts of men today should find shining leadership and glowing inspiration in these educational institutions established in this land in the name of Jesus Christ. In them should be trained the master-builders of a better world.

5. It is fortunate that a National Christian Council has been established in Japan. As this central Christian body gains in momentum, the time should come when it will become a powerful coordinating and unifying force in this whole large work of Christian education, and when its offices in Tokyo will become a clearing-house for such exchange of information and stimulus as will go far to give a new *esprit de corps* and a new momentum to the whole endeavor. If also under the auspices of this Council, with perhaps a few experts from abroad added, the whole situation could be studied by a competent commission, much good would result. At the Conference held under the auspices of the Council at Kamakura in December steps were taken looking toward a closer inter-relation of the existing institutions. This will be an excellent forward step.

In ways like these, even though haltingly and imperfectly realized, the vast and far-reaching mission of this beneficent work will more and more be fulfilled. Faith, courage and hope will be needed every step of the way, but the result achieved in the history of this nation will not be small.

THE PRESENT CHRISTIAN EDUCATION SITUATION

(2) Female Education

Miss L. L. Shaw

The most striking fact in the present educational situation for women is the amazing development of facilities for higher education which the opening of some 800 institutions is now giving. When one remembers the decided opposition to college education for women even a few years ago, the present change in public sentiment is nothing short of a phenomenon, and plainly shows the steady resistless demand of the girls of the nation for education equal to that of their brothers. The college courses now open to girls carry them nearer to their goal and the way is open for women to obtain degrees similar to those granted to men. A few specially qualified women have been allowed to enter the Imperial Universities and to obtain a full degree the same as men.

The surprising success of the private colleges has at last induced even the conservative Educational Office to open a few schools of college grade for women, which in time, may become universities. One of the first acts of the recently formed Girls High Schools League was to approach the Educational Office with the request that the Men's Higher Schools and universities be thrown open to women. The officials soothingly replied that they did not consider the time ripe for co-education but that the problem of pro   th   t, , , t   , t , r   r   r education was being sympathetically considered.

This change of public sentiment in favour of higher education for women, is due in no small measure to the Christian Girls schools which have consistently held to the ideal of a complete course from the kindergarten to the university, equal in every respect to that given to men. Up to a few years ago, with the exception of the Higher Normal Schools, most of the higher education for girls was either under Christian auspices or open to Christian influence. These colleges have not only sent out many strong Christian teachers but they have also furnished many of the leaders in the women's movement. In order to hold this position of leadership, it would seem wise for our Christian women's colleges to agree among themselves to emphasize certain departments, so as to use the limited means and forces we have to the best advantage. Such a policy would greatly strengthen our position and enable us to keep our Christian colleges well in the lead.

The second outstanding feature is the slow but steady trend toward an understanding of the value and place of religion in education. After the recent conference of the principals of Girls High Schools where the need of religious instruction was voiced so strongly, a leading Japanese Christian said, "Congratulations to the Christian Girls schools. This change of sentiment is due to your work. Carry on, you are winning." The attitude of the government was made clear by the representative of the Educational Office stating, that though the government could not endorse religion as part of the curriculum, yet any principal was free to speak himself on religious subjects and also to invite others to speak.

This gradual recognition of the value of religious teaching as the foundation of character has given so much more elasticity and freedom to schools with government recognition, that it has encouraged many of the Christian Girls schools to become regular Higher Girls' Schools for they find no difficulty in continuing their regular Christian instruction and worship. Our next great movement should be to establish Christian Primary schools. The weakest point in Japanese education to-day is not that which all seem to emphasize—the deficiency of higher schools—it is something far more fundamental, namely the inadequacy and inefficiency of the primary schools. Poorly trained teachers, huge classes, crowded buildings and poor equipment, long hours for the teachers six days a week and often meetings on Sunday—Is it any wonder that the teachers lose energy and enthusiasm? Or that individual children receive little attention? Or that the principals of high schools do not see their way to admit this medley of graduates without applying the sieve of the eliminating entrance examinations to remove the unfit?

Some of the wealthy merchants of Osaka have lately put up fine concrete buildings, with roof gardens and excellent modern equipment, as their contribution to the city schools. These are steps in the right direction, but as yet there is no attempt to get at the heart of the matter, which is not buildings, necessary though these are, but *personality*. Has not the time come, in the large cities at least, for the Christian communities to get together and establish joint primary schools which shall be model Christian institutions? Such schools should carry our Christian kindergarten system into and through the primary school. Freedom of movement, opportunity for initiative, and ever the child in the midst looking up to the Father, looking *out* on the world, working *with* his fellows—the children and the teacher cooperating together to make all those adjustments to life which are so essential for the well-being of any community.

The Christian Nursery Schools, which are proving so successful in London, Night schools for girls in business, clubs and educational centers for girls in industr.

Christian leadership which our schools can and should give. We must make it our aim to put before the girls the crying need for workers in all these fields.

What then is the contribution to education that the Christian Girls schools have made and are making? Many of the results are intangible but some can be plainly seen. Christian education for girls in Japan from the kindergarten to the university stands for certain ideals and the first of these is woman as an individual. It refuses to consider that women's life can be merged in that of husband or child or state. As an individual then the girl must receive and fulfil all the privileges and responsibilities which belong to each human being. It is therefore the endeavour of Christian education to show the girl her relationship to her Creator, to her fellowman, and to the world around her, so that she can make the best possible contribution to her generation.

The outstanding feature of the Christian Girls schools in contrast with the government schools, is a spirit of friendliness, of comradeship between pupil and teacher. The spirit of independence and initiative is encouraged and there is more freedom and elasticity. These schools have made no small contribution to the progress of women in Japan and have no cause to feel ' ashamed. It was through their pioneer and uphill work that the government was persuaded to include girls as well as boys in its schemes for public education. It is again due to their steady persistent effort that the movement for the higher education of women is finally gaining public approval. And it is largely due to their influence that the importance of religious teaching in the schools is today gaining adherence in high places.

One of the by-products of the influence of the mission schools of the country is seen in the adoption of western dress by many of the government schools, in order to get the freedom of movement and out of-door games so necessary for modern ways of life.

Already the result is amazing and is revealed in an amusing way in the modern request for brides. Formerly the request was for girls with pale, oval faces and subdued gentle ways. Today the demand is for tall, energetic, athletic girls, with round faces. So we are making progress.

This change toward the western mode of living in dress and in the home is significant and is no mere whim of fashion. It notes a definite movement of the women toward a new freedom..

In fact the Christian educated women are the leaders of the woman's movement. It was these women who introduced the petitions into Parliament asking for equal opportunities for men and women in education and in politics, and the bill for the abolition of the licensed quarters. They are the real leaders of the suffrage and all movements for social reform. Also in any general women's meeting, such as those held by a town or one of the newspapers, the Christian women take a prominent part. The steady poise, the quiet power, the unassuming ways, and the practical ability of these Christian women, win the confidence of the delegates and they are usually given positions of trust and responsibility.

The day has now come when the leadership in our girls schools should naturally pass into the hands of our Japanese co-workers. It is to be hoped that it will pass into the hands of women. Unfortunately few women are left free in Japan to devote themselves to a career but even here the women missionaries have wrought a change. A few thoughtful leaders are advocating the single life for women who feel called to special work, but married women are being allowed to carry on their work as teachers, writers, etc. So we see Mrs. Moto Hani, Mrs. Yamakawa and others working out their ideals in their own schools and publications, but we need many more as principals of our schools and colleges. Our schools under the manage

admit of personal contact, direct Christian teaching,
influence by personality and, therefore, carefully
selected teachers.

We wish we could have carefully selected pupils.
But to get them we need equipment, salaries and a
pension system equal to that of the Government
schools; we need the cordial support and understanding of the Christian community. Above all we need
a far greater measure of cooperation and coordination
in all our educational work, such as was recommended
at the Mott Conference at Kamakura. For instance if
the two colleges and three higher departments for girls
in the Kwansai region could work out some plan of
affiliation such as has been attained in London and
Toronto Universities, we should have a much stronger
centre for the higher education of women in West
Japan. This would be further strengthened if different colleges agreed to develop special departments and
so reduce overlapping to a minimum.

We have worked and are working with poor
tools, but when we see so many Christian women in
positions of responsibility and leadership, and when
we remember the growing influence of the Christian
home throughout the length and breadth of the land,
we can thank God and take courage. Though we
count not ourselves to have attained yet we press
towards the mark of our high calling in Christ Jesus.

CHAPTER IX

THE DEGREE OF SELF-SUPPORT REACHED IN JAPAN

(1) In Evangelistic Work

Rev. David S. Spencer, D.D.

The first requisite to a clear understanding of any discussion like the present is a definition of the terms used. Under the above heading, the following nine items are included in Evangelistic work: (1) Churches; (2) Kogisho; (3) Evangelistic Touring; (4) Bible Classes; (5) Visiting & Woman's Meetings; (6) Street Preaching; (7) *Tenmaku-dendo;* (8) Evangelistic Literature including Newspaper Evangelism; (9) Sunday Schools & Young People's Societies. Hence all funds belonging to educational or eleemosynary work, or to missionary sustenance are excluded.

The facts revealed come in answer to a questionaire sent to every Mission doing evangelistic work among Japanese in Japan or Formosa.

Occasionally a Mission has felt delicate about revealing the results of its accomplishments on self-support lines, and therefore, as a rule, the names of specific Missions co-operating will not be given. Nor can all Missions be measured satisfactorily by one standard. In a testing of this sort, a small Mission, started among a special salaried class, and with a special objective, such as merchants, artizans, clerks, doctors and the like, may become self-supporting from the start; whereas a larger Mission, carrying on various line   f   m   f   l.,

seems not to be able to make so good a percentage
showing. A mission or Church that stresses educational or eleemosynary work, will find difficulty, especially in its earlier years, in developing self-support
in its evangelistic department.

Again, the nature of the relations existing between Churches and Missions,—Japanese and foreigners,—has much to do with the question under discussion. In this respect, Japan offers a most interesting study. Here are organizations in which all real
authority is practically exercised by the Mission, the
Japanese being advisory. Others there are, from
which the missionary has been practically eliminated,
the Japanese exercising entire control; and there are
grades of adjustment between these extremes. There
can be no doubt that the question of ultimate control
has a powerful influence upon the question of self-
support in all lines of work.

As to present attainment in self-support, the survey shows a great divergence. The lowest showing
is where 3% of the funds used are from Japanese
sources, and 97% from foreign sources; while the
highest showing credits the Japanese with furnishing
92%, and the foreigners 8% of the funds used. To strike
an average proportion at this point is difficult because
of incomplete returns. A fairly safe guess would be
that, taking the field as a whole, present day evangelistic work gets 40% of its support from native
sources, and 60% from foreign.

Then immediately comes the questions, what
changes if any are taking place? Is self-support gaining ground, not only in aggregate amount, but in average gifts per member?

To answer these questions scientifically for the
country as a whole would require a little more pains-
taking attention to the questionaire on the part of
Mission secretaries making reply; and therefore a conservative statement is still required. But enough is
reve~led to m~k~ ~l~~ the fact that there is a steady

gain being scored in self-support.

One leading group spends 405,069 Yen per year in evangelistic effort, 373,069 Yen of which comes from Japanese pockets. Another has spent more than 525,000 Yen in 1925, more than 410,000 Yen of which the Japanese gave. Still another reports for ten years past: "Church membership has just doubled during that time; native contributions have increased five-fold; the Mission grant has just doubled. Native Christians are paying a larger proportion of Church expenses than ten years ago."

Another witness is definite: "In 1914, the Japanese raised 18% of all monies used in Evangelistic work. In 1919, 23.7%; in 1924, 35.7%. During the last five years there has been an increase of 84% in contributions by the Japanese for the whole Church."

This writer has recently made an intensive study of the Japan Methodist Church, and of the three Missions now co-operating with that Church, from the very beginning of the work of each in this country, covering a little more than fifty years. The total cost of establishing this Church, with all that belongs to it, on educational, publishing, eleemosynary and evangelistic lines was found to be $14,067,379, U.S. Gold, of which the Japanese giving totalled 7.3%. But this simple way of stating the matter is entirely misleading, unless explained. The $1,038,945, or 7.3%, given by the Japanese, was wholly for the evangelistic work of that Church, and omits their large gifts to education, while the $13,028,434 of foreign money covered all foreign expenditure for the large united missionary force, the schools, publishing interests, and all property investments of all three Missions. But a more satisfactory statement is found in the fact that since the erection of this autonomous Church in 1909, its membership has doubled one and a half, and self-support has increased five fold. It thus gave in 1907, Yen 3.18 per member for self-support; in 1924, Yen 17.50 p   · ' · ·

The above four samples represent four of the prominent Missions, and seem clearly to point the way to what is taking place in other Missions generally, though not all have spoken with equal clearness on this point. In the interests of future evangelization, it would be well to have this survey carried on until all Missions and Churches were accurately represented and definitely recorded. Reports received show that they might thus really aid each other.

Incomplete as the returns received are, they make pretty clear the following conclusions:

1.—Self-support in evangelistic work in Japan is steadily gaining ground. If the gains made are not entirely satisfactory, they are largely so.

2.—Where co-operation between Japanese and foreign workers is closest, self-support is advancing with greatest rapidity, *providing* the acquisition of administrative control by the Japanese is made to depend in some fair way upon Japanese giving. There is a necessary relation between authority and financial responsibility. Granting autonomy without financial responsibility is shown to be unwise. *"Push* the Church on to self support" is the silent but implied conclusion.

3.—Where Japanese Church and foreign missionaries, belonging to the same communion, work independently, the results are clearly "disappointing," even discouragingly so.

4.—More than one witness calls attention to the necessity of saving the Church from "the benevolent missionary."

5.—While the resources for self-support in the present Japanese Church have not been exhausted, it becomes increasingly evident that the limits of such support are not so far ahead, unless the Church's membership can be largely augmented. The *sine qua non* to complete and genuine self-support is a mighty spiritual baptism that shall fill the churches and set souls free.

THE DEGREE OF SELF-SUPPORT REACHED IN JAPAN

(2) In Educatinoal Work

Prof. Y. Ichimura

Among all the present existing Christian schools in our country, the oldest is the Yokohama Kyoritsu Girls School, which was established in November, 1871 (Fourth Year of Meiji), that is to say fifty-five years ago. The newest is the Kyushu Jogakuin of Kumamoto, established in May 1924 (Thirteenth Year of Taisho). During this half century there have been established throughout the entire country 91 Christian schools. Among these there are 17 Middle Schools, 35 Girls Schools and 39 Universities or Junior Colleges. The graduates number about 40,000. The present number of students is 26,500. Comparing these figures with the number of public schools existing in the Tenth Year of Taisho, we find the Middle Schools are about one twentieth of the total, the Girls' Schools about one thirteenth and the Universities and Junior Colleges about two thirds of the whole.

	Middle Schools	Girls Schools	Universities and Colleges
Public	303	465	62
Christian	17	35	39

In addition there are very many Christian Kindergartens and ten or more Christian Primary Schools. Even if we consider only thus far we see that Christian ed.

lopment of culture in our country. Especially is this true in the sphere of woman's education and kinder-gartens.

Especially meritorious service has been rendered in the sphere of spiritual education. Because our national school education has until now discarded religious faith, it has lost the foundation of moral education, and moral authority has failed; our Christian education alone, by emphasizing the education of character based on faith and established moral authority, has made its great contribution in this sphere. Again, in the sphere of the curriculum, it has in English and in music a special character which defies all imitation. Also Christian education has produced from among its 40,000 graduates many leaders in the world of religion, learning, politics, education, business, etc., and has thus made a great contribution to the development of the culture of our nation

Most of the Christian schools of our country have been established by foreign missionaries. It is true that two or three have been established by Japanese but these have come into being with the assistance of foreign missionaries. Among these are the Doshisha established by Jo Neejima, the Tohoku Gakuin by Masayoshi Oshikawa and the Baika Jo Gakko by Benra Sawayama. Only such schools as the Theological Schools established in Tokyo by Masahisa Uemura and Kodo Ozaki have been from the beginning entirely the undertaking of Japanese. Other than these there are none without some sort of relation to Foreign Missions. Therefore it has been the custom to call Christian schools simply Mission schools.

Again, the number of teachers employed in all Christian schools is 2452. Subtracting 804 special lecturers, there are 1648 teachers, but of these the number of foreign teachers is 370, or about one fourth of the total number. These are indispensable teachers in Bible teaching, English and Music.

Next we come to the matter of expenditure. The total current expenditure for all our Christian schools for the year 1924 was Yen 2,994,596.00. Of this amount what percent was contributed by foreigners? It is a great pity that as there are no reliable statistics on this point, it is impossible to ascertain the degree of financial self-support attained.

But it is certain that all Theological Schools, Junior Colleges, Universities, etc., are receiving far more assistance than the organs of middle school education. Among middle grade schools, if a school has about five hundred students, it ought to be able to become self-supporting.

Out of our 94 Christian schools, 22 are Zaidan Hojin, 20 are Shadan Hojin, 16 are independent Zaidan Hojin. All the others are in Foreign Mission Board Hojin or Holding Corporations. 21 schools have endowments and the total of these endowments amounts to Yen 3,687,381.00.

There are fourteen middle grade schools with more than 500 students. Two or three of these have more than 1,000 students. Such schools as these are in a position easily to become self-supporting, without either support from outside or even an endowment. But suppose that all form of Foreign Mission support, spiritual and personal, should be cut off, how many Christian schools could continue to support themselves? This is a very important question. Under the present circumstances, if we leave out of consideration two or three schools, it would mean a tremendous blow to Christian education. But I believe that ten years from now by far the greater part of our Christian schools will have reached a level where they can support themselves. There are three reasons for this expectation.

The first is that by ten years from now, evangelist

and l . . .   11

have increased; along with the independent self-support of the churches, the schools will receive endowments, etc., and will be able to become self-supporting.

Secondly, it is a fact that as the spirit of independent self-support is remarkably springing into existence among our Christian churches and schools, dissatisfaction is being felt with depending only on assistance from Foreign Mission Boards and progress is gradually being made in organizing independent Zaidan Hojin.

Thirdly, we should note that society in general in our country has gradually come to understand the intrinsic worth of Christian education and in consequence people are sending their children to schools of Christian type; graduates of such schools are being welcomed in all directions, our Government is giving financial support of grants of land and is encouraging the graduates by giving them various privileges, and private friends are raising endowments for and are assisting Christian schools.

In short, we are now in a transition period when all Christian schools, separating from the guiding and protecting hand of the Foreign Mission Boards, are progressing toward independent self-support. But we need to pay great attention lest we hurry on merely to independence, using forced methods, discarding the spirit in which our schools were founded, compromising with the world, etc. Truly it may be said to be a critical time.

THE DEGREE OF SELF-SUPPORT REACHED IN JAPAN

(3) Self-Support in Other Lines of Work

Prof. Roy Smith

Social work institutions, or those organizations which are neither educational nor evangelistic, are so numerous and so varied in their nature that anything like an exhaustive treatment of them here is out of the question.

The great increase in general social work is easily apparent. Last year in Tokyo-fu there were at least five times as many social service institutions as ten years ago. Eight years ago the amount of money spent throughout Japan by the government increased in one year from one million to twelve million yen, and has increased substantially since. Tokyo City is reported to have spent six million yen last year in 180 institutions in comparison with Y.200,000.00 in 20 institutions seven years before, while Osaka City reported an expenditure of Y.2,200.00 in 1923 against nothing expended in 1916.

Such facts, while gratifying in themselves, are relevant to our subject of self-support among Christian institutions doing social work only in so far as the latter may have served as a stimulant to the national and city governments in their efforts to solve the many and great social problems confronting them. And if one of the fundamental motives of Christian Social rightly consider that any influence that is serving to increase the amount of work done by the government or by the people is vitally related to the question of self-support.

However, we are concerned in this paper with the situation among Christian institutions. In an attempt to get reliable information on the point of self-support the writer applied to over 160 institutions scattered throughout Japan. He was successful in getting reports from a little less than half of these. Therefore anything that may be said here cannot be taken as exhaustive, but we can, however, draw some general conclusions.

Self support may be looked at from several points of view. First of all we may consider the matter of the property—buildings, land, equipment, etc.—which the organization is using.

Reports on this point were not uniform enough to justify very definite statements. In a few cases the land was reported as having been received from Japanese while the buildings were received from foreign sources. Several institutions have received half of the amount for their property from Japan and half from abroad. Over half of the 35 institutions making a clear report on this point state that all of their property was received from Japan while in no case was it reported as all coming from abroad. These 35 institutions estimate their property at about two million yen. Less than one-fourth of this amount came from abroad.

Sixty-seven organizations report an aggregate yearly income of Y.1,607,345.84. In one case the income is being received entirely from one individual. Forty-eight of these are receiving at least small amounts from some government source, the total amount from this source being a little above one hundred thousand yen, or one sixteenth of the total income.

Strictly speaking it may be said that in order

to be entirely self-supporting an organization must receive its· entire support from its own members or from those served. However, so far as our reports go, only a little over one-fourth of the yearly income comes from this source. But since a goodly proportion of the institutions reporting are homes for orphans, lepers, old people, poor children, and others of a similar nature, it could not be expected that they would be entirely self-supporting in this sense of the word.

It is difficult to tell from the reports just how much of the annual income of these institutions comes from local churches connected with the institutions. In a very few cases it seems that practically all of the support comes in this way. One Christian organization for the relief of orphans and poor children reports no receipts from any church, saying that the "churches are unkind." On the whole, between six and seven percent of the annual income was reported to be coming from local churches or individuals closely connected with the institutions. And for our purpose it does not much matter whether the money is given by individuals directly to the institution or through the church to the institution. We can say, however, that in the neighborhood of one-third of the yearly income of these sixty-seven social work organizations, amounting in all to Y.1,607,345.84, is received from the people whom they help, from their own members, from local churches, or from individuals close at hand. This in one sense may be taken as a pretty good indication of the degree of self-support at present reached by these associations.

Eighteen out of the sixty-seven reports state definitely the amounts which come from foreign mission boards or from foreign churches. The aggregate thus reported is about eighty thousand yen, or about one-twentieth of the whole income. As a considerable propc .   . '   .   . . I '   l·c that some more should be credited to the foreign missions and churches. And furthermore, it should not be thought that this amount is the total of what is being given by mission boards and foreign churches to social work in Japan. This survey does not cover the whole field, as many institutions failed to report to us at all. Others reported by general statements without stating definite amounts. However, it seems to be pretty clear that church people in foreign countries are not at all bearing the big end of the Christian Social work load in this country.

If, however, we are looking at this matter of self-support with the idea of asking ourselves the question as to whether or not the time has arrived or is arriving when foreigners may withdraw from Christian Social work in Japan, we must consider the personnel of the workers as well as the financial support. Here again we must speak in comparisons rather than in absolute numbers. Fifty-five societies reported 496 paid Japanese workers. Nine out of these fifty-five societies have twenty-nine paid foreign workers. Thus we see that less than six percent of the paid workers are foreigners. Our reports do not show whether the expense of maintaining these foreigners is included in the amounts stated as coming from foreign sources or not. It is altogether likely that in most cases such items of expense do not pass through the accounts of the local societies at all.

Nearly all of the societies that have paid workers also report volunteer workers. Here the proportion of foreigners to Japanese workers is much higher, as over one-fourth of the volunteer workers are foreigners.

As was stated above, only a few of the institutions get along entirely with volunteer workers. Of such volunteers one-sixth are foreigners and the rest Japanese. Of the sixty-six organizations reporting regarding their workers, sixty percent report no foreign workers at all. Taken as a whole, only a small fraction more than ten percent of the paid and volunteer workers are foreigners.

Thus in view of the fact that sixty percent of these societies have no foreign workers at all and that nine-tenths of the total number of workers are Japanese, it may be rightly concluded that from this point of view they have reached a pretty high degree of self-support.

In order to get a general idea of how the leaders in these various societies feel regarding foreign help we asked three questions:

(a) How has assistance from foreigners or from foreign countries helped your work in the past? The replies to this question show a deep appreciation of the value of the assistance from foreigners. In several instances it is stated that the work was established entirely by foreigners and that it is because of the effectiveness of their influence that the societies are now able to get along so well with Japanese workers only.

(b) Would you suffer any serious disadvantage if support from foreign countries were discontinued? Naturally those societies not now receiving support from abroad would not be affected. The others, however, with some exceptions said that the disadvantage would be "Serious." A few said that their activities would have to stop entirely, be greatly decreased, or changed in form. One or two expressed the opinion that the Japanese would be "encouraged toward independence and hard work." Two or three said the disadvantage would be "for a while only."

(c) How can foreigners living in Japan or in foreign countries help your institution? In over two-thirds of the replies to this question "subsidy" or "contribution" was mentioned.

One definitely asked for Y.200.00 per month. One said "I

countries, but it is better to send money." In four
cases it was said that they could help best by coming
and preaching the Gospel. Eight preferred to have
the foreigner help in the educational work by advice,
lecturing, teaching English, teaching English Bible
classes, etc.

In conclusion it seems to the writer that the foreigner who has been connected with the promotion
of Christian social work in Japan need not be disappointed at the degree of self-support at present attained, nor on the other hand does the person who
is desirous of entering into the work need to feel that
the job is done or that there is no room for him or
her.

*

PART III

THE FUTURE

CHAPTER X

THE FUTURE PROGRAM OF THE JAPANESE CHURCH

(1) In Organization

Rev. K. Matsuno

Cooperation.—The present Christianization of Japan is still in the state of cooperation of the Japanese Church and the foreign missionaries. Compared with the first stage of missionary work there has been great progress. We are now in the second stage of the transition, and have not yet reached the third. As to when this second stage of cooperation will pass away, different people have different opinions, but unless a sudden, unexpected change should come, it will most probably last at least thirty years longer, that is, till 1956. The Federation of Japanese Churches lasted for ten years and now has ceased to exist. Now the present Japan National Christian Council will doubtless prove a most valuable instrument in the future Christianization of Japan, and will not easily pass out of existence. Hence, in regard to this new organization it will be necessary also to view it as a cooperative instrument of Japanese and foreign workers

Union of Churches.—It is difficult to think that
the many denominations will always continue to exist
in their present form. In response to the demands
of the time it will be necessary, sooner or later, for
these denominations to come together as one united
Church. The desire is general to get rid, as soon
as possible, of the denominational divisions brought
in from foreign lands and to form a large and united
Japanese body for the Christianization of the Country, both spiritually and economically. At the Conference in Gotemba in 1918 there were present 116
persons who decided to endeavor, in the spirit of
Christ, to unite the different Japanese Churches for
the Christianization of the Country. In pursuance of
this decision, several committees set to work visiting
different Church bodies and inquiring into the condition of things regarding the feasibility of Church
union. And even before this concrete attempt there
were various movements and discussions bearing on
the question of Church union. Mr. Nagao Hampei
and others, seeing the impossibility of a general union,
effected a local union of churches at Moji. At the
Missionary Conference in 1925 a resolution was passed
appointing a committee to look into the matter of
Church union and in the Congregational Mission a
committee for the same purpose was appointed.

The Way of Church Union.—In Canada the Methodist, Presbyterian and Congregational Churches
united last year (1925) after twenty-five years of
effort. As for Japan, there are the different denominations and the different missions concerned, hence
it may seem that union would be a task requiring
months and years of efforts and various kinds of pro-
cedures. But in reality this is not so. By earnest
endeavors of the National Christian Council together
with the Missions, it may not take such a very long
time; probably it can be accomplished within ten
years.

I will now set forth in general outline the future plan and expectation of such union.

1. Let the "Church of Christ in Japan," the "Kumi-ai" (Congregational), and the Methodist Churches appoint a joint Committee for conference on the question of union and submit a proposal for the same.

2. Let the Baptist, Christian (Disciples) and the Christian Convention Churches consider the question of union, as to whether they shall unite in the first place with the "Kumi-ai," or enter at once upon union with the three Churches named above.

3. Let the Methodist Protestant, Evangelical, United Brethren and Free Methodists consider the union question, as to whether they shall unite with the Methodist Church or with the first-named group.

4. Let the "Friends," Lutheran, Holiness and other remaining Churches consider whether they should freely unite with this or that Church or with the first-named group, or whether they will go on separately.

5. It is a question whether, as outlined above, the larger Churches should unite in group and the smaller likewise, or whether they all should try to unite without distinction of size.

6. As for the Episcopal Church, it has not yet. as such, come into the National Christian Council and doubtless in the matter of union it would create great difficulty, but even this is not altogether without hope, and I believe that ultimately they will unite. In case the Episcopal Church should go into union, the Anglican Church will likely follow, I believe.

As for the Roman Catholic Church, no one thinks union with it can be easily effected. But if, as of old, the time came that again they would have to bear witness to their faith unto death, we would gladly place ourselves on their side as martyrs for the faith.

7. If those who direct the affairs of the various Churches and Missions should neglect the opportunities for union and not avail themselves of the methods of its possible accomplishment, in such a case unions like that at Shimonoseki, or other unions, disregarding denominational lines, might quickly take place.

The Furtherance of Union.—To appoint Committees for investigation, propaganda, conference and addresses may be useful, but the very best method would be to have the Churches and Missions that desire union appoint a representative committee which should meet for making preparations, and enter upon a definite campaign of united movement by public addresses and education, all under the direction of said Committee. Thus by addresses and conferences the subject of union would become prominent and its blessings and benefits would become apparent.

Cooperation after Union.—Even though union might be effected, the Japanese Church would not be strong enough, either in personnel or in financial means, to bear alone the burden of Christianizing Japan. For the present there would still be need of the earnest cooperation of Foreign Missions. I think that Foreign Missions would gladly cooperate with men and money under the banner of a United Church.

The Japanizing of the Union Church.—The United Church would have to consider questions of selecting from each denomination the best and eliminating the worst, of making combinations, and thus build up the best Church possible to the possible satisfaction of all.

Whether this United Church would be largely constituted along the lines of outward ceremony, as in the Roman Catholic Church, or more along informal lines, like, viz. the Friends Church, cannot be positively asserted beforehand. But reasoning from the fact of Buddhist influence and character in the past, it is very probable that at least some such forms as obtain in the Low Church Episcopal would flourish to a certain extent in the United Church in Japan of the future.

THE FUTURE PROGRAM OF THE JAPANESE CHURCH

(2) In Evangelization

Rev. S. Tada

1. A GLANCE AT EVANGELIZATION WORK OF THE PAST AND THE PRESENT.—The preaching of the Gospel having begun only a few decades ago, we are compelled to say that its present results move us to astonishment at the evidences of the display of God's power. Speaking from the view-point of statistics, compared with those of the other religions, the result seems exceedingly small. But when looking at the influence and power of Christianity, people in general will doubtless agree that it is by no means to be despised. The seed sown with tears and prayers of foreign and Japanese workers, and the saints who today with steadfast faith are bearing the cross in strenuous effort, are undoubted evidences of their desire to dedicate the country to God. It is essential, I think, to anew stir up courage and with thanksgiving and prayer to plan for evangelization in the future. But, a review of the work of evangelization in the past must necessarily be accompanied by repentance and regret. In point of numbers the foreign and Japanese preachers were not a few, (in various activities), but compared to that, the efficiency attained did not come up to the mark. The efficiency by laymen in evangelization, both in the past and at present, is as yet hardly worth mentioning. If we compare it with what is set forth from year to year in the statistics

of each denomination is cannot be gainsaid that there is a pessimistic aspect in the situation.

In the task of evangelization, making the training of Christians the main objective, it is plain that pastoral care and activity should go hand in hand. Where this is lost sight of the Church is usually able to maintain attendance upon the services throughout the years at a certain level, but as regards attendance upon the regular evangelistic meetings, is it not true that these are all in a dismal and deplorable condition? Even though there are candidates baptized, when we consider that in even larger numbers Christians are back-sliding, we cannot but think in silence, and with a shudder, about the future of the evangelization of Japan. In short, it is matter of unspeakable regret that in the Church at present we do not find, like in the Church of the Apostolic times, individual believers going here and there, from place to place, zealously doing evangelistic work. To be sure, evangelization work is done, but the ministry of training a body of men who in holy consecration will go forth as a picked body of Christ, is still in its infancy; and carelessly lying down is surely one of the main causes of the stagnation in evangelization. Still more, when one observes the plans and policies of evangelization work, the places chosen for preaching, the rifts in foreign and Japanese cooperation, etc., and everywhere discovers deficiencies, in the face of these failures one deeply feels how essential it is to put the program of evangelization upon a firm basis.

2. THE CHURCH STANDARD IN EVANGELIZATION.— Evangelization thus far is spoken of as only skin-deep, but the evidences as to the future of yielding to haphazard ways of working are already there. Evangelization has come to a sort of dead-lock, and while on every hand difficult problems are setting in, are we not . . . .

of evangelization? The work of foreign evangelization at present also is being involved in various
troubles. Some look upon the future so pessimistical-
ly that we hear of their withdrawing from the field
and returning to their home-land. I hear that some
even raise the foolish question as to whether the foreign missionary is still needed in Japan. But are
there not scarcely a few hundred-thousand believers
only, among the 70 million of people in this country?

The work of evangelization is, beyond dispute, of
tremendous importance. Looked at from that point of
view the question as to whether the foreign missionary
is needed or not cannot even be reasonably discussed.
Does not such a question arise from the faults in our
evangelistic ways of working, our plans and our cooperation? I am of opinion that the evangelistic work
of the missionary in the future ought to be in vital
connection with the Church. The results of evangelization must head up in well established individual
independent churches. Let the local church determine its own sphere, and let the results of evangelistic
efforts swarm, like bees, to form a new church.

When we look at city churches, even cities with
millions of people, the hundreds of churches existing
in such a city, all having made the city their principal
sphere, as a rule are not in a position of acquiring
firm foundations in their respective neighborhoods.
This is the very defect which ought to be thoroughly
considered in regard to city evangelization. If we
do not devise some way of settling upon our spheres
of church operations and some methods of evangelizing the indigenous citizens, it can by no means be
said that the Church has set up a program for a
century.

Without departing from the policy of attaining
our former purpose, the Church ought to become, in
the second place, the centre of religious instruction
for the children. I would like to advocate as one

program that the Church push forward, full of ideal and ambition, becoming like a light-house in social service, training of men, and other activities that fall within its sphere of operation.

3. COUNTRY EVANGELIZATION.—Just as the city Church has as yet no sound foundation as an autonomous body, so the local village Church, as far as one can see, appears like a floating castle. As for the church members, the officers are mostly such as have come from other places, and the church as such has no real roots among the people of the place. Viewed from this point also, the present Church must be said to be as yet very weak in its foundations. The spiritual and physical conditions of our villages is becoming more and more deteriorating and pitiable, as everyone who has knowledge will observe, and this makes the problem of the country villages a most important one. The problem first of all regarding the deteriorating condition of the villages is a spiritual one; it is a problem of personality. Learned men today are trying to solve this problem by statistical figures or reports from various sources, but, living in the city such discussion, by men who do not come in touch with the real condition at hand, is to us like "scratching the itch on one's shoe."

The most important question in connection with the work of education is that of building equipment. And in evangelistic work likewise there is the problem of the Chapel. Viewing the evangelistic work till the present, at first private residences were rented at which Sunday meetings and preaching services were held. Without much outward attraction, these places were not equal to the task of shouldering the spiritual problem of the place. The amount of rent paid out for such places must be immense. Besides, nothing is left of all this expenditure. Hence, would it not have been wiser to have built chapels from the be cal point of view, the chapels could have been built with the rents paid.

In the next place, in country work, next to pure evangelism, attention must be paid to the religious education of children. In lower grades kindergarten work is easy and has many practical possibilities. Centers for local young men and young women associations are necessary. By meetings for special courses in agricultural subjects which will increase the output of harvest, and by purifying physically and spiritually the village atmosphere, we begin to get a real foundation for our religion. Having secured a number of genuine Christians as a nucleus, we may look forward to a strong church. Then, as individual Christians by their faith influence other individuals, so a church will beget churches, and thus true evangelization will really bring about results.

4. CULTIVATING EVANGELISTIC ENERGY.—It goes without saying that evangelization is a spiritual warfare, and those who take the field are the evangelists. In a plan of evangelization for a century, the question of training preachers must not be overlooked in the program. Different denominations have a number of theological schools. The number of schools may not be few, but as far as numbers of students and their quality are concerned, sad to say, this is rather discouraging. It is doubtful whether their curriculum and methods of instruction are such as to adapt themselves to the present and future evangelistic and pastoral activities. To unify the different theological schools within one denomination for the sake of economy in men and money, and thus improve the spirit within the Church, while a desirable plan, its adoption is not easily seen, and hence the unifying of schools of different denominations will likely be still more difficult. Nevertheless, unless the Churches in Japan can bring about great improvement in the training of ministers, they will not have a great

future. A system of students' support, details of instruction, division of chairs,—these are subjects that need to be thought about. But leaving these aside for the present, the most urgent question is the training of superior men as pastors in the Church and as leaders in country evangelism. It is not desirable to rely on large numbers and give theological training to students who will prove to be failures or to have unworthy motives. Specially should we not allow a lower grade of preachers to do the work of country evangelism; that would be a clumsy policy.

5. COOPERATION.—Evangelism has no national boundaries. We have the commission from the Lord to preach the Gospel anywhere. In the preaching there is no foreign and native; but as both in the Missions and in the Churches there are various instrumentalities at work, it becomes necessary to find proper ways of cooperating with men and means, and especially in matters of evangelistic policies, plans, etc. As we, both foreign and native, are working in God's vineyard, we ought to work in unison. Whether such cooperation in the future should be in the local churches, or in the district or Presbytery, is a question which I would like to see tried out. At any rate, there is plenty of scope for missionary cooperation in evangelistic work, or in Conferences, or in some league or Council,—but after all, its success depends not upon these, but upon our personal endeavors. There is too much discussion about the power of money, numbers of men, all kinds of conferences and agreements, but the efficient result of them all is very little.

Those who are preaching the Gospel in our country facing the thought-world with its changes, must not fall behind in observing these changing conditions. National consciousness and self-realization have become vigorous, and as a result the question of deit⋅　　⋅　⋅⋅⋅　　⋅⋅⋅　　⋅　⋅⋅⋅　⋅．

Whether in the future an aggressive attitude on the part of our country is a wise ·policy or not is also a live question that needs very careful attention. But as for me, I think the determination of Paul expressed in his words, *"I determined not to know anything among you save Jesus Christ and him crucified,"* is the most important thing for future evangelization. What is above all things necessary is to preach the Gospel of peace which is able to deliver men from the bonds of sin and to thoroughly convert them to God.

CHAPTER XI

THE PLACE OF THE MISSIONARY IN
THE FUTURE

(1)   Rev. Charles Wheeler Iglehart

If the work of the missionary is to be related to
anything in Japan or to have any roots at all it must
be rooted and integrated in the Japanese church.

It is to the Japanese church, therefore that we
must look for an answer to the question "What is to
be the future of missionaries in Japan?" Increasingly large numbers of missionaries are asking this question, and are anxiously awaiting a coherent answer
from the Church. It must be remembered that the
average church member in this country is not thinking about the question at all. It has not come above
his horizon. And yet eventually he must be the one
to answer it. In the meantime we have the opinions
of the "church leaders." These are usually the elder
statesmen of the various denominations, and their
views are colored by the fact that they themselves
are largely the product of foreign missions and missionaries. They therefore are usually either very
chivalrous in their reticence about passing judgment
on the missionary or else in their struggle to develop
independence of foreign money and control they have
become prejudiced. They also have on their shoulders
the care of the churches, and this burden compels
them to modify their opinions of the ideal in view
of re' .... Th .... h ... . for
the v..   . . . .: the

church in trying to answer the question now so
urgently being put by many missionaries, "What do
you want us to do, and where and how?" One feels
a misgiving that they have not dreamed that the foreigner would be willing to sincerely and genuinely
take his commission from the church and work under
it. Nor is their surprise to be wondered at. They
have never been consulted as to our selection for
missionary service, they have had no part in our
training, no opportunity of passing judgment on our
work before furlough, or on the advisability of our
return thereafter. They have not determined our place
of residence nor our mode of life, our salary or equipment, and in many cases never even receive a report
of our work. We are not here at any cost to the
church in Japan, but purely as a gift from abroad;
and who can look a gift-horse in the mouth? Nor
have the missionaries, once they have developed any
work, shown any great desire hitherto to subsume
themselves and it under the Japanese church. Even
at this late date very much of the work in church and
school,—possibly half of it,—is under the administration of missionaries; under them because of indirect
or direct money control. In the more developed type
of denomination where there is a really independent
church organization the associated missions have had
a tendency to clearly define their zone of activity,
draw sharp lines about themselves and their work,
and go their own way under a policy of practically
mutual exclusion, so far as the Japanese church is
concerned. This protectionist policy on the part of
the missions is in large share the cause of the fatal
isolation into which much missionary work is now
on the verge of falling. If the church rightly or
wrongly believes that we missionaries force on it the
dilemma of either operating under our control, or
else of strictly going on its own way without us,
deplorable consequences may be expected to follow.

What, then, are the spheres of service offered the missionary by the church today? From the article "The Missionary's Task" by Dr. Kawaguchi in The Christian Movement for 1923 we get much light, and also from the opinions of the church leaders, as well as from observation of the actual situation in the various churches. We may summarize the offered opportunities as follows:

(1) Rural Evangelism
(2) Social Welfare Work
(3) The Use of the Home
(4) Associate Pastor in large Churches (for special groups)
(5) English Teaching in Schools.

There are many other scattered suggestions, but this pretty nearly completes the circle of suggestions that have come out of every recent conference on the subject. The more we study these ranges of work the more we are impressed by two facts. One is, that they are none of them an essential part of the rock-bottom working program of the church at present. There are things that the young Japanese church is desperately trying to get done, and for these things it is spending its wealth and strength, but the things on the list above scarcely can be said to be included. They are almost all types of work that the missions in the past have been interested in developing, or personal work such as the missionary can very naturally do, without much cooperation on the part of Japanese colleagues. It is this fact which leads us to think that the Japanese church has not yet "gone to the mats" in any serious way with the question as to what the missionary is urgently needed for; but has rather reached out for a set of obvious and rather conventional answers to it. And yet in any of these spheres of work large opportunities are wide open for the missionary who will engage in them.

Th

include many of those activities which the missionaries in the past have been most engaged in and have rather thought their special field: such as supervision of churches and evangelists, administrative offices in the church, management positions in schools, the teaching of general subjects, especially of religious and theological subjects, the creation of a Japanese Christian literature, preaching and lecturing, organizing district activities, supervision of work for women, work in Sunday Schools, and particularly all financial and advisory work of every description. The fact that these things are none of them being emphasized as the missionary's work by the church today is no reflection on the way such work has been done by missionaries in the past or even in the present, but it is an intensely significant fact in conjecturing what the work of the missionary will be in the future. With full appreciation of the help it has received in the past the church is plainly settling down to the quiet conviction that these are all things it ought to be doing for itself. Undoubtedly it is right. The transfer of all such work can not be made in a day, but the sooner it can be put under the direction of the church the better. It will then be possible for the church to re-commit to well-qualified individuals among the missionaries as much of this sort of work as it wishes them to undertake.

Summarizing the sort of work the church seems to want of the missionary we may say that it is more humble than the traditional task, but more human; it is less official, and more personal; it has less of finance in it, but more of fellowship. We never again, even in the most liberal sense shall be masters,—but the way is wide open for us to be servants. Why, if nothing were offered us but the opportunities clustering about the use of our home alone, every man and woman misionary in Japan could round out a life of the most satisfying personal service to the Christian cause. But there is no fear that eventually the church may not give us full work of an urgently needed sort, provided they are convinced of the sincere willingness of the missionaries to receive the commission of the church and serve in it, without distinction or favor.

In order, then, to establish a permanent sense of reality between the church and the missionary's task in the future three sets of adjustments are necessary, --all complex and difficult. If they can be made the church will want missionaries indefinitely and without reference to numerical limits   (It is noteworthy that no Japanese seem to care much as to how many missionaries shall be needed, nor how long. What they want to know is what sort of folks they are and what work they can and will do.)   These adjustments must begin in the mind and heart of the rank and file of us missionaries as individuals, through a humbling process by which the weeds of race pride shall be torn up by the roots from our Anglo-Saxon hearts, the love of place and power killed, and our reluctant wills bent to lowly service. But more than this, our mission organizations must suffer much change. Unless as missions we unconditionally surrender the traditionally protected areas of missionary finance and personnel, and heartily throw open the gates to Japanese participation from the beginning to the end of the process, there can be no vital future for missionary work. We must give up our security if we would find life as missions. How fearful we are, and yet how little cause we have to fear! Finally, the supporting church in the home lands must move on into the new day when foreign missionary motive no longer roots in pity and in a sense of spiritual superiority, but in humble Christian brotherhood. There is every hope and indication that it can be brought to do so   •

If we individual missionaries will submit to being humanized, and if the mission organizations will become more nationalized, and if the home church will become internationalized there need be no fear for the future of the missionary in Japan.

THE PLACE OF THE MISSIONARY IN THE FUTURE

(2) *By Rev. Akira Ebizawa*

INTRODUCTORY.—The Mission Boards have already done much in helping to build up the kingdom in this Empire, and no one would ever doubt the contribution by the missionaries in bringing about the present status of Christian influences in the social and educational world as well as in direct evangelism. And we believe a missionary has a brilliant future, at least for the next fifty years, provided he be well qualified in learning and personality, and be properly located so as to meet the real needs of the community. There seem to be prevailing some doubts now-a-days in regard to the future of the missionary in Japan. We know that the time has come for us to stop and think; not because the Japanese-American relation with the immigration problem has cast a stone, but because the change in our social condition as well as the growth and progress of our national life make it imperative to re-examine our plan and program in the light of the new situation, with the experience of over half a century.

WHAT WE EXPECT FROM THE MISSION BOARDS.—It goes without saying that each Mission field has its own peculiar needs and characteristics, and that the missionary must be allowed a large measure of freedom as to method of work and as to his theological standpoint. There seems to be a growing tendency with some Boards, through the present-day economic and ca consciously to overrule even the methods of work in the Kingdom. We have heard some such utterance as this: "The hand that writes the check must rule the Mission field," but this arises certainly from a mistaken idea which never ought to be introduced in the work of the Master.

Let us touch here in passing on the problem of Church Union in Japan. Some missionaries seem to be afraid that their stay in this country will hinder the progress of that movement. We believe that it is only a matter of the attitude of the Boards and our missionary friends, and we wish them rather to push forward the movement, staying among us.

What Gospel we expect from the Missionaries. Our people are burdened with too many systems of various religions, and if it means only to replace superstition with another kind of superstition, they will no longer need the missionary. We need no more heathen teachings gilded with nominal Christianity. It is a plain fact that some class of people show their cravings for the "signs and miracles" as did the Jews, but that can never be a reason for making the Gospel cheap, or Christianity will have nothing more to give than Tenri or Omoto-kyo. If it attempts to appeal to the utilitarian motive, Konko-kyo will work much more efficiently. These religions have recently been putting forth their strength in their propaganda. If Christian preaching remains on that same level our ordinary people will cease to think of their need of the true Gospel.

What we need in Japan is not the Jewish garment of Christianity, nor the dogmatic coat of the Apostolic age, but the kernel of the spiritual life embodied in the person of Jesus and revealed in the life and death of our Savior. Our nation can never be Christianized by a mere cheap sensational Gospel, but only by the fundamental Christian truth which appeals to the very depth of human nature.

Certainly this is the most difficult field in the world, but there is also a special opportunity for a missionary, we believe.   We are of the opinion that to thoroughly Christianize Japan really means to Christianize the entire Orient.   Then, after all, it is not a question whether or not we need the missionary.   Let him go ahead heedless of the feelings of even the whole nation if he has his own distinctive Christian message he ought to impart to this nation.

THE KIND OF MISSIONARY WE NEED IN THE FUTURE. —First of all he must be a student in scientific research.   Not necessarily to teach the sciences but to strengthen his own belief.   Secondly, he must be well trained so as to be able to teach religion.   The world seems to back-slide now and then, and there still remains a wide field even for a worker without much culture; but we must think how such a worker may repudiate the belief which he professes.   We are passing through a transition age, and the line of work of our missionary must necessarily change as the time advances.   A specialist in some line of study, for instance, in religious education, in Social or in Agricultural work, will find rare opportunities among us. Gradually it seems the industrial problem is giving way to the agricultural, and it is certainly desirable to prepare for the solution of the rural problems from our Christian standpoint.

WHAT WOULD BE THE METHOD OF WORKING?— There are many things we owe to the missionaries, and they will have a wide field open and great opportunities given in the future.   Their work might well be studied along two lines—the *Educational* and the *Evangelistic*.

(A)   No doubt the educational missionary has a great future so long as the Mission School does not lose its distinctive Christian influence.   Care must be taken to maintain the Christian principles when there is a tendency to secularize the Christian schools.

A plan of Exchange Professors for courses of lectures of Government and in Mission Schools by those competent in such branches of study as would be advantageous for nations that live so closely together as America and Japan, on both shores of the Pacific.

A term of service in teaching work in his mother tongue, both in Government institutions and in Mission Schools, should also be valuable for many years to come.

(B) As to the future work of the Evangelistic missionaries, there are many aspects of work to be taken into account according to the personnel. Just for the sake of convenience, let us consider the matter under two headings: *city* and *rural* evangelism.

(1) THE WORK OF A MISSIONARY IN THE CITY

(a) We need at least one from each of the denominations to be located in the Capital as an ambassador of Christ,—not less significant than the representative of the Vatican. He would serve to influence the whole atmosphere of political and international affairs, trying to Christianize the relationships in order to prove the nations from falling into heathen ways of dealing with things when problems arise.

(b) In a great city, as the educational and industrial center there should be developed a well organized institutional church, really functioning to meet the urgent needs of the community. The missionary may be appointed there as an associate pastor to share the real responsibility, for instance, the teaching work or in leading the English service. The writer has such a privilege of cooperation now in his present pastorate. A specialist in the line of social work for young people could also be appointed and he or she would be able to utilize his strength and ability to the full.

(c) Term service for two years of a student missionary fresh from College was tried, probably for the first time, in purely church work, while the writer held a pastorate at Sapporo. A veteran missionary, writing about the plan said: "The essentials to success would naturally be; first, a University seat or some similar place where there are English learning students, and secondly, an English speaking pastor to welcome and help a young American as his Associate." This plan was carried out quite satisfactorily and the young missionary left the city when his term expired, carrying back much experience and leaving behind some good impressions among the youth. Let him speak for himself about his experience: "The teaching of English is a splendid drawing card to reach the young Japanese. Thus through the medium of an English night school we have been able to draw under the roof of the church many young people who are perhaps receiving for the first time the germs of the Christian spirit. A deep and sincere longing for help in the attainment of the highest values of life dwells in the hearts of the young men and women. Now opportunities come almost every day to put in a word or deed which may start them in the Christian life. The chances to influence them for Christ are as numerous as time and strength allow. To guide the lives of these Japanese youth is an inspiring challenge, the proper acceptance of which will bear untold fruit."

Such a plan will relieve the young missionary from the trouble of language study, and has the advantage of bringing his power to bear right at the center of actual work.

(2) The Work of a Missionary in the Rural District

(a) A missionary in a country village will find a unique place which perhaps none of the city dwellers can ever dream of. The advantages of inconvenien pleasure given in contact with the simple-minded people. A rural missionary will find ample time to deal with the living personality while the city dweller is liable to be absorbed in dealing with the mechanism. A missionary and his home would be the center of new information and learning as well as in the social life of the village. Nothing can surpass in strong influences a right family living in a remote country place. His method of work must needs be different from that of the city worker, but there is nothing to compare in efficiency with country evangelism.

(b) If he is a touring missionary over a wider field, he has another unique opportunity of his own, provided he is well equipped with the language and with good health. But it is much more desirable if he could remain in one place even for a few months, thus moving from one place to another just as Paul used to do. Probably he may be able to make good use of some religious films or some other kind of equipment for illustration to help on his work.

We have written about the future place of our missionary, and we wish again to lay stress on the fact that Japan is a peculiar field where Western civilization meets face to face with that of the Orient, so that to a Christian worker in this land is given the rare opportunity to discover and build up real universal civilization upon the Christian principles. We might think of this field as a testing-place for the missionary work in the world. So long as Christianity remains inactive, unable to thoroughly Christianize Japan, the world will remain with its dark hemisphere. The challenging voice from the land is clearly heard.

CHAPTER XII

THE FUTURE PLACE OF THE FEDERA-
TION OF CHRISTIAN MISSIONS
IN JAPAN

Rev. A. J. Stirewalt, D.D.

Since the future is always an outgrowth of the past and present, in considering the future of the Federation of Christian Missions in Japan, it is necessary for us to get its setting from this viewpoint.

The Federation is an organization composed, at present, of thirty-two Missions, two of which are in Formosa. As the name implies, it is a federation and functions as an advisory body, without any authority whatever over its constituent Missions. In its constitution, we read (Art. III—Powers): "The Federation may confer, investigate, give counsel, and take other action regarding matters of common concern to the Missions represented in it; it may also undertake such co-operative work as may be agreed upon by the constituent bodies; but no action may be taken affecting the independence of the Missions represented or dealing with ecclesiastical principles, or questions of Christian doctrine." Article II— Purpose, reads: "The purpose of the Federation shall be to promote fellowship, mutual understanding, and the spirit of unity among Missions comprising it, and to form a medium for such co-operative effort as may be advantageous to the common cause."

The

upon the Missions is sufficient to make us wonder why such an organization was not called into existence long before 1902, especially since its powers are limited to an extent which securely guards the feelings and rights of the constituent bodies.

The various Missions working in Japan, while representing churches in the home-lands which have no organic connection, in most cases, are here on the mission field possessed of one common purpose, meet like conditions, and are confronted by the same problems and difficulties. For any one body to ignore the experience, or advice, of others would be most unnatural. Just what means existed for comparison of ideas and discussion of mutual problems before the formation of the Federation must be told by those who were on the field at that time, but it would seem that the Federation must have been called into existence through constraint. Since its organization, its annual conferences, especially since they have been held in the Summer, at Karuizawa where the larger part of the missionary body has access to them, have become very valuable, as regards the exchange of ideas, comparison of methods, the compilation of facts, recommendations, inspiration, etc.

The Christian Literature Society is a child of the Federation. This is an institution which no one Mission could sustain. All Missions look to it for literature and are benefitted thereby; but without some such coming together of Missions as the Federation has effected, this institution would not have come into existence, and each Mission in its own feeble and limited way, would perhaps be attempting the publication of its own literature, at an enormous aggregate cost.

The Japan Evangelist, recently turned into the Japan Christian Quarterly, and the Christian Movement, are publications of the Federation, and either one alone would have justified the existence of the

Federation. These publications have not only afforded opportunity for the exchange of ideas, but they have preserved these ideas and various facts in printed form, and these publications will be very outstanding to those who, in the future, write the history of Christianity in Japan.

The Federation has sponsored Newspaper Evangelism, and has a very close relationship to the Language School.

It is the official medium through which the missionary body in Japan speaks. It has afforded occasion for Missions and missionaries to associate, and thus better understand each other, in a way that would have been impossible without some such organization.

There are yet other features which contribute to the evaluation of the organization. Were we to stop here, without considering another factor which has, within the last few years, come into existence; it is quite certain that all bodies connected with the Federation would consider its continuation decidedly essential.

In May 1922, there was held in Tokyo, a conference of representatives of Missions and Japanese Churches which led to the organization of the National Christian Council in Nov. 1923. The Federation of Christian Missions had already existed for twenty-one years, and the Federation of Churches had existed for eleven years. The desire to have a single medium through which a united Christianity could express itself was the reason for the new organization. Since then, the Federation of Churches has ceased to exist. The Federation of Christian Missions still exists, though many of its functions have been transferred to the new organization whose conferences are attended by 51 Japanese, 34 missionary, and 15 co-opted delegates. But the question has be .   . .   .

continue to exist, for an indefinite period, and if so,. what shall be its character?

At its 1925 conference, the organization voted: "The continuance of the Federation of Christian Missions in Japan for fellowship, education, and inspiration," and authorized certain alterations in the constitution, with due regard to the functions, purpose, and powers of the National Christian Council, and in consequence of having turned over to the Council many of its former functions.

It is very clear that the Federation will never again function in such a wide sphere of activities as heretofore, but it also is quite clear that some organization distinctively missionary is essential to the welfare of our common cause. These thirty-two Missions and their missionaries desire to help each other, as well as to be helped by each other. To pool experience, knowledge, ideas, and in such fellowship mutually encourage each other, and foster inspiration for the work before us, constitute a program of sufficient importance to continue the Federation.

But there are other considerations. For example, the Christian Literature Society has been put on a new basis, with enlarged activities, and independence apart from the Federation, and it is now seeking a government charter. But twelve of the twenty-four members of the Society are, in its constitution, designated to be elected by the Federation. This constitution might be changed, but it is a question if such representatives could be so satisfactorily elected to represent the participating Missions as through the present method.

The Japan Christian Quarterly, and the Christian Movement may eventually be transferred to the Council, but until that is done, the continuation of the Federation is necessary for financial and editorial reasons, as well as to afford anchorage and authority for these publications.

Newspaper evangelism will likely soon be transferred to the Council. It might be a question if the Council would be willing to concern itself about the Japanese Language School, even if the Federation desired to sever relationship in favor of the Council. The Missions have an interest in the American School in Tokyo, and in the Canadian Academy in Kobe, for the education of their children. It would not seem reasonable to consider such problems within the sphere of the Council, and the Missions can best express a united relationship to these schools through some such organization as the Federation.

The Conference of Federation of Christian Missions is made up of approximately ninety delegates who represent thirty-two Missions which include nearly all of the 1206 Protestant missionaries in Japan. These missionaries are working harmoniously and for a common cause. It would be very strange if, in their efforts to make Christ known to these people, there should not be problems of sufficient importance, common to all, to justify the existence and functioning of an organization such as the Federation. Problems which distinctively concern Missions continually arise, and these can be discussed freely and decided properly only by those whom they primarily concern.

Each Mission has its own annual meeting at which such problems may be discussed, but there is enhanced value in such discussions when carried on in the light of the nation-wide movement, and by those most capable in the entire mission body, rather than in any given Mission. Even if the excellent papers read at the annual conferences could be produced by individual Missions, it would be unfortunate if their value should be limited to such. The missionary body needs just such a clearing-house of information as our annual conferences provide. The annu: ·· t l·i t···   · · ·· ·   ··· · · · ·   · · '·

tunity for the new missionary to get a ready acquaintance with Christian work in this country. It would indeed be a dull Summer to many, if the Federation ceased to exist, and they were deprived of the conference inspiration they had received in former years.

Unfortunately we are divided by denominational lines, and the least we have to do with each other, the more prominently the divisions appear, and the greater the occasion for offence to the people among whom we work. It is true, most of us have contact with each other in the Council, but it would give an unfortunate impression were it to appear that we can mingle with each other only with the Japanese as a medium. It strengthens our front, in our own eyes, and before the public, when we are organized, even in a limited sense, as one unit.

The Council has its own sphere, and it will increase in importance, while the Federation gracefully decreases. This is the natural consequence that should follow as the Missions succeed in the work they have set out to do.

The time may come when the Protestant missionaries in Japan will be so few, and so scattered, and so divested of responsibility in helping to plan for the young church that the organization may no longer be needed, but that time is not near.

The Council will never become a place where the missionary can freely enter discussions and be benefitted by the discussions of others. It will never afford to the missionary the devotion and the inspiration the Federation is capable of giving. There are several considerations which militate against these things, and the language problem is not the least. At present, the Federation is essential to our highest efficiency; and the more effort we invest in it, the more will be the benefits we derive from it. Just as the Federation of today is not what it was before the Council was organized, so the Federation of the future will more and more emphasize those things which distinctively pertain to the missionary, recognizing the things which pertain to the young Church as the sphere of the National Christian Council.

———————

CHAPTER XIII

THE FUTURE PLACE OF THE NATIONAL CHRISTIAN COUNCIL

(1) The Japanese Viewpoint

Bishop K. Uzaki

It is a matter for rejoicing that after many efforts year by year the Japan National Christian Council has now been organized and is increasingly becoming a strong united body. The Council is an instrument for setting forth the united strength of the different Churches in a representative character. There are now 42 bodies constituting the Council and of these 22 are foreign Missions. The Council is entirely democratic in its working through representative committees. The present different Committees are: Evangelistic, Educational, Literary, Social and International. These five Committees represent the Council in all their activitivities. After the great Earthquake in the "Kwanto" (Tokyo District) the reconstruction of Christian forces was rapid. Taking advantage of this opportunity, it was thought the best time for fostering cooperation. Union Theological Schools, Union Newspaper, Union Building, were much spoken of and discussed but they did not get beyond the point of discussion. But in the midst of all, the matters of a Union Building and of a Union Council have come about to fruition. The former has not yet entirely materialized but is still somewhat in the state of discu·   ｊ· ｌ．· ᵗ ·ｌ ᵗ Cᵗ ᵗ ·· Cᵘᵗ ᵗᵗ,

carried on a nation-wide campaign in 1924-5. In its
nature it was a kind of demonstration. When the
America-Japan question arose, Christianity was thought
to be no good. At that time the movement of the
Council demonstrated the power of Christianity. It
also gave a good opportunity to explain to thinking
men the nature of Christianity. The cooperation of
local churches was also fostered and strengthened.
At least, it was demonstrated that what could not
be accomplished by one Church could be accomplished by united effort. It also opened the way splendidly for non-christians to get close to Christianity. The
Home Office and the Bureau of Education assisted
the movement by giving facilities in the way of lending offices and other places for holding meetings.

In the future also, the Council is an important
organ for representing the Christian groups before
the Government and the masses of the people. The
day has not yet come for the union of all the Churches
or for just laboring to foster the idea of the power
of one united Church. The present-day Church in
Japan must have its eyes wide open to the Christianization of the country and to world-wide evangelization. In this present century it is vain for one to
strive by himself, or even for one denomination or
one group. All must join their strength for the
struggle. To my mind there are three or four objects
for which the National Christian Council should
strive.

1. The cultivation of friendship and fellowship
among the different denominations. This, everyone
will admit. We often hear that in general the Japanese are indifferent to religion, but really this is not
true. The ideas of one's own Church or one's own
denomination are pretty strong. There are even some
who would promulgate Church-ism more than Christianity. It seems unavoidable that, just as in political
and intellectual circles, here also the sect in the

religious world. But the present is not the time to encourage the spirit of denominationalism. It may be difficult at once to do away with all denominationalism and form one Church. The National Christian Council assumes responsibility for the task of bringing together the various denominations in friendly spiritual fellowship.

2. The second thing is, cooperation in the evangelistic field. Money for evangelization must be used with the utmost skill. Both in men and in money we must be careful. For each Church to just go to work independently anywhere in its neighborhood must not be continued. The Council must face this situation and counsel thoroughly in regard to this matter. For example, on virgin soil the Council should map out the spheres of operation so as to avoid overlapping. Also, in cases of too many Churches in a comparatively small place, the Council, by conferences, should endeavor to have the number of Churches lessened in such a place. In large cities also, the opening of new localities should be decided upon by conference with the committee of the Council constituted for that purpose. To put up a new church in the close vicinity of an already existing church ought not to be possible under the working of the Council. To allow this would be very detrimental to the fellowship of the believers and the maintenance of a friendly spirit. In this respect the Council has in the future a very important task to perform.

3. As an Instrument for Investigating Christian Social Movements.—In the Council there is a Committee on social service which has already gathered an amount of valuable material on Christian Social Movements and has in part made publication of the results.

This Social Service Committee is not a rival of the Reform Society, Purity Society, Temperance, White Cross, Educational Society, . . .

them in investigating conditions and setting forth suggestions as to the carrying on of such work. All this agrees·with the aim and object of this Council. Thus far the Social Section of the Council has confined its efforts to investigating conditions, and has not yet entered upon the actual work of Social Service. But gradually work of this kind for social and other improvements will doubtless be undertaken in the name of the Council. Also, cooperation with similar local movements in various places will most likely be possible through local sub-committees of the Council. If the finances allow, it is also very desirable that a specialist in Social Service be appointed by the Council. If some Church or Mission could furnish the Council with such a specialist it would be splendid.

4.   In the fourth place, the Council ought to serve for the purpose of encouraging the tendency towards Church union. The Council will be in a position to specially assist in this movement. The question of Church Union is at present one of public discussion. That this question of union, no matter by whom or where initiated, is thus on the tapis is a matter for rejoicing. That the present several Churches may become one is doubtless the prayer of all.

In this matter of Church Union there are specially two ways that must be considered. The first is, that those Churches which are nearest together come into organic union. After that, groups that have different histories and thus far different regulations, should come together and form new regulations for union. But, according to the Constitution of the Council it cannot directly concern itself with this method of Church Union.

But a second method is, that the local Churches by themselves make adjustments for union. In such an event there might result the necessity for some Church rather to give up its own work in a certain place. This could only be effected through the broad-

mindedness of the Church leaders. To create opportunities for such union efforts would be one of the
great tasks of the Council.

One easy step towards Church Union would be
to have Christian Schools of similar nature get together. I would approve of the Council assisting in
conference on such endeavors for union work in
Christian education. In the publication of Christian
Literature a union of the Kyobunkwan (Methodist
Publishing House) with the Christian Literature Society has already been effected. The erection of a Union
Building is also in progress. Church Union is at
present apparently only an ideal without realization,
but its realization is not an impossibility, but a real
possibility. The Council is at present the proper instrument to serve as a centre for encouraging the
union efforts of the various Churches. In the great
evangelistic campaign of the Council this year, it
is hoped that all the Churches will unite. Church
Union is not a question of individual interest or
feeling, but one of spirit and of conviction. Where
the mind of Christ is in us there Churches will come
together, begin to talk about union and offer some
basis for such union. If Church Union is the ideal,
should we not face it and steadily advance towards
its realization? Is it not a wise procedure to use
even small opportunities and ways for such union?
Is it not the duty of leaders to take advantage of
the present opportunities for union that are offered?
I believe that the Council has the duty of important
leadership in this matter. It is the duty of the Council, with great composure, to consider the future position of the Christian Church in Japan, to think not
only of the advantages of the Church as such,
but also of the great final purpose of bringing into
conformity to Christ the nation of Japan, yea, the
entire Orient. The Council must act f . . .
for the a . . . p . . . .

I would also like to say something about the Council serving as an instrument, in a representative character, for conference on international questions. but will omit this because I think someone else will present this phase of the work.

THE FUTURE PLACE OF THE NATIONAL CHRISTIAN COUNCIL

(2) The Missionary Viewpoint

Rev. T. A. Young

The Edinburgh Continuation Committee of 1910! The Japan Continuation Committee of 1913! The Japan National Christian Conference of 1922! The Organizing Committee of thirty-five members! The National Christian Council of Japan in 1923! Thus one sees the outstanding events by which this experiment of nation-wide and world-wide cooperation in the things of the Kingdom of God has come to its present fruition here in Japan.

If one will study the functions of the Japan Continuation Committee as they were stated at the time of organization it will be seen that, even from the beginning, the destined goal was more or less clearly perceived—yet with the years the ideals and purposes of cooperation have assumed more and more definite form until we have the Constitution of the National Christian Council embodying the following:—

1. "To express and foster the spirit of fellowship and unity of the Christian Church in Japan; to give expression to its oneness with the Church throughout the world."

2. "To be the medium through which the Church may speak on such matters, social, moral, religious, and the like as affect the entire Christian Movement in Japan."

3. "To represent the Christian Church in Japan

in communication with similar bodies in other countries and to express its voice and to make its contribution in the International Missionary Council and in other international relations."

4. "To take counsel, make surveys, plan for cooperative work, and to take suitable steps for carrying on such work, and to act on behalf of the cooperating bodies in all matters of common interest."

5. "In the above mentioned functions this Council is understood as having no-authority to deal with questions of doctrine or ecclesiastical policy, neither shall its actions in such matters be interpreted as being in any way mandatory."

While the cooperation thus expressed in the articles of the Council has been defined as "the simplest form of federation" yet it marks the highest point thus far reached in Japan of united effort and cooperation of the Christian communions for the building of the Kingdom of God. Better still, it is accepted by many as the harbinger of the time when an indigenous church, in its own power, shall go forth conquering and to conquer; as the promise of the time to come when the Church in Japan shall help guide and mold Christian thought and activities in all the Far East—when the voice of the Church shall be heard and listened to in all the world-wide missionary and Christian Councils.

The Council already has two full years' work to its credit and is entering upon the third year. These may be used as a basis of judgement as to its degree of success and as to its promise for the future. A fair consideration of all the circumstances surrounding the work of the Council for these first years brings one to the conclusion that the Council has stood the test. It has more than fulfilled the hopes and expectations of those most earnest and zealous in its organization.

What is the future of the Council? What is the

place that it is to occupy? What is the work that it is to do? The past work of the Council and its present work and place offer the only basis upon which, with any degree of certainty, prophecies may be made of its future. The natural growth and development of the spirit and desire for unity and cooperation to the degree now expressed in the Council, its two years of excellent work, the growing interest in the Council and its work, the plans which have been made for the next few years, all unite in justifying the statement that "in the future of Christian work in Japan the National Christian Council has an assured place." As one seeks a more definite statement with regard to this "assured place" he naturally comes upon certain conditions, the fulfilling or the not fulfilling of which, will define and largely determine the sphere of the future activity of the Council. The future of the Council is not in question —simply the fact that its degree of future success must depend upon certain conditions being successfully met.

The matter of its finances, an adequate central business office and an efficient staff are all of importance but these are not the most vital to the future life and work of the Council. More vital things were expressed in the impressions given by certain delegates attending the General Council Meeting of 1925. A Japanese delegate voiced the following, "The lack of progressive action in the Council with special regard to the matter of Christian union and the need of applied Christianity in view of the messages of the fraternal delegates." A missionary delegate sensed the lack of spiritual unity—another "the lack of a large body of devout and economically powerful Christians behind this comparatively small body of educated and talented leaders." Yet all were united in recognizing the great possibilities of the Council— in bel'''·'··· '' · '' '· · · .'' '····' ·'···· ·' '· '· · · '· ' ·' ·' ··'· · ·' · ·
tian J·;·   · ·· ·.' · '·   .' · '·· ·   ·' · ·· ·

tional Christian Council is a necessity. The above impressions emphasize the outstanding problem for the future of the National Christian Council—namely whether it will become indigenous and, binding to itself in loyal and sacrificing support the various Christian communions, whether it dare seek to meet and to try to solve the great problems confronting the Church to-day in the spirit of Jesus Christ. If the Christian Council measures up to this it may go on—more richly influential and strong—with the advancing years—the voice of a united vigorous Christian constituency—the real representative body of the Christian movement in Japan. If the Council cannot measure up to this it will doubtless continue to have "an assured place" but it will be a place exceedingly limited —so far as real influence and work are concerned.

It was perhaps inevitable that the Christian Council should have developed and should have been organized while still largely dependent upon assistance from sources not a vital part of an indigenous church yet this condition cannot continue and the Council be able to do the work it seems so clearly destined to do. Moreover this condition will not go on. The clearness with which the outstanding need of the Council is recognized is promise of this. With the advancing years the Council will more and more stand upon its own feet—more and more becoming the representative body of a vigorous, united, aggressive, spiritual Japanese Christian constituency.

To the missionary the National Christian Council of Japan brings a challenge for his utmost effort, his loyal support, his unceasing prayer, and the remembrance that "there are times when God requires of a man nothing except that he be patient."

CHAPTER XIV

ORGANIZED ACTIVITIES OF THE CHRISTIAN MOVEMENT

THE PROGRAM OF SOCIAL SERVICE

I. Temperance and Prohibition

Rev. Mark R. Shaw

TWENTY-FIVE YEAR LAW CAMPAIGN

A definite advance in the temperance movement in Japan was made on January 27th, 1926, when the secretaries and officers of twelve reform and religious organizations met at the National Y.M.C.A. building and formed the "Association to Promote the Twenty-five Year Law." The purpose was to give united effort to the campaign to raise the age of the present Juvenile law from 21 to 25 years, thus making it include all students and those in the military service. As the Association included both Christians and Buddhists and the fourteen members in the Diet who later introduced and sponsored the bill represented all five political parties, the movement is both omni-religious and omni-partisan. It seems to be also something of a youth movement, as six of the organizations in the Association are young people's associations and it was noticeable that it received most active support from the younger members of the Diet. Mr. Kanji Koshio, executive secretary of the Association, graduated from Waseda only in 1925, where he was active in the student prohibition society. Mass meetings and public demonstrations were held in Tokyo and elsewhere. The bill was not brought up, however, until the closing day of the session, when it was briefly explained by Rep. Masaji Yamaguchi and rushed thru, without debate, by a nearly unanimous vote, but too late to be considered in the Upper House. An indication of the growing sentiment for temperance is given by the fact that several leading daily papers, including the *Osaka Mainichi*, Japanese and English editions, *Osaka Asahi*, *Tokyo Asahi*, *Tokyo Jiji Shimpo*, *Yomiuri* and *Miyako* as well as a number of local dailies editorially endorsed the revision of the law.

The fact that even the present law is quite generally ignored however, apparently being regarded by many an official expresssion of an "ideal" rather than a measure to be observed, would indicate that much educational work must be done if the drinking customs of even the young are to be materially changed. The 24,973 cases of infringement of the Juvenile law, reported by the police during 1925, are probably only a fraction of these that occurred. In 73 of these cases sake was confiscated, in 252 fines ("not exceeding ten yen") were assessed upon parents and guardians—the law specifically exempts the minor himself from punishment—and the other 24,648 cases were dismissed with an admonition. The revised law would likewise exempt minors from punishment but would make those between 21 and 25 and parents of minors, who cause or permit minors to drink, subject to the fine. "Although the prohibition law for minors was enacted in 1922," says the *Hochi*, "only a few have been aware of its force. Parents, factory-owners and shop-keepers may have no knowledge of the existence of such a law. How can young men have sufficient knowledge of its operation?"

NATIONAL TEMPERANCE LEAGUE

The National Temperance League has had a good year, and a very enthusiastic three-day convention in April, at Osaka, 133 delegates being present representing 89 of the 166 local societies affiliated with the League. The total membership is about 25,000.

More than fifty resolutions and proposals to the government had been submitted by the local societies for consideration and twenty-seven of these were endorsed by the Convention. The most important were those recommending: (1) the continuance of the campaign for the revision of the Juvenile Prohibition Law —raising the age from 21 to 25 years—and concentration upon this measure by all local societies, (2) especially intensive work by each society with the members of the Diet from their district, (3) the election of new, dry candidates to the Diet, (4) the application of the present Juvenile Law to Korea and other colonies, (5) the posting of this Law in all sake shops and drinking places, (6) the appointment of a special policeman at each station for enforcement of the Juvenile Law, (7) sending posters from the League to all Young Men's and Girls' associations, (8) scientific temperance instruction in the primary and middle schools, (9) regulations requiring abstinence of teachers, policemen and others, (10) more field lecture work by the league headquarters, (11) the use of moving pictures in educational campaigns and (12) a commission for investigation of the social and economic aspects of the alcohol problem in Japan.

The OFFICIAL PROCLAMATION called for renewed effort for the Twenty-five Year Law, urged the election of only dry members to the Diet, stressed the necessity of prohibition to help solve the present social and economic problems of the Empire, re-stated the non-partisan attitude of the League, demanded the purification of politics, urged greater consideration for the welfare of the masses of the people, emphasized the

essentially social as well as personal nature of the
drink problem, and appealed for earnest and aggressive cooperation by all classes and creeds in the campaign for ultimate national prohibition.

Greetings were brought by representatives of the
Home Minister, the Minister of Education, the Govern-
or of Osaka Prefecture and Mayor of Osaka, the president of Osaka Chamber of Commerce, the *Osaka Asahi*
and *Osaka Mainichi* (newspapers) and others. Nearly
all mentioned America's example and revealed an increasing interest in the significance of the alcohol
problem. Following these Mr. Mark R. Shaw brought
greetings from several of the temperance organizations
in America and spoke briefly about the actual conditions there during this transition period.

The general enthusiasm of the convention, the
sympathetic interest expressed by the officials who
brot greetings, the large attendance at the four public
mass meetings—there being over 2,000 in the Central
Public Hall in the closing night, the frequent applause
given the speakers by these audiences of the common
people, as well the passage of the 25 Year Law by the
Lower House, indicate a growing appreciation of the
importance of the anti-alcohol movement in Japan.

WOMEN'S CHRISTIAN TEMPERANCE UNION

With their usual enthusiasm and earnestness the
women of the Japan W.C.T.U. held their thirty-fifth
national convention in the auditorium of the Nagoya
Chamber of Commerce, April 6-8, with 126 official
delegates present representing 45 of the total of 155
local unions in the organization. The total membership is now 8,086, a gain of over 800 since a year ago.

A Memorial Service was held for Madam Yajima and
others who had been called during the year. In her
opening address Mrs. Gauntlett, recalling the words
of Paul in I. Cor. 3:9-10, reminded her hearers that
"Madame Yajima's spirit is still with us. She laid the

foundation of this work in Christ and we must continue to build thereon." Miss Azuma Moriya reported on the L. T. L. work, especially the sending on April first of the new posters,—two showing the effect of alcohol upon organs of the body and one giving the text of the Juvenile anti-smoking and prohibition laws, —to each of the 26,000 primary schools. Cordial greetings were brought from several ken and city officials revealing an awakening interest in these women's work. The delegates bravely accepted the responsibility for raising the Yen 5,000 needed to make up the fund that formerly came from America, thus relieving the directors of this extra burden this coming year.

II. Purity and Abolition of Prostitution

OPPOSITION TO JAPAN'S RESERVATION

Following the publication in English and Japanese last summer of the *Report on Prostitution in Japan*, which the Social Welfare Committee of the National Christian Council prepared in response to the request of the League of Nations Committee, quite a strong protest developed against Japan's reservations to her ratification of the treaty prohibiting international traffic in women and children. Some members of the Privy Council protested that Japan's reservation in 1920, making the age of consent eighteen instead of twenty-one and its non-application to Korea, Formosa and other colonies, were nothing less than a national disgrace. Several newspapers were outspoken on the issue and a protest meeting was held in Tokyo addressed by Dr. Masataro Sawayanagi, head of the Imperial Education Association and other prominent educ.... . . v..l .. .I. ..d .and r.t...... l. .l.. . A

resolution condemning the reservation was passed and
sent to government officials and wirelessed to Ambassador Ishii at Geneva. So strong was the growing
protest that government officials promised that the
reservation would be removed—as soon as the proper
time came. It is understood that they contend that
it can not well be withdrawn as long as eighteen years
remains the age of consent in Japan, as the age regulations should be the same for domestic and foreign
traffic.

CONFERENCE OF POLICE OFFICIALS

On May first, 1926, a conference of police officials
from thruout the empire was held with the Police
Bureau of the Home Department to consider revision
of the regulations for licensed quarters. The present
rules, adopted in 1900, were felt to be too antiquated
and out of conformity with the spirit of the times.
There seemed to be a strong conviction that present
conditions are intolerable. Among the various remedial measures discussed were those of raising the age
limit to twenty-one years (the brothel keepers convention had urged that it be lowered to sixteen years)
and enforcement of the provision, now existing in
theory only, permitting the prostitute to leave the
brothel if she wills. Mr. Matsumura, head of the
Police Bureau of the Home Deparment, however, said
in his opening address that there can be no other
way to reform the system but to abolish it. Chief of
Police Saito, of Gumma Prefecture, staunchly advocated the total abolition of the public prostitution system,
on the ground that in his prefecture where there is
no public prostitution, the moral and health conditions
of the people are no worse than in other prefectures
where the licensed quarters flourish. Encouraged by
this support from official circles, Mrs. Kubushiro, chairman of the Social Welfare Committee of the Council,
lost no time in making up the petition asking the
Minister of Home Affairs, Mr. R. Wakatsuki, to abolish

the licensed system of prostitution. It has been signed
by many prominent Educationalists such as Dr.
Hayashi, President of Keio University, Dr. S. Tanaka,
President of Waseda University, Dr. Asoh, President
of Women's University, Dr. T. Yasui, President of
Tokyo Women's University, Madam Hatoyama, Dr.
Yoshino and others.'

The wide discussion in the Diet and the daily
press of the Matsushima scandal, many politicians
being implicated in the real estate bribery connected
with the removal of the Osaka licensed quarters, has
served to keep the sordid matter before the public
mind and perhaps to quicken the national conscience
as to the inherent evils of the whole system.

ORGANIZATIONS

The Women's Christian Temperance Union (Kyo-
fukwai), The Purity Society (Kakuseikwai) and The
National Christian Council Social Welfare Committee
are the leading agencies educating and awakening the
public conscience. They feel much encouraged over
the evidences of growing support in official circles.
The W.C.T.U. at its April convention, decided to stress
this year as its immediate objective, and as a practical
measure towards the final goal, the campaign to keep
any new quarters from being established. This movement was launched by sending telegrams from the convention to every prefectural governor. The "ten sen
bags" will be used as heretofore both to raise funds
and to create thousands of opportunities for discussion on this urgent problem. The Kakuseikwai, tho
small, is doing an effective work and publishes its
monthly magazine, *Purity.*

THE PROGRAM OF SOCIAL SERVICE

(2) Settlement Work

(A)

Miss A. E. Cary

By the time this goes to the printer, Osaka will boast seven settlement houses, three of which are less than six months old, and all but one started within the last five years. This one, the Aizen-en, has a history of sixteen years of service, having now reached the enviable position of feeling that its work in its present neighborhood is done, and that a more needy part of the city must be its future field. Of the seven settlements, two are municipal, one is Buddhist, and of the four Christian institutions, one, the above mentioned Aizen-en, is supported by a wealthy Japanese Christian, one is under the leadership of Mr. Toyohiko Kagawa, and the other two are missionary enterprises, the Mead Shakaikan (Baptist), and the Yodogawa Zenrinkan (Congregational).

In Osaka, as has, of course, been true the world over, the beginnings of so-called "social work" were almost entirely relief or remedial in nature. Fortunately we are passing beyond that stage and there is a growing desire for more constructive and preventive types of endeavor. This is being manifest in the increasing interest in settlements and in the churches branching out into institutional phases of work.

Among the kinds of social work being done in common by both Christian and non-Christian settlements, the most outstanding are (1) work among children, (2) night schools and classes, (3) reading rooms, and (4) consultation and advice clinics. It is most encouraging to see that in most cases the children's work includes regularly organised kindergartens, though there is one institution which has only a day nursery. In some cases the work started with the day nursery type, but developed, in addition, the kindergarten, calling for trained teachers, and regular class work. Classes and meetings for mothers, emphasizing the training and care of children, have already done much in neighborhoods where there has been nothing of this kind before. The night school and classes are of all kinds, from work in English, commercial courses, vocational education along many lines, common school subjects for those who have not had the opportunity of going to school, to special classes for young women in training in home economics, as preparation for marriage.

Reading rooms are very popular, especially among children and young people, each institution usually choosing what class it wishes to reach, but also having books of general interest to all. Legal advice, help in the more perplexing personal problems, and discussion groups are all means for gaining the trust and friendship of the neighborhood, and are almost forced upon an institution by the community needs and demands.

Municipal settlements, with their much larger funds to draw upon, can branch out into a wider field of activities, such as free dental and medical clinics, money lending, pawn-brokerage, orchestra training, and similar lines. Since they are city work, and because their classes are advertised through the newspapers, they draw a constituency from all over Osaka, with the Tenroku Shiminkan averaging over seven hundred people a day.

In contrast to this, mission and other Christian institutions have, in the very nature of the case, developed into a more intimate and personal type of neighbo.. ... .

formal clinics, classes, and lectures, they are in a position to make a distinct contribution along the lines of recreational activities, organized club work as we know it abroad, and such phases of work as those which depend especially upon strong personal interest and personal leadership. Peculiarly necessary to these is a staff of workers chosen for character and winning personality. To find these we have the great advantage of being able to draw all our workers from the Christian society of Japan, and beyond the regular members of the staff, to count upon the help of volunteer workers, whose enthusiasm comes from a religious motive.

This will cause, we hope, the development of a Christian community in the neighborhood, a community which will, of its own volition, wish to organize into a church, making of the settlement the best type of institutional church. This seems to be a more natural sequence, than the making over of a present day church into one with institutional features.

Judging from our Christian point of view it is very easy to say that the work of non-religious settlements is superficial and not lasting, but that is hardly fair. Many in such institutions feel just the lack we note, but their hands are tied, and we can only commend them for the really splendid things they are accomplishing. Their work is doing much good, and as we cannot hope to compete along their lines, nor they in ours, the two types ought to supplement each other and through them evolve a better community and a better city.

Osaka, with its over two million people, needs many more settlements. Althought the growth in the past year has been astonishing, hardly an impression has yet been made. There is a boundless opportunity open to Christian forces to join in a work which, among the working people, will commend Christianity with greater emphasis and with a more permanent influence than could possibly be done by the older method of *kogisho* preaching or ordinary church work alone.

The Yodogawa Zenrinkan, Honjo, Osaka.
        30 January, 1926.

THE PROGRAM OF SOCIAL SERVICE

(2) Settlement Work

(B)

Rev. G. E. Bott

In a discussion of the place of Settlement Work in the Christian Movement in Japan, it is necessary to bear in mind what Social Settlements are and the forms of work in which they are engaged. The Settlement may be defined as a center in which men and women who have had the advantages of education and a reasonable amount of culture and leisure "may meet on terms of neighbourly friendliness the less fortunate citizens of their community where each may learn from the other, and through friendship render service to each other resulting in enlargement of vision, development of personality and united action for social betterment." Christian Settlements in Japan are, I believe, making an honest effort to carry on their work along the lines suggested in this definition.

The following are some of the activities in which the Social Settlements in and around Tokyo are engaged: (*a*) Educational Work, including Kindergartens, Primary Schools, Night Schools of primary, middle and commercial grades, (*b*) Day Nurseries, (*c*) Play-grounds, (*d*) Medical Work, including, dispensaries, visiting nurses and midwives, mothers' clinics, and teaching of hygiene, (*e*) Neighbourhood Visiting, (*f*) Case Work, (*g*) Employment Bureaus, (h) Legal Advice, (*i*) Community Recreation (*j*) Religious Education, (*k*) Clubs for boys, girls, young men and young women.

Why should Christian organizations engage in this sort of work? As one Settlement worker has said, one good reason is, the work needs to be done. Christian individuals and Christian organizations are a part of the community and cannot be indifferent to the needs of the community. "The Son of Man came not be ministered unto but to minister and to give His life a ransom for many." There is always some ministry which is urgently needed. The need should determine the form of service to be engaged in, for example, the Shin Rin Kwan is situated on the edge of the industrial section of the City of Tokyo where the labor movement is best organized and most active. During a strike of the women operatives in a certain factory the strikers asked permission to use the building. Permission was granted and during the protracted strike the women were given useful employment. At the conclusion of the strike the Settlement was asked to open a Night School for factory girls and as a result a flourishing Night School is now in operation. Undoubtedly, education is one of the primary needs of both men and women workers and that need is being met in this Settlement. In Nippori it was found that a large number of unregistered children were roaming the filthy streets of the slum quarter unable to go to school because their parents had neglected to register their birth, so a primary school was started for them. Similarly, the work of the various Settlements is determined by the needs of the community in which they exist.

It is a matter of common knowledge that, up to the present time, Christianity in Japan has made progress chiefly among the middle and professional classes. The masses of laborers, farmers, fishermen and the dwellers in the slums of city and country are, as yet, practically untouched by the Christian spirit and message. There are, of course, some who are living and working among the poor and among laborers w: k   a   I m   pk   a wards in Tokyo, there has been a considerable increase of Christian centers but the number is still entirely inadequate to meet the needs. It is the consensus of opinion of workers in this field that ordinary methods of evangelism can never be successful. If the Church is to reach the masses of the people with the Christian message it must make the problems of the people its problems and work with them as neighbours to find a solution. This does not mean that Settlement work should be used as a bait to get people to Church but that Christian brotherhood demands it. If the so-called lower classes are to be saved and a new society created, the Church must be as active in helping people to a better life as the saloons and brothels are active in leading them to perdition. The sympathy and goodwill which exist in the membership of the Church needs to be organized and educated and directed so that its expression may be as effective as consecrated, scientific effort can make it. Large, expensively equipped Settlements may be necessary in places, but more important than that would be the establishment of hundreds of smaller Christian Settlements in the slums and industrial sections of cities and the rural districts.

It was suggested that "Hostels" be included in this discussion. A brief experience of a little more than one year in connection with a dormitory for labourers, has convinced the writer of the need for this sort of work. There are thousands of homeless labourers in the large cities who welcome clean, wholesome dormitories where the atmosphere is helpful rather than degrading. Furthermore, contact with the men in the dormitory is a great help in the understanding of their problems and their point of view. It is a commonplace to say that the labour problem is one of the most serious problems not only in Japan but throughout the world. Unfortunately there is, at present, somewhat of a gulf between the Church and the masses of labour. Dormitory work may be most useful in bridging that gulf and teaching those on either side that the others are human and that brotherhood is not an idle dream.

I am convinced that the Christian movement in Japan should give more thought and effort to these forms of work in the future than it has in the past. It is unfortunate that social service and evangelistic work are sometimes regarded as antagonistic. Social service which is not evangelistic in spirit or evangelistic zeal which does not issue in service are alike out of harmony with the spirit of the Master and inadequate to meet the modern situation.

THE PROGRAM OF SOCIAL SERVICE

(3) Health Crusade

Mrs. R. D. McCoy

In the spring of 1924 in Chicago, a New Era in Health Education was opened by the National Education Association. Certainly it is high time that educators everywhere were shouldering their responsibility in putting "Health in Education and Education in Health." The world war made all too plain the need for training in the three fold path of "health habits, health attitudes and health knowledge." This movement is becoming known throughout the world. It is most encouraging to record what has been done along the line of education in health in a few of the Christian institutions here in Japan.

The following centers teach balanced meals, nutritious lunches, proper care of the body, proper sleep habits, health habits and ideals:—Baiko Girls School,—in Domestic Science Course, with emphasis upon health: Amanuma Gakuin,—in cooking classes and women's meetings; Misaki Tabernacle,—in its two dispensaries and two children's clinics, by means of tracts, posters, and a visiting nurse; Omi Sanitorium, —to sanitorium patients, in the homes of the missionaries and at church services; Soshin Girls School,— Domestic Science Course and Housekeeping Course; Shokei Girls School,—in all grades lectures on health and sleep habits and infectious diseases; Ferris Seminary,—proper lunches are on sale to the students. Lectures on etiquette, dress, social problems are given,

as well as talks by doctors on health and diseases;
Joshi Sei Gakuin,—in Domestic Science Course, sewing and gymnasium classes; Toyo Eiwa Girls School
and Kindergarten,—Domestic Science Course, lectures
by specialists at cooking classes, and milk supplied
every morning to kindergarten children; Lambuth
Girls School,—in Domestic Science Course, through
courses given by Child Clinic physician; Kobe College,
—Household Science Course, and Hygiene taught as
a part of the curriculum,—a one hour course; Y. W.
C. A. Centers,—in Cooking Classes (one dietitian), use
"keep well" chart; Friends' Girls School,—Domestic
Science Course, balanced meals on sale for day pupils,
emphasis on health habits in dormitory, Institute, and
to day pupils; Matsugae Cho Primary School and Kindergarten,—use Dr. Saeki's balanced menu, lectures on
health habits, nutrition, doing of health chores, use
of "keep well" chart; Okayama Kindergarten,—intensive teaching for one month on the Organs of the
Body, their care, use and misuse, right and wrong
habits of eating, nutrition, sleep, germs and how to
avoid them, doing of health chores; Meguro and Higashi Murayama Leper Hospitals,—sanitation rules strict
ly enforced; East Tokyo Institute,—directed lunches,
regular clinics, use of "keep well" chart, emphasis
on rest period and play in sun-shine. "Children, like
flowers, thrive best when they have, beside the right
kind of nourishing food and care, plenty of sunshine
and out-of-door air."

Open-air classes, nutrition classes and baby garment demonstrations have been held at Kobe College.
The Better Baby Movement with contests and clinic
has been successfully tried at the Baiko Girls School,
the Friends' Girls School, and the Y. W. C. A. Centers.
In each case necessary instruction was given to the
mothers of the babies. At Baiko, the movement was
started because of the high death rate of infants in
that immediate Province and to celebrate the wedding
of the two Roy... Contest the past include si-

partment made house to house visitation throughout the neighborhood of the school. These Better Baby contests were attended by approximately 150 babies. At the Friends' Girls School one Better Baby contest was held at which 90 babies were examined by a baby specialist, a card system of the height and weight being kept. There was also a demonstration class of proper foods for babies, charts and recipes, and temperance posters for the mothers.

Measures are taken to prevent White Plague by means of posters, special addresses, personal advice, at Misaki Tabernacle; at Omi Sanitorium, Joshi Sei Gakuin, and Baikō Girls School, through individual teaching; in special classes at Shokei Girls School, Amanuma Gakuin, Ferris Seminary, Lambuth Girls School and Friends' Girls School. At the latter place attention is paid in a practical way to each individual student. The school recommends Dr. Takata's Sanitorium (Christian) at Chigasaki. At Kobe College a special schedule of four days was arranged for Dr. Elliott of St. Luke's Hospital. The subject of prevention of tuberculosis was especially stressed at these meetings.

Medical inspection is reported as being a regular item on nearly every school program. The Lambuth Training School and Kindergarten has very careful inspection and holds a regular weekly medical clinic for little children. At Kobe College weight records are made each month, and through the Parent-Teacher Association educational and protective measures are emphasized. At the Friends School special emphasis is put upon the throat, nose, teeth and spine. At Baiko Girls School inspection is made three times a year, eyes and teeth being carefully watched. At Eiwa Girls School a competent school nurse cooperates with the homes. At Misaki Tabernacle, Omi Sanitorium, Amanuma Gakuin, Soshin and Shokei schools protective measures are stressed for the child in the home. At Ferris Seminary protective measures are taught through a Social Problem Class, with emphasis on personal investigation of cases. At Lambuth Girls School the homes are educated through the Mothers' meetings and clinics. Kobe College observes Good Health Day, which is recommended by the Educational Department, as well as an annual Mountain Day in the spring.

At the meeting of the World Federation of Education Associations in Edinburgh last July where sixteen hundred black and white, brown and yellow alike, came from 47 different nations, the living truth was affirmed, that "even as we educate our youth, so also shall we reap."

THE PROGRAM OF SOCIAL SERVICE

(4) Work for Mothers

Mrs. R. P. Alexander

Mothers' Meetings in Japan have made great strides since the first one was organized by Mrs. Chappell in 1898. While at home on furlough she had attended the Second National Congress of Mothers at Washington and was greatly impressed by what she saw and heard of this great world movement. Soon after her return to Japan she organized the first Mothers' Meeting at Aoyama. This pioneer organization has held its regular monthly meeting ever since. Scores of sister associations have been established all over the Empire. These were early organized into a Mothers' Union. An Annual Meeting was held in Tokyo. Delegates from Yokohama and Tokyo attended, other more distant societies sending written reports.

In 1918 a National Mothers' Association (Naikoku Katei Kwai) was organized, with Mrs. Draper as President. This Association holds a yearly meeting in November. We have been fortunate in securing interesting speakers for our Annual Meetings. Among those who have delivered educative and inspring addresses are such names as, Mr. T. Namaye, for many years connected with the Social Reform Bureau of the Home Department, Dr. T. Saeki, head of the Government Food Investigation Laboratory, Mrs. Kubushiro, of the W.C.T.U., and Mr. K. Tomioka, President of the Tokyo Union of Social Workers and head of a Boys' Reform School.

Frequent requests from country places for material to be used in Mothers' Meetings led us to publish each month, a short leaflet on some topic helpful to the home. At first only 614 copies a month were sent out. This number has gradually grown until now we send out every month to regular subscribers 5,500 copies. In addition to these, special orders bring the average monthly sales to at least 10,000 a month.

It is the aim of the Mothers' Association to contribute as largely as possible to moral, mental, and physical upbuilding in the home. The following are some of the leaflets we have sent out: "Home and Purity," "Moral Benefits of Manual Training," "Clothes for Little Folks," "Mothers and their Boys," Social Relations of Young People," "A Father's Influence," "Temperance in the Home," "Teaching Truthfulness," "Proper Physical Development," and "A Happy Home."

The Katei Kwai is working with an efficient committee of Japanese ladies, and the leaflets are growing more and more popular. One of the members wrote that she was constantly surprised at the scope and variety of our literature. One great encouragement is the interest the women themselves are taking in the work.

The various Mothers' Meetings carry on a variety of activities. Better Baby Contests, Health Crusades, Sewing and Cooking Classes, instruction for young mothers—anything and everything that goes toward the building up of body, soul and spirit is the aim of our National Association.

Special attention has been given to leaflets appropriate for Christmas and Mothers' Day. This past year orders for 11,800 extra Christmas leaflets were filled. For Mothers' Day 21,000 extra copies of a sermon, "Mother," and 65,000 one page leaflets explaining the meaning of the day were sent out from the office.

M··· ·· · ·ui ·· · ··;· · · ·· t f!·· ··· · · ·· ·· ··f

these 'Mothers' Day leaflets have come to us. One Church using it as a model had 1,000 extra copies printed, giving the address of their church, and an invitation to the special Mothers' Day service. These they distributed in Banks, Clubs and Business Houses. Some people expressed surprise that Christians as well as Buddhists believed in filial piety. At one of the Kindergartens, children invited their mothers to a party, and gave them each a Mothers' Association leaflet in a pretty envelop which the children themselves had made. A University student whom I had never seen before came up to me as I was riding in the tram, and pointing to a package which he was carrying, said, "I am sending this present to my mother for Mothers' Day." "I will write her a letter tomorrow." The pupils in one Girls' School began several weeks beforehand to prepare remembrances to be given to their mothers on Mothers' Day. The Principal of a Primary School had 1,000 extra leaflets printed and gave one to each of the children in his school, asking them to tell him the next day what they had done to make their mothers happy.

Last year Mothers' Day coming on the Silver Wedding Anniversary of their Majesties, the Emperor and Empress, Mrs. Draper suggested that if it were possible, it would be very appropriate for the National Mothers' Association to send twenty-five carnations to the Empress as a token of our sincere congratulations. Through Count Chinda we inquired if such a thing would be permitted, and if we might with the flowers send a copy of our leaflets "Mother" and a letter from the Mothers' Association. A favorable answer was received, and we had a special copy prepared. It was very dainty, bound in white silk with silver lettering on the outside and a pale pink carnation painted on the upper right hand corner. This with the letter and a silvered willow basket containing twenty-five carnations was presented through Count Chinda. Our Mothers' Association esteems it a great privilege and honor to have been permitted to present this token of our affection to One who in so many ways has shown Herself an exemplary Mother not only to Her own four stalwart sons but to all Her people.

———————

CHAPTER XV

CHRISTIAN LITERATURE, PRESENT AND. FUTURE

Rev. S. W. Wainright, D.D.

Japan is a field where the conditions are peculiarly favorable to the production and distribution of literature. The output of Christian literature has not been adequate to the opportunity the situation has presented. Education has prepared the way: Popular education for general reading and the higher education for an appreciation of technical and other learned writings. The production of literature of a secular type has been far in advance of that of Christian literature. This is to be explained in part by the advanced stage of secular higher education beyond that of Christian higher education, and in part by the wider market demand for secular books.

Japanese readers are now supplied with three distinct types of books representative of western ideas. First, are the publications available in the original languages of Europe, for the most part in the English language, now being widely read. Secondly, are the numerous translations on the market. The schools have turned out many who are competent to translate from the European languages. By visiting the book stores one will find that a large proportion of the books on the shelves have been translated from European languages into Japanese. Then, the literature that is native output of or and writings, modern in character, and composed in the style of Japanese writing in current use. The literature of the past in Japan is being republished in modernized editions and is being interpreted afresh from the standpoint of the modern mind. The great impetus both to writing and publication, in the present, comes from the west. Literature in Japan indeed is being reconstructed and recast in a vastly larger mould through contact with the west.

Christian literature has been published by agencies established for the purpose, while not a few secular publishers have added Christian books to their list. The foremost Christian publishers have been the Christian Literature Society, a union enterprise representing organized Protestant Christianity, and the Keiseisha an independent Christian Publishing House. The Methodist Publishing House has been the outstanding importer of religious books from western countries and has done some publishing besides. The Christian Literature Society and the Methodist Publishing House have been recently merged. Other agencies are the Japanese Book and Tract Society, the Seikokai Shuppansha (Anglican), the Fukuin Shokwan (Southern Baptist at Shimonoseki), and the Y.M.C.A. and Salvation Army Presses. The American and British Bible Societies, dividing the country between them, have published Scriptures in the Japanese vernacular and widely distributed them. These publishing enterprises have been working under distinct disadvantages. Their capital funds have been small; the market demand has been limited; the literary productive power of the Churches is as yet undeveloped; and the publishing houses have been without profit earning sources of income, such for example, as is derived from Sunday School literature, or school text books or fiction, in other countries. The Keiseisha has covered a wider field than the Christian Literature Society and its business has been more profitable on that account. The Christian Literature Society has limited itself to such publications as its supporting constituencies would approve.

Notwithstanding limitations, there has been a steady improvement. When the day of larger things comes in Japan, the Churches will be prepared for it. Work of standard quality are beginning to appear. We may reasonably expect, with the development of Christian schools into higher institutions of learning now taking place, to see a larger output of standard Christian writings. A widening demand will insure a greater degree of publication of such books, when authors write them.

The future is full of promise. The present justifies such an outlook. The growth of the import trade in English books, for example, in this country is truly amazing. Every year marks an increase. An adverse rate of exchange on the money market seems to produce but little effect on the demand for foreign books. The latest phases in this import business are shown in the increased demand for school text books from abroad and in the growing demand for foreign periodical literature. This vast volume of imported literature is significant. It shows the extent and reality of the desire for reading among the Japanese people. This literature certainly will reproduce itself in the future in the vernacular literature. When we think of the parallel literature already being produced, both book and periodical literature, in the Japanese language, on a scale unequalled outside of Japan except in Christian countries, we are justified in looking to the future with a feeling of assurance that Christian literature will command a great place.

When the Chinese ideographic symbol for writing, still in use in Japan, is done away with, a great advance will be marked in the printing and the publis   · · · · · · · · · · · · · · ·re shown in book designing at the present time, in the publication of books made up in the style of the West. But the clumsy characters keep the industry back. The use of modern machinery cannot go very far until a simpler symbol is adopted.

Some idea of the scope of the literary production going on in Japan may be had from the published statistical returns. In 1924, for example, 14,361 distinct publications were issued. These do not include periodicals, the total number of which, published throughout the country, was 23,433. Among the books published those on education, literature and music headed the list. Text books are probably included under education and apart, therefore, from fiction, books on religion, 763 in number, no doubt occupied the first place.

Western books imported, as shown by the customs returns, have greatly increased in number since the European War. The imports of foreign books before the War in the aggregate amounted annually to about Yen 500,000. After the European War, there was a marked increase. The annual imports amount roughly to Yen 2,500,000. The books from England head the list and those imported from the United States and Germany stand about equal in amount. One disadvantage suffered by American books is the high price they are sold at. Books· produced in Europe are much cheaper than those published in the United States. High prices are an obstacle to the dissemination of literature in Japan. The cost of production greatly increased during the European War and the high level reached then has been maintained since the War.

THE PRESENT AND FUTURE OF CHRISTIAN LITERATURE FOR WOMEN AND CHILDREN

Miss A. C. Bosanquet

In planning literature for women and children there is a close relationship to be considered. Much is said on the upbringing of children in the publications intended for women. But as more women in Japan are remaining unmarried and have independent careers, they are demanding literature to help them with their new problems. As a result, literature for women is becoming more sharply divided from that for children; and less sharply divided from that for men. Though the majority of women still need the literature for home and children's problems, the other class is gradually increasing. Women graduates of Colleges have minds trained to read any available books without difficulty and we must meet their needs. Besides these College women there are thousands of intelligent girls who are studying books on many subjects, including religion. So Christian literature for women should include books and magazines of the highest quality on a variety of subjects, as well as the more simple books and magazines for the less keen minds.

The subject of children's reading is so highly specialized, and has so many possibilities, that it should be made into a separate department in every publishing society. There is already a fairly long list of but evangelistic booklets are much needed. The earthquake of 1923 destroyed so many books that it became necessary to spend funds on reprinting the books most in demand, instead of producing new ones. Much has been done for women and children by the Christian Literature Society, the Methodist Publishing House, the Japan Book & Tract Society, Keiseisha, Church Publishing Society, Fukuin Shokwan, and by the National Mothers' Association; and yet, only a beginning has been made. Though faithful work has been done, it is the general Japanese opinion that Christian books for women are, as literature, below the level of secular publications in beauty and force of style. For this reason, in spite of the present demand for good reading and the great lessening ot prejudice against Christianity, these books are not being read as they should be, outside of Christian circles. We must change this and produce more books which will capture the reader by the wonder of great thoughts in noble language. So far we have relied upon translations and imitations, rather than upon original spontaneous creative work. Much of the beauty of thought, imagery and diction, is necessarily lost in translation, while loyalty to the original restrains the translator's native eloquence. Christian translations compare well with others, as to accuracy, but those for women and children are often done by conscientious but insufficiently trained persons. Our women translators have nearly all been educated in Mission schools with a knowledge of English rather than skill in Japanese style, though there are a few notable writers who excel in both. Mission schools which teach modern Japanese literary style and give full opportunity to their students to perfect themselves therein, are rendering a great service to the Church and to the general public.

Despite these facts, Christian literature today has a real influence, because of the life giving power of the saving truth on which it is all based. After the great earthquake many found comfort and new courage in some Christian book. Christian girl students, far from home, welcome the spirit of love in Christian writings. Grateful mothers are glad to read books which help them in the moral and spiritual training of their children. Young people turn to our literature in the hope of finding answers to their questions. There is a magnificent sphere awaiting the coming poets and prose writers of the Christian Church.

With the merging of the Christian Literature Society and the Methodist Publishing House at the end of 1925, backed by the fine representative body of Japanese Christian leaders and missionaries, established in a new enlarged center on the site of the old Methodist Publishing House, a great advance may be confidently expected.

Perhaps we can best serve the future by indicating some of our greatest needs for development.

I. GENERAL

1. More vigorous, varied, constructive work, (a) for evangelistic teaching, (b) for women with higher education, (c) for the home, (d) for the school and student class, (e) for the country people, (f) for children of all ages.

2. More masterly *translations*, in purer, freer Japanese, which would be easily understood by people who do not know the English idiom.

3. More Christian *artists*, able to enter into the deeper spirit of Christian books and produce worthy gift volumes, as well as the cheap editions hitherto aimed at.

4. A more complete system of distribution making Christian reading accessible to all women and children throughout the Empire.

II. FOR WOMEN

1. Definitely Christian magazines for women and for th.... .. ..th

a great mind, once said that one of the greatest needs is a magazine in Japanese corresponding to the English magazine "Sunday at Home."

2. The introduction of *Christian influences* into the ordinary secular women's magazines, which have an enormous circulation. Some of them welcome good articles and stories by Christian writers. This might even develop into a kind of "Newspaper Evangelism" for women.

3. More *devotional books* to help in prayer and to uplift and comfort the hearts of busy mothers, girl students, the sick and sorrowful, as well as to refresh the spirits of the advanced disciples of Christ.

III. For Older Boys and Girls

1. Biographies, which are of special value in character building of the adolescent stage when the character and the ideals of a future life time are beginning to "set."

2. Biographical studies of the great Bible Characters, keeping close to the Bible record, while making scholarly use of all the genuine historical and geographical background. (There is a wide-spread tendency now to use the Bible as a source of romances, embroidering the original facts with purely fanciful materials, too often quite inconsistently).

3. *Original Japanese fiction;* dealing with real life in a hopeful, purposeful way, picturing the ideal Christian home, suggesting what is good and beautiful to the young imagination, without preaching. Such fiction might give higher ideas on love and marriage than the current novels, and suggest the holiness and dignity of marriage and motherhood, birth and death.

4. *Books* and *Pamphlets* seriously considering the special problems besetting older girls, written from a Japanese Christian point of view. These are often asked for by mothers and school teachers.

5. *Books* and *Magazines* suited to girls in train-

ing for various forms of Christian work are also asked for.

IV. For Children

1. Bible story picture books for the children to read, others for mothers to read aloud and show to their little children.

2. Any amount of wholesome, happy reading. The prevailing taste for melancholy stories, and the indifference to horrors and tragedies, need to be changed by substituting good reading. Really good boys' books are perhaps even rarer than those for girls. Translation alone can never make a satisfactory children's library. We hear complaints of the bad, foolish stuff children read, and the only solution is to be found in the speedy provision of a much more varied, much more interesting supply of genuine, original Christian books. Fiction, books on animal life, birds, trees, adventures, travels, mission work in other lands, etc., all from the truly living Christian standpoint are needed.

Insufficient and imperfect as the present supplies may be, some children love their Christian books and magazines in a touching way. A Christian boy who had been taking the Christian magazine, "Shôkôshi," for a year was asked if he would like to continue it during 1926. His answer was, "I shall take it till I die!" When the children show such a spirit, we must respond with equal fervour in the great work of helping forward the Christian literature cause.

CHAPTER XVI

THE PLACE OF NEWSPAPER EVANGELISM IN THE FUTURE

Rev. W. H. Murray Walton

A recent and very wise book on the subject of the relation of religion to science devotes the whole of the first chapter to a discussion of definitions. In considering so big a subject as the place of Newspaper Evangelism in the future it may be well for us to do likewise. For what is Newspaper Evangelism? It may be described as a method utilized by the Christian Church, which aims at the extension of the Kingdom of God by means of the systematic presentation of the Christian message through the secular press and the effective following-up of the same.

This definition is, strictly speaking, more ideal than actual, since the work is still in a comparatively pioneer stage, yet it contains the three essential elements in Newspaper Evangelism, both present and future. These are the Christian Church, the use of the secular press and the effective follow-up.

1. THE CHRISTIAN CHURCH

The future of any Christian work in a country is irrevocably wrapped up in the future of the Christian Church in that country. The Church is the Body of the eternal Christ; the individual 'militant here on earth' is but a temporary phenomenon. He comes, he makes his contribution to the Church of his day, and he goes beyond the veil; he dies, but the Divine Society, which bore him and blessed him and benefited by him, goes on.

The place of Newspaper Evangelism in the future depends largely on the extent to which this truth is realized. If Newspaper Work is regarded as but the work of an individual, or a missionary society, while at the moment it may do work of real value, yet as a method with a future it can safely be disregarded. This does not mean of course that much of its success will not depend on individuals; it inevitably will. But these individuals will do their work as workers for a Church rather than free-lance Christians or agents of a missionary society.

Now when we study the Newspaper Work that has been done hitherto, we see that the Japanese have given valuable help, both in writing articles and in attending to the work of the office, but the pioneers and leaders and supporters have almost without exception been missionaries and their friends. And even though they have doubtlessly emphasized the importance of the Church in their dealings with enquirers, yet they themselves have done the work first as missionaries; they have owed a greater loyalty to the Board which supports them than to the Church for which they work. Even the cooperative work which they have done has been cooperation between Boards rather than between Churches. It is this fact perhaps which accounts for the comparative lack of interest in the method on the part of the Japanese Church. Not until the change in emphasis suggested above is brought about will it get the enthusiastic backing, which it deserves.

Someone, however, will ask, 'In view of the nature of Newspaper Evangelism, its wide appeal, its broad message, and its use of such an instrument as the public press, would it not be better if it were made one of the activities of the National Christian Council? There is no doubt but that in certain matters the Council can give valuable help, especially when circumstances demand some authoritative statement in the Press by the Christian forces as a whole, such as was published for example at the time of the American Immigration legislation. But as a general rule it seems for several reasons to be a task much better handled by the churches. For in the first place, while the Council represents the Christian forces in Japan, it is the Churches which are scattered up and down the country and have to do the real spade work. To the average reader an article by the National Christian Council would conjure up in his mind some high and mighty authority residing in the capital, whereas an article by a Presbyterian would be inevitably linked up with the little tabernacle in the town he knows best, to which hitherto he had not paid much attention, but which he now sees standing in the Press for 'righteousness, temperance and judgement to come.' Again, it is a very moot point if it is the Council's function to do such work. The proclamation of the Gospel is the first duty of the churches. The Council is a convenient channel for cooperation, but it will be little short of disaster if, by usurping the function of the Churches, it appear to offer a substitute for unity. We must recognize its limitations no less than its achievements. Denominational articles may reveal in all its ugliness the fact of our present divisions, but to attempt to conceal them under a conciliar cloak is no solution of the problem.

As a matter of practical politics, however, there is no reason why the several churches should not use different leading papers as well as the local papers in defined parts of the country as at present.

The first great principle, however, which will determine the future of the Newspaper Work is that it become an integral part of the campaign of the Churc

2. THE USE OF THE SECULAR PRESS

The first question that arises under this head is what kind of articles should the Church insert—ones containing definite Christian teaching, or ones discussing the Christian attitude to present day ideals? In a country like Japan, where Christianity has already won a recognised place in the national life and where there is less reserve on the subject of religion than in the West, there seems to be little need for articles of the last type, though of course there is no objection to them. But with regard to the first two, the definite presentation of Christian teaching will by the simple presentation of facts go far to eliminate mistaken ideas so prevalent in the Japanese mind about Christianity, e.g. that it is equivalent to abstinence from some evil habit. It will enable the Church to set forth something of the attractiveness of the Gospel, which it has to offer, and its power to satisfy the deepest longings of the human soul. Or again, articles having a definite relation to present-day problems will not only elicit a large response from the reading public, as experiments have frequently proved, but they will also shew that Christianity has a real and living message for modern life.

Articles of this kind have also some relation to another point we must consider under this head, the matter of cost.

It is true that here and there papers have been persuaded to publish Christian articles free, and a courageous step has been taken by the 'Yomiuri' in starting a religious column which is open to Christianity. Yet the fact still remains that in most cases advertising rates of some kind or another are paid to secure the insertion of the Christian message. Now the average Newspaper editor regards the matter, quite naturally, not as a religious proposition but a business one. He puts into his paper just such matter as he thinks his readers will want; other material

must be paid for. Now if the Christian article is such
as to provide good 'copy,' there is no reason why
the shoe should not be on the other foot; in other
words, why the Newspaper proprietor should not pay
the Christian journalist for his article. Perhaps one
of the reasons why this form of work has cost so
much hitherto is that we have thought more of what
our readers ought to have than what they will take.
Jesus Christ drew the crowds because there was a
point of contact between his message and themselves.
The fact that the Japanese Newspapers inserted the
National Christian Council statement referred to above
without cost is proof that they are not unsympathetic.
This fact is certain, in the near future at all events
the Japanese Church will not be able to shoulder the
expense of paid articles for many years to come,
whereas by wise action there is no reason it should
not win for religion a place in the press such as
literature and art and the drama enjoy today.

Another point under this heading is that of cooperation in the production of the message. A series
of articles on 'Christianity and the sex-problem' such
as was put into the Tokyo 'Nichinichi' by the Seikokai
office, does not necessarily require a Seikokai mind
to compose it. If a first-rate Christian journalist were
forthcoming there is no reason why his articles should
not be syndicated to the different churches, provided
their freedom is respected. As a matter of fact in
all the Newspaper Work so far there has been a happy
ignoring of the Copyright Law by mutual consent; the
work of the Kingdom is too serious a matter to be
hampered by patents! It should not be impossible
to pay the salary of such a writer by charging a small
fee for the right of reproduction. The gain in expert
advice would be immense.

There are some, however, who urge that what the
Church in Japan really wants in the future is not so
much Christian articles in the secular press but a Chris-

tian Newspaper of its own. They point to the 'Christian Science Monitor' as an example of what they mean. Apart from the fact as to whether the above paper is as successful in producing good 'scientists' as it is in giving good news, it is nevertheless a debatable point if more effective work is not done by utilizing the secular press. In addition to the serious question as to whether it would be financially possible to maintain such a paper at a sufficiently high standard to make its Christianity felt, there is the more fundamental question as to whether we as Christians are not meant to use a weapon already placed in our hands by the providence of God. At all events let us try this former method first.

3. The Follow-up Work

When the Newspaper Work is done by the Churches it stands to reason that the effectiveness of the follow-up will depend largely on the extent to which it links up the results with the Church. In England and America this may be a comparatively simple process, but in a country like Japan where the churches are almost entirely confined to the towns and the bulk of the readers live in the country districts, the difficulty is a serious one.

Two lines of development suggest themselves. By a chain of circumstances, which it is unnecessary to describe here, practically all the Newspaper offices in the country have adopted the name 'New Life Hall' (Shinseikan) prefaced by the title of church or place. The enquirers in connection with these are banded in 'New Life Societies.' Is there any reason why this term should not be adopted by the Church as a whole? 'Shinseikai' is certainly a more euphonious term than 'kyudoshakai' (enquirers' societies) and the meaning has more purpose. If such a plan were possible, and each church had its own branch of the 'New Life Society' the country member of his visit to his town friends would naturally ask, if there were a local branch of the Society and so the first link with the church would be forged. The Japanese have a love for societies of one kind and another. By such a plan the Christian Church would be taking advantage of a psychological opportunity, which might bring untold results.

A second feature of the follow-up work, which is potent with possibilities, is the magazine issued to New Life Society members. It is a suggestive fact that the two most influential Christian leaders of recent years, Uemura and Uchimura, have been men who have had their own magazines. The Editor of 'New Life' would have through the mass of correspondence which comes into his hands an opportunity of gauging the spiritual needs of his members to a degree even greater than that of a successful pastor. For it is a striking fact that the Japanese are often quicker to reveal their spiritual desires on paper than by word of mouth. By making use of the knowledge thus gained to frame his message, by cultivating the 'group-spirit' among his readers, and by making the magazine in a perfectly natural way an organ of the church to which he belongs, there is no limit to the effectiveness of the work that a wise editor can do.

Such in brief outline are some of the possible ways that Newspaper Evangelism will play its part in the Church of the future. In conclusion a brief word must be said on its place in the whole Christian campaign. One of the most striking facts in the world today is the increasing part being played by propaganda. Ludendorff admitted with chagrin that it was a decisive factor in Germany's defeat. There is nothing which statesmen fear more today than Bolshevist propaganda. Political leaders have been quick to realize the value of the press and the printed page. The Christian Church of course admits its use, but it importance. The progress of Christianity in Japan today is steady but it is painfully slow and utterly incomparable with the growth of ideas and of population. One of the great reasons for this is that the people do not know what Christianity is. The great majority of them are beyond the reach of the Church, and present conditions suggest that they will be for at least another generation. The only hope is for the Church to make such a revision of her methods as will transform the whole situation. In a land where everybody can read and where there are nearly 300 daily papers, it is not too much to claim that Newspaper Evangelism has a vital part to play in the evangelization of Japan. The Word of God is not bound. It is not limited to human lips. The Bible is an eternal testimony to the value of the printed page. There is no reason why nearly everybody in Japan should not be within the regular reach of the Gospel within the next ten years.

CHAPTER XVII

ORGANIZED WORK FOR YOUNG PEOPLE

Y. W. C. A.

Miss J. N. Scott

In an article whose purpose it is to discuss the place of the Y.W.C.A. as a factor in the development of the Christian Movement in Japan, it would seem to be fitting to consider those features of its work which, at least in a measure, distinguish its program from that of other organizations similar in their aim. Many of these have their origin and incentive in the fact that the Y.W.C.A. is working among a homogeneous and somewhat specialized group. About six thousand girls and young women compose its membership and its activities are planned with this definite group in mind. In these days, when so much is being said and written about a somewhat nebulous thing which we call "group consciousness" it is a task at once fascinating and alluring to try to express in terms of a particular group certain concrete definitions.

To this end, the Association has been working through a number of different channels. The most inclusive of these is the self-governing clubs which offer opportunity both for training in group action and for development of individual initiative in leadership. The leaders of these clubs are, in most cases, themselves young girls who have taken the training offered

Association and who work under their guidance. The
activities of the clubs are varied according to the
needs and desires of the members. One of the most
interesting of these has been the production of plays
and pageants. The girls throw themselves into these
with the greatest zest, often making their own cos-
tumes and the results which they achieve would be
creditable for a much longer experience than most of
them have had in this direction. Principally through
these clubs the Association has found one of its
choicest opportunities for service in a ministry to
young business women who need help and guidance
in forming standards in the comparatively new world
in which they find themselves.

The educational program is perhaps the one
which is best known to the average person. Crowds
of girls trooping into a building in the early evening
hours and the hum of interested activity are easily
intelligible to the casual passer-by. But interest in
the matter is vastly increased when it is understood
that these programs· are planned with reference to
varying groups of those who participate in them—the
"continuation school" for the girl who, under heavy
economic pressure, was obliged to leave school and
go to work; the morning classes for the so-called girl
of leisure who desires to extend her cultural life; the
class in household science for the girl who is getting
ready to be married or for the young matron who
wishes to enlarge her horizon in the management
of her home; and always, and most important of all,
the classes in Bible and religious education which are
the goal and the crown of all the Association's activities. A small beginning has been made in physical
and health education. The Association looks forward
to a wide extension of work along this line in cooperation with the government agencies and with those of
other organizations and it is hoped that through this
may be gradually developed . t pe of work closely
articulating with the woman in her own home.

Only a passing reference can be made to the industrial work. This follows, in general, the lines which are being followed by workers among industrial groups who are connected with other organizations, some of whom have carried their programs for a much longer time than we have done. But a good beginning has been made, and at our National Convention in October of last year, a commission was ordered for a study of industrial conditions as they affect women, and for definite recommendations to be made at the next biennial convention. A study group has been formed and plans are under way for an ordered approach toward a program of education of public opinion.

Almost since its earliest beginnings, the Association has been known as a pioneer in the holding of summer conferences to which, in the twenty years of its history, thousands of girls have come. Reference has been made in an earlier volume of this book to the fact that we now have our own conference grounds. To these grounds, now fairly well supplied with buildings and equipment, came last year nearly eight hundred girls and women in attendance upon the three conferences and the National Convention held there. Our program for this year calls for four conferences, at least, made necessary by the experience of last year. The Association leaders hope to extend this service more and more as time goes on, not only by more and larger conferences held at our own grounds but also by many smaller group conferences in different parts of Japan.

For several years the Association has been offering a short course each spring in training for the secretaryship. The response to this has been most encouraging, and we are looking toward a considerable extension and development of it. In this we hope to work out some kind of cooperation with other agencies offering training as well as to plan for brief course

ferent centers and for varying kinds of service. In
common with all Christian workers, we believe that
we can do nothing more fundamental than to help in
the training of the coming leadership among the
women of Japan.

CHAPTER XVIII

ORGANIZED WORK FOR CHILDREN: KINDERGARTENS

Miss M. M. Cook

Fifty years ago the government introduced the kindergarten into the educational system of Japan. Eight years later the first Christian kindergarten was opened in 1884. In 1925 the "Christian Movement" reports 269 Christian kindergartens with 12,680 children. Government statistics, issued December 1925, report as follows for 1921 and 1922:

	1921	1922
Kindergartens in Higher Normal Schools	2	—
Public Kindergartens	250	—
Private Kindergartens	464	—
Total Number Kindergartens	716	747
Total Number Children	63,063	65,094

These public and private kindergartens are scattered all over Japan,—in Tokyo and Osaka-fu and in 45 Ken—and the private ones include probably most of the Christian kindergartens.

Allowing for the difference in dates in the above statistics and the uncertainty regarding the inclusion of all the Mission kindergartens in the government report, it is yet apparent that the number of Christian kindergartens is about one-fourth of the whole; the num.. : , .. , ' , ; '. th of all in kindergarten.

In the "Christian Movement" for 1914 a brief
history was given of the first three decades of Christian Kindergarten work in which it was stated that
the number of kindergartens had increased to 111.
In the "Christian Movement" for 1915 a hopeful outlook was taken of the beginning of the fourth decade.
That fourth decade has ended, with report showing
an increase during that ten years greater than the
increase of the previous thirty. The 111 Christian
kindergartens have become 269. This gives an encouraging impression, but the bigness of the task yet
unaccomplished is emphasized by further study of
government statistics.

The total number of kindergarten children in 1922
was 65,094, of whom less than one half would be
ready to enter school in April. The number of children reported as actually entering first grade was
0,083,477. If of these only about 30,000 came from
kindergartens and of these not more than 5,000 or
6,000 from Christian kindergartens, can we be satisfied? What about the millions in primary schools
all over Japan who have never come under Christian
influence?

Three facts as regards the kindergarten are encouraging, in spite of the relatively small numbers
as yet reached.

First, a most encouraging fact is the distinctive
character of the training given the individual child.
In the "Christian Movement" for 1924 in a study of
education in general are found these significant words:
"At present the Christian kindergarten is doing by
far the most effective piece of Christian education
found in Japan. . . . . In the first place the kindergarten gets the children very early in life and therefore has a unique opportunity to start them on the
'Great Highway of Life' which leads God-ward. In
the second place the kindergarten is in a class by
itself as an educational institution. If you want to

know what education really is, frequent a well re-
gulated kindergarten where pupils and teachers are
engaged in sharing in the experiences of living. You
will find a social group characterized by warmth and
enthusiasm, purpose and cooperation. You will find
here child problems arising out of the actual situations
which are vital to the children. . . . . Of these splendid institutions. . . . . Would there were ten times as
many. . . . . Ten times as many would go far toward
bringing in the Kingdom within a generation or two."

Second, another encouraging fact is that the principles and practice of the Christian kindergarten are
attracting the sympathetic attention of some of the
best educators in Japan. This makes possible an in-
fluencing of ideals and standards in the public school
system *if* the kindergarten really demonstrates the
value of its unique contribution to education. To
realize such a possibility places upon every Christian
kindergartner a heavy burden of responsibility to
measure up educationally, in order that her kindergarten may influence the thinking public as well as
the children under her care.

Third, the kindergarten is the starting point and
center of definite influences in the community. Perhaps not one of all the 269 kindergartens reported is
without its mothers' meetings and visiting in the
homes. Word comes from many, of organized clubs
for fathers, mothers, older brothers and sisters, as
for graduates of the kindergarten. Some, like the
Zenrin kindergarten of the Baptist Mission in Kobe,
have transformed their communities and inspired
others to undertake likewise to lift whole neighborhoods thru the little children. The Zenrin kindergarten is repeating itself in Liuchu. More and more
the kindergartens are being linked up with larger
social enterprises as at Hanabatake in Okayama in the
recently opened Zenrinkan in Osaka, both of the Congregational Church. The Baptist Tabernacle in Tokyo
is an   t   .l. .   .   . .,. .   . . t.   pl. .   t. .f   . .   1.9

given to kindergarten and day-nursery work in connection with an institutional church. More than others Methodists have multiplied kindergartens in close connection with the ordinary church or chapel. The Episcopal group is second in this respect. Thirtyfour missions representing the various Churches report kindergartens in 1925. The Methodist group, representing the Japan Methodist Church, report 75; the Episcopal group representing the Sei Ko Kwai, 49; the Presbyterian group, representing the Nihon Kirisuto Kyokwai, 28; the Baptist group, 24; Congregational and Kumiai Kyokwai, 20. Other Protestant Missions and Churches range from 1 to 10; and the Roman Catholics report 18. These statistics speak for themselves regarding the fact that the Church in Japan is appreciating the kindergarten as an evangelistic agency and the kindergartner as an evangel of Jesus Christ.

Not only, however, are the Missions and Churches working individually along kindergarten lines but in close cooperation. In the third decade of work, in 1908, the foreign Christian kindergartners, led by Miss Annie L. Howe, organized for mutual help. The Japan Kindergarten Union now numbers 70 active members and 14 associate members, including not only graduate kindergartners but others connected with Christian kindergartens. A continually increasing number of missionary kindergartners keeps fresh inspiration always available in the annual meetings at Karuizawa. The inspiration of these meetings is carried all over Japan thru branch meetings which extend the influence of the Union and make work more intensive for the Japanese kindergartners. Membership in the Union and its branches is limited to Christian kindergartners, but cordial relations are encouraged with kindergartners in the government schools. For two years a representative has been sent from the Christian kindergarten Union to the larger body of kindergartners who form the National Kindergarten Association.

The Christian kindergarten work creates a constant demand for teachers equal to the task. Here is the place of the Christian Kindergarten Teacher Training Schools, of which there are eight. The responsibility rests with these schools to cherish ideals and hold up standards, that make possible thru their graduates what is going on to-day, and will make possible the larger things toward which the whole kindergarten movement is tending in the general progress of Christ's Kingdom in Japan.

THE ORGANIZED WORK FOR CHILDREN IN JAPAN

(2) *Mr. H. E. Coleman*

A lady visiting a new mother in the hospital the other day found the proud father and the mother of the seven day old baby planning her college education. When we speak of education we quickly think of school, but yet those same parents realized that the education of the child had begun before the mother had left the hospital where the wee thing was born.

When taking dinner with the parents of a young boy a few nights ago we were discussing dishes, when the adopted father proudly remarked, "We shall have no more pretty dishes in this house now until that young man (a four-year-old) graduates from college."

Now if we can think of the church as analogous to the home, can we ask the same question, Who is the most important individual? Or what is the important work of the church? Can we not say that one common object for both the home and the church is to maintain its own life and to work for the good of society in which it lives? To maintain its own side the most important duty, surely, is to bring up all the children that are born into the church in the Christian way of living. This the church for hundreds of years has failed to do as well as it should, because it was obsessed with the idea that its work was to save "sinful men." The workers were so busy in saving the lost, that the work of reclaiming them kept the workers from preventing other children from going into sin.

This question of the most important work of the church was asked to pastors in the middle west of the United States last year. Six hundred of them said that the connection of the pastor with the home was the most important work; and that the *second most important was that of providing the religious training for the children of the congregation and the community*. This religious education, it is being realized, must be a part of his growing life. It must mean the child so that he comes to experience the Christian attitude of mind in all his relations.

This new attitude of mind realizes that a Christian is not made in one evangelistic meeting. Moreover, the largest number of earnest workers in the church today are those who have been brought up by this slow process of religious training from the younger years.

Some people in Japan are beginning to realize the importance of this work for the children. The Rev. Seimatsu Kimura gave a splendid testimony at our Training School recently, saying that he realized that the real results that came out of his evangelistic work, i.e. those people who finally came into the church, were those who had first had a definite training in the Sunday School.

So important is the work of religious education that the Sunday School with one hour on Sunday is no longer considered enough to fulfil the obligation of the church toward the children, or to make use of its opportunity for the good of the children of the community. The week-day school of religion is being established all over America and Canada with the cooperation of the leaders in education. It is considered necessary as a part of the system of education. Another way of securing additional time for this work, and another evangelistic means of reaching the children and homes of children, is the Daily Vacation Bible S

been so rapid in the last twenty years that last year
there were more than a million children enrolled in
Bible Schools for giving religious training during the
summer time.

During the last two years the work has been
strengthened by the publishing of a new Sunday
School Hymnal, new graded lesson texts, and other
literature. This hymnal provides material for putting
new content into the worship period of the Sunday
School, enabling this to become a real contribution
to the devotional life of the child. It has been very
well received and we hope that soon no Sunday
School in the country will be without a copy

After the new graded lessons were destroyed in
the great fire the work of completely revising them
was taken up. A committee of experts in Sunday
School work and with literary ability was gotten together and they have been at work most conscientious-
ly. The second text for each of the first four departments will be ready for use by the first of April this
year (1926). The next work will be the preparation
of leaflets for children and note books for the older
boys and girls. Sets of pictures are now being assembled for the use of the teachers in class work.
These are being selected from the Perry, Wilde and
Brown copies of famous pictures, and thus it is
hoped to maintain a higher standard in the art side
of our religious education than has generally been the
case in the Sunday School work.

By the first of April this year (1926) two courses
will be available for each department and by the first
of April next year the eleven years will be completed,
hence those schools who wish to put into operation
the complete course of eleven years can do so.

A splendid magazine for teachers is now being
published each month. This has been greatly
strengthened by the cooperation of the Boards of
Religious education of the Methodist and Congrega-

tional Churches. This is a splendid example of the advantage of cooperative enterprise in the general religious work for children.

The training of teachers is one of the most important phases of Sunday School promotion work In realization of this fact the National Sunday School Association has taken entire responsibility for the Training School at Karuizawa and we are now planning to organize a second Training School for teachers and officers in the Southern part of the country. The buildings of the Baiko Girls' School at Shimonoseki have been placed at our disposal for this purpose Our texts for teacher Training were all burned in the fire but since then four books have been issued. We also recommend a book on organization by Rev. A. Ebizawa, so that five books are now available for class or group study.

In Japan one of the greatest hindrances to regular Sunday School Work is frequent absence on the part of children due to Government school functions held on Sunday which they are practically required to attend. To make up for this lack of time for religious education in the church, the Daily Vacation Bible School affords a splendid additional opportunity.   Three different pamphlets have been issued explaining the purpose of the Daily Vacation Bible School and also giving details of carrying out the program. One hand book of seventy pages was published of which one edition has been exhausted. One text for the Junior Grade was published last year and one other new text for the Primary group will be published this year.   Sets of pictures will also be available for these courses. Short intensive institutes will be conducted this year (1926) for training college students and other young people for this important work. The International Association of Daily Vacation Bible Schools is now operating as an auxiliary of the International Council of Religious Educ ʼ   ʼ . ʼ   ,   ʼ   · ay

School Association definitely represent them in countries outside of American Continent. They are definitely helping to promote the work in Japan.

A fuller realization of the value of the child in the church is still a great need among Christian workers in Japan. As that vision broadens, the work of the religious education of children will take deeper root and the church will receive a new impetus in its growth.

CHAPTER XIX

THE CONTRIBUTION OF BIBLE SOCIETIES TO THE CHRISTIAN MOVEMENT IN JAPAN

---

(1) American Bible Society

---

(2) *Rev. K. E. Aurell*

An officer, in early days of missions in Japan (1875), wrote to a certain missionary. "Give us the Gospel first and the hospital afterwards for we cannot afford to wait for the Gospel." This statement expresses the innermost condition as well as longing of the hearts of the Japanese, such as king David in ancient times expressed when he said: "As the hart panteth after the water-brooks, so panteth my soul after thee, O God. My soul thirsteth for the living God."

An eminent Japanese Christian emphatically asserts that the Japanese are very religious. The mythology and history of Japan bear him out. The comparatively well preserved shrines and temples throughout the empire today prove it. The more one truly knows of things Japanese the easier it is to join Saint Paul of olden times in the statement: "I perceive that in all things ye are too superstitious." Their conceptions and expressions of religion differ from that of the Christian, nevertheless the bent of their hearts is tow.   ᵗ   ᵗ   ᵗ   ᵗ   ᵗ

gion of the Bible is preeminently spiritual or mystical
—"Great is the mystery of Godliness"—it suits them.
Christianity rose in the Orient and is not so difficult
for the Japanese to understand as is often thought
and said. Interpretation of Christianity by occidental
instruction and living not infrequently makes it diffi-
:cult of appreciation.

One of our good American ambassadors once said:
"Give the Old Book a chance." That is what the
Bible Societies have done and are continuing to do.
It is the Bible which stands true to life and brings
knowledge of verities the hearts of men everywhere
long for, and it has won a great and lasting place
for itself in Japan.

The fruits of Christianity are found all over
Japan but, after all, that is not what grips and converts hearts. This people as well as any other cannot be satisfied with the more gifts, their hearts long
to get into vital touch with the Giver. Therefore
Bible spreaders have no hesitation in claiming that
it is the unadulterated religion of the Bible—"God's
wisdom in a mystery, even the wisdom that hath been
hidden, which God foreordained before the worlds
unto our glory" that appeals to the true inner self of
this people.

The Bible Societies are giving them this Book
without note or comment or man's interpretation.
Every year thousands of letters to the Bible House in
Tokyo indicate that the Japanese all over the country
are profoundly impressed by it. Without a doubt
there is a great future for Bible circulation in Japan.
Give the Bible a chance and it will surely take and
hold this empire for Jesus Christ. For, as some one
has strikingly said: "The Bible is not a wayside well
built over a single spring, but a mighty river into
which a million springs have poured their waters."
"Therefore with joy shall ye draw water out of the
wells (rivers) of salvation."

THE CONTRIBUTION OF BIBLE SOCIETIES
TO THE CHRISTIAN MOVEMENT
IN JAPAN

(2) British And Foreign Bible Society

(1) *Mr. F. Parrott*

The work of the Societies engaged in translation, publication, and circulation of Holy Scripture in Japan can be reviewed for fifty years. The Societies issue and circulate the text and the text only. The dictum, "the Church to teach and the Bible to prove" has been adhered to,—since no note or comment has been published by the Societies at work in Japan. Yet who can measure the contribution to the growth of the Kingdom of God achieved by this very abstinence from "comment"? Throughout the length and breadth of the Japanese Empire, the divinely opened door of freedom of religious belief has enabled the Bible Societies to disseminate God's own Word to millions more than have ever listened to preaching.

From time to time, our Colporteurs hear from the lips of men and women accounts of their having found peace through believing and acting upon what they have read; and only the Recording Angel has an account of the Baptisms of those who in simple faith have confessed their sins and have repented and turned to God. Has the Christian Movement in Japan received any more momentous dynamic (apart from the infinite of God to the Spirit, than the readition and circulation of Holy Scripture? Consecrated service and consecrated lives of God's servants are immeasurable in their influence: and Japan has richly enjoyed those who have given their all to Him Who called and sent them here. The Bible Societies have had a great responsibility in the great privilege God has given them of providing Japan with God's own Word in its fresh purity. To the honor of those that toiled and prayed in those early days of the seventies and eighties, their work remains to-day marvellously good and acceptable. That a first translation should have proved vitally serviceable for over forty years was a contribution to the Christian Movement in Japan which those who come after us will freely acknowledge.

The Bible, in whole or in part, has been circulated far below cost. It has been circulated far beyond the region where churches have been planted. This work still goes on in mines, in factories, among emigrants, persons in prisons, among lepers, and in hospitals. And this work is but in its infancy; because the Church (by reason of her poverty of manpower), cannot yet go where Colporteurs brave scorn and abuse from ignorance and prejudice, patiently toiling through torrid heat and biting cold, in season and out of season, and make their contribution to the Christian Movement in Japan.

CHAPTER XX

THE CONTRIBUTION OF THE TRACT SOCIE-
TIES TO THE CHRISTIAN MOVE-
MENT IN JAPAN

George Braithwaite

Some one has said, "It is a trite saying that Christian literature is indispensable, and like most trite
sayings, this one is trite because it is so absolutely
true." The Christian Church has recognized this need
from the very first and has laboured to supply it.
Not that the press can ever take the place of the
preacher, but the printed page can go where the
living preacher can never penetrate, and can be
read and studied wherever the possessor may be.

The first Tract ever printed in Japanese seems
to have been one prepared by Dr. Hepburn and printed
in Shanghai in 1864. Another, "The Story of the
Cross," published a few years later, is noteworthy
because some of the Christians in Hawaii sent it over
together with enough money to pay for its translation
and publication in Japanese.

The American Tract Society began work here in
1874, and the Religious Tract Society of London a
few months later. Looking back over the half century
that has since passed, it is found that these Societies
and their successor the Japan Book and Tract Society
were enabled up to the end of 1925 to place in the
hands of this people 875,784 Books; 23,223,189 Tracts;
and 6,053,806 Cards, a total of over 30 million. These
figures .   .   .   .

other Societies such as the Kyobunkwan, the Christian Literature Society, and other publishing departments which are in more or less close connection with individual missions.

In the early days the production of Christian books and pamphlets was beset with many difficulties, indeed as late as 1874 a Japanese gentleman was arrested merely for having distributed a few copies of a small Tract by Rev. J. D. Davis, D.D., and nearly two years passed before he was finally released. Now of course this is all changed and though before any publication can be sold, two copies of it must be presented to the Home Department, no objection has ever been raised to any of the numerous issues which the writer has sent in during the past twenty-five years. Not only so, but the Government officials have again and again given special facilities for the distribution of the Society's literature. This was markedly so throughout each of the three sad wars in which Japan was involved. In the World War the naval authorities not only made it easy for us to place some of our publications on board the Japanese warships at the Cape, but assured us they would be glad for the selection to be sent, and the commander of the squadron afterwards himself sent us a grateful letter acknowledging the small parcel we did send.

In the early days our literature was mainly distributed through missionaries who received it as free grants for use in their work. But as costs increased and the financial help received from the homelands lessened, this method of work became increasingly difficult till now it is only in very special circumstances that we give such grants at all. The very fact that during 1925 we received Yen 55,567 in cash for our sales gives some idea how essential our work is.

While the missionary community still furnishes a large number of our customers, it is interesting to note that each year more and more of our publications are being bought by the Japanese. Moreover the demand now comes, not only from those who may be thought of as professional religious workers but also from the more general public, the wealthier class of whom do not hesitate to pay large sums for Christian books both in English and Japanese. Surely there could be no greater proof that there is a most important place for the work of the various Christian publishing houses.

Whether in evangelistic effort or in pastoral work there are few places where Christian Books and Tracts are not vital to efficiency. In all the various modes of travel, whether by land or sea, and even in the ordinary contacts of everyday life there are constant opportunities for passing on the little printed messengers. That this method of evangelism has been greatly used of God is abundantly proved by the many testimonies received through the years from those who in this way have for the first time heard of the Gospel of the grace of God. Some who were thus reached are now well-known leaders among the Christian forces in the empire.

The opportunity for using literature is not less in pastoral work, for in order that the man of God should be throughly furnished unto all good works he needs an ever fresh supply of literature that will help him to a right spiritual understanding of the Book of Books and to that personal knowledge of the Lord Jesus Christ without which he cannot be used to win and build up others.

One feature of Japanese life that makes literature work particularly important is that such large numbers of the people are so unsettled, indeed it has been said that one third of them move each year. In this way they come for a few weeks or months to a meeting or bible class and then off they go to other part of the empire or it may be to South America or some other distant place where there is no church to which they can be introduced. If therefore Chris- tian influences are to be continued, it must be mainly done by means of the printed page. Thus the publication·houses are the supply stations, not only for the islands of Japan but are centres from which packets constantly go forth over the world wherever Japanese readers are to be found.

In a word, the supply of fresh Tracts, Books and Cards for our evangelists, pastors and Sunday School teachers whether they be missionaries or Japanese, is as vitally essential to the success of their work as was the provision of ample ammunition to the soldier on the battle front.

CHAPTER XXI

THE PLACE OF THE LANGUAGE SCHOOL IN THE CHRISTIAN MOVEMENT

Rev. H. V. S. Peeke, D.D.

The place of the Language School in the Christian Movement depends entirely on the place of the missionary in the Christian Movement. If direct evangelism by missionaries, men and women, is a spent force, there will be one answer; whereas if it is thought that there is still work for missionary men and women as direct and aggressive evangelizers amongst the millions of people that are at present not touched by evangelistic operations, there will be a different answer.

If the missionary force is not to be kept up to its present strength, or increased, if it is not to be considered as having a very real contribution to make to the evangelizing of the nation, there is no great necessity of a language school. When the numbers of new missionaries coming to a work in which a knowledge of the language is imperative once begin to fall off, it will fall off rapidly. And while it may be readily admitted that a school for language is very helpful, it is hard to maintain in a satisfactory manner when on the down grade. This is very evident whether we look at the question of morale or the question of finance. Missionaries have done very well in the language without a school, and they can do so again whenever the numbers of new comers fall be. t ' ...tt (' .t ' ·j ' · '' t.

As far as teachers in schools are concerned, an increasing number of so-called short-termers is being sent out. Even those who come out to schools with a life time of service in view are apt to be set at work at once, and there is always the question whether it is desirable or worth while for a school worker to make the effort necessary to acquire a proficient use of the language. There are many ready to argue that a school-worker is quite as valuable without as with a knowledge of the language, unless such knowledge be as extensive as can be acquired only by long years spent in evangelistic work.

In view of the above, a succinct reply to one of the alternatives can be given by saying that with a waning missionary force in direct evangelism and in administrative positions in mission-schools, we will have a waning language school for a few years till on account of expense the extinction point is rather abruptly reached.

The other alternative is that matters will so-adjust themselves that missionaries will be direct evangelizers alongside of the Japanese church rather than within it as heretofore; that both men and women missionaries will work in hearty sympathy with, but administratively outside of, the organized church, much as the women evangelistic workers have functioned in the past. Also some missionaries at least will take up that work in the schools for which a knowledge of the language is necessary.

If the alternative outlined in the last paragraph, or something approximating it becomes the program for the future, the missionary body would for possibly a score or more of years maintain its present size through a constant inflowing of young men and women whose first step in preparation for usefulness would be acquiring considerably more than a smattering of the Japanese language.

With a constant reinforcement of the missionary body the language school would be as greatly in demand as ever. Well trained and independent students are able to make good progress in the language with private teachers. There are drawbacks connected with living in Tokyo or any other large center during the language study period; but the opinion of the majority undoubtedly is that in view of the methods that seem to be in practice in the world at large, a language school is a necessary part of the equipment of any mission field. That is the conclusion reached in Japan, and previous to the earthquake of 1923 the Tokyo Language School had a history of constant development and had made a good name for itself, had accumulated sufficient to acquire school property, and looked forward to a prosperous future.

After the earthquake the school divided into two sections, both directed from Tokyo, where the Executive Committee functioned, and there the correspondence work was centered. The Tokyo section is the school proper, and the Kobe section a sort of branch school that receives its teaching materials and most of its teachers from Tokyo. There are roughly two dozen pupils in each division, and good work is done in each. Certain large missions are insistent that if not a branch school then an independent school be maintained in Kobe, and some very good reasons are advanced.

Without entering into an extended discussion of the subject, the writer would say that experience has proved that two independent schools, or a main school and a branch is an economically impossible plan. At least two thousand yen of capital is wasting away each year on account of the division, and vigor and enthusiasm that would attach to a single large school become impossible. A unified school of fifty or sixty pupils, with a single principal giving his whole time to the work, and with the further ideal, in addition to fitting for missionary work, of linking up with some existing Japanese University in such a manner that work done, in the language school could be credited in American universities, might reasonably hope to go on from strength to strength.

A majority of the directors of the present school are persuaded that the Kobe branch should be discontinued and the work concentrated in Tokyo. While the students of the school are almost entirely missionaries, yet the school enjoys in its management the assistance of such men as Barons Sakatani and Fukuoka, and Prof. Murakami, principal of the Ueno School of Music, who for several years, out of pure love, has acted as dean. The entire history of the school is linked up with Tokyo, and in spite of disadvantages that might possibly be lessened or absent in another location, the opportunity for obtaining instructors and qualified persons to assist in the management of the school, seems to make Tokyo its logical location.

It is perhaps not impossible for an independent school to be maintained in Kobe or Kyoto by missions whose work lies largely in the south, but in practice it would be found that there is much difference between a branch school sponsored from Tokyo and provided with teaching materials and direction from that source; and an independent school obliged to make its own plans, train its own instructors and build up its own methods of instruction. And it should be remembered that while this doubtful experiment was being worked out in Kobe, it might make it impossible for the Tokyo school to carry on alone. There is such a thing as Divide and conquer, but there is also such a thing as Divide and court defeat.

The most uncertain element in the problem is the supply of new missionaries; but granting that the average of the past decade is maintained, the writer ventures the opinion that the reply to the question of the Place of the Language School in the Christian Movement of the next few years, is that with its forces concentrated once more in Tokyo, the prestige that the school enjoyed during the years previous to the earthquake will be restored, and that it will more and more be viewed not as a convenient and desirable aid to the Christian Movement, but as one of its necessities.

CHAPTER XXII

THE FUTURE OF THE OTHER RELIGIONS IN CONTACT WITH THE CHRISTIAN MOVEMENT*

Rev. A. K. Reishauer, D.D.

This article must in the very nature of the case be largely "guess work," for it deals with so many unknown and unknowable factors. The limits set by the editors force us to be dogmatic in this "guess work—not a very attractive combination." The only reason for attempting the impossible is because it seems high time that Christian workers in Japan realize that the non-Christian religions may yet play a considerable role, either as helps or as hindrances (or both) to the Christian purpose.

By the "Other Religions" we mean, of course, Shintō and Buddhism. Confucianism, though once regarded as one of the "Three Religions" of Japan, is really not a separate religion but a general ethico-political philosophy permeating the Japanese social structure, especially its upper section. As such it has made a vital contribution to Japanese life, and Christianity has little difficulty in coming to terms with much of the practical wisdom that centers around Confucianism's Five Relationships. Some of Japan's strongest Christians have been men for whom Confucian ethics had been a real discipline preparing

---

* For a fuller treatment see the author's "Studies in
[illegible]

them for the fuller life in Christ. As Christianity
has brought to them the ideal of the Supreme Relationship, man's relationship to God, it has established
a new nucleating center around which the Five Relationships are being reshaped and supplemented. Thus
Confucian ideals are finding a more natural fulfilment
in contact with Christianity than they ever had in
connection with Shintô and Buddhism.

Shintô. In general, the future of Shintô seems
destined to be that of any primitive cult coming into
contact with a rising tide of culture. It must either
lose its hold on all but the illiterate classes or undergo
such a radical transformation that it will be difficult
to identify the new with the old. As a matter of
fact, both these things are taking place to day. The
old Shintô of the *Kojiki, Nihongi* and *Yengishiki* is
losing its hold among the educated and has its adherents largely among the ignorant masses; even many
of these do not take their beliefs too seriously.

The attempts that some are making to restate
Shintô in terms suitable to the modern mind often
do such violence to the old that it is difficult to take
this restatement seriously. If Buddhism had not in-
corporated Shintô into its own system back in the
eighth and ninth centuries these primitive myths
which constitute orthodox Shintô would long ago have
disappeared or been reduced to Japanese fairly tales.
To pretend to construct out of these primitive elements
a religion suited for a modern educated Japan by
merely "restating things," hardly seems honest. Of
course, much may be smuggled in by such a "restatement," but a religion that must live on smuggled goods
can not hold its place among intelligent men.

There is, however, one element in Shinto which
is of permanent value, namely, the spirit of loyalty
to Ruler and Country which Shintô has always in-
culcated. Though this spirit of loyalty was bound
up with Shintô mythology in the past, and though

many still think that it must have its sanctions in Shintô beliefs, it is becoming more and more clear to many intelligent Japanese that as these primitive Shintô myths are being recognized as mere myths there must be found a new basis for this wonderful spirit of loyalty. That is the meaning of the action of the central government which separates Shintô as a religion from Shintô as a patriotic cult, in which latter all true Japanese might have a part whether in religion they be Shintôists, Buddhists, Christians or what not.

This action of the government has, of course, created some confusion and for the present this new non-religious patriotic cult seems to stand with one foot in old Shintô and with the other to be stepping out into a non-Shintô world. It faces in two directions. The ignorant masses see only the face that looks towards the past and for them the spirit of loyalty still finds its sanctions in Shintô mythology which pictures the emperor as heaven-descended. They see, e.g. in the new Meiji Shrine only one more national Shintô temple and regard the late Emperor Meiji as one more Shintô deity. But the educated classes see the face that looks towards the future. They are as loyal as their fathers were but their loyalty has a new basis. To them the new Meiji Shrine is a fit memorial to a great emperor. They are loyal to Ruler and country as Americans are loyal to the Flag and as British are to King and the Empire. Around this Meiji Shrine is developing a new life. Near by are the huge stadium and athletic field, an art gallery and the large hall of the National Young Men's Association. Here as a center is developing something like a new cult with patriotism as its core and athletics, æsthetics and all that makes modern life interesting, as its outer form. It is not a religion but rather a sort of substitute for all religions. Its devotees are not exactly anti-religious. They simply do not feel the need of religion. They are like so many people the world over had to enjoy the good things of modern life and even ready to help some in making these the possession of others, but not going beyond that. They take over from applied Christianity all that splendid emphasis on physical training, clean sports, wholesome recreation, good fellowship, etc., but they do not worry as to the spiritual roots from which these things grew.

Now it must be clear that Christianity can find in this new movement an ally in working out its own great purpose in Japan, but it must be equally plain that Christianity must bring something more than these good things which it has helped to inspire in this generation of Japanese. Unless it can infuse into this new movement something of its own spirit of loyalty to humanity and to the Father of all, then this new cult may easily develop into a chauvinistic patriotism which may yet prove a real enemy to the higher ideals and purpose for which the Christian movement stands.

Buddhism. Though Shintô may gradually be volatilized into a non-religious patriotic cult, Buddhism can not become so completely secularized, for it is too deeply grounded in the transcendental world and is destined to have a future *as* a religion. Buddhism still has a hold on the religious consciousness of the Japanese people. The masses are Buddhists if they are anything. They may know nothing about Buddhist philosophy nor have a clear grasp of even the more simple elements of the Buddhist faith, but the religion of the Buddha has still a real hold on their hearts and imagination. Buddhism has been a power in the past and this will go a long way to keep the masses Buddhists in the future. Out of a sense of loyalty to *things Japanese* they will be loyal to Buddhism to the temple and the temple court in the villages and the towns where dwell about eighty per cent of Japan's sixty millions and where Western thought and ideals have not made very serious inroads as yet. An occasional visit to the village temple, a small offering to the Buddha or saint enshrined there, a short mumbled prayer for prosperity and good luck, or a formula repeated again and again to earn merit, paying a small fee to a priest to say mass for the beloved dead, in youth sharing in the fun of the temple festivals and when old age and inevitable death approach expecting to be buried properly with Buddhist rites—this, in a few words, is what popular Buddhism means. Some take it fairly seriously, others not so seriously. It is not much of a religion but most people can get along with a very beggarly religion. Buddhism demands so very little of its ordinary adherents and yet seems to promise so much, if not for this life then for the next, and so the investment which the average Japanese makes in his religion seems not so bad after all. Any way, it is what the masses have inherited from the past and this will hold them unless some extraordinary influences are brought to bear upon them. Even then they will more naturally try to assimilate the new to the old than allow the new to become a new center for their life.

But Buddhism's hold is not confined to the ignorant masses. Though most of the educated classes seem indifferent to popular Buddhism, many of them have a profound respect for Buddhism as a philosophy. Few of them know anything about Buddhist philosophy but they somehow have a respect for its profundity. They realize that it is not altogether fitted for the practical needs of life, but they vaguely feel that if the Buddhist philosophy were combined in some way with the more vigorous and practical elements of Western civilization, Japan might develop a religion suited for the modern man. And there is a growing number of progressive Buddhists who are attempting to infuse into their religion this new vigorous element. It is too early to know whether they will succeed in giving Buddhism a real re-birth or whether this is only an effort to stave off as long as po

This "re-birth" manifests itself in many ways. There is first of all a revival of learning among Buddhists. Five universities, ranking as full-fledged universities, are being conducted by Buddhists. Learned societies are publishing new editions of sacred texts and making them more available to the masses. General works on Buddhism are appearing. A daily paper, two weekly journals, monthlies, quarterlies, pamphlets and other publications are disseminating Buddhist ideals. Secondary schools, special schools, lecture halls, summer schools, etc., are all a part of the program today. Sunday schools, Y.M.B.A. and Y.W.B.A. and even something akin to the Salvation Army, represent activities of present day Buddhists. Perhaps most significant of all is the missionary work which some of the sects are conducting among Japanese living in foreign countries. Wherever Japanese have gone in large numbers there Buddhism is following them; in one land, at least, namely, in Saghalien, Buddhist temples are built, as it were, on the ruins of a retreating Christianity.

Now it takes little imagination to see that this new activity is the direct outcome of the impact of Christianity on Buddhism. In some cases it is a wholesale borrowing from Christianity, not only as to method but also as to message. How far will this process go? Will Buddhism in the name of Buddha bring to the Japanese the life of Christ?

From the standpoint of Buddhism this would not be at all inconsistent, for it seems to be the genius of Buddhism to take up into itself whatever it encounters. All along its march from India through Central Asia, China, Korea till it reached Japan, Buddhism compromised with the most diverse elements. The local cults of primitive peoples, Chinese Ancestor Worship, Confucian Ethics, Taoistic Naturalism, Korean Devil Worship, and Japanese Polytheistic Nature Worship—all have become a part of Buddhism. It is, therefore, not at all strange that Japanese Buddhism should today try to absorb whatever Christianity and Western culture have brought to Japan. Buddhism's very inability to cope with this mighty stream from the West, which is engulfing everything in Japanese life today, leads it to grasp at elements in that stream which will enable it to keep afloat and therefore Buddhism would somehow link up with Christianity to save its own life.

Naturally this situation creates a real problem for Christianity and it is not at all clear just what attitude Christians should take towards this semi-Christianized Buddhism. On the one hand it is, of course, clear that Christians should rejoice to co-operate with any force that is working for righteousness and bringing new life to an ancient people. "Whether in pretence or in truth, Christ is proclaimed," we should rejoice. But on the other hand, it is equally true that if Buddhism continues to stand for all the rubbish that it has gathered into its all-inclusive system and it it does not stand a little more positively for *some* things, then Christians can not go hand in hand with Buddhists. If, e.g., it is true, as a speaker at the recent Far Eastern Buddhist Conference said, that Buddhism can pass from Atheism through various stages of Pantheism until it lands in Theism (and presumably reverse the process) without committing any heresy, then Christianity can not merge with Buddhism and remain true to its founder. However broad-minded a Christian may be he can hardly become so shallow in his beliefs about essentials that it makes no difference to him whether there *is* or there *is not* a Heavenly Father. Not even to be brotherly towards his Buddhist brother can he afford to betray his Master to whom it *did* make a tremendous difference what a man really believed in his heart. If Buddhists to-day went serious to *accept* the great vital things for which Christianity stands then they must be willi   ·   ·   · y still seem to stand. It may have been possible in the past for Buddhism to gather up into its "big bag" all that it encountered. It can not do that with a vital Christianity without ejecting a great many things. In fact, in most cases it would be more simple to throw the old bag away entirely, for "no man putteth new wine into old wine-skins; else the wine will burst the skins, and the wine perisheth, and the skins."

At any rate it is the chief business of Christians to bring into the life of modern Japan a vital Christianity and not depend very much on others to do this work for them. If Buddhism more and more takes up the Christian way of life, so much the better. We would, however, not bank much on this. Buddhism has been too much a Cameleon-like religion readily taking on the color of its environment rather than transforming that environment. Christianity's message must ever be, "And be not conformed to this world: but be ye *transformed* by the renewing of your mind."

PART V

OBITUARIES

Mrs. Russell T. Barr

Mary Winn Barr, wife of Russell T. Barr, was born in Yokohama, Japan, on August 9, 1878. She was called from her earthly home in Germantown, Pennsylvania, on August 21, 1925.

It is fitting that her name should appear upon these pages for she was the eldest daughter of the Rev. and Mrs. Thomas C. Winn, missionaries for many years under the Presbyterian Board of Foreign Missions, and for four years a missionary herself under this same Board, first in the Hokuriku Jo Gakko in Kanazawa, and later in the Wilmina Jo Gakko in Osaka. Her missionary service did not end with her return to the United States and her marriage in 1904 to Mr. Barr of Quincy, Illinois, for she was ever about her Heavenly Father's business, promoting missionary enterprises in the First Presbyterian church after their removal there. She was a gifted speaker and constantly drew upon her own experiences of childhood or young womanhood, and upon the letters of her parents, two brothers, and a sister, all of whom were missionaries in the Japanese Empire, for material to use in her addresses.

Her death came to her at the end of seventeen months of invalidism, during which she did not lose her characteristic cheerfulness in spite of intense suffering. A week before she was called Home. She sent f . . . .

which she wished to leave to her friends. First, she wished the young to realize the importance of accepting Christ early in life, before "the evil days" come upon them. Second, (she urged) that those who love Christ should be faithful witnesses for Him.

Her husband and three children survive her, and theirs is the memory of a loving devoted wife and mother, a comrade in play, and a wise counsellor. These earthly contacts of hers were enriched and mellowed by the deep conviction in her heart that God lives and to love and serve Him is man's highest purpose.

Georgiana Baucus

Georgiana Baucus was born at Dryden, New York, November, 12, 1862 and died at Pasedena, California, April 8, 1926. She came to Japan July 12, 1890 under the Women's Foreign Missionary Society of the Methodist Episcopal Church and after a few months of preparatory work in Hakodate went to Hirosaki and there laid deep the foundations of her knowledge of the Japanese language and people.

In 1895 she joined Mrs. Mary C. Nind on her trip around the world. It was on this tirp that Miss Baucus met in Jerusalem Miss Emma E. Dickinson with whom she was to be closely associated during the remainder of her life.

In 1897 they came to Yokohama as enthusiastic adventurers in Christian literature and established Tokiwasha, from which there was soon to issue a steady output of cards, leaflets, tracts, booklets, pictures, songs, in addition to a monthly magazine called Tokiwa. A new approach into the homes and hearts of women and children was obtained but Miss Baucus continued to seek opportunities for direct personal contact. She had come into a rich experience in her youth which seemed to lift her above all doubts and fears. She lived as one ever conscious of her Master and the glory light was always shining through the frail tabernacle trying to communicate its joy to others.

At the time of the great earthquake the home of Miss Baucus and Miss Dickinson collapsed but they escaped unhurt. Their chief thought was for their literature and it was salvaged from the wreckage and safely housed. In the following spring they returned to America but not to cease their joyful labor of love, for Japanese printers were sought out in California and from beyond the seas came back the printed message.

The beautiful word—tokiwa—chosen to symbolize the message may be applied to the faithful, loving messenger who being dead yet speaketh.

Margaret Mabel Boutflower

Miss Mabel Boutflower, daughter of the late Archdeacon of Carlisle, England, and sister of Dr. Cecil H. Boutflower, for some years Bishop of South Tokyo, was well known in Japan, for she came out to this land with her brother in 1909 and soon won general love and respect. She was an ideal friend; she had much to give, and she gave unsparingly, taking infinite pains for those whom she could help spiritually. And these were many, among Japanese and her own people. When the Bishop returned to England in 1921, she decided to remain in Japan a little longer and lived chiefly in Yokohama, where many will remember her work among English-speaking girls and for the "foreigners" Mothers' Union. She re... d ... ...

and at once threw herself into Girls' Friendly Society and other work there, though she was far from strong, until, after a very short illness, she entered into rest on June 3, 1925.

Miss Boutflower was born in the beautiful English Lake Country, and was laid to rest there "in the exquisite churchyard that watches the sun set behind the Langdale Pikes at the head of Windermere." There was much of the steadfast strength of the mountains and of the sky-reflecting peace and radiance of the lakes in her. Young people were attracted to her by her motherly spirit, her happy nature and spontaneous sense of humour, her power of insight, her generous, hopeful outlook. Her life was felt by her Japanese friends to be one lived very fully "in Christ." We seldom meet anyone so free from self-consciousness of self-seeking. It has been truly said of her that "in her there was less self than in most of us, to stand between others and the Indwelling Christ."

James McDonald Gardiner

"Mr. Gardiner was born in St. Louis, Mo., on May 22nd, 1857. He was educated at schools both in the United States and in Scotland, the home of his ancestors, and at Harvard University. He came to Japan in 1890 to take charge of St. Paul's College in Tsukiji, Tokyo, after having had a brief experience in an architectural office in New York.

Always loving the beautiful, and with refined artistic taste, Mr. Gardiner naturally turned more and more to architecture, which eventually became his permanent occupation.

Until 1908, when he retired from the active list of the Mission, his architectural skill was almost exclusively employed on its behalf alone; but upon retirement he set up in business for himself. However, he remained until his death in close connection with his Mission, a trusted and beloved adviser and member of its most important committee.

His public spirit was manifest throughout the whole of his 45 years in Japan, but always in a quiet, self-effacing way. He was for most of the time prominent in the Council of the Asiatic Society of Japan, in the Tokyo Club, in the old American Peace Society and its successor the American-Japan Society, the newer American Association, and above all in the Harvard Club, of which organization he was one of the prime movers.

His final illness was not of long duration, and up to the day of his last seizure he was active as ever, though recent years had seen him often suffering from illness all of which he had borne with true Christian patience. The final cause of death was hardening of the arteries, accelerated by serious hemorrhages, and he fell asleep surrounded by all his immediate family, with a faith that was most impressive, at about noon on November 25, 1925, at St. Luke's Hospital."

(Condensed by permission from an "In Memoriam" in the Japan Evangelist, December, 1925).

Lora C. Goodwin

Miss Goodwin was born in Orange, Ionia Country, Michigan, October 9, 1886. She was a graduate of the Chicago Training School for Home and Foreign Missions and held the degree of A. B. from Albion College. Several months were spent in the Battle Creek Sanitarium studying nursing a year in the Tokyo Language School she was appointed to evangelistic work in Sapporo, but in 1919 was transferred to Hakodate to take charge of Kindergartens and City work, and this continued to be her appointment until the time of her death which took place in Karuizawa, August 30, 1925.

The funeral was at Hakodate where her body was interred in the British Concession, on a sunny hillside overlooking the sea.

The joy of service seems to have been the very breath of her being. Those who knew her as a student, as a missionary worker, as a friend, and, last of all, as a sufferer, unite in testifying to her courage, to her sympathy, to her patience. And what a response she had! She made the Kindergarten in which she lived a center not only for children but also for mothers. The story of how these mothers entered into the joy of service by making another Kindergarten possible for less favored children than their own is the finest tribute to her influence.

The spirit of Laura C. Goodwin has returned to God who gave it; her alabaster offering has been completed.

Miss Louisa Imhoff

Miss Imhoff was born at Siskilwa, Illinois, June 18, 1852. She came to Japan in 1889 and joined the Industrial Department of Kwassui Jo Gakko at Nagasaki. After two years she went to Yonezawa as an evangelist. On April 29, 1894, Yonezawa's greatest festival in honor of a former Daimyo was held in the park. Miss Imhoff felt she must take the Gospel message to the people. With some fellow-workers she went and distributed tracts and held a short meeting. While they were singing, a boy threw a stone which struck Miss Imhoff's right eye, resulting in its entire loss. The boy could not be found and consternation prevailed among the officials. But when they were assured that Miss Imhoff bore no ill feeling toward them but was praying that the accident might be the means of helping them to know the Spirit of Christ, they were much impressed.

Last year the Y.M.C.A. of Kobe held a welcome meeting for the officers and men of a Japanese Man-of-War. When the Captain arose to thank the members for their kind welcome, he said; "I am a Christian. When I was a Chu-gakko student in Yonezawa, there was a festival in the park and a company of Christians held a meeting there. I threw a stone hitting a woman missionary in the eye. I fled to the woods and hid for three days. Later I heard that the missionary did not want me to be punished but was praying that I might become a Christian."

Miss Imhoff also did effective work in Tokyo, Sendai and Sapporo. But the climax of all was her loving service for the children of the Sendai Christian Orphanage, of which she was Superintendent for about ten years.

She went to her Heavenly Home from Blair, Nebraska, on September 11, 1925.

Rev. Herbert Buel Johnson, D.D.

Mr. Johnson was born in Fairfield, Herkimer Country, N. Y., on April 30, 1858. He attended Ilion Academy in New York State. In 1878 he was married to Miss Emma J. Leach of Frankfort, N. Y., but the young wife passed away after only five months of married life.

In 1880 Mr. Johnson entered Drew Seminary, Madison, N. J., where he graduated in 1883. In this same ye...

Clara E. Richardson of Dover, N. J., and in 1887 the family arrived in Japan under appointment as missionaries of the Methodist Episcopal Church, taking up work in connection with Chinzei Gakuin at Nagasaki.

In 1904 Mr. Johnson was transferred to the Pacific Coast, U.S.A., to be the Superintendent of the Pacific Japanese Mission of the M. E. Church, which post he held till the time of his death in November, 1925.

From his Alma Mater Mr. Johnson received successively the degrees of Bachelor of Philosophy and Doctor of Divinity.

"He was moving in the line of his special duty, on a train in Nebraska, en route to Indiana to attend a Convention—when the stroke fell that called him home. His toil is over. He has run the race honestly, sincerely and well.

Herbert Buel Johnson was a vigorous Christian. With him Christianity was a business, a life service, a grand commission. He has won the goal.

To his bereaved widow and five sons will go the sincere sympathy of a host of friends on both sides of the Pacific."

William Yates Jones

"He saved others; himself he could not save." Only because the spirit of these words was followed is it save from sacrilege in applying it to a human being.

William Yates Jones was born in Illinois, Sept. 6, 1864. Early in life his parents moved with him and an elder brother to a farm three miles west of Somerset, Miami County, Kansas. His father combined the pastorate of the local Presbyterian Church with farming. An early recollection of Dr. Jones

is when he indignantly opposed a bit of bullyism
in a cornfield. This with an incident at the Ikao
hot springs in the year of the Boxer Rebellion, when
he compelled the cessation of an unsavory story,
gives the measure of the justice and purity of his
character.

Entering Park College, Parkville, Missouri, in
1886, he literally worked his way through academy
and college with his hands, making an enviable record for ability, reliability and faithfulness. He
graduated in 1892 with high honors.

Three years were spent in McCormick Theological Seminary, Chicago. His scholarship, assiduity
and dependability were such that he was the unanimous choice of his classmates to represent them
on the program at the graduation in 1895.

He was one of the student volunteers and arrived
in Japan in September 1895, joining the then West
Japan Presbyterian Mission and serving first in Kanazawa and Fukui on the west coast. The qualities
early manifested made him a missionary of rare
ability, excellence and acceptability, so that he was
greatly useful, and beloved by all who knew him,
fellow-missionary and Japanese alike.

In January 1899 Mr. Jones was married to Miss
Mary Ellen Brokaw who was then on the faculty of
Ferris Seminary, Yokohama.

The ill-health of Mrs. Brokaw took them for a
while to Shimonoseki and then to Kyoto; and finally,
in 1907, ended their missionary career.

From that time till his death he cared for his
invalid wife with a tenderness, understanding and
manliness unsurpassed.

In the inscrutable providence of the All-wise
Father, his prayer that his wife might go first was
denied him. Stricken while on vacation and while
visiting his wife's younger sister and family, peritonitis

who loved him and whom he so generously served.
He departed to be with the Father, November 18th,
1925, dying in a hospital in Summit, New Jersey.
A friend wrote: "If ever anyone will be perfectly
at home over there, it is William Yates Jones. "Blessed
are the dead who die in the Lord."

Mrs. James M. McCauley

Mrs. McCauley, (nee Jane C. Kooser), born 1848
in New Wilmington, Penn., U.S.A., sailed for her first
Mission field, Siam, in November 1877. A year later,
November 6, 1878, she was married to the Rev. James
M. McCauley, of the same Presbyterian Mission. After
a period of two years in Siam, owing to Dr. McCauley's failing health, they were transferred to Japan
in 1880.

Mrs. McCauley taught English in the Meiji Gakuin and opened her home and heart to her students.
But the work into which she threw her boundless
energy for nearly forty years was that of the two
primary schools for Japanese children at Shiba and
at Tsukiji, and the Sunday-schools connected with
them.

Mrs. McCauley will too always be remembered
for her faithful visiting and counsel at the "Kozen-
sha" Leper home, her ministrations to the sick and
wounded Japanese soldiers during the Russo-Japanese
War, and above all for the long and zealous work
in the W.C.T.U., especially in connection with its
Ji-Ai-Kwan Rescue Home at Okubo, where she lived
for years literally "fighting wild beasts at Ephesus."

Mrs. McCauley was a woman of rare generosity
of spirit and ardent kindliness. Hers was that unusual combination of humour with deep spirituality.
Another trait was her amazing energy. Nothing was

too hard for her that made for the comfort of her
friends, and everyone was her friend. "She had a
Japanese heart" was the verdict of one of her head-
teachers who had grown gray in the work with her.
Cordial, unconventional, overflowing with humour,
absolutely loyal to the Lord she loved,—when shall
we look upon her like again!

On April 26th, 1925, she suffered a stroke of para-
lysis in her home in Los Angeles, after which followed
seven weeks of illness but of little pain. The end
came on June 11th, 1925, after a second stroke. The
end was beautiful, joyous. She opened her eyes with
an expression of joy and great surprise, then closed
them. A short breath, and she was gone.

Miss Lida B. Smith

Miss Lida B. Smith was born at Collamer,
Onondaga Country, New York, May 5th, 1859. Her
early years were spent in this rural region. When
the time came for higher schooling than furnished
in her home section, she was trained in Potsdam
Normal School, and at Cazenovia Seminary, graduating from the latter in June, 1885. In the following
November, the New York Branch of the Woman's
Foreign Missionary Society accepted her as a worker
for Japan, and she was at once on her way to her
new field of work, arriving here December 12, 1885.
She was an elder sister of Mrs. Flora Smith Long,
who, with her husband, Dr. C. S. Long, had pre-
ceded Miss Lida to Japan by five years.

The first five years of Miss Smith's work were
given to the Fukuoka Jo Gakko, when health failed,
and she was compelled to spend five years in search
of health in the home land. Returning in 1896, she
was again employed in educational work, first at

Nagasaki and then at Fukuoka. Her work from this time was in the evengelistic field, residing most of the time at Kagoshima, 1906—1909 being Superintendent of the Evangelistic work for women in South Kyushu, and in Loo Choo, making trips to the latter islands occasionally. Leaving the field in April, 1910, she was thereafter unable to return to her work on account of ill-health. Her residence had been in New York State, and finally at South Orange, New Jersey, where she fell on sleep, April 9, 1926.

Miss Smith was a willing worker to the limit of her strength, a genial spirit, gifted in winning friends, earnestly Christian, and giving her whole self to the endeavor to make Christ known to the people of this land.

William H. Brokenshire

William Henry Brokenshire was born in Kingston, Ontario, Canada in 1866 and, with his young wife, came to Japan as an independent worker in 1891, remaining about four years.

He was born in a fervidly evangelical home, his father being a class leader and local preacher of the earliest Wesleyan type. Foreign Missions early claimed his attention and, with his wife, shortly after college graduation and marriage, he went to London, intent on getting General Booth to send him to Japan as a pioneer worker of the Salvation Army which he had joined. Instead of doing this at once, the Booths naturally put him and his wife through a gruelling test in the slums of London, in poverty, almost in rags—the heroic thing ordinarily required of Salvation Army officers. The strain proved too great for the young Canadian couple and they resigned to come out to Japan on their own account, Mr. Brokenshire taking service as a teacher of English in the Middle School at Mito, Ibaraki prefecture. In 1893 he was engaged by the Bible Societies' Committee to take charge of the agency in Yokohama in the furlough absence of Mr. George Braithwaite, and it was shortly after the return of Mr. Braithwaite to Japan that the family went back to Canada.

The rest of William Brokenshire's life was spent, first in seminary study in several institutions, and later in ministerial work in the United States and Canada, with a short period in Scotland in the United Free Church. His last years were given to a Presbyterian congregation near Kingston, his home city, and it was while thus engaged that he broke down in health in 1925, retiring to Kingston for his last half year of gradually failing strength. He died on March 14, 1926.

FORMOSA

CHAPTER I

UNITED CHURCH OF CANADA THE NORTH FORMOSA MISSION, 1925

Rev. Duncan MacLeod

I. THE PAST

1. The place of the missionary in the past. During the first thirty years Dr. G. L. MacKay was chief administrator of the Mission. For several years previous to his death he had two ordained native pastors as helpers, but being alone for the most of his life as pioneer missionary there was no Council, and the time had not come for the organization of a native presbytery. His only colleague and successor was Dr. William Gauld, who was the helper during the last two or three years of his life.

Two or three years after the passing away of the pioneer missionary a presbytery was organized. In the year 1904 the North Formosa presbytery was organized. In the year 1904 the North Formosa presbytery was organized. In the following year two ordained missionaries were sent. Henceforth all missionaries became ipso facto voting members of the presbytery.

2 The beginning of the North Formosa Mission. In the year 1872 Dr. G. L. MacKay began his missionary work in North Formosa. The first few years he devoted himself to evangelistic work. He travelled from place to place with a group of evangelists, teachi

kind of a peripatetic school of theology. By this method many new stations were opened. In 1880 a hospital was erected, and, with the help of the foreign community doctor, the medical needs of both Christian and non-Christians were met, and the knowledge of the Christian faith was very widely disseminated. In 1912 the hospital location was transferred to Taihoku, where a new hospital building was erected in memory of Dr. G. L. MacKay.

3. Educational beginnings. In 1882 a new theological college was built in Tamsui. During Dr. MacKay's first furlough the Christians of Oxford County, Ontario, raised money for this purpose; for this reason it was called Oxford College. In 1883 a Bible School for preachers, wives and Bible Women was erected next to the college. In 1905 two lady missionaries were appointed to North Formosa. After two years of language study they organized a Girls' School in the old building. In 1916 a new Girls School was erected. This School has a Primary, Public School, and a High School Department. In 1910 a new Bible School for women was built.

In 1914 the first Middle School was organized, under the supervision of Mr. G. L. MacKay, son of the Founder as principal. In 1925 a new Middle School was completed.

In 1914 a new theological college was built in Taihoku, the capital of Formosa. At present negotiations are carried on between the North and South Missions with a view to the establishment of a Union College in some centre that may be finally decided on by the Synod.

In 1918 a missionary was appointed to Kindergarten work. Encouraging work has been carried on. Land has been secured for the purpose of kindergarten School building. The hope is that such schools will be opened at several important centres.

4. Financial beginnings. During the larger

part of the life of the pioneer missionary the Christians suffered much persecution. There was a great deal of political strife, as well as attacks from the outside. The Christians suffered most on every occasion. Their property was often destroyed, and their lives threatened. Only the poorer class, who had but little to lose financially and much to gain morally and spiritually, dared to enter the Christian Church. Since the arrival of the Japanese the situation changed entirely. Life and property has been safe, and financial prosperity has been the result. In 1904, the year the presbytery was organized, the total givings of the native Church were about three thousand Yen. In 1907 the presbytery undertook to bring before the whole Church the duty of assuming the responsibility of self-support as speedily as possibile. Ever since a process of education has been carried on with a large measure of success. In 1924 the total givings of the North Formosa Church were over twenty eight thousand dollars The amount raised in 1925 is recorded in the statistical report. Last year there were no new churches built hence the apparent decrease since 1924.

II. THE PRESENT

1. The Modern Development. So far nothing has been organized that may be called modern. We have no Institutional Churches. The Sunday School Department can scarcely be called modern. This Department has never had any outside help, such as the Churches of Japan have been receiving from World-Wide Organizations. Some years ago the Synod called into being a Sunday School Committee, to be responsible for the literature, the methods of work, and the securing of financial support. For years there has been a Sunday School Quarterly, based on the International lessons. This is being prepared in Japan by   the

list. and is printed in the South Mission Book-room. There has been a strong demand for suitable literature, especially for the Christian workers. Last year a new periodical was started in the North Mission. But the whole problem is soon to be taken up by the Synod. For Sunday School work and the new periodical nearly two thousand Yen were raised, over a thousand yen of this amount was for Sunday School work.

2. The Present place of the Missionary. In the past the foreign missionary was the leader in every department of Mission work. For many years, however, he has been taking his place as a co-worker in matters of Church government. In many matters the Formosan pastors and elders are ready to accept many responsibilities which they can shoulder to the relief of their foreign colleagues. In all the institutions, on the other hand, the leadership is still in the hands of the foreign missionaries. The young Formosan men, some of whom have been in Japan Proper for years, prosecuting their studies, are now returning gradually to take their place in our institutions. Native Christians are on all the Councils of the various schools. These members are chosen from the graduates of the schools, as well as from the presbytery.

The missionaries are also responsible for the pastoral supervision of all the congregations that are not self-supporting, or those which are not under the pastoral care of native pastors. In the North there has not been felt any restive spirit on the part of the brethren. They feel that to give the Gospel to the million and a half for which they are responsible, there is need for more foreign help for many years to come. The wise plan is to prepare them for undertaking large responsibilities before such a feeling has been felt. It is well to know that the feeling

may be there before the foreign missionary is aware
of it.

The missionaries in Formosa are in a very difficult position. The native Churches North and South
united under one Synod in 1912. There is one
Presbyterian Church, but there are two Mission
Councils. Their Funds are separate, thus rendering
a real consummate Union impossible. The only perfect solution would be to have one Mother Church
responsible for the evangelization of the whole island, or for an equal share in the financial support.
This is a problem still waiting solution.

3. The Present Christian Educational situation.
(a) The only institutions for male students are the
Middle School and the Theological College. The
Middle School has no government recognition. The
object is to get such recognition providing an assurance is given that there will be no restriction in
matters of Christian teaching.

(b) There are two institutions for the training
of female students, viz. the Girls' and the Women's
Schools. There is at present a demand for a higher
institution for the religious training of young women,
graduates from the High School Department. The
question of co-education in such a higher institution
will be raised in the near future.

4 The degree of self-support. (a) In evangelistic work. There are nine self-supporting congregations with ordained pastors. The rest of the congregations are partially self-supporting. There are several Funds entirely administered by the native presbytery. The Mission Fund was established several years
ago with the object of starting Christian work among
the Aborigines. The Formosan Government has not yet
given permission to enter this so far closed territory.
The interest of this Fund is being used for special
evangelistic work. 'A Widows' and an Aged and In-
firm M. · ·   ·   ,.   ·   ,   ·   ·   ·

ration for years. Three years ago the Christian women organized a Women's Missionary Society. They
now engaged their own women evangelists. This is a
very prosperous cause. The Augmentation Fund has
been meeting the needs of the weaker congregations
for some years.   The Forward Movement Fund is
used in meeting the expenses of purely aggressive
evangelism. Last year about twenty four thousand
heard the Gospel in districts where there are no
chapels. Only Yen 260.00 of the expenses came from
foreign Funds.

(b) The educational work is practically all
carried on by Foreign Mission money. The Kindergarten work from its inception has had native financial
help, and is expected to be carried on along this line.

III. The Future

1. The future progress of the Formosan Church.

(a) In Organization.   Reference has already
been made to the peculiar situation in Formosa. We
have one native Church, but two mother Churches,
one in England and the other in Canada, bearing the
financial responsibility for the two Missions. It is
a very unsatisfactory arrangement. The need for
deciding the policy for the future is pressed upon both
the native Church and the missionaries.

(b) Evangelization. There are about four million souls in Formosa. The Aborigines number about
100,000. Nothing has been done so far for this spiritually destitute people.   Permission for Christian
work is not given. Probably on the East Coast plain,
work could be begun by Japanese Christian missionaries among the semi-civilized people. We are of
the opinion that the Formosan government would not
permit Formosan Christian workers to enter this so
far closed territory.   We are also convinced that
this problem ought to be seriously considered by

some Christian organization in Japan. Any Church undertaking this important task no doubt would get financial support from many outside sources. The two Missions in Formosa have considered the matter on many occasions. A Japanese organization might be able to make a definite request from higher authorities, either in Formosa or in Japan.

The Japanese population numbers about 180,000. There are very few Japanese Christians in Formosa. There are five Presbyterian congregations, most of them are very weak. There are two Episcopalian congregations, and one Congregational Church. There are not more than 2000 nominal Christians in the whole island in a population of over 180,000. These Japanese congregations are in no way capable of undertaking the evangelization of such a large population. It seems, furthermore, that this problem does not find a place in the discussions of our annual conferences on the mainland of Japan. The Missions at work in Formosa have never assumed responsibility for the evangelization of the Japanese population in the island. The personal opinion of the writer of this article is that the United Church of Canada, which has a large staff of missionaries in Japan ought to consider the problem with a view to beginning a new Mission in Formosa, in conjunction with the other missionaries already at work among the Formosan people. We have to report that the only Japanese in Formosa who may be recognized as lovers of the Formosan people, in the true sense of the term, are the Japanese Christians. There is a real fellow feeling of Christian sympathy between them Should the United Church have a Mission among the Japanese we feel it would be a happy day for the Japanese Church in Formosa.

There are many young men coming to Formosa every year who have been taught in Christian institutions in Japan. Several of them take letters of introduction, and some disjunction certificates, which were never delivered. They have in most cases gone adrift in the midst of the manifold temptations of a new land. We have met many of them, and they confessed they never looked up any Japanese pastor. Nothing is done to seek out such young men. The Young Men's Christian Association is merely a small institution whose sole aim seems to be to teach a few young men a little English. In fact this Institution has never had any considerable influence on the youth of the city. Several attempts have been made to try and establish a Y.M.C.A. for the youth of the two races, but they have so far failed.

The Formosan population number about 3,700,-000. About 200 churches have been established among this population. One in every 128 is reckoned within the Christian community. The non-Christian community is growing much faster than the Christian community. There must be a forward movement on a much larger scale than has ever been launched before in Formosa. The North Formosa Mission is looking forward hopefully to a larger recruit for this most urgent work. Never before have the people been so ready to listen to the Gospel. The North Formosa Mission staff has been very seriously depleted of recent years through death and the withdrawal of missionaries on account of illness.

2. The place of the missionary in the future. In the matter of self-government he will have less and less a place for the simple reason that in this department they can manage their own affairs quite competently, yet the presence of the missionary for a long time will be like the oil on troubled waters. He helps to subdue the element of self-interest, and of officialism which may at any time spring up in a much more injurious manner than the apparent leadership of foreigners themselves. As long as the missionary is willing to accept the position of a

co-worker, and helper, he is needed anywhere. We see no reason to doubt but that the missionary will be needed in Formosa for a long time, not because the Church cannot do without him, but because our fellow-workers will want our presence with them until the evangelization of this island has been undertaken with zeal and competency.

We have great cause for thankfulness for the comradeship that has existed from the very beginning. It will be our fault as missionaries if the attitude changes. As the native leaders grow in competency, and assume positions of responsibility it becomes the missionary to fall in line and accept the places for which they are most fitted, though these may appear even less conspicuous. There is a place for any man who loves sincerely, and serves humbly the people to whom God has called him. It is not God that makes mistakes, but rather frail men who have in the past made mistakes in the choice of their life calling. As long as we love for Christ's sake, we remain indispensable in any spot on God's needy earth. Let us love as He does and we need not worry about our place in the great harvest field into which He has thrust us.

UNITED CHURCH OF CANADA.

Statistics of the North Formosa Mission for 1925.

Communicants on the Roll at 31st December

1924 2595

Additions.—

    Adult Baptisms during the year.... 105

    Received to Communion (Baptized

        in infancy) 36

    Received by Certificate.......... 65

    Restored to Communion.......... 3

Deductions:—

Deaths	39
Suspended	7
Gone elsewhere and other causes..	81

Total Deductions....... 127

Communicants on the Roll at 31st December 1925 2677

Children on the Roll at 31st December 1925.... 1908
Adherents 3075
Sunday School Scholars.................... 2062
Formosan Workers
              Ordained Pastors 9
              Preachers (Non-ordained). 45

Total Givings of the Formosan Church during 1925....................Y.24,579.84

Needs for the year 1926—1927.

Ordained Missionaries 5
Medical Doctor 1
Literary and Sunday School Worker............ 1
Middle School Teacher........................ 1
Lady Missionaries 12

CHAPTER II

ENGLISH PRESBYTERIAN MISSION, SOUTH FORMOSA

By Various Contributors
Compiled by Rev. Edward Band

PAST

1. THE PLACE OF THE MISSIONARY IN THE BEGINNING

The work of the English Presbyterian Mission in South Formosa began in 1865. It is impossible for any one now on the field to speak from personal knowledge about the beginnings of the work. That could only be done by our senior missionary, Dr. Thomas Barclay, whose missionary career dates back to 1874. Dr. Barclay, however, left in January for a short furlough, hoping to return at the end of this year to Amoy, to undertake translational work.

The present writer arrived in 1895, and is able with thankfulness to say that the foundations of the work were well and truly laid by his predecessors. The first attempt to start work was made by Dr. James Maxwell, Sr. in the city of Tainan in the summer of 1865, but he was soon obliged to remove to Takow.

At the outset constant vigilance was necessary to guard against the Church being used for worldly ends by interested parties. Happily this evil had been well eradicated by the time of the Japanese occupa'   ı ı ı   ı   ı ı

2. THE BEGINNINGS OF THE FORMOSAN CHURCH AS AN INSTITUTION

From the outset our missionaries had always kept before them the ideal of building up a Church which should be self-governing and self-supporting, —a truly Chinese Church, not a branch of the Home Church from which they themselves had come.

The most important step towards this end was taken in 1896, when a few preachers and elders constituted themselves into the Presbytery of South Formosa, after which they invited the foreign missionaries to become associated with them in the management of affairs. During the thirty years that have since elapsed, the Formosan Presbytery has gone on from strength to strength. At first very much dependent on the guidance of its missionary members, it has latterly shown itself a body well competent to manage its own affairs.

3. EDUCATIONAL BEGINNINGS

In former days education in Formosa differed in no respect from that which had prevailed for ages in China. In our own field we endeavoured to establish elementary schools in connection with all churches in town and country. Owing to the illiteracy of the people and the extreme difficulty of the Chinese written character, our Mission from the outset has always laid great stress on the importance of the Romanized vernacular, with the result that there are now in the whole island, north and south combined, about ten thousand readers of this system, which is the acme of simplicity.

4. FINANCIAL BEGINNINGS

As regards finance, for the earliest years of the Mission I have no statistics available. In those days, of course, almost all expense had to be borne by the Home Church. Yet the aim was ever before the missionaries' of making the Chinese Church self-supporting, and of increasing the burden to be borne by the Christians as they were able to bear it. If the sum now spent by the Home Church is no larger than it was fifty years ago, this is because the Formosan Church has grown so greatly, and has undertaken an increasingly larger share of financial support. Almost from the first each local congregation has been urged to pay direct to its preacher up to the level of its ability, only that portion which it could not raise being paid by the Mission. In this way the people have been gradually brought to realize clearly their direct responsibility and privilege of providing for Gospel ordinances. In the case of ordained pastors, the entire salary must be provided by their own congregation.

Detailed statistics cannot be given here. However, to take the earliest available figures, it may be noted that in 1885 the total givings of the South Formosan Church were 1570 Mexican Dollars. In that year the congregatiosn numbered 31, and the communicant members 1412. At the end of 1925 the Formosan Church membership was 6412, belonging to 110 congregations; while the givings for the previous year (1924) amounted to Yen 50,884. Of course the money is derived not only from communicants but also from many adherents, who cannot be reckoned in exact numbers.

PRESENT

(1) The Modern Development of the Formosan Church

Formosa with a population of nearly four millions has a Christian community of over thirty thousand. It is ˙ ˙ i ˙ ˙ ˙ d th ˙ ˙ ˙ ˙ 1˙˙ of th˙ ˙˙˙˙l˙t˙˙˙ ˙s

Christian. During the last ten years the whole population has increased 15 per cent, while the Church has grown 50 per cent. An annual increase of only five per cent is not satisfactory. This slow growth is due mainly to three causes, (1) a scarcity of Formosan preachers, (2) a shortage of foreign missionaries, (3) a lack òf vigorous spiritual life.

(1) The Southern Church has some sixty pastors and preachers for 110 churches, with the result that some congragations are seldom visited, and the brethren have to conduct the services themselves. In some places the churches without preachers hold together faithfully, but the membership rarely increases. The four or five theological students that graduate annually are not sufficient to fill the vacaucies.

(2) The evangelisation of Formosa does not ultimately depend on the missionary, and the natural tendency in a healthy Church is for the number of missionaries to decrease. In spite of these truths, it is an indisputable fact that the missionary body in Formosa is inadequate for its task. A glance at last year's statistics shows that if Japan with a population is sixty million has a total of 1610 missionaries, Formosa with four million inhabitants ought to have 107 missionaries. There are only fifty. Has not the time come for another Presbyterian Mission to join forces? This is a question for the National Council and the Formosan Presbyterian Church to discuss.

(3) Of course if every Christian in the Formosan Church became an earnest worker, eager for the salvation of his fellow-countrymen, we could do without more missionaries; but the level of spiritual life is low, except in a few churches. In the present situation there is a need for intensive rather than extensive work. The level of spiritual life in the churches needs raising before the heathen can be

gathered in. The life of the Church is not rich and abundant enough to win lasting victories. The heaten are attracted but they are not held. They will not be fully gathered in, until "like a mighty army moves the Church of God." (E.B.)

2. THE PRESENT PLACE OF THE MISSIONARY

The place of the missionary in the Formosan Church is a difficult one at the present time. Possibly not so difficult as in some other fields, but still calling for the forbearance and the insight that a loving interest in the progress of the Church alone can give. It is a sure sign of progress that this position should become increasingly difficult. It means that the Formosan Church is realising its responsibilities, is consicous of its growing ability to undertake them, and is anxious to undergo the test of experience.

All our institutions at the present time are controlled by foreign workers, with help and advice from the Formosan Church, but it seems probable that in a very few years time, the position will be reversed, the foreign workers occupying subordinate positions.

The Formosan Church realises that the time has not yet come when it can dispense altogether with foreign help, and is anxious to advance step by step with the co-operation of the missionary. There will be scope for many years to come for educational workers, for teachers in the Theological College, and above all for evagelistic missionaries. The foreign worker still seems better able to do pioneer work in the unreached parts of our Field, than his Formosan colleagues. (W.E.M.)

3. PRESENT CHRISTIAN EDUCATIONAL SITUATION

(a) Male

A t. t , t t.t t   t ys

in Formosa, one in the North at Tamsui, carried on
by the Canadian Mission, and ours in the South at
Tainan, two hundred miles away, we cannot be ac-
cused of overemphasizing the educational aspect of
our work in Formosa. Neither of these schools has
obtained Government recognition, though we are
negotiating for this privilege at Tainan. Our Middle
school contains 230 pupils, all boarders, with a staff
of 13 teachers, made up of 6 Japanese, 5 Formosans
and 2 foreigners. About one-third of the boys come
from Christian homes. Scripture teaching is given
in schools hours. All the pupils attend church on
Sunday, and the school religious exercises on week-
days. About twenty-four boys join the Church each
year. Too many of our pupils leave school half-
way for us to acquire a great educational success.
Government recognition would repair this leakage.
Whether recognised or not, the school provides ample
opportunities for evangelistic work; yet we must not
cease our endeavours to make it efficient from the
educational standpoint. (E.B.)

(b) Female

In South Formosa there is only one Christian
Girls' School, having both an elementary and a secondary course, four years in each. There are 140
boarders and 60 day-scholars. About two-thirds
come from Christian, and one-third from Non-Christian homes.

The curriculum is the same as in the Japanese
Government Girls' school, with two hours a week
Scripture teaching extra, as well as daily worship.
The greater number of teachers are Christians; the
ideal aimed at is that all should be. Education with
Christian training is the aim of the school. Oppor-
tunities for practical training in Sunday school work
are given to the senior girls and are readily used.

Some graduates become teachers, others nurses

in the Government or our own hospitals. Some have gone to Japan for further study, and numbers are now wives of preachers and pastors in the Formosan Church. (S.E.M.)

4 Degree of Self Support Reached

(a) In Evangelistic Work

This term, "evangelistic work," may include various forms of work, more or less directly evangelistic.

(1) The Pescadores Mission. The Pescadores islands contain a population of over 50,000. For many years this has been the Home Mission Field of the South Formosa Church, and the work there is entirely supported by themselves.

(2) The preaching in churches in over a hundred towns and villages, Sunday by Sunday. This is part of the regular worship of the Church, but it is to these services that the more earnest church members bring their friends to "hear the doctrine."

(3) Special "Missions." These are organised from time to time in different centres, held in the local church, and duly advertised by posters, and sometimes by a band! The speakers are neighbouring pastors, preachers or some other gifted Layman, and occasionally a missionary.

Towards the regular work of the preachership, the Presbyterian Church of England contributes about one-third of the support. Otherwise, these various forms of evangelistic work are supported by the gifts of the Formosan Church. (C.M U.F.)

(b) In Educational Work

The Middle school receives an annual grant from England of 4000 yen only, in addition to the salaries of two foreign teachers. The rest of the income is deri

being raised among the Formosans. We are aiming
at a total of 100,000 yen, spread over a period of
five years. Mr. Lim Bo-seng, the chief promoter, has
already obtained promises for 80,000 yen.   If all
these promises are kept, the school can be put on a
sound financial basis. Teachers' salaries form the
heaviest item. Japanese teachers in Formosa get one
and a half times the salary they receive in Japan.
(E.B.)

The Girls' School has as yet no Endowment Fund.
A grant of about 3300 yen is received annually from
England.   All other expenses are met by fees.

A few years ago, a new school building was an
absolute necessity. The cost was over 60,000 yen,
almost half of which was contributed by Formosans
themselves, the remainder being a grant from home.

It is hoped to raise an Endowment Fund in a
similar manner in a few years time, as the growing
needs of the work, and specially the increase in
teachers' salaries, will become too heavy a drain
on existing funds.   (S.E.M.)

(c)   In Medical Work

For many years the Medical Work of our Mission
has been self-supporting. Apart from the salaries of
the foreign doctors at our Tainan and Shoka hospitals, no grant has been received from abroad. The
income has been derived from various sources. Donations have been received from those interested in
the work and from grateful patients. Special mention must be made of generous gifts from the Imperial Charities, amounting to Yen 1000 annually to
each institution.

A charge for medical treament is made from
all who can afford it. The really poor are treated
free. For those who desire it, private wards are
provided; and the rent from these very materially
assists the finances of the Hospitals.   (D.S.)

FUTURE

1. FUTURE PROGRAMME OF THE FORMOSAN CHURCH

(a) Organization

The future organization of the Formosan Church does not seem at the moment any very serious problems. The situation is simplified by the fact that there is only one church, the Presbyterian Church, for Formosans, and there is plenty of room for it to develop without fear of overlapping. In the Southern half of the island, for which we are responsible, there appears to be nothing more formidable than the organising of new Presbyteries as the need arises. What concerns us more than the organization is the spirit permeating it.

We hope in the immediate future to have a Union Theological College, which will adequately meet the needs of the whole Formosan Church. Should this become an accomplished fact it will go a long way to make the Union of the North and South Churches a real, permanent one.

A strong central department for Christian literature, fully representative of the whole Church, could easily be built up, if the present agencies were slightly re-organized.

(b) Evangelization

The prospects of aggressive evangelistic work are bleak indeed. With the exception of our hospitals, where most of the effective evangelistic work has always been done ,there is little definite evangelistic work being attempted. Our missionaries are all occupied, inevitably it seems, in institutional work. Even those who came out definitely to do evangelistic work have been swallowed up by the "lean kine" of Institutionalism! There is no more urgent need than that of evangelistic workers, both men and women. (W.F.M.'

2. PLACE OF THE MISSIONARY IN THE FUTURE

Has one in eighty-five of the Formosan population heard the Gospel intelligently? How many of the Church members have a growing personal knowledge of Christ, and are able to lead their families in His ways? How many of the Sunday School teachers have had a good general education, not to speak of special preparation? How many of the preachers are equal to their exacting task, or are able to get uplifting fellowship?

With such questions as these in mind must the future of the missionary be considered. The Formosan Church is bearing its own burdens with a will; for many years the foreign staff has been very small, and perhaps for that reason the ever-growing work has been carried on with the minimum of direct missionary influence. Is the missionary then unnecessary, or, if he is needed, will he be welcome?

What has he, or she, to give? With a background of generations of eduacted Christianity behind him, with knowledge of the Church in other lands, he ought to have a width of vision, a balance of mind, and a depth of Christian experience that can hardly be found in the leaders of a young Church. He ought to be able to be a guide in the constantly changing circumstances of the time, and to hold up a light in the problems of the Bible that will more and more assail. His work will increasingly be that of a friend, might one say a "Comforter" in the Biblical sense? He may not be the principal of the schools or the Convener of Committees, he will be an invited guest and helper. He must know the people and the Language and the Church, and then be willing to wait for the opportunities to serve. "Ourselves your servants for Jesus' sake." And the opportunities will come.   (C.M.D.F.)

3. FUTURE PLACE OF FEDERATION OF CHRISTIAN

MISSIONS

It is necessary to bear in mind that whilst we form a part of the Federation, our work in Formosa is very different from that in Japan, in that we scarcely use Japanese at all. Our work is wholly for the Formosans, and carried on in the Amoy Chinese dialect. We have more points of resemblance with the Church in China, but for political reasons it would not be advisable to be affiliated to the Chinese Church. Our educational missionaries, who require Japanese for school work, are more in touch with things Japanese, and they derive more profit from the annual Conference at Karuizawa. Because of the long expensive journey and the different nature of the missionary problems that arise, we cannot expect a large attendance of our missionaries at the conference. In future as the Formosan Church becomes more Japanese in its outlook we shall feel the need of keeping in closer touch with the Federation in Japan. (L.S.)

4. FUTURE PLACE OF NATIONAL CHRISTIAN COUNCIL

The above reasons also prevent us from taking an active part in the National Christian Council. Yet we should value visits from leaders of evangelistic, temperance or other social service campaigns, or from Sunday School experts. Interpreters can always be arranged for, if necessary.

Great help might also be given to the Japanese pastors working among their fellow-countrymen, who number about 200,000. They need all assistance possible, whether from foreigners set apart for Japanese work, visits from leaders in Japan or by literature a ;   f ;

ORGANIZED ACTIVITIES OF CHRISTIAN MOVEMENT

1. Social Service

Owing to the smallness of our Mission staff, there has been no time or opportunity for special crusades for temperance, purity or public health beyond the regular work of our two large hospitals. There is a great field here for a more active campaign, if there were an adequate staff. Along certain lines especially much might be done. There are thousands of lepers in Formosa, who are a misery to themselves and a danger to others. We are hoping that in the near future a definite campaign will be started to rid the island of this dread disease, which is now so amenable to treatment.

Hookworm too is a great scourge here. A very large proportion of the population appears to be infected, especially in the country. This leads to stunted development both physically and mentally, and lowers the general standard of efficiency. Much might be done to eliminate hookworm, dysentery and other parasitic infections by an active campaign of eduaction and improvement in sanitation. The Government must lead the van in this fight against these enemies of public health and progress. The authorities have already done much to improve sanitation and stamp out cholera and malaria The people in infected districts are submitted to blood tests and are supplied with free quinine. The undoubted success already obtained ought to encourage the Government to make further efforts in other directions. (D.S.)

2. Present and Future of Christian Literature

The function of Christian Literature in the evangelization of Formosa involves the problem of spreading a knowledge of the Gospel by this means among

a people who are on the one hand illiterate, yet, on
the other, possess not only a traditional, but a very
real reverence for learning.

The distribution of Christian Literature in the
South of the Island centres round the Tainan Book
Room. It is in part a printing establishment, which
devotes its energies almost exclusively to the production of literature in the Romanized Formosan vernacular (practically identical with the dialect spoken
in the Amoy region of Fukien). Just forty years
ago, in 1885, there was started by Dr. Barclay a small
monthly magazine, which has appeared without a
break ever since as the Church News (Kyokaiho),
and has now a circulation of 1700 copies. We also
publish quarterly Notes on the Sunday School Lessons, a Golden Text Calendar, and a large number of
miscellaneous books and leaflets.

The other side of the Book Room's activity consist in the purchase and distribution of books and
magazines in Chinese Character obtained from
Shanghai, Amoy, and elsewhere. As yet the sale of
Japanese publications is very limited, the work of
our Mission being exclusively among the Formosan
people. With our limited staff we can do almost
nothing among the Japanese.

As to the future, two lines of development seem
to be necessary. First, the present book-room ought
to be re-organised and made more representative of
the whole Formosan Church, both North and South.
It has been too much a missionary concern, and not
enough use has been made of Formosan initiative
and enterprise. Secondly, the Japanese side ought
to be developed and use made of the Christian Literature publications The number of Formosans able
to read Japanese is rapidly increasing and there is
a large and educated body of Japanese officials and
teachers ready to read suitable Christian books, if
not prepared to attend them   .A.B.N.

3. NEWSPAPER EVANGELISM

Of this there is little to be said, for at present nothing is being done. An attempt was made some years ago on a small scale by our Canadian friends in the North of the island but was shortly afterwards discontinued.

There are three daily newspapers published in Japanese with one page entirely in Chinese character (Kambun) Not many Formosans can read the character freely, and we have nobody free to prepare suitable Japanese copy, and follow up the work. (A.B.N.)

4. WORK FOR YOUNG PEOPLE

As far as our South Formosa field is concerned we might say that Y.M.C.A. and Y.W.C.A. work do not exist. Nominally there is a Y.M.C.A. in Tainan but it is practically without activities. Racial feeling is not strong, but young Japanese and Formosans do not mix intimately. A joint institution might be satisfactorily run with a minimum of three trained workers, Japanese, Formosan and foreigner. In Tainan alone there are over three thousand students of middle grade, for whom nothing is being done. (L.S)

5. WORK FOR CHILDREN. SUNDAY SCHOOLS

In Formosa, Sunday School work is specially important, because in recent years Missions have been discouraged by Government regulations from opening elementary schools, thus throwing the main burden of Christian education upon the Sunday Schools. Intelligent Christian teaching in the homes of church members is as yet so meagre and unsystematic that it unfortunately counts for little.

Each of our 110 churches in South Formosa has a Sunday School, and though much willing work is done, the standard of teaching efficiency in most places is still very low, so that the progress of the children is slow. We are also handicapped by having to teach Romanised Chinese, for only a small minority learn to read at home, and the Bible cannot be read till the Romanised is mastered.

In spite of these drawbacks, the S.S. work is encouraging, and last year the Presbytery appointed a Sunday School Committee consisting of four Formosans and two missionaries, to overlook and help forward the work. Local Sunday School Conferences lasting fully two days are being held throughout our field, in which about 6 churches join, and though all the teachers cannot attend, most of the schools are represented. At these Conferences Organization and Teaching Methods are taught and discussed, and of course time also given for the devotional side.

Two or three times within recent years large Conferences, lasting a week, have been held during the summer vacation. In all of our Sunday Schools the International Scheme of Lessons is followed, and very useful Quarterly notes in Romanized are issued.

This year both our Mission and the Formosan Church are considering how best to arrange for the training of Sunday School teachers. At present the only regular training given is in our Theological College and the Boys' and Girls' Schools, which latter each have a weekly preparation class for the senior pupils who teach in Sunday Schools. Another crying need is that someone should be free to devote full time to supervision of S.S. work. Owing to a sadly reduced Missionary staff, ordinary itinerating work has been almost nil for the past two years, so that even this means of occasional help has been lacking. As yet no attempt has been made at holding Vacation Bible Schools. (A.A.L.)

6. BIBLE AND TRACT SOCIETY

Lil

yond measure to the great Bible Societies, our needs
being supplied chiefly through the Shanghai depot
of the British and Foreign Bible Society. We are
helped in a lesser degree by the National Bible Society of Scotland. With the aid of these two societies
we are enabled to give steady employment to a
colporteur, who is allowed to include tracts in his
sales. He meets with a favorable reception almost
everywhere, the chief drawback to extensive sales
being the prevailing illiteracy of the people. Though
many of the younger people have by this time passed
through the Government elementary schools and a
small proportion through schools of higher grade, yet
there are still very few who can read Japanese books
with pleasure or real profit. At the same time, the
study of Chinese is even more neglected than before
the advent of Japanese rule, so that the diffusion of
the Gospel through the written word is even more
difficult than before. Last year our one colporteur
disposed of about 7000 Scriptures' (chiefly Gospels)
and nearly 3000 other books and tracts. There are
few tangible results, but one may surely trust that
such broadcast diffusion of the word of life cannot
be in vain. The great bulk of our literature is, however, sold through the post from the Tainan Book
Room and chiefly to Christian purchasers, though
quite an appreciable amount is bought by those interested though not professing to be Christians.
(A.B.N.)

7. OTHER RELIGIONS IN CONTACT WITH THE
CHRISTIAN MOVEMENT

Speaking generally, bodies come in contact only
when they move. If there is no vigorous movement
there will be no violent contact. If the Formosan
Church moved more vigorously, it might come into
contact with more opposing bodies. The pity is
there is no opposition. The matter is there is no-

thing the matter. The authorities are impartial, the heathen have ceased raging, though they may still ridicule. Evangelistic meetings are well attended, the people listen with interest, and yet nothing happens. Lord, how long?

The only "other religion" that attracts the people is the idolatrous superstition that centres round the worship of Ma-so, the "Holy Mother," at Hokko in the centre of the island. Huge crowds attend the annual festival, for which cheap trips are provided on the Government railway. Also the merchant guilds of different towns will invite the idol to pay them a visit, knowing that crowds of country-folk will flock in to see the procession, and so the tradesmen and inn keepers will profit. Commercial gain and a love of merry-making, rather than religious devotion, are the main motives of these festivals. They do not rouse the deepest religious instincts of the people. Only the work of the Holy Spirit can create a longing for the one true God. Only the one Saviour can satisfy. (E.B.)

KOREA

PART I

FOREIGN MISSION ORGANIZATIONS

CHAPTER I

NORTHERN PRESBYTERIAN MISSION

Rev. C. L. Phillips

MISSIONARY ACTIVITY

In the providence of God, the year 1925 has been an excellent year for missionary work. In numbers of missionaries at work on the field, there has probably been a decrease. Many have been home on furlo, in some stations one-fourth of the missionary force having been absent during the year. There have been few reinforcements—only three new members having been added to the missionary body. But the men and women at work on the field have been blessed with good health and have been given wide-open opportunities to witness for Christ. But "pitifully inadequate" have been the activities of the missionaries of our nine stations. Somehow the idea has gone forth that our Korea Mission is now well manned. But a visit to the stations would soon show that our present force, especially in evangelistic and medical activities, is utterly insufficient to cope with the pressing needs and opportunities. For example, one ordained man is trying to take care of a territory as large as one-half the Sta

40 of these churches being without a pastor and dependent on this one missionary for pastoral work.
Or take the medical situation—two of our nine stations
without a doctor, four stations with only one physician
each, where the needs of the medical work would
require at least two men, many of our hospitals patiently hoping and waiting for foreign nurses to come
and help carry the burdens.

NATIVE CHURCH ACTIVITY

We have every reason to believe that in native
church activities, our Northern Presbyterian work
has decidedly moved forward. There has been an
increase of over 8,000 men and women in average
attendance at Sunday services. Bible classes of a
week or more still flourish, with an increase of 4,000
men and women over last year, in attendance at
these classes. Our church, in spite of hard times,
flood and famine, contributed Yen 97,000 more for the
activities of the church than they did last year. Especially has there been a large increase of native contributions for the upkeep of church property and for
new church buildings. And in 1925 our native church
scored a hundred per cent increase in contributions
for local and foreign missionary work and benevo-
lences at home and abroad. But better than to quote
dry statistics, would be to write the story of "What
one woman saw." At the close of the year, in a
Korean home in the city of Pyengyang, there lay dying
a very old lady, well known and beloved throughout
our Presbyterian Church. Her name in English would
be Mrs. Walking-by-Faith Lee. She lived and died
triumphantly. Mrs. Lee was the first woman to believe in Jesus in all our northern territory. Like her
Master's life on earth, her life of faith covered a
period of 33 years. And, like her Master, she saw
many miracles performed by the power of God in
that time. For the great changes in all Korea are

the miracles of the present day Korean Christian women. When Mrs. Lee became a convert in 1893, it was in the face of severe persecution. At that time women were nothing. They could not read nor write. Mrs. Lee learned to read and became a zealous preacher of the Word. She brought in many women converts. Through her efforts there was organized the Pyengyang Women's Missionary Society, of which Mrs. Lee was the President for 20 years. Even at the time of her death this remarkable woman was still the President Emeritus of this active society which has done a wonderful work in uplifting the women of the city and in sending out evangelists even to far-off country districts where many churches have been established by this woman's organization. During these 33 years, beginning with her own life of ignorance, Mrs. Lee has seen, thru the efforts of evangelization and higher Christian education, her own Korean women rising up to their present plane of happiness and freedom and activity. What a triumphant close to a life of faith and sacrifice! As Mrs. Lee lay dying, she was listening to the sound of church bells in Pyengyang city, calling together a Bible Class of 500 Korean women, who were meeting for one week to read and study the Bible.

School Activity

The most difficult problems of the past year have centered around our educational institutions. In the lower schools, carried on entirely by the native church, the situation has been discouraging. Hampered by the lack of funds, distressed by flood and famine in some districts, driven to the wall by competition of other schools, discouraged by the impossibility of bringing the schools up to the government requirements, during the past year 46 of our boys' and girls' lower schools have been discontinued, with a loss of some   .   .   .   .   .   .

The situation in the higher schools conducted by the Mission, has been one of feverish effort and patient waiting all the year—effort to bring the schools up to the government requirement, and waiting for the government designation papers to come. The mission is thankful that during the past year the Union Christian College at Pyengyang has been granted a government charter as a "special school," with recognition in the literary department. This college, with its newly completed Science Hall, now has brighter prospects of continuing as an institution approved by the government and by the Korean Christian constituency. Of the eight academies under the Mission, only one has yet been granted government designation as an approved school. The remaining seven have spent another year striving to bring their equipment, curriculum, budget and number of qualified teachers, up to the government requirements. In one instance tireless efforts had been put forth, apparently all the requirements had been met, with every indication that the long hoped-for designation would be granted, only to be told at the last minute that the government would not give approval. As this school was in the fairest position to obtain designation, the government's refusal to grant it has left the other schools in a state of perplexity.

Hospital Activity

The seven Mission hospitals have enjoyed another year of large service to the Korean people, nearly every hospital working up to the limit of its equipment and the strength of its staff. The outstanding feature of the medical work this year, has been the increased success of evangelistic work in the hospitals. The "Taiku Plan" has become famous thru-out our mission. Heretofore all our hospitals had their evangelists and Bible Women and a great deal of preaching has always been done in the sick wards. But it remained for our

Taiku Hospital to perfect a preaching organization
that has been so successful as to attract the attention
of all the Mission. The Taiku hospital staff is organized into a missionary society, everybody being a
member, from the superintendent down to the janitor.
This preaching society has a budget separate from
the hospital funds. The aim is not merely to give
the Gospel to the inpatients, but to follow them back
to their homes and establish churches in their villages. Besides the regular evangelists and Bible women
working within the hospital, there are men and
women "deputies" whose work it is to travel in the
country, following up every patient who has been to
the hospital, and thereafter making regular visits to
him and his fellow villagers. By this method the
Taiku Hospital Missionary Society establishes new
churches every year, sometimes as many as a dozen
groups being started in one year, in the country. Our
other hospitals are taking up with this plan, with
most gratifying results. Even with incomplete statistics, we discover that there were 2,300 more converts
in our hospitals this past year than we had in 1921
Our Union hospitals in Seoul and Pyengyang have
done a fine work this year in evangelization along with
medical service.

CHAPTER II

SOUTHERN PRESBYTERIAN MISSION

Rev. J. C. Crane

The South-west section of Korea, being the best rice-producing section of the country, has at once developed the more leisure-loving people, and attracted the energetic Japanese settler with whom the farmers are unable to compete, from sheer lack of experience, handicapped by the enervating effects of the milder climate.

PERSONNEL

There is about one ordained missionary for every 150,000 people in this section, and an average of a little more than one native pastor and four helpers or colporteurs for each missionary's circuit (tho many have no co-pastor). Each missionary is responsible for about 21 groups, of which about 4 have elders, each native pastor has an average of 3 groups, while a native helper visits from 4 to 7 groups, leaving at least three-fourths of the groups without resident leadership. Practically none of the native leaders have a college education and many have not even a High School training, tho most of them are well versed in the Bible and Chinese.

LOSSES

The past year has witnessed a net loss of three members of the Mission, including the death of Rev. Eugene Bell D.D., for 30 years pioneer worker in South

Tate, both pioneers, Mr. Tate being one of our first seven missionaries. Two of our physicians and families retired from the field, but their places were promptly filled by young and promising recruits.

The Mission has organized a sixth station at Pyeng Yang, where two families are located in connection with the Union College and Seminary, in addition to Mr. Namkung, M.A. B.D. (Princeton), now a member of the Seminary Faculty. Our dentist, tho greatly handicapped by ill health, has made, with our faithful medical staff, a substantial improvement in the general health of the mission.

ATMOSPHERE

The increase of Government schools and general literacy among non-Christian young men, including some with higher education, has presented the embarrassment in many communities of church leaders who can no longer hold the position of social or intellectual leadership, but are actually "despised" for their ignorance by those whose "little learning" has become a "dangerous thing." The Christian leader, once the pioneer of western learning and civilization and in breaking bands of superstition and antiquated customs, is now simply (and rightly) a humble witness of the "lowly Nazarene"! This situation, together with the *age of adolescence* which characterises the consciousness of Young Korea and of the Korean church, has demanded a general *rapprochement* toward all lines of work and in the general attitude of the missionary. Mission schools are considered inadequate, with their poor equipment, and the missionary himself, no longer an object of blind worship, has become the subject of keen criticism and observation. A year or so in the college of awakened mentality has equipped Young Korea, he feels, to reappraise all moral and social standards, and to choose his teachers, even tho they be counsellors of de peration from the Bolshevistic North. All the physical extravances of western dress and recreation, added to the mental extravaganza of *socialism*, has driven the bewildered searcher for Life to "cash in" his last resources for an education which he thought would solve all difficulties without undue labour or discipline, only to find himself in more abject poverty and desperation than ever before; yet any suggestion of restraint is charged to a sympathy with capitalism and monarchism! Impatience with language or personal deficiencies, and with any sort of monetary control, extreme sensitiveness, wielding the bitter weapon of newspaper notoriety, searching in western clothes and automobiles for the slightest imperfection in missionary, pastor or helper, inconsistent with "the spirit to new Korea"—this is the stifling atmosphere in which the growing church is struggling, and Christians are called to their knees as never before, for strength, wisdom and guidance.

Appraisal

It is not surprising, under these circumstances, to find a general decline in the rate of growth, as shown by statistical tables, and at the same time to find an encouraging sense of independence within the church itself, with its cry for equal rights, equal responsibility and equal share even in gift-fund distribution. 500 fewer catechumens are reported this year than last, with 22,000 fewer on the roll.

The addition by baptism (1,358) is 58 less than last year, a gross gain of 13% but a net gain of only 100, or 1%! 5,000 fewer are reported in the Sunday Schools, and a similar decrease in church attendance; yet the general interest in Sunday School work, as manifested in convention attendance, Daily Vacation Bible Schools, extension Sunday Schools, etc., is decidedly greater than ever before!

Contributions show 30,000 Yen less for medical work.

Yen 1,000 more for general church work and Yen 3,000
more for native Pastors—one Presbytery only 5 years
old, with this year calls its tenth pastor on native support; Yen 6,000 less for *General education*, with the
attendance at Mission schools is at least 30% less for
boys than last year, tho the girls school, with greater
prestige and more successful self-help, shows only 500
less (10%). The experiment of an industrial school
in Kwangju is meeting with favour and is a hopeful
solution, in part, for the problem of educating a
poverty-stricken church. Unless we can secure Government recognition, or a substantial improvement in
equipment, etc., for our schools, our entire system,
upon which the critical need of leadership depends,
is threatened with annihilation! This serious situation
was thoroughly considered at a special meeting of the
Mission upon the occasion of the visit of Rev. H. H.
Sweets, D.D|(General Secretary of Christian Educa-
tion for the Presbyterian Church in the U.S., and an
earnest plea was made to the home church.

ENCOURAGEMENT

In spite of the gloomy situation outlined, the
average Korean village is more receptive to the Gospel
than ever before. A common economic desperation
is driving non-Christians toward the Church more
surely, we believe, than the discouragement of weaker
Christians in poverty. 17 more organized churches,
19 more unorganized groups, 30 more elders, and a
number of new prayer-meeting places are reported.
In fact, this important advance line is limited only by
the ability to furnish any sort of leadership for Sunday
services. A large increase is shown in attendance
upon women's classes, Institutes and Bible schools,
and a church with devout women need not fear for
its future.

ADVANCE

The church is now making splendid progress

in self-government. It is likely that very shortly the actual planning and running of our Men's Bible Classes and Institutes will be largely in the hands of the native Church. A Board of Trustees, composed half of native leaders chosen by Presbytery, will direct the work of our Mission schools in each Presbytery, to the extent, at least, of reviewing the budget, qualifications of teachers, general rules, etc., and a union Board of the three Presbyteries in our bounds will have general oversight of the co-operating schools as a unit. One of the younger Presbyteries has successfully supported a Presbyterial evangelist. A Union Mission Committee of the three Presbyteries to conduct the entire work on Quelpart island, is under way—in fact such a committee has been functioning between two of the Presbyteries. One of our missionaries has received substantial equipment and is planning shortly to begin large tent meetings in important centers in each Presbytery, by special evangelistic effort. Another Presbytery is planning to support a Sunday School evangelist. With cooperation in Evangelistic, educational, and Sunday school work, it may be an embryo Synod is in the forming—in fact, one of the Presbyteries is so petitioning General Assembly this year.

The physical and spiritual welfare of our Mission, and we trust of cooperating Missions, bids fair to receive great benefit from a mountain resort being established within our bounds—the only mountain resort in Korea for missionaries—for which a generous fund has been contributed by Mrs. C. E. Graham, of South Carolina. The visit of Rev. Edward Mack D.D. to our Annual Meeting in 1925 was of great spiritual value. His Christ-like spirit, added to his scholarly expositions, united with a Gibraltar-like faith, has stirred each of us to a closer walk with Jesus, the Son of God, for whose Kingdom we work and pray and wait. "Even so, Come, Lord Jesus."

CHAPTER III

THE METHODIST EPISCOPAL MISSION

Rev. Chas. A. Sauer

The Korea Annual Conference now has a membership of seventeen ordained missionaries, one hundred Korean pastors and six lay missionaries as associate members. The missionary groups consist of five men in medical work, six in charge of district evangelistic work, the remainder being in educational institutions and connectional work.

MISSION REORGANIZATION

Under the wise leadership of Bishop Welch, the work of this mission has for three or four years been gradually passing from missionary to joint missionary and native control. This is so far true that mission meetings have been practically eliminated, there being possibly one full day each year devoted to exclusively missionary problems. This day is chiefly occupied with the appointment of such committees as must be selected by the Mission and to the hearing of a few reports dealing with the missionary's relationship to the home base.

In order to secure the cooperation of the Korean church as a whole in plans and policies for advancement of the work, provision was made for a joint council on policy, consisting of two Korean pastors or laymen elected by each district, and an equal number of mis   . .   l.. .d ' \ l. . .,s.,.t   l l.. .. s

a council of about fifty leaders who meet just prior
to the session of the annual conference of pastors,
and after considering such matters of policy as may
have been referred to them, or may have been initiated
by them, they prepare a report of their recommendations to the annual conference, the finance committee
and other controlling bodies within the church. It is
significant to note that most of the recommendations
of this council have been approved and adopted by
the annual conference of pastors at the ensuing session.

The Mission finance committee has also been re-
organized in order that the Mission might have the
benefit of the counsel and the best thought of the native
church, in its disposal of Mission funds.   The re-
organized finance committee consists of eight missionaries elected by the Mission and a like number of
native pastors or laymen elected by the annual conference. All moneys appropriated by the Board of
Foreign Missions for the aid of schools, hospitals, the
extension of evangelistic work—in short, for any purpose except missionary salaries—are distributed to the
various parts of the work through this joint committee.   The purchase and sale of property, and the
purchase, sale, or removal of Mission buildings, are
likewise within the control of this joint group.

The reorganization has been more than justified
by its result; not so much in revolutionary or forward looking movements which have immediately
arisen out of such joint control, but in the mutual
understanding which has arisen between the missionary and the native worker as they have faced together
the financial and other problems and tried to work
out a solution.   No longer does the native pastor have
to inquire as to how much money is available for
any particular institution.   No longer need he feel that
there are some mysterious doors in this missionary

enterprise which are not open to him. This spirit of cooperation has been especially manifest during this last year of cuts in funds from the home base. Knowing the workings of the system, there was little need of explanation why such a cut should come, and all could proceed at once to face together the problem of how best to meet the situation.

FINANCIAL HANDICAPS

The work of the year has been greatly handicapped by a cut of forty per cent in receipts from the Board of Foreign Missions for the year 1925. This meant the elimination of all subsidies to primary schools and the cutting by four per cent of the subsidies to church groups, with similar slashes in the appropriations to schools, higher schools and hospitals. In some cases this meant reduction in the number of circuits, with corresponding decrease in the efficiency of the work; in some cases the local churches were able to more than make up the deficits caused by such a decrease in receipts from foreign sources. Institutions were much reduced in efficiency, so much so that another similar year would probably mean the forced closing of at least two schools and one hospital. Unfortunately it does not as yet appear that the next year will be any better financially.

This situation is made harder because of the increased economic pressure under which the Korean is living. As the economic situation is to be discussed more fully in another chapter, suffice it to say here that four years of what one district superintendent describes as "flood, hail, drought and flood again," has made it exceedingly difficult for pastors to continue on the salaries they have been receiving, while at the same time the laymen have not been able to make the increa‧ ‧ ‧ ‧ ‧ ‧ ‧ ‧ ‧ ‧ ‧ ‧ ‧ ‧ ‧ ‧ ‧ ‧ ‧ ‧
increa‧ ‧ ‧ ‧ ‧ ‧ ‧ ‧ ‧ ‧ ‧ ‧ ‧ ‧ ‧ ‧ ‧ ‧ ‧

living under extremely trying economic condition for a
year in the hope that a new year might bring increased
foreign funds. As this now seems unlikely, the coming
year will doubtless see the forced retirement of some
of these men.

CHAPTER IV

METHODIST EPISCOPAL MISSION, SOUTH

Mrs. V. H. Mayor

The Mission of the Methodist Episcopal Church, South, in Korea, has work in five important cities in Korea: Seoul, Songdo, Chul Won, Choon Chun and Wonsan. It has well established institutions in each of the three usual lines of missionary work, Medical, Educational and Evangelistic.

We have well-equipped hospitals in Songdo and Wonsan with capable medical missionaries, both doctor and nurse, at their heads, and they are assisted by Korean doctors and nurses, more successful always than a missionary in pioneering among their own people. In Choon Chun, we have the capable missionary doctor and nurse and a new hospital which is being equipped. In Seoul, we cooperate in Severance Union Medical School and Hospital.

In all of these hospitals the number of in-patients is limited by the hospital space, but each hospital has a large clinic where thousands of sick people find relief from time to time. The Choon Chun Hospital has pushed its clinic work into the surrounding country districts, the doctor and nurse going out for previously announced clinic days. Another interesting phase of this hospital's work is the Baby Clinic. The Wonsan Hospital has extension work in the country too, with a doctor regularly stationed at a village some miles down the coast from Wonsan.

All of our hospitals have extensive evangelistic progra.   1. H . . .   .   s

and Bible women who do some very thorough "follow
up" work among previous patients. Other hospitals
have other plans but the evangelistic motive is at the
center of all the medical work and it truly ministers
to sick souls as well as to sick bodies.

Feeling that education is always a strong arm of
the church, our Mission has established throughout
its territory schools of varying grade and character,
from the unregistered three or four-grade schools in
the country districts to those of college grade. We
find that the money invested in the simple little country schools brings a good return in strengthening the
church and giving a bit of training looking toward
church and community leadership.

We have three Higher Common Schools for Girls.
Holston Institute at Songdo has had government recognition for several years and, with its system of
common schools and, kindergartens in various parts
of the city of Songdo is offering opportunity to some
1,200 or more girls. Lucy Cunninggim School for
Girls in Wonsan has made considerable progress this
year. The Primary building has been completed and
is in use, and the school has been granted government
recognition as a regular Primary and High School. This
represents a considerably enlarged program with a
corresponding increase in equipment and teaching
force. The location of this school in a part of Korea
where there are almost no High Schools for girls gives
it a peculiar advantage. Carolina Institute, the third
of these High Schools for Girls, is located in Seoul,
and enjoys the distinction of being the oldest institution established by our Women's Department in Korea.
This school, too, received full government recognition
in March, 1925. Thus all our girls' schools are placed
on a par in the eyes of the government and enjoy
the privileges of regular government schools, our
graduates being able to enter higher schools and receiving, by virtue of their diplomas, qualification as

teachers in Primary Schools. Carolina Institute has put in this year considerable new equipment and a new High School building, now in process of construction, will be ready for use by Sept. 1926.

It is the purpose of all these schools to give to their students the best educational advantages possible, and train them into strong Christian characters who will be able to take places of leadership in church and in that greatest of all duties, wifehood and motherhood. We believe that if our schools can accomplish these purposes they will have rendered this people an invaluable service.

The Boys' Higher Common School in Songdo shares with Holston Institute a strategic location in an old city of many traditions and unusually pure Korean life. This school has a large student body and already its graduates are finding places of responsibility and large usefulness in the life of their people. Our Mission cooperates in Chosen Christian College (for boys) and has two missionary professors and some Korean professors on the faculty. With the Methodist Episcopal Mission we have united in our Theological Seminaries, one for men and one for women. All of these schools have no other ambition than that of serving Jesus Christ and His little ones.

Like all missions, we desire that all our work be thoroughly evangelistic in spirit and results, but we would say a little too, of the churches and Social Evangelistic Centers and of our more specialized forms of evangelistic work. In each of our stations there are strong growing churches, and each station is the center from which we try to serve large country districts with many churches.

Just at present our churches are giving especial attention to self-support and revival activities, thus showing that they are thoroughly alive in both material and spiritual activities. . .

Especial notice should be taken of the splendid work in the Social Evangelistic Centers. W   t

big institutional church in Songdo, with a Social Evangelistic Center for Men, and almost within a "stone's
throw" from it is "The House of High Aims," a like
institution for women. Along with the other usual
activities of such an institution, this Center also has
a clinic for women, with their own woman physician.
The Center for Women in Wonsan has been doing
good work for some time in the rooms of the Bible
School building and a well developed work is ready
to be moved into the new building which is now being
erected on a beautiful spot facing the sea.

A little more detailed account of the work outlined for the Union Social Evangelistic Center for
Women in Seoul, in which our Mission cooperates,
will give some idea of the general lines on which
all these Centers will be developed. A school is to
be conducted for women sixteen years old and over,
in which two courses are offered, the Home Maker's
Course and the Bible Course. These courses each
cover three years and include a good many of the
common school subjects as well as special work in
the lines designated by the names of the courses.
However, certificates will be given at the end of each
three months' term, making the term a unit. A competent missionary nurse, with a Korean woman physician and nurse, has built up a well organized
clinic which ministers to hundreds of babies and
their mothers. Constant home visiting follows up
all these contacts and endeavors to tie the whole constituency to the church and lead them out into the
abundant life which the Saviour has for them.

Our Mission is not a large one but we desire
humbly to stand in our places, shoulder to shoulder
with all others who are praying and working for the
coming of the Kingdom in Korea.

CHAPTER V

MISSION OF THE UNITED CHURCH
OF CANADA

Rev. W. R. Foote, D.D.

In previous years the article occupying this space was under the caption "Mission of the Presbyterian Church in Canada." That Mission was opened in 1898 and the change in name was made in July, 1925. A month before, about two-thirds of the commissioners of the General Assembly of the Presbyterian Church in Canada, meeting at Toronto, decided to enter the proposed United Church of Canada. As a majority of the members of the Mission decided to follow the lead of the Assembly, the new title adopted was that which stands at the head of this report.

The territory occupied by this Mission is in northeast Korea, extending over a distance of some 300 miles. It includes two provinces, which contain a population of 2,000,000 people. Churches and schools are scattered throughout the whole area. All of the former and most of the latter are administered by three Presbyteries whose bounds coincide with those of the Mission. The missionary staff comprises 10 men, all but two of whom are married, and 16 single women. These are located in five stations (including one just over the border in Manchuria). There are two more ordained pastors than last year making a total of 25, and 22 more evangelists, 28 outstations, 1,164 communicants and 1,195 catechumens were added to the list.

stages of training preparatory to becoming members
in full communion. Although it has been a year of
financial stringency, and in the north the crops were,
in some districts, from lack of rain, a partial failure,
the receipts from the Koreans reached a total of Yen
165,500, which is above that of any other year.

BIBLE CLASSES AND INSTITUTES

In the different congregations at least a
week a year is set apart for Bible study. At
these seasons other duties are set aside and
numbers gather to become better acquainted with
the Word of God. The best leaders available take
part, and in the evenings special revival services are
conducted, with a view to leading non-believers,
through faith, to experience a new life. Growing out
of these Classes are Bible Institutes for those who
are already leaders, or who are looking forward to
leadership in the Church. The course covers four or
more weeks each winter and extends over five years.
It is arranged so as to cover most of the Bible, and
carries related subjects. Missionaries find here a
fruitful field of service and give most of the instruction. Such gatherings develop a Bible-loving people—
a healthy foil to much of the light and .unreliable
literature in circulation. From these Institutes come
the elders, Sunday-school teachers, evangelists and
theological students. Summer Retreats are becoming
quite common and at these, too, Scripture instruction
is given. The leaders are away from the routine of
their surroundings, and by study, prayer and consultation, obtain a better view of the responsibilities of
their office; they thus gain vision, strength, and courage
to better inspire and guide those to whom they minister.
Similar Institutes are held in each station, for women,
with the best of results. From these the best women
enter the Training School for Bible Women located
at Wonsan where they receive a three years' course

in advanced Biblical studies. All missionaries speak in the highest terms of the work done by these graduates. There are 70 women, graduates and under-graduates, many of them supported wholly or in part by Korean funds, employed under the direction of the Native Church as Bible women and evangelists—five more than last year.

EVANGELISTIC

While there has been much to encourage in the number of places of worship dotting the area, 322 in all, one cannot forget the great evangelistic problem still before the Mission. Only one in a hundred of the population is a professing Christian, leaving 1,980,000 still to be reached and won. For this task the foreign staff is at most 8 men and 5 women, each of whom is also engaged, some to a considerable extent, in other departments of work.

Besides attending the various classes and Institutes which absorb the best months for country work, every missionary sets before himself the goal of visiting each group under his care at least once a year. For want of time this is often not realized, leaving almost no opportunity for coming into contact with the larger non-Christian centres. Experience shows that such work would be richly rewarded in good results, as the people are friendly and the door stands wide open for evangelistic effort. Often among the young men there is a readiness to accept the gospel. This is a waiting field for the Korean Church to cultivate, and we hope for increased effectiveness in the men and women who devote themselves to this form of service, with its promising future. In this connection there is a class of workers worthy of mention—the teachers of boys' and girls' schools in country churches. These schools are permitted by the civil authorities. The pupils are from the believing L.   : the community and are children whose heathen parents approve of their being Christians. They grow up loyal to the Church and are well trained in Scripture knowledge.

Another evangelizing agency is that of Sunday-schools for heathen children. The total number of pupils under training in the Sunday-schools is 20,835. Central and county Institutes have been organized to train teachers for this line of service. No less stress is placed on older methods by which the Church has grown to its present size, but this added and most effective instrument of evangelism is being employed as well. Not only do thousands from heathen homes thus bear the gospel, but young men and women who otherwise would find no sphere of Christian activity, are being enlisted and trained as teachers. Through the hottest week Daily Vacation Bible Schools were in session. The sacrifice and devotion of the teachers were most commendable. The schools were numerous and surprisingly well attended. It is a decided step forward when numbers of children through such agencies learn of a Saviour and become attached to Sunday School and Church, thus coming under continued influence and instruction.

Worthy efforts have been made in Church building. In Wonsan an elder, by no means wealthy, contributed Yen 1,700 towards the erection of a handsome and commodious church. Several others have been built during the year and the liberality of this individual was an illustration of what others did, according to their means.

Other Activities

A good Middle School for boys was erected at Hamheung at a cost of $25,000 (Can. cur.) and has been occupied since September. The Mission schools for boys, including two Middle schools, and for girls, with also two of Middle school grade, have been well attended and with good results. Several of our best

' leaders were once students in these schools. The three Mission hospitals, with a missionary doctor at the head of each, have had an unusually active year. In each case the hospital ever keeps before the eye of the Church the fact that the doctors are first of all Christians, and that the healing of the whole man is the one great object of their being in Korea. These are evangelic centers as well as efficient hospitals, each with a capable staff.

The Mission cooperates in the Severance Hospital and Medical College, in each of which Institutions we provide a missionary, and with the Chosen Christian College and Pierson Memorial Bible Institute, all of Seoul; also in the Union Christian College and the Presbyterian Theological Seminary in Pyeng Yang. In the latter we have one man on the staff and 27 students in attendance.

CHAPTER VI

AUSTRALIAN PRESBYTERIAN MISSION

Miss Edith A. Kerr

The spirit of unrest and dissatisfaction which rose as a whirlpool out of the placid waters of Eastern calm some years back, seems now to have separated itself into a racing current forcing its channel through the lethargic, clinging in its eager search for the alluring ocean stretching wide and free beyond.

In every branch of the work in Korea today the problem confronts us—the bursting away of the young people from the traditions of the past, and the lack of understanding and response on the part of the older folk who gladly would hold them back in their ruts of thought and custom. This advance movement among the young people—this intense longing for education, culture and intellectual development, barely touches the masses. It is the urge felt by the comparatively few, who, often in the face of cruel obstacles and almost insuperable difficulties, are turning to the light.

But these few we cannot disregard, even if we would, for it is they who are going to be as the axle on which this old wheel of Korea is to be turned out of the rut into better conditions of life, both social and religious. They are the little lump of leaven which is to leaven the whole, and already we see evidences of intolerance of the darkness of the old days, impatience with many of the restraints, and dissatisfaction with much of the teaching.

A

Lranches in the spring, so a people must testify to
their vitality by advance in thought and activities.
We must rejoice in these signs of life and growth, but
while we rejoice, we realize that, if we would look
for a full crop of fruit in the summer, there must
be *teachers* who are mentally and morally equipped
to train the minds of these young people aright,
a *literature* that will inspire true motives and
noble ideals and a *faith* that will satisfy their souls'
deepest needs, that they may know in whom they
believe and worship Him in spirit and in truth. We
must realize with President Coolidge that, "As the
Christian nations have assumed the responsibility for
bringing new and higher civilization in touch with
all peoples, so they must recognize their responsibility
to press on and on in their task of enlightenment.
education, spiritualisation, Christianising. There can
be no hesitancy, no cessation of effort."

Therefore, in Korea today, we must not cease to
press on with our educational program as expressed
in Bible Schools, Institutes, Normal Classes, and Secondary and Primary Schools. While the Australian
Presbyterian Mission realizes this fully, we have not
yet been able to carry out our educational policy as
we desire to do. The Bible Schools for both men and
women are still being carried on at Fusan in very
cramped and unsuitable quarters, although there is
the prospect of the special building being erected for
this work in the near future.

In accordance with our policy for the education
of the youth of the Southern Province, two Secondary
Schools are now established, one for girls, just out
of Fusan, and one for boys, at Masan. Although we
have not yet received Government "designation" for
these two schools, with both staffs and equipment
right up to requirements, we hope that that will soon
be granted.

One of our three complete Primary Schools for
girls has recently been informed by the local Govern-

ment authorities that its pupils will henceforth be admitted to the Government Secondary Schools on the same condition as the pupils from their own lower schools.

Our special instructress for Normal Kindergarten Training has arrived on the field but so far plans have not been completed for the establishment of this centre.

Kindergartens continue to be carried on in all five stations. In most cases fully trained teachers are in charge, and the increasing appreciation of the Koreans of this most valuable work amongst the little tots is very gratifying.

Evangelistic work is still crippled through lack in numbers of missionaries—especially is this true on the men's side. One of our stations has been carried on without a resident ordained Missionary in charge, since 1921, and another station, during the past eighteen months. The statistics from the latter station seem to indicate that the time for the foreign missionary to give place to the native worker has not yet arrived. There is a drop shown in baptisms, from 137 last year to 33 this year, and in new cate-chumens, from 260 to 35. As against these discourag-ing figures from one station, we have a total increase of 1,599 church adherents, making the total now for the field 13,009.

There were 4,964 communicants for the year! To 484 adults and 1,052 infants was administered the sacrament of baptism; and 2,840 were admitted to the catechumenate. The total membership for Sunday Schools was 12,518, showing an increase of 2,070.

Work on the women's side has been carried on systematically and has shown progress. There is more and more demand for the regular instruction given in classes lasting from one to two weeks, and less satisfaction shown with the short itinerating visits. A very interesting and important addition which should be of great importance as an evangelizing factor, is the increasing desire of the churches to employ a Bible Woman of their own for the purpose of doing intensive work in their district. In some places several of the weaker Churches have clubbed together in the support and use of such a worker.

The Women's Missionary Union of the Province has shown new life during the past year. A fine Christian woman has been engaged as their Bible woman by the Union, which is organized and supported entirely by Korean women. She has been indefatigable in her preaching, and many churches testify to the spiritual uplift and growth that have followed the visit to them.

Medical work is concentrated in one Hospital at Chinju. There is also a Leper Station at Fusan, and some co-operation in the Union Medical College, Seoul.

The Chinju Hospital reports a marked increase during the year in inpatients, outpatients, and also in receipts. A preaching society has been organized by the staff with the object of following up, where possible, those patients who have decided to believe, and also of doing regular evangelistic work, both inside and outside of the Hospital.

Last year marked an increase of interest in the Sunday School Movement, and an attempt on the part of the workers to gain greater efficiency. Two small Institutes and one large Group Meeting for the whole of the Province were held. At the latter, Bible study conducted according to the Study Circle method, proved a great inspiration. Consecration meetings were held in various centers, and Sunday School workers proved their spirit of service during the hot summer months by conducting Daily Vacation Bible Schools with great success, in several places.

In this, the day of the young people of Korea, when they are seeing visions and dreaming dreams, the development of Sunday School work offers a great opportunity for helping them to give adequate expression to their aspirations.

Throughout the year there has been somewhat of discouragement and sense of failure, but much of encouragement and joy, while always there has been the deep consciousness of the fulfilment of the promise, "Lo I am with you always."

———————

CHAPTER VII

THE ORIENTAL MISSIONARY SOCIETY

Rev. II. W. Woods

For the benefit of new readers of the Christian Movement a restatement of previously mentioned facts is sometimes profitable. The Oriental Missionary Society is a faith mission maintained by funds sent in answer to prayer. It was founded in 1901 by the late Rev. C. E. Cowman upon a definite call from God, with *direct evangelism* as its sole object. Rev. Cowman, with his wife and Rev. E. A. Kilbourne, began work first in Tokyo, Japan, and a number of years later came to Korea, at which time they started the Oriental Missionary Society in Korea. They do not minimize the value of educational or medical work that has as its only object the personal salvation of the recipients, but, feeling called upon to engage in a ministry that is wholly evangelistic in its nature, they maintain no work of that kind.

To carry out the policy of the O.M.S. and to better fulfil its calling, a Bible Institute was established in Seoul for the training of a Native Ministry. This Institute has a Men's and a Women's Department with a Three Years' Course of Training. The course includes Studies in the Old and New Testaments, Doctrine, Church History and Methods of Personal Work. With the Preachers and Bible Women that have been trained in the Bible Institute, the Oriental Missionary Society has established fifty churches or missions and others whose members are not or prayer-meeting points. Of the number, seven were opened in 1925.

In keeping with Christ's command to preach the Gospel to every creature, the Oriental Missionary Society has been carrying on a systematic distribution of the Gospel message into every home in Korea. With the aid of maps, each home in every village of several Provinces (with the exception of a few counties) has been given a Gospel Tract which consists largely of Scripture and sufficient explanation to awaken in the heart of the reader a conviction of sin and to acquaint him with the Christ who is able to save him from sin. In connection with the work, street meetings have been held in many places and we have great reason to believe that many have found and will find the Savior as a result.

The Oriental Missionary Society maintains a Publishing Department which has published the following during the past year: 150,000 Tracts (pamphlets), 60,000 sheet tracts, 2,000 copies of "A Guide to Holiness," 1,000 copies of "New Gospel Songs," and a Monthly, "Living Waters, or H'whal Chun," having a circulation of 850 subscribers. All publications mentioned above comprise a total of 6,170,000 pages. Knowing the power of the printed page we feel that these silent messengers of the Master are speaking messages of hope and life and peace for Him.

CHAPTER VIII

THE SALVATION ARMY

Lt.-Colonel W. E. W. Twilley

During 1925 the Army's work under the leadership of Commissioner Lt. Commissioner Palstra was carried forward on the same lines as hitherto. There were many evidences of Divine blessing in the advances made in the different parts of the field so that our numbers and centres of work were increased, new interest aroused and many who hitherto had known nothing of Jesus and His power to save, heard for the first time the Gospel message and cast off their old belief and habits, acknowledged their sin and accepted Christ as their Saviour. This, together with many other signs of God's hand at work, caused us to "take courage and go forward."

SHELTER WORK

The winter of 1924-1925, whilst not unusually severe as far as the weather was concerned, yet gave rise to much anxiety, it being discovered that distress in and around the City was unusually great. 'Oms' or 'dug out' were multiplied and, on Army Officers visiting these, conditions were revealed which would not fail to touch a sympathetic chord in the hardest of hearts. At a meeting called by members of the Community in the Morris Hall to look into the matter, the writer was asked to make a statement and outline what the S.A. intended doing—being also asked to take ... d ... th f ... th ... d ... l ... th the question of General Relief throughout the winter. The Army did its share of this along with other Societies, distributing daily to needy families.

The Army's particular work, however, was that of Night Shelters for the positively destitute. First one house was taken and equipped, but this proving too small, an adjoining one was added and finally a third, so that until the end of March, two men's and one women's shelters were running.

Where a charge was possible, 5 sen was asked, but the majority, being without means, they were entertained free of charge. By the close of the winter, it represented a high figure, 10,998 beds having been provided, and 10,623 meals. The cost was met by voluntary contributions, the Community being interested, and generous in their gifts.

Boys' Home

The working amongst ex-beggar boys has been continued, and many of them, rapidly growing into manhood, have shown great signs of becoming earnest Christians. The Brass Band of some 12 players, is able to render very acceptable music and is often in demand for services of various kinds. The Tailoring Department has developed and a number of boys are becoming quite efficient, under the direction of an able teacher. Looms have been fixed, and, with a first class teacher, the boys are rapidly becoming competent, whilst the bootmakers are turning out good wearing articles of very creditable appearance. Each of these Departments are housed in the Workshops recently erected and opened in the early part of the year.

Girls' Home

In the beginning this home was handed to the Army by the Misses Perry and Paysh on their retirement from the Korean Field, and useful work was done in it. For long, however, it was felt that the premises were too small and unsuitable, so that in connection with a recent visit to Australia by Mrs. Commissioner Palstra, special efforts were made for raising funds— these being forthcoming, and with aid given by our Headquarters in London, it has been possible to take down the old building and erect a two-story one on the same ground, with living and dining rooms, work room, Matron's Quarters, sick room and the necessary conveniences, so that we have reason to hope for a good increase in this branch and in its utility also. Some of the girls from the Home have already passed through the Training Garrison and are now Officers—two of them being at present touring with a party in Canada and the U.S.A. in the interest of Korea.

Flood Relief

When the great flood overtook Seoul and the vicinity in July last, relief work was at once started, particularly in the Ma-Po district—a suburb of Seoul near the Han River—food and clothing were given, and particularly wood, to a number of householders, that they might rebuild. Assistance was also given for the acquiring of higher ground, so that many of them were able to erect their dwellings in a position. so as not to be overtaken again by a similar disaster.

Halls

In a number of villages halls have been erected, chiefly the result of labour and contributions from the people themselves. In addition to this, in two Centres, namely Chun Ju and Yong Dok, larger buildings have been put up, with consequent improvement in the work done.

Officers to England

For the first time since the S.A. started work in Korea,

the purpose of receiving training in the International Training Garrison—Clapton, London. It is expected that this will have a very beneficial effect, widening their outlook, so that they will return in due course, to carry on more ably the work they had already commenced.

Touring Party in Canada and U.S.A.

In addition to the above, Major and Mrs. Hill, who have charge of the Boys' Industrial Home, left at the close of the year with six Korean Comrades, for a tour thro' Canada and the United States. It is anticipated that the meetings, etc., held in this connection, will result in great interest being aroused in the work in Korea, whilst its chief object is the raising of funds with which to erect a new Training Garrison in Seoul.

Campaign Against Drink

Again the Anti-Drink War Cry was published during the month of March, a total of 50,000 copies being disposed of. Employers bought copies for their employees, teachers for their pupils, church workers for their members, etc., and evidence goes to show that great good was done. Pledges were taken by goodly numbers of people, the forms being sent to our Headquarters, whilst the following letter was received from one purchaser, this being a fair specimen of many others:

"Thank you very much. I was a sinner passing Chong No last night, with some of my friends, dead drunk. We met Salvationists on duty selling the War Crys. I was so glad to see them and bought one for myself and advised my friends each to buy one, but I could not read it last night. When I woke up this morning I cannot tell you how much I was sorry, and I read the Anti-Drink War Cry which you have issued for us, from the first line to the last. I felt how much money I had spent in drink without looking after my family, and how I had lost all the confidence of others, but now I have decided to cut it off for ever, and enclose my pledge. I have never smoked before."

———————

CHAPTER IX

BRITISH AND FOREIGN BIBLE SOCIETY

Korea Agency, 1925

Mr. Hugh Miller

Throughout another year the Agency has pursued its work of providing the people of this peninsula with the Holy Scriptures in their own tongue. The Board of Revisers have revised Genesis, Leviticus and Deuteronomy. Genesis has been prepared in Mixed Script as well as in Eunmun, and in Mixed Script with the Eunmun characters along side of the Chinese—the same style as that of the Japanese Scriptures.

We published 5,450 Bibles, 5,500 Old Testaments, 45,500 New Testaments and 667,000 Portions—a total of 723,450 volumes for the year.

The circulation for the year reached 611,476 volumes, an increase of 6,000 volumes over the circulation of 1924.

The 111 colporteurs and 8 Bible women that we were able to support, sold no less than 538,000 of the total circulation, by their careful hand to hand methods. This work is hard on those who do it but it is one of the best ways of successfully getting the Scriptures where they should go. Mr. Hobbs who has just returned from furlough, is continuing, with his assistance, the work of visiting the colporteurs from time to time. This is fruitful not only in increasing the sales, and in the number of evangelistic meetings held, but in encom. in the region the in creating an esprit de corps. The men, working day after day, facing alone non-Christian influence, are apt to get discouraged and lose their keenness. And anything that cheers them on their way and adds to their spirituality and knowledge of the book they sell, increases their efficiency as they do the pioneer work of the church in this land.

Bible Sunday was observed, as is now the custom, on the last Sunday in May. Suitable literature is distributed among ministers and church leaders, to inform them and through them their congregations, as to what the Society is doing in this and other lands. The response is very gratifying and the donations and collections from the Koreans, Japanese and foreigners amounted to almost two thousand yen.

CHAPTER X

THE CHRISTIAN LITERATURE SOCIETY
OF KOREA

———

Rev. D. A. Bunker, D.D.

The Christian Literature Society of Korea was
founded with much the same object in view as has
led to the founding of all such institutions. The
Society under discussion. from a national point of
view, is the youngest Literature Society in the world.
There may be younger local societies but this one
is national in its scope. Korea is its field.

The Christian Literature Society of Korea was
founded about 35 years ago under conditions that
augured success from the very start. What were
these conditions? Korea had no literature of her
own. The Chinese language held the literary classes
of Korea in its mighty embrace—had held them for
so many centuries, that not only was there no effort
to throw off the embrace, but all literary ambitions
had cuddled down—were asleep so far as any knowledge, or desire for knowledge, through its own
written vernacular, was concerned. Oonmum—the
name of the Korean written language—was considered the "dirty language"—the language of the scullery,
the coolie, the donkey and the pony driver. No
scholar would belittle his pen by guiding it while
it traced the native characters—far from it. Just as
in our own history we do not have to go back many
centuries to come to the time when no "cup and
gown" v· rl·l des r·   il   · utt r··   · · , ·*· ·-

or public address in warm Anglo-Saxon. Latin was the tongue of epistle and public speech. Away with the mother tongue. Then came along the King James Version and other literature in the speech of the people. A miracle was wrought. Every man spoke in a tongue that was understood by every other man.

Results were much the same in Korea. If ever there was good soil for growing and maturing a mother tongue it was Korea forty years ago. The great majority of the 18,000,000 people of Korea were sitting in darkness waiting for a light to shine. All the needed elements were ready-made to hand. The 25 letters of the alphabet were prepared; a working vocabulary was on the tongues of the people; it was simply a matter of learning the alphabet and adapting the letters to the sounds as known. It needed only an agent to cause the printed page to speak, and light would flood the land.

Such an agent was found in the Christian Literature Society of Korea. The Society came into existence at an opportune moment. The great majority was waiting, longing for deliverance from the darkness of centuries.

The presses of Japan gave the first pages of printed matter in the vernacular; then came the Trilingual Press of the Methodist Mission in Korea; then came, in ever increasing number, local printing establishments. Presses were a song with psalm and story, telling them forth far into the night:—O, Come let us sing unto the Lord; Rock of Ages, cleft for me; Come unto me all ye that are heavy laden and I will given you rest; stories of the wonderful Christ and his works among the children of men. Stories, stories, stories.

How the heart of Korea responded! New life was infused into the dwarfed, shrivelled vernacular. Intellects that had lain dormant for two score, three score, three socre and ten years even, were vivified. The desire to read and study and think intelligently became a consuming fire. Edition after edition of alphabet primers, printed in large type for eyes dimmed with age, came to, and were passed out from, the shelves of the Society. Thousands of pages grew into tens of thousands-millions; such was the demand of a people thirsting for knowledge. A missionary and his secretary-teacher could no longer care for the increased work in the little godown attached to the missionary's home. The staff of workers necessarily increased. Permanent quarters in the center of the city were secured; still the work grew. A general secretary was secured for the work. The staff increased. A second foreign secretary was added. The work has grown till within the fiscal year of 1925 1,971,932 individual publications were sent out from our stock-room.

Prosperity congestion, in all its parts, best describes the condition of the Society today. The offices where the clerks do their work are unsanitarily overcrowded; twice the present floor space is needed here; the stock-room resembles a wrecked box-car, loaded with all lines of stationery, that has been in a head-on collision.

A new building we must have or we are stalemated. Further expansion in the old quarters is out of the question. The will to do, the Christian Literature Society has; the Korean world is before us to be moved. Give us the fulcrum and the job will be done and well done.

PART II

THE KOREAN CHURCH

CHAPTER XI

SHORT HISTORICAL SKETCH OF THE KOREAN PRESBYTERIAN CHURCH

Rev. C. F. Bernheisel, D.D.

Protestant mission work began in Korea in 1884 and almost from the beginning the blessing of God seemed to be upon it. Perhaps It was that the hearts of the Korean people had been specially prepared of God for the reception of his Word. In whatever way the work is explained the Gospel seed fell upon fertile soil and was not long in germinating and bringing forth fruit to His glory.

Itineration was carried on far and wide over the country and in an astonishingly short time groups of believers, incipient churches, were to be found scattered all over the country. During the summer of 1925 the far-famed church in Sorai Village, in Whanghai Province, celebrated the fortieth anniversary of its organization, which means that this church, so far removed from Seoul, began its existence within two years of the arrival of the first missionary.

In this short account we shall pass over the intervening years and come down to the year 1907 when

Korea Presbyterian Church started its separate corporate existence and took its place as one of the Presbyterian bodies of the world.

The four Presbyterian Missions of the country had been working in close co-operation from the beginning and now united their forces and efforts in the establishment of one native Presbyterian Church of Korea. The first organization was called a presbytery and was effected on the 17th. day of September 1907 in the city of Pyengyang. Thirty-eight missionaries and forty Korean elders comprised the membership.

This newly organized church represented a total of 11,061 communicants scattered over the thirteen provinces of the country. The total adherents at that time numbered 37,047. These adherents were gathered together in 417 groups, 394 of which groups had provided themselves with church buildings. There were 129 primary schools, enrolling 3,730 pupils. The contributions for all purposes for the preceding years amounted to Yen 31,576.

The first presbytery took three actions of special significance: First—Seven men who had just completed their prescribed course of study were ordained to the ministry. They were all men of mature years. It is an interesting fact that six of these men are still living, two of whom have been honorably retired and four of whom are still in the active service.

Second—A Confession of Faith and a Form of Government were tentatively adopted for one year.

Third—A Board of Missions was organized and it was decided to send one of the newly ordained men as a missionary to the island of Quelpart to preach the Gospel to the hundred thousand Koreans living there. That work still continues and many churches have been established in that island.

Organization of the General Assembly

For years after the organization of the first presbytery it was decided to divide the one presbytery into seven presbyteries and to meet the next year as a General Assembly. This Assembly met at Pyeng-yang beginning Sept. first 1912, Dr. H. G. Underwood being elected the first moderator. The Assembly was composed of 52 Korean ministers, 125 elders and 44 missionaries.

The number of communicants had now risen to 53,008 with a total adherence of 127,228. These were distributed in 2,054 groups, 1,438 of which possessed church buildings. The total church contributions had risen to Yen 148,764.

The most important action of the Assembly was the decision to begin foreign missionary work, and the province of Shantung, China, was selected as the field for such activities. Three men were selected to begin the work and they soon sailed with their families and the beginning of what has grown into a good-sized mission work was laid. The Korean missionaries have been well received by the Chinese and the work has been followed by the evident blessing of God. Two stations are now operated.

Three years previous to the meeting of the General Assembly a missionary had been sent to work among the Koreans living in Siberia. That was the beginning of a great work among the Koreans living in that distant section of country. There is now a presbytery organized there under the Korean General Assembly.

Just as an indication of the way the church has developed from that time to the present, it may be stated that there are now twenty presbyteries under the General Assembly, eighteen in the mother country and one each in Manchuria and Siberia where there are hundreds of thousands of Koreans living. There

are now 315 ordained ministers on the roll, 260 of
whom are in active service. There are 199 theological
students, 1,569 elders, and a total of 12,529 church
officers of all kinds. There are 794 organized churches,
1,515 unorganized churches or groups and 876 other
places where prayer meetings are held. There are 2,232
church buildings. The total number of communicants now reaches 89,879 and the adherents total
193,823. For the first time the contributions have
passed the million yen mark, the exact figure being
Yen 1,000,779.12.

The Korean churches support 590 primary schools
and 25 middle schools. The support of these schools
is a tremendous drain on the financial strength of
the Christian believers but they are willing to give
thus generously in order that their children may have
the benefit of studying in Christian schools and under
Christian influences. However, many Christian children attend the government schools.

BIBLE STUDY

Bible study classes continue to flourish in
the Korean Church. From the very beginning
this has been one of the outstanding features
of the work in this country. Nearly every church
and group gets its membership together at least once
a year for a week or ten days of intensive Bible study
and evangelistic work. The latest report to General
Assembly shows that 1,405 such classes were held
for men during the year and 1,252 for women. The
total attendance at these classes was 40,670 for men
and 51,870 for women. This is believed to be the
largest number ever reported.

SUNDAY SCHOOLS

. . ., ... able
is . . . . uly. the . are the

Sunday schools. Sunday School work has been stressed for the last few years and the increase has been large. The interesting fact is that the Sunday School attendance is larger than the total adherence of the church. 2,811 adult Sunday schools are reported, the men and women often meeting separately. The adult attendance at Sunday Schools is 121,878, while the children numbered but 85,035. This does not mean that the attendance of the children is small but that the attendance of adults is unusually large. In fact, in Korea at least, the whole membership of the church is found in the Sunday School.

CHAPTER XII

THE METHODIST EPISCOPAL CHURCH IN KOREA

Rev. E. M. Cable M.A. D.D.

The introduction of Methodism into the world was not an accident. Dr. Stoughton says, "The rise and progress of Methodism may be regarded as the most important ecclesiastical fact of modern times." Isaac Taylor, the great English ecclesiastic, says, "The Methodist movement is the starting point of our modern religious history." The introduction of Methodism into Korea is by God's appointment and therefore, has a very real message and contribution to make to the sum total of Christianity in the peninsula.

In 1884, at the request of the Board of Missions of the Methodist Episcopal Church, Dr. Robert S. Maclay, a missionary of the same Board in Japan, came to Korea to investigate the field. He was the first Protestant missionary designated by any evangelical church to reach the Forbidden Land. Through the good offices of the American minister, Mr. Foote, the emperor of Korea consented to the opening of mission work along medical and educational lines. Upon Dr. Maclay's report to the Board, an appeal for funds was made and in 1884 Rev. and Mrs. H. G. Appenzeller and Dr. and Mrs. W B. Scranton were appointed the first missionaries. Mrs. M. F. Scranton, the mother of Dr. Scranton, accompanied her son as the first representative of the Woman's Board. Owing to the p... as ... ...

above mentioned missionaries were not permitted to land until later. Dr. and Mrs. Scranton reached Chemulpo May 1st., 1885, followed shortly afterwards by Rev. H. G. Appenzeller and wife. The first meeting of the Mission was held in Seoul August 1st., 1885.

In 1886, Mrs. M. F. Scranton founded the first girls' school in the Hermit Kingdom, and so pleased was the Emperor that he gave it the name of Ewha (Pear Flower), a name which it still bears. It remains the only institution offering higher education to women in Chosen.

In the same year Rev. H. G. Appenzeller founded the first modern boys' school in Korea, to which the emperor gave the name of Pai-Chai, (Hall for rearing useful men). This school was the first Mission school to comply with the government's regulations and was recognized as a Higher Common School. Methodism has always been interested in the cause of education. It is looked upon as the hand-maid of religion. It was Edward Everett Hale who said, "No church in the country (United States) has so successfully engaged in the cause of education as the Methodist Church; no one that, during the last twenty-five years, has done more for the advancement of the same."

On October 9th., 1887, the first religious public service was held in Korean at the Bethel Chapel and it was here in the same year that the first Korean woman in the peninsula received baptism. On December 7th., 1889, the Methodist Espiscopal Church was formally organized and its work grew steadily until, by 1892, it had extended its work to Pyengyang, Wonsan, and Chemulpo. Later the church opened up stations in Haiju, Kongju, Yengbyen and Wonju. At the 20th. Annual Meeting of the Korea Mission the Korea Mission Conference was organized and continued to function until 1908 when it was organized into the Korea Annual Conference, with a member-

ship of 'two Koreans and twenty-three missionaries.
The General Conference of 1908 electced Merriman C.
Harris Missionary Bishop for Japan and Korea, with
his residence at Seoul. This office the Bishop filled
with satisfaction until failing health made it impossible to continue. The General Conference of 1916
elected Herbert Welch, president of Ohio Wesleyan
University, Bishop, and he was appointed to the Japan-
Korea Area with his residence in Seoul. This office
the Bishop has continued to fill with dignity and
signal success. Under his administration the church
has made steady progress along all lines.

The Methodist Episcopal church has grown from
childhood to maturity. At the last Annual Conference, June 1925, there were present 93 full members,
27 Probationary members, a total of 120 Korean members and 18 missionary members, making a grand
total of 138 members of the Korea Conference. The
Membership of the Church in 1925 was 19,480, with
360 organized churches, 598 Sunday Schools, with a
total of 33,990 Sunday School scholars. The membership contributed in the same year a sum total of
Yen 191,975 to all causes of the Church. The total
number of missionaries, including the Woman's Board,
is 93.

The Methodist Episcopal Church in Korea,
though an integral part of the Methodist Church in
the United States, to all intents and purposes, exercises autonomy. It has been the determined purpose
of the church to commit all the interests of the same to
the Koreans as fast as they are ready to assume them.
Following out this determination there was organized
in 1922 a Policy Council, composed of an equal number of missionaries and Koreans, to discuss, frame
and present to the Annual Conference for action and
approval all matters of church policy, so that the
matter of cut and dried policies manipulated in mission quarters and presented to the native church for

approval, has ceased. Even meetings of the Mission, except for a few matters which relate solely to missionaries, have been dispensed with, removing a cause of suspicion, to say the least. Great bodies of missionaries, meeting for days at a time in Mission Meeting, does not help to make for better understanding and relations with Korean workers. Furthermore, the Methodist Episcopal Church in Korea has committed all its financial interests to the hand of a Finance Committee, composed half of Koreans and half of missionaries. These brethren sit down together, make all redistribution of mission funds and discuss all financial matters. We have felt more than repaid for the confidence we have placed in the Koreans in this respect. They have in every instance proved themselves to be capable, fair and brotherly, all causes for suspicion of one another have been removed and there exists the frankest and best of feeling between missionary and Korean workers. It will be noted that the Koreans in the governing body outnumber the missionary members five to one, yet we have the first instance to record of any racial lining up on any question that has come up for consideration.

The General Conference has created a Central Conference for Eastern Asia of which the Methodist Church, in Korea is a member. Here matters pertaining to the indigenous churches in China and Korea are carefully considered and large liberty is granted in matters of ritual, education and church policies. This body is a delegated one, composed of missionaries and natives. More and more it will come to a position of influence and power in the administration of its church policies.

The Methodist Episcopal and the Methodist Episcopal Church, South, have united in ministerial training. In 1910 the Union Methodist Theological Seminary was established in Seoul. Both Churches

share equally in expenses and teaching staff.   The
Seminary has already graduated 153 men.   Two
courses are offered, one in English and one in the
vernacular.   This year witnesses the first English
graduates.   The school stands for the great doctrines
of our common founder and seeks always to emphasize the things which have made Methodism so sig-
nally blessed in the years past.

PART III

SPECIAL LINES OF EVANGELISTIC WORK

CHAPTER XIII

SWALLEN'S BIBLE CORRESPONDENCE COURSE

Rev. W. L. Swallen, D.D.

Nothing is more important in the life of a Christian or community of Christians, than a systematic study of the Bible. Almost any system, perhaps, is better than none at all. But there is much gain in the use of a proper workable system—one that is not too easy, nor yet so difficult as to be burdensome. Generally speaking, the Bible is not an easy book to read, unless it is read in the proper way. It is necessary to recognize the Bible to be the Word of God; necessary to come to it with a real consecrated purpose; prayer is necessary; and above all, it is necessary that the Holy Spirit be present to guide and enlighten the understanding. Consecutive reading is always absolutely necessary for the better understanding of the precious Word.

The Bible should be studied by Books and read consecutively. We should think of the Bible as a letter from God, and read it with a mind to know what

over again and again, it will not be long until the
truth begins to appear; and when all the books from
Genesis to Revelation are thus read, the relation of
the various parts to each other will also appear.

This Bible Course lays stress upon the consecutive reading again and again, of the whole Bible,
book by book, beginning with the New Testament,
which is divided into 12 sections, of as equal length
as possible, combining several of the shorter epistles
in one section. There are from 45 to 50 questions
on each section, or about 600 on the New Testament.
There are two Courses, a First Course and a Second
Course. When the student enrolls he is given the
book of questions, and a grade-sheet upon which to
paste his grade-cards as he proceeds with the work.
The book of questions contains the lists of questions
on each of the 12 sections, and a very brief introduction to each book; also in the preface of this book are
the rules directing the student as to how the work
is to be done.

The student is to read each section twice over
consecutively from beginning to end, as he can take
time to do so. Then, after studying carefully the introduction, he proceeds to answer the questions, searching out the answers from the text of that section
on which he is working, and writing them down as
he finds the proper answers. The answers are all
found in the text, and there is no need for any other
helps. When he has answered all the questions on
a given section, he mails the sheet to me. The answers are gone over in my office, graded and corrected
in red ink, and returned with the grade-card for that
section. The 12 sections thus completed constitute
the First Course.

For the Second Course the student prepares on
the same list of questions, the correct answers of
which he now has, and takes a written examination
before any pastor, who selects 10 questions from the

50 questions of the section on which he is being examined. When the Second Course is thus completed he is given a Diploma. The Old Testament is divided into 20 sections and the work is done in the same way. A Diploma is given upon completing the Second Course, as it is for the New Testament.

The report for the last year is as follow: New enrollments during the year, 1421; present total enrollment 3,064; graduated during the year, 65; total graduates, 122; examinations on First Course during the year, 2,038; on the Second Course during the year, 874. The amount of work done in one year is equal to that of 170 persons who have completed the whole New Testament in the First Course, and 73 persons in the Second Course.

CHAPTER XIV

THE SEOUL CITY MISSION

Rev. M. B. Stokes

The Seoul City Mission is a new enterprise in mission work in Korea. It is unique in several respects: meetings are held every night; its activities are confined to active evangelistic work, and definite conversion, rather than merely a decision to become a believer in Jesus, is the end in view at all times.

Work was begun on the evening of the 20th, of September, 1925, in a rented hall situated on one of the busiest streets in the center of the city. Since that evening, for more than four months now, a service has been held every night. The attendance has been surprisingly good. Sometimes we have had the hall packed with people, and almost always a goodly company of earnest hearers to whom to bring the Gospel message. The average attendance for the first four months, in spite of the fact that much of this time has been in the coldest and most disagreeable time of the year, has been about seventy.

In the meetings we use no attraction other than the singing of good lively songs and the preaching of the Gospel. People are brought in mainly by workers on the street in front of the hall, who simply state that we are having a salvation meeting and would be glad to have them attend. Someone is on hand inside to welcome those who come in. Often a word or two of friendly exhortation is spoken. While service is held. We have a good song-leader who knows how to sing himself and understands the art of getting others to sing.

This song service runs into the preaching service without a break. After the last song the preacher in charge of the meeting at once calls upon all to join in a word of prayer to God. This is usually, it ought to be always, short, simple, and to the point. Immediately after the prayer comes the sermon. This is usually a short, simple, earnest presentation of the good old Gospel message. At the end of the sermon, either by the same speaker or by another, a short exhortation is given. This is in the nature of an application of the message to the present needs of the people, and a call upon them at once to seek to find God. The aim is not to get anyone to decide to become a believer in Jesus in a nominal way, but to seek salvation from sin by repentance, confession, and a living faith in Him.

After the sermon and exhortation an urgent invitation is given to those who want to be saved from sin to come forward for prayer. As soon as a number have gathered this prayer service is held. Usually, first of all, a few words of explanation of the way of salvation are given and then all are urged to pray. Each worker takes one or more of the seekers and endeavors to lead at once to the point of true repentance and saving faith. It is wonderful how the Spirit sometimes moves in these services. Often the seeker has never uttered a prayer in his life before, and his first prayer is like that of the man who went up into the temple to pray, "Lord, be merciful to me a sinner"; and like him, too, often he meets His Lord there on his knees, and goes down to his home "justified."

After a season of prayer and personal work a service for testimony is held. This is often a most interesting part of the meeting. Any who feel that they have been blessed are urged to speak a word of testimony. Many and various are the experiences given. Sometimes a backslider will tell of how he once knew the Lord, but had drifted away, and has now been received again into the fold. Sometimes a man will tell of how he had no thought of seeking God, but in passing in front of the hall was invited to the service, came in, heard the message, and sought and found the Lord. Sometimes a man will tell of an awful life of sin for many years and of how God has this very night given him the strong purpose to lead a new life from now on, trusting in Jesus to save. And sometimes, too, a man will tell of how he came to the hall with the purpose of becoming a Christian and of how God has met his need.

Let me close this paper with just one illustration out of many that might be given. Soon after our meetings started a young man who had recently come up to Seoul from the country was very definitely converted. He was at once filled with a zeal to work for others and kept coming nightly to the meetings. He got concerned about some of his companions back at his home village and wrote them a letter telling them of his conversion and urging them to come to Christ. In a short time he got a reply saying that they had decided to become Christians. After a few months he went back home. It was a three or four days, journey over land by foot, and he went those weary miles with a heart burdened for the salvation of the members of his family. In a letter he tells of how he arrived at just about dark one evening, his father and mother with the other members of the family rushing out to welcome him. And then he says: "I went in and told them of how God had given me a new heart." Soon they, too, became Christians, and he was able to write to us the glad news that now "the sound of singing is heard in the home." But he y . . t . . . . :

companions together and they commenced to go from
house to house proclaiming the glad news of salvation. Surely if nothing else had been accomplished
during the past four months in the work at the mission this one result alone would have well repaid us
for all of our labors there.

———————

PART IV

THE EDUCATIONAL SITUATION

CHAPTER XV

EDUCATION FOR BOYS

Rev. H. D. Appenzeller

Western education was introduced into the peninsula of Korea by the missions and Pai Chai high school is the first school of modern learning in the country. From this beginning forty years ago the work of education for boys has grown until we find that the government has a well-developed system, from primary, through middle schools to colleges, special schools, and finally a university, to be opened this year. We of the missions started this work, and there are times when we forget perhaps, that with our necessarily limited resources, we have been outstripped by other schools. It is only fitting and proper that the government should take over, increasingly, the education of the youth of the land. What is our place in the system, and what our distinctive service?

First, let us see how much of a quantitative part the missions have in general education for boys in Korea. The government report of schools for November 1925 gives the total number of primary and common schools, for Japanese and Koreans, at 1703, with 374,377 pupils; middle schools (and higher common) 33 with 14,748 pupils; colleges at 9, with 1,736 pupils. These schools without recognition. This is a very important item when we realize that the majority of the mission schools, other than those of higher learning, are not registered. The latest mission figures available from the report of the Federal Council give the number of boys' primary schools (up to six years) at 627 with an enrollment of 34,899, schools of middle grade (above six years), at 25 with 5,651 pupils, Bible and other special schools at 5, with an enrollment of 242. Comparing the figures for Korean boys only, we find a total of 40,792 students in 657 mission schools with an annual expenditure of Y.900,940 as compared with the government figures of a total of 422,321 Korean boys, and a total educational budget, boys and girls of 24,263,473. Thus is forced upon us that quantitatively the missions are hardly a tithe in the education al system. And it is inevitable that this tithe diminish as more government and non-mission private schools are established.

Second, from a general quantitative viewpoint let us try to estimate the place of mission schools for boys in Korea. Here only the most general standards can be used as one finds it impossible to gauge individual schools. Rather must we look to general qualifications. Something very similar to the Northwest Association and other standards set up for and followed by high schools and colleges in the United States obtains in the distinction made by the government between registered and unregistered schools, or in more familiar terms, accredited and non-accredited schools. Mission schools are now distinctly divided into two classes, those which are and those which are not accredited, and the latter form the greater majority. In fact there are only four boys high schools accredited, and there remains among these four the further distinction of being "registered" and "recognized," 3 and 1 respectively, the conditions of which were fully explained in the volume of last year, 1925. All three of the mission colleges for men have been

recognized as fully accredited schools, and as a result the graduates from unaccredited high schools
cannot matriculate in these colleges any more than
they can in government colleges or any other school
of higher learning. There is a special arrangement
whereby they can attend classes in the mission colleges as special students, but they cannot receive
their degree until they pass a government examination
covering all high school subjects. This examination
is so difficult that few are able to pass, in fact this
year out of some four hundred taking the examinations
only 3 passed!

In like manner graduates from unaccredited high
schools, (the missions having only 4 accredited ones)
are hindered in securing teacher's certificates and
positions in government offices, banks or business
houses. Says the principal of one of these unaccredited (undesignated or unregistered) schools, "The road
forward for the graduates of undesignated middle
schools is rough and discouraging. Because of this
the future of undesignated schools is uncertain. They
must either meet the government standards and become designated, or stop. But you ask, Why do not
all get designation? The answer is that is hard for
all the schools to meet the government standards as
long as they are dependent upon the limited mission
appropriations. The government standards touch on
buildings, grounds, apparatus, annual budget, teachers' qualifications. When the requirements are met
there is no doubt that the schools are bettered. There
are between fifteen and twenty mission schools that
are facing a crisis precipitated by the new regulations."

When, then, is the place of the mission school
if, as we have seen, quantitatively it must decrease
and qualitatively it has fallen short of standards set
up by the government? The answer seems obvious,
that ours must be a qualitative and not a quantitative
service. W   ll , t   f   t i   l t i

but do better what we do. Dr. Russel of Teachers College, Columbia University, a member of the China Educational Investigation Committee, says, "It has been my judgment for some time that the program of higher education on the mission field can only be perpetuated by elimination of most of the colleges by raising their standards and promoting them into first class middle schools and confining all institutions of collegiate grade to not more than five institutions." If this is true in China, one wonders how it must apply to little Korea? Whatever the numerical figure, it is patent that without some unforseen increase in current funds and then in endowment, even the present educational work for boys cannot be carried on successfully. That the church of Christ which has been the proponent of enlightenment should come to be content with sponsoring second rate education seems unthinkable. The best will always crowd out the better, and it is for the best that we must strive. We firmly believe that the government standards, good as they are, can and ought to be vitalized with Christian contacts, that education may be not the donning of new mental furnishings but the transforming of the life for greater service. Not more schools but better schools, not a quantitative striving to cover the whole territory, but a qualitative and intensive effort in chosen centers, not a servile, inferiority-complex education, but a serving, confident education that shall produce men who will lead this people in the way God would have them go.

How "Designation" Works in the Kyung Sin Hakkyo

In the "Christian Movement" for 1925 there is an article in which THE EFFECT TO "DESIGNATION" ON A MISSION SCHOOL was explained as far as known at that time. These notes are to be read as an addition to that article, bringing it up to date— April 12, 1926.

Designation has been extended to schools in the whole Japanese Empire, including Formosa and the Leased Territory around Dairen.

In the face of severe competitive examinations, 15 graduates of this school, in the classes of 1925 and 1926, were accepted as regular students in schools of Sen Mon Gakko grade, in Chosen and Japan Proper. As the whole number of graduates for these 2 years is 37, and several of them are in salaried positions, the proportion who have succeeded in their ambition to enter higher schools is very satisfactory. It proves that in the examinations the graduates of a designated school have fully as good a chance as those of a Private Higher Common School.

They have also the same eligibility as teachers, in Private and Public schools.

What was said last year about improved *morale*, on the part of school teachers and students alike, is more noticeable this year. The quality of those who apply for admission is much improved.

But there are draw-backs even yet. The first is that the graduates, while eligible as regular students in any school, including the Keijo Imperial University Preparatory Department, are not in line for official positions. So far this has little weight, but it must not be forgotten, and should be removed in due time.

Second, the school is still listed among the "unclassified schools," not among the Higher Common Schools. This is a matter of "face," but is a real consideration. The situation is anomalous, and no one can tell just how it should be amended.

Third, there is a Government School of Sen Mon Gakko grade, that annually advertises to accept without examination the top ten percent of graduates from any Higher Common School. Both years I have asked to have this apply to my graduates, and both times have been refused. The explanation is "Your graduates result is that boys of lower rank in the graduating class take the examination and enter the school, but the school loses the chance to get the top boys. However; this discrimination works against the designated school. Legally, we have all the privileges that were promised, for our graduates are eligible for the higher schools. Practically, there is still a spirit of discrimination against the school, and we all feel it.

I have been asked about the Government's policy as to designating more schools. I have been categorically assured by an official who stands very close to the Governor-General, that the Government has not wavered in its intention, and will designate schools as fast as they prove themselves worthy.

The present difficulty seems to be in the proficiency of the students. Equipment, teaching force, school rules, can all be brought up to standard, but when the students are examined, they do not meet the severe requirements of the Educational authorities, and designation is not granted. This is a matter that time and persistence can solve, and the attitude of the Educational Department is uniformly sympathetic and encouraging.

Notes

(a) I have since learned that the school referred to in item Three, has discontinued the plan of taking in certain students without examination, and that in fact, none were so received into the entering class this April.

(b) The Governor of this Province is inviting 10 schools to send one teacher each for an excursion to Japan Proper, in May, and is paying Yen 200.00 toward the expenses of each person so sent. This school was among the 10 schools to which this privilege was extended. This has a bearing on the matter of a "spirit of discrimination against the school," spoken of in the article.

(Signed) E. W. KOONS.

CHAPTER XVI

PRESENT·DAY PROBLEM IN EDUCATION
˙FOR WOMEN

———————

Miss E. Wagner

The trend of public opinion in Korea to-day in matters pertaining to education for women is part of the tendency of the times to look to general enlightenment for all things worthwhile and desirable. Hence the, unprecedented rush into the schools in which rush the mission school has shared with all others. This condition only makes plainer the imperative need to strengthen the mission girls' school and to raise the faculty and equipment to the highest standard possible.

The achievements of such institutions has been remarkable in view of their meager resources,—now, however, we have come to the parting of the ways,— the time has come in Korea when the mission that can not organize and equip her schools, bringing them up to the government standard and adjusting them to the government requirements, had better close such schools before that step becomes necessary. The temptation in the past has been to meet the great need of the unschooled Christian population in putting quantity before quality in establishing a greater number of schools than could be carefully and properly equipped. It is to be greatly regretted the few mission schools above primary grade can equal the government schools, which though few in number have splen··· ··· ··· ··· ··· ··· ··· ··· ··· ··· ···

therefore, is re-organization, a conservation of forces and resources in supplying the adequate institutions for training Christian leaders for Korea.

Several of our girls' schools during the past year have faced the necessity of the present conditions, and these have met the situation squarely. The Methodist Episcopal Church, South, has put two of her schools on a new basis during 1925, and brought them up to standard qualified high schools,—these are Pae Wha in Seoul, and Lucy Cuninggim in Wonsan, while other missions have taken preparatory steps toward the same action.

During the past centuries woman's subordinate position in Korea, as in all the Orient, was in marked contrast to the present general turning toward freedom. The breaking down of old standards, the influx of new ideas and strange influences has not only changed things, but is bringing about some of the most difficult and complex problems of the student class. In many cases it is regrettably true that the parents either can not or will not control the younger generation, and the young people feel that they are free of restrictions. Korean youth of to-day has not passed through the transition years between complete separation of the sexes and so-called freedom, and this naturally brings about difficult situations and much suffering. The Committee for Student Work of the Federal Council is seeking to inform people of the conditions and dangers of Seoul, and to present the need of Christian hostels, and co-operation on the part of the schools in gaining properly chaperoned boarding houses. Mrs. W. J. Anderson, who has made a study of conditions among the girl students in Seoul, in connection with this Committee, says: "There are approximately 4,000 girls studying in the middle and higher schools of Seoul, and it is a conservative estimate that half of them come from outside of Seoul. They come from every province in Korea, even from Manchuria and Sib... missions, government and

private schools." Indeed Seoul is the Mecca toward
which the student feet more often turn these days,
and in many instances the young women prefer the
greater freedom outside the dormitory to the more
restricted though safer boarding place. In facing the
difficult and perplexing temptations of the modern life
our young people have left the shelter of the old restrictions, and have come with the youth of all the
world to the place where it is necessary for the to
realize that only the spirit, the principle within, only
a right valuation of moral worth, can keep their feet
firmly set in the path of righteousness. Young Korea
must have the conscious life with Christ in God in
order to solve her problems, and those who have the
responsible positions of teachers and leaders need
above everything else, Love that never faileth, courage
and the understanding heart.

There are two essential elements in every school,
—the pupil and the teacher. There is surely no lack
of the former in Korea, but the question of the teacher
is a very vital problem. With the new education goes
the necessity of new methods of teaching, and new
methods of teaching demand new training for teachers. In fact this demand is so much greater than the
supply that all schools, government as well as private,
find difficulty in meeting this need. It is not sufficient
that Korean young women receive the equivalent to
a high school education. Some of them—the leaders
and teachers of future Korea,—must be given the privileges granted to young women of other lands through
Christian Colleges. The Methodist Episcopal Church
has in Seoul the beginning of the first real college for
women in Korea. In writing of this, the President,
Miss Alice R. Appenzeller, says:--

"The year 1925 must be especially marked in the
annals of women's higher education, for Ewha College
became the first "Semmon Gakko" (special school or
college) for women in all Korea. Later on the "Chris-

tian Movement" told of plans and eager hopes that
such registration would be granted. The old College
Department of Ewha Haktang, which had been the
pioneer for 15 years, graduated its last class in March,
making a total of 29 young women who are serving
Korea as her first college graduates. They have received college credit in accredited institutions in
America, some graduating with distinction, one of
them having been admitted to the Phi Beta Kappa
Fraternity. The undergraduates took qualifying examinations to enter the new Ewha College, which began its history in April with 55 students enrolled in
the Liberal Arts and 15 in the Music Courses. These
students represent almost every Christian body in the
country, forming a *real* union college, although as yet
the women of the Methodist Episcopal Church bear
the burden alone. Ewha College looks forward to
losing herself in the larger life of the college that is
to be, *The Women's Christian College of Korea.*

"This name has been assigned to that college of
our dreams which is to occupy the beautiful site of
45 acres near the Chosen Christian College. This
spring an architect will make tentative plans for buildings and grounds. So far an unofficial committee of
Koreans and missionaries from the two Methodist
Churches has been directing the plans for the proposed college. Before the year passes it is hoped that
definite plans can be presented to all the Christian
bodies, so that together they may begin this important
work."

We have set our hand to the educational plough
in Korea and we may not turn back with honor. We
have here a special responsibility; the ministry of the
Christian school is more needed than ever before. We
have not occupied the field adequately. Our schools
are numerous enough,—in fact we have too many;
what we need is concentration, specialization,—a field
definitely limited by the ability to do what we do

supremely well. Let us have fewer, but better schools. Let us spare neither men, nor money nor effort in carrying our educational program to its successful, completion, and share the best we have with our Korean sisters.

———————

PART V

MEDICAL MISSIONS IN KOREA

CHAPTER XVII

MEDICAL WORK

Dr. A. G. Fletcher

DEFINITION

The work of Medical Missions in Korea may well be defined in the words of Dr. Fletcher Moorshead "as that section of the missionary enterprise of the Christian Church which seeks to spread the knowledge of "The glorious Gospel of the Blessed God" through the healing of the sick.

DATE OF BEGINNING

Medical Missions were initiated by Dr H. N. Allen who came to Korea in the year 1884. Since then the work has gradually grown until at this time it is being carried forward by 40 Foreign Doctors and 26 Foreign Nurses assisted by a large force of Korean Doctors and Nurses in 27 medical institutions, and a great many Korean Doctors and Nurses in private practice. The following information was gained from replies to questionnaires sent to 16 hospitals represer

NEED FOR MEDICAL MISSIONS IN KOREA

1. As yet the people have no sense of responsibility (except for one's personal relatives) for the sick. In the light of our replies there is not one organization, endowment or institution for the free care of the sick, outside of Mission or Government or foreign control. This need is very evident, however, for in the Mission hospitals anywhere from 10 to 95, or an average of 43 per cent of inpatients, are free cases while in the outpatient department from 13 to 80, or an average of 39$ per cent, are charity cases.

2. As yet about 50 per cent of patients suffer because of superstition, ignorance, neglect or crudeness and cruelty of old style, native methods. For instance, sprained or dislocated joints are infected with needle (ch'im), Vesico-vaginal fistulae follow burn treatment of uterine prolapse, Pneumonia follows Measles, due to exposure, also blindness often occurs, due to neglect of eyes. Other causes of blindness are Trachoma, Gonorrhoea and injuries. One man with a bad compound fracture of lower leg had his leg dressed with a split chicken, the warm entrails being placed over the protruding bones, and came to us after a day or two. The odor was horrible and maggots wriggled in the wound. One of our Girls' School graduates after being treated by us for Pulmonary Tuberculosis with improvement and not being pleased that we still reported bacteria in her sputum when she thought she was well, left us and went to eating snakes, of which she has already eaten thirteen. A man with Syphilitic Dementia refused our treatment and went and bought himself one small root of wild ginseng for which he paid Yen 2,000. The owner of a native drug room in Taiku feeds a deer that he may cut his horns each year. The price of one year's growth is Yen 300.

PRACTICE OF MEDICAL MISSIONS IN KOREA

The centre of our work is the Severance Union Medical College and Hospital and Training School for Nurses where Korean Doctors and Nurses are prepared for service in the country hospitals and for private practice. Here, also, a start in Public Health work has been made, while a Public Health Department and Baby Clinic are in operation at the Seoul Evangelistic Centre. In Fusan, Kwangju and Taiku work for lepers is carried on. In the three institutions an average of 500 lepers is cared for in each place. Two or three doctors do more or less itinerating. The great bulk of medical mission work is being done in the different Mission Stations throughout all parts of the country.

HOSPITALS

Staff. While Severance has a staff of 9 foreign doctors, 2 dentists, a business manager, with 3 foreign and 12 graduate and 30 student Korean nurses, the country hospital, on an average, has 1¼ foreign doctors, 1½ Korean doctors, 1½ foreign nurses, 2 graduate and 6 pupil nurses.

Beds· While Severance has 92, the average number in a country hospital is 38—the smallest number being 12 and the largest 80.

Buildings: While three or four new hospitals are asked for, with the exception of an isolation ward, or similar small unit, the majority of institutions have no further building programs.

Heating: 87 per cent of the hospitals have central heating plants – of these 40 per cent are steam, 27 per cent hot water, 20 per cent hot air and 13 per cent native style and stoves.

Lighting: 87 per cent are lighted by electricity— the rest by kerosene.

Wat.. . . ..

87 per cent both hot and cold water. Apparently, therefore, most of our hospitals, from the view-point of buildings, heat, water, and light, are now prepared for efficient service. However, only about 60 per cent have isolation wards, only 47 per cent X-Ray machines—Only 47 per cent a definite method fo filing and indexing records of patients, while only 13 per cent have a method of following up cases from a medical view-point, and these only for special cases. About one half the hospitals make some effort to follow up cases from an Evangelistic view-point, and on an average two Evangelists are attached to each hospital.

Administration: Staff Meetings are held in 30 per cent of the hospitals—30 per cent have Administrative Councils while 40 per cent have neither. Ten per cent of the Councils do not function well. Only 30 per cent of the hospitals have Advisory Boards and 10 per cent of these do not function well.

Finances: Country hospitals receive on an average Yen 3,822 from Foreign Mission funds for current expenses—the smallest amount received being Yen 600 and the largest Yen 12,500. In addition to these funds a few hospitals get special appropriations for supplies and equipment. Of the total receipts of hospitals an average of 60 per cent is from native fees—the lowest percent being 30 and the largest 85.

Dispensaries: At Severance 66,132 treatment were given to out-patients during the year while the country dispensaries averaged 11,090—the minimum number being 7,145 and the maximum 31,567. In addition, an average of 385 visits were made to homes of patients from each dispensary—the smallest number of visits being 46 and the largest 974.

Policy of Medical Missions in Korea

As yet not well defined but all the Missions seem

to have decided not to extend medical work.

As yet no definite action has been taken to reduce the amount of foreign funds now being appropriated for medical work, though some effort has been made to reduce the number of institutions.

Foreign doctors and nurses are being supplied for vacancies only and any increase over the present number is not anticipated. Only a small number of hospital beds is being planned for and this increase is due to the three or four new hospital buildings asked for.

SUGGESTIONS OF NEEDS

More equipment, such as of X-Ray machines and laboratory apparatus.

Provision for caring for contagious cases in each hospital.

Method of filing and indexing records of patients in each hospital.

A system of following up all cases, both from medical and Evangelistic view-points.

Workers, Council, Advisory Board, Staff Meetings, etc in each hospital, that Koreans may assume a greater responsibility for the control and policy of our medical institutions.

A deputation of Medical Secretaries from, the Home Lands invited to visit Korea to help formulate a definite policy for the future of Medical Missions.

PART VI

OTHER ACTIVITIES

CHAPTER XVIII

WORK AMONG YOUNG PEOPLE

Rev. J. Gordon Holdcroft, D.D.

Probably no better statement of the general conditions as affecting Young People in Korea could be made than that prepared and adopted by the group of Christian Leaders and missionaries which met at the "Mott Conference" in December, 1925. The report of the Conference on "The Attitude of the Korean Youth Today toward Christ, His Church and His Program." is as follows:

"In the minds of those in closest touch with the rising generation in Korea today there is little doubt that there is a spirit of unrest which in part is manifesting itself in an attitude of antagonism to the Church and criticism of the existing religious order. This attitude is in evidence among the student class and the unemployed, especially in the larger cities In which, in a few instances, it has become outspoken. The unfriendly spirit toward the Church gives no evidence of serious antagonism to Christ or to His program.

"The source of this unrest can be traced in part to influences from Russia and to the literature which is in ci   ·   ·. · · !   T   · · · ·

consists of newspapers, pamphlets and magazines, printed not only in Korea but more especially in Japan, which are frequently critical of the Church and of religion in general. Even among those sympathetic to the Church there is a feeling that the program of the Church should be enlarged, its educational program rendered more practical, and its ministry made more effective to meet the intellectual and spiritual needs of the younger generation and t o lead them in their legitimate aspirations. The main source of discontent and complaint, however, not only against the Church but against government and authority and the existing social order is found in the present economic situation in Korea which is rendering it increasingly difficult for the Korean people to acquire a livelihood.

"In view of these facts it is our opinion that the situation demands greater exertion in winning our young people and in maintaining sympathetic personal touch with them. We feel also that there is need of more strenuous effort in reaching the non-christian students, and that to this end our Christian young people should be thoroughly prepared, intellectually and spiritually, for a leadership which shall command the respect and confidence of the rising generation whose minds have been confused by the sudden transition of Korea from the ancient order of life to the complex conditions of modern civilization with the concomitant doubts and perplexities of a materialistic education. An urgent call should be sent out to our Christian young men and women to devote their lives to consecrated and unselfish service in seeking to confront the youth of Korea with Christ in Whom they may have the abundant life of joy and peace."

As a general report the above is admirable and seems to be fully borne out by such information as reaches the writer. There is unrest both within and without the Church, and there is antagonism to and criticism of the Church. Almost every day, instances of this are discovered, and yet, often it is found, that much of this antagonism and criticism is due either to complete ignorance unenlightened, or to perversion brought about by the causes named above. Nevertheless even so, when this criticism and antagonism are intelligently met, often they are dissipated. A case recently occuring in Southern Korea is in point. A large gathering had come to criticise and to oppose. But when Christianity was clearly explained many left saying, "If that is Christianity we have no fault to find with it."

In the midst of this admittedly difficult situation such a possibility is enheartening. It is still further encouraging to know that more is being attempted for young people than ever before. Nearly every center of Christian work and influence has some provision for special work among young people, in addition to the schools which are provided.

Much of the work for young people, however, very properly, centers about effort for students, and in many of the larger cities special effort is being made for students. The Federal Council of Evangelical Missions' Committee on Student Work, for instance, has conducted a survey of student conditions in Seoul and report that there are about 10,000 boys and young men and about 4,000 girls and young women studying in the middle and higher schools of the city. Some few meet the need, the Committee is earnestly considering how it can do something to meet it, especially as the majority of homes in which students find lodging are non-christian and the owner of the house assumes no responsibility for the conduct of his boarders. Girls seem to be as free as the boys, to go and come at any hour of the day or night and to receive callers whenever they please. A number of places have been found

where students can be cared for under Christian
influences and it is found that the students respond
to this thought and care for their well-being. The
situation in Seoul is, without doubt, much the same
as in every student center in the country.

In regard to young people's work in general,
the Y.M.C.A. and, to a lesser extent, the Y.M.C.A.,
are becoming increasingly active and plans are in
course of preparation which will plant these organizations in many centers which hitherto have had
none. The Christian Endeavor and Epworth League
are also active and each reports that, while statistics
are not at hand, yet there is a rising tide of interest
in these forms of work and they are prized particularly because of the opportunity they furnish for
expression of the life within.

In regard to the possibility of enlisting Christian
young people in various forms of work, encouraging
success is being encountered. Perhaps one of the
most notable cases is the response to the need for
teachers of Daily Vacation Bible Schools. These
Vacation schools were held in every province in
Korea in 1925, to the number of 258 at least. They
enrolled 25,000 boys and girls and employed about
1950 teachers, the overwhelming majority being
young men and women. The great majority of these
teachers gave their time, free of charge, for at least
four weeks during the summer. This is notworthy
as indicating the spirit of Christian youth today.

All this show that while the situation as respects
Korean youth is now and in some respects startling
or even dangerous, yet young people are what young
people have always been, that is, eager for life, easily
led either wrongly or rightly, responsive to every
disinterested effort on their behalf, willing to listen
to the claims of Christ, willing to dedicate soul and
life to His keeping when they understand what is
involved, and ready for Christian service when there

is opportunity offered which is within power to embrace.

The future of the young people of the Church is, therefore, with Christ, if they are properly led, and there is a wide open path to the heart of the youth of Korea today, as never before, for all those who come with friendship, understanding and an earnest presentation of the Gospel.

———

CHAPTER XIX

FOLLOWING THE KOREANS ABROAD

Rev. C. A. Clark, D.D.

Korea, considering its lack of industrial and factory enterprises, is a densely populated country. It is only about the size of Minnesota or Kansas, or England and Scotland combined, and has but half the area of the main territory of Japan, but in this farming territory, where there are few large cities, is packed a population given by the census completed this month as just a little short of 20 millions.

Even before the annexation of the country by Japan in 1910, the movement of Koreans abroad had begun. Korea may conceivably be thought of as an island, for the Yalu River flows west to the Yellow Sea and the Tumen River east to the Pacific and both have their rise in the same beautiful lake high up in the crater of the Everwhite mountains on the border. Up and down the valleys of those two rivers all the years since the Mongols of Genghis Khan and the Manchus of later days ceased attacking the borders, Koreans have spread out on both sides of the river and at least 20 miles beyond to the great wall of mountains parallel to those rivers, which stands as a natural rampart.

Before 1900, little bands of them scaled that rampart and made homes for themselves in Kando, that No Man's Land of relatively unoccupied territory that used to lie between the thickly populated parts of Ch

The first Protestant Christians ever converted were those who came in touch with the Scotch and Irish missionaries as far north as Mukden and Newchwang. The first Korean baptised under Dr. Mc Intyre's preaching in Newchwang in 1875, was Mr. Saw Sang Yoon, still living in Whang Hai Province. From 1875 till 1900, these Scotch and Irish missionaries did much for the Koreans, particularly Dr. John Ross of Mukden who superintended the translation from Chinese into Korean of a Gospel or two and had them printed and sent in over the border while Korea was still a forbidden "Hermit Land."

In 1891, Drs. Moffett and Gale made an exploratory trip by pony and Chinese cart from Wiju to Mukden and then across Manchuria to Kangkei and to the east coast of Korea at Wonsan.

The first official movement of the Church in Korea to follow up these colonists across the border was in 1902, as we see from the Minutes of the Presbyterian Council that year, where a Committee was appointed "to consult with the Scotch Mission to see whether we or they were to be responsible for the Koreans in Manchuria." They asked the Korean Church to take the burden and from that time till today, North Pyeng An Presbytery has continuously maintained from one to a dozen pastors and local preachers, mainly in the province of Mukden, but also going far north into Siberia and west even to Lake Baikal.

Between West and East (or as it is called, "North") Manchuria, there are high mountains and dense forests, and no traffic goes through the barrier. The Northern Presbyterian work has been in "West" Manchuria and straight north up into Siberia. It early became so well established that strong churches were founded there and many of them were fully self-supporting altho the weak churches were assisted by the Korean Church . . . . ever put into the work until 1920 when the Scotch Mission agreed to form with the Northern Presbyterian (U.S.A.) Mission a joint Station at Hingking, they to care for the Chinese of the district and we for the Koreans. Two missionary families were sent from Korea. There are now 100 Korean churches connected with that Station, with 3,200 adherents of whom 2,213 are baptised. All of the, expense of the work, except the personal expenses of the missionaries, is paid by the Koreans of the district or those in Korea. There is a separate Presbytery in this field.

In 1921 the Northern Methodist Church in Korea opened work in this field, so it has been divided roughly between them and the Presbyterians for purposes of evangelization. They have nine pastors working in this field, one of whom is District Superintendent. They have 18 churches with about 1,100 adherents. Their total budget is Yen 11,550, of which Yen 2,500 yearly comes from America, Yen 4,000 from the Korean home churches and the balance from the churches themselves.

"North" Manchuria, the half over towards Vladivostock was first entered by the Canadian Presbyterians and Southern Methodists about 1908, but the latter did not follow up the work. In 1909 the Canadians established a Station at Yongjung which now has 12 resident foreigners. Around that Station are 106 churches with 6,049 adherents. This field is also a self-governing Presbytery's field.

The Southern Methodists from Korea again took up work in North Kando in 1922, and they now report there 10 preachers, 19 church buildings, and about 1,800 adherents who gave last year for their own work over Yen 4,000.

The national Presbterian Church of Korea was organized as an independent body in 1907. To celebrate the event they raised a Thank Offering to send a Fore   " t   t t,   ,   d t On b t   the

Yellow Sea south of Korea. Of their first seven ministers ordained that year, one was sent as a missionary. There are a score or more of churches on the island now and the work is nearly self-supporting though assisted somewhat by the Presbyteries of Chula Province.

In 1909, a call came from Siberia, and the Presbyterian Church sent one member of its second group of ordained ministers to be a missionary to the territory around Vladivostock and through the Maritime Province south of there. Since that time, churches have multiplied in that field until there are now 57 with 827 believers. · In 1922 a separate Presbytery was set up there. That year Dr. Foote, of the Canadian Mission, moved there to found a Station and stayed until driven out by the authorities.

Rev. J. O. J. Taylor of the Southern Methodist Mission opened work for his Church also in Vladivostock in 1920 and stayed there until driven out by the authorities. ·

There are churches now scattered all across Siberia to Lake Baikal and missionaries (Korean) of the various churches sent by the Churches of Korea or of Manchuria are caring for them, since American missionaries are not allowed to do so.

Between 1901 and 1905 great numbers of Koreans flocked to Hawaii, and in 1905 a petition came urging the Presbyterian Assembly to send them missionaries. It was found upon investigation, however, that the Methodists from the mainland were well able to care for them and so no missionaries were ·sent from Korea. There are now many strong, thriving churches there. ·

About 1905-6 a great body of Koreans migrated to Mexico to the neighborhood of Yucatan. No missionaries were sent from Korea to them, but, from individuals who have drifted back, we hear that there also the banner of the Cross has been upheld and

Christians have been true to their faith.

In 1909 the Presbyterian Church sent a worker to minister to the great number of Korean students who were flocking to Tokyo. In 1912 that work was made a union work with the two Methodist bodies, the Methodist and Presbyterian missionaries financing it and managing it on equal terms, Presbyterian and Methodist pastors being sent over alternately. That work has continued till today and the Korean Church in Tokyo is one of the largest Christian congregations in that city, about 200 meeting regularly. There are 586 Christians there, 179 of them baptised. There are seven meeting places in the neighborhood of Tokyo and Yokohama.

In 1924 the above work was enlarged by sending a pastor to the Kobe-Osaka-Kyoto district of Japan, and the American missionaries of that district personally contributed Yen 785 to help carry it on. There are 13 Korean Churches in that district and 400 Christians, of whom 114 are baptised.

In 1925 all of this work in Japan was turned over to the Korean Federal Council which corresponds to the National Councils in Japan and China and other countries. It hopes soon to send two more workers to Japan. There are said to be 150,000 Koreans now in Japan, according to the Government figures. These figures are usually old, however, and some claim that the number is nearer 300,000.

There are about 1,000 Koreans in Peking, of whom 600 are students and 100 are Christians. In 1924 the missionaries there were persuaded to subsidize a Korean Church to the extent of $500 Mex. The Chinese Churches gave $100 Mex., the Koreans there $270 Mex., and Yen 300 was sent for that year and this, and a pastor is in the work.

There are several hundreds of Koreans in Nanking who have a Korean pastor looking after them, suppor there, and the Presbyterian Church in Korea has promised Yen 300 a year.

For ten years there has been a Korean Church in Shanghai where there are several hundreds of Koreans. The work there has been assisted somewhat by individual missionaries there but no money has been sent from Korea for fear of political complications. Those are past now and the Presbyterian Church is hoping this year to send some help.

In America, there are thriving Korean churches in Seattle, San Francisco, Los Angeles and at other places on the Coast, and there are also groups of Christians in Chicago, New York and other cities. All are self-supporting so far as any help from Korea is concerned.

From the above it will seen that the Koreans have gone north, east, south and west. Perhaps a full million of them are now living outside of their native land. Wherever they have gone they have taken the Gospel with them, and, so far as possible, the Church in the home-land has followed them. The Presbyterian Church in Korea has also a real Foreign Mission fully supported by itself, working among the Chinese in Shantung, China, with a budget of Yen 17,000 annually and a force of three pastors and a doctor, with their families. The Korean Church is profoundly affecting the nearby Chinese Churches and stirring them for their task. We hope for the time when anyone meeting a Korean in a foreign land will know at once that he is a Christian and a soul-winner.

CHAPTER XX

THE EVANGELIZATION OF THE JAPANESE IN KOREA

Rev. F. H. Smith

As I look from my study window I see a famous old tree just beside the new Pai Chai School, which, it is said, was planted by Kato Kiyomasa, a famous Christian general, in June of 1592. He was one of the leaders in the invasion of Korea planned by Hideyoshi. The old tree stands as a mute reminder of the close relations that have always existed between Japan and Korea. In the arts and literature and religions of Japan one may find much that was passed on to her by Korea.

While the relations between the two peoples were of various kinds during the centuries of history, it was not till the close of the Japanese-Russian war that they really became very close. With the coming of Prince Ito as Resident General in 1906, and especially since the annexation in 1910, the connections between Japan and Korea have been increasingly intimate.

As late as 1912 two small boats of 1200 tons each, the Iki and Tsushima, one each way every twenty-four hours, were sufficient to accommodate the traffic. These were supplemented by two fine new boats built in Scotland which took the night runs each way, but soon proved inadequate and were in turn two years ago replaced by three fast 2300 ton liners which ran the day run in eight hours

night run in nine hours. They provide a morning
and night service both ways every day. In the busy
seasons in the spring and fall, when Korean students
and workmen are going to Japan and various types
of Japanese are coming to Korea, they do not suffice
and an extra boat each way must be taken from
the freight service to carry the passengers. There
are from 3,000 to 4,000 passengers a day in the busy
seasons. In addition to this ferry service of the
Railway Bureau there are other direct steamship
lines from Jinsen, from Genzan and from Seishin, so
that on some days there may be as many as 5,000
travellers on these connecting lines.

The increase in the Japanese population has
been a steady one of from 10 per cent to 15 per cent
a year since the establishing of the Residency General in 1906. When the writer was appointed to
Korea in 1914 the population was rated as 171,543.
By 1925 it had risen to more than 415,000. Even so,
they are not a very large percentage among the
more than 19 million Koreans.

As to the type of Japanese who are coming over,
one may say without fear of contradiction that they
are improving each year. In the earlier years there
were many of the adventurer, swash-buckling type
and many who were keen to get rich quickly no
matter by what means. Count Terauchi did a very
fine service in clearing out the worst of these and
sending them home. In the period just after the
war with Russia it was not uncommon to see a
Japanese kicking or striking a Korean but in the
past seven years of wide and constant travel the
writer has not seen one case of such ill-treatment.
The great majority of the Japanese settlers are merchants, tradesmen, teachers, officials, employees of
companies or banks, or those engaged in the transportation business, or on the railways, or in developing
some afforestation or irrigation plan. In the south there

are a good number of Japanese farmers and in other
parts of Korea Japanese are engaged in agriculture,
apple-raising, sugar-beet or silk-worm culture.   It
has been said that Japanese farmers are crowding
the Koreans out into Manchuria but the Koreans who
go to Manchuria are from North Korea where there
are almost no Japanese farmers. In South Korea
there may be a tendency for the Koreans to sell more
land than is for their best advantage, but the price
of land has advanced very greatly everywhere and in
some places hundreds of per cent. In any case the
Japanese have developed and reclaimed more agricultural land than they own. A recent investigation
by a reliable Christian gentleman places the Japanese holdings at 5.7 per cent of the total. At the
present time the increase of Japanese farmers is only,
about 100 per year which is less than the influx of
Chinese farmers. To succeed they must have some
capital, so the number is few. One often reads of
the failure of the Japanese as immigrants in Korea
and Manchuria. They fail in the same way and for
the same reason that American immigrants might fail
in Mexico. In Manchuria they can neither buy nor
lease land. As day laborers they cannot compete
with the Chinese or Koreans any more than an American laborer could compete with a Mexican, so there
are few of that class of people here.

Thus their distribution is largely determined by
their occupation. In Seoul there are 80,000, in Fusan
30,000, in Jinsen, Heijyo and Taikyu 20,000 each.
Fifty other cities, mostly ports or provincial capitals,
contain most of the others.   A few are found in
every village and hamlet. There are at least a general store keeper, a post-master, a school teacher and
a policeman.   Many of the officials by the time
they retire have acquired land, paddy fields or or-
chards, and settle in the country. With a large prop

of the higher and better officials, it has been a cust

there to live on their pensions. The change in the population and thus in the church membership too, each year, is tremendous.

The change to a new environment, the loneliness, oftentimes the temptations and the hardships, the freedom from the restraint of the family and its traditions fixed through the centuries, have all been factors favorable to evangelistic work in Korea, especially in the smaller centers. There has often been strong and bitter opposition on the part of the Buddhists who have been most faithful in following the Japanese wherever they go. They have had no success with Koreans but have been very successful with their own people, and one finds temples everywhere. But all in all the results obtained by Christian workers have been very satisfactory and the Nihon Kirisuto Kyokai, the Kumiai and the Methodist Churches at least, are strongly established in both Korea and Manchuria.

It has been interesting to watch the relations between the Koreans and the Japanese and observe how they influence each other. Many Korean missionaries would say that the coming of the Japanese into Korea has greatly slowed up, not to say, hindered their work. The change in government, the bringing in of a rushing, modern, materialistic civilization, the licensed brothel and in places direct opposition to Christianity by officials or educators, are some of the factors to be noted. The improved methods of communication, the excellent order maintained throughout the peninsula and the extended common education have been and are advantages more and more appreciated. At times, especially during the Independence Uprising, many missionaries thought the government anti-Christian, but it is doubtful whether any think that today. At the Mott conference no dissatisfaction was expressed as to the government rules or regulations governing

the churches or evangelistic work. On the other
hand the impact of the much advertised Korean
Church on the Japanese has been most disappointing.
I do not know of any Korean preaching to Japanese
though they have missionaries in China.
The results of Christianity in manhood,
character, honesty, industry, cleanliness, sanitation and order are not yet sufficiently clear.
Last August I asked a non-Christian police official
at Heijyo if they had much trouble in their work
with Korean Christians. He said that aside from
political matters the distinction was perfectly clear
and that the Christians were far superior to the non-
Christians. Nor can the Korean missionaries be
asked to give much time for the Japanese. The
language is an obstacle. They are burdened with
their own work. If they are too friendly to Japanese
it alienates the Koreans. Some of them have held
Bible classes, English classes and cooking classes for
Japanese, and some have taught in Japanese schools.
The Koreans as a whole find it very difficult to love
the Japanese, even the Christians, and though we
have tried to promote fellowship between the two
groups there is as yet no common standing ground.
At Seoul especially, the Japanese Christian leaders
have made several efforts to become friends with
the Korean pastors but the older pastors cannot speak
either Japanese or English and even to carry on
conversation is difficult. Of course too their hearts
are sore at losing their country. The younger pastors and leaders all speak Japanese, many of them
having studied in Japan, and one hopes for more
fellowship and mutual love and appreciation in the
not distant future.

The Japanese work in Korea was given a serious
set-back by the American Immigration Law but began to recover toward the end of 1925 as people
realize

Christianity. During the year the Congregationalists at Seoul erected a beautiful and well-appointed modern church building. The Methodists acquired a new self-supporting circuit with Shariin as a center. The Kanko Church attained self-support from the first of April.. Just now new buildings are in course of construction at Kanko and Taikyu which will strengthen the Methodist work in those cities. The total membership of the Japanese Christian churches is now given as 5,169.

The various missions in Japan have gradually come to see the needs of this field and have sent a few men. The Methodist Episcopal, Northern Presbyterian and American Board Missions are represented in Seoul, while the Anglican Mission assigns two or three men and women from the Korea Mission for this work. Miss Bertha Starkey was sent last year by the Womens' Foreign Missionary Society of the Methodist Episcopal Church. On a recent trip the veteran, Dr. R. E. McAlpine, was so impressed with the needs of the Southern Presbyterian field that he secured from his Mission permission to spend his time till furlough in southwest Korea where no foreigner penetrates. The Methodist South, the Union Church of Canada and the Australian Presbyterians ought to have one family each for Japanese work. In the large centers the Japanese pastors can pretty well take care of the situation but in the scattered towns and villages and among the students there is a limitless and fruitful field for the missionary. He finds numberless opportunities to help the Korean missionaries and Christians with the Japanese and can make his life count for international goodwill in a way that is not possible where he would deal with only one people. Seoul has become a great student center with Japanese and Korean students together in the new Impeiral University Preparatory School and the Technical, Medical and Law Colleges.

In addition there are two Japanese Middle Schools, two Girls' Higher Schools, not to mention a score of higher schools, public and private, for Koreans. It is hoped that several more families may be spared from Japan for this field of peculiar need and opportunity.

CHAPTER XXI

THE LAND PROBLEM

Rev. R. A. Hardie M.D.

The most hopeful sign in Korea today is that the most persistent complaint on the lips of the people is that they are losing their land. Great as was the loss of their political independence it was small compared with what the loss of economic control of their national resources would be, and if the cry we hear so constantly indicates that the Korean people are beginning to realize how serious a matter the loss of the agricultural possibilities is, and that they will undertake to put a stop to it there is still hope for them as a race, but if without action they simply bemoan what it is within their power, and theirs only, to control, the future is dark indeed.

Under the grasping despotism of the old hermit regime the people had no incentive to earn more than was necessary for a bare subsistence. There was no foreign market and if there had been, there was no adequate means of transportation, and if both had existed the farmers would have been squeezed dry by rapacious officials who valued their office mainly on account of the cold cash it brought them. Today the exports of Korea, which are mainly the product of the farm, are more than ten times what they were fifteen years ago, and the area of cultivation and the amount of production per acre is increasing so rapidly that in fifteen years more it will perh that Koreans are awakening to a realization of the future prosperity of agriculturists, and feel sorely the loss of their land.

When asked why the land is passing out of their hands Koreans say that when Annexation took place all crown lands were appropriated by the State,, and that later when all owners were required to register their lands and take out new deeds many were ignorant of modern legal procedure and consequently many villages and families lost their hill and ancestral lands through neglect to comply with the regulations. They say too that many country people were enticed into selling their farms by wily carpetbaggers or through the introduction of irrigation projects which in many cases cost more than they would or could pay; and that in others the old water sources were diverted so that they were soon forced to sell. Advantage is also taken of their weakness for borrowing, not only by avaricious money lenders but by loan associations which, on good security, lend at a much lower rate of interest than the exorbitant rates charged by Koreans. There are also semi-politico-religious organizations which prey upon the credulity of their fellow country men: for example, the agents of the Po-Chun-Kyo tell the farmers that Communism is certain to prevail in Korea in the near future and that as all land will then be equally divided among the people it will be to their advantage to sell even cheaply now because they will get back their share free when that fortunate day comes. Intelligent Koreans condemn the foolishness of men who are taken in by such propaganda but they also claim that it is winked at by the police and petty officials throughout the interior.

It is impossible to state definitely and up to date how much land is in the hands of the State, and of Japanese Companies and private owners. In the two South-West provinces (North and South

Chulla), generally spoken of as "the granary of Korea," it has been estimated that 75 per cent of the rice land has been mortgaged or sold for debt." The majority of the nearly 200,000 Koreans in Japan proper came from the four southern provinces (North and South Kyung Sang and Chulla) and as most of them say they were forced to leave their homes in search of some means of livelihood the conclusion is that a larger proportion of land has been bought by the Japanese in these provinces than in those farther north. According to the reports of the Governor General of Chosen for 1922-23, in addition to 22,800 Cho in actual use of the Government General itself at the end of March 1922, the State then controlled "about 7,020,600 Cho of forest and uncultivated lands, making the area, exclusive of land in military use, 7,043,000 Cho or about 30 per cent of the whole area of the country." In 1921 the State sold 17,499 Cho of rice-land, 15,855 Cho of upland, 926 Cho of residential land and 520 Cho of other land of 81,490 buyers, most of them probably Japanese, for the sum of 14,648,958 Yen. In 1922 8,273 Cho of rice land, 2,848 Cho of upland, 253 Cho of residental land and 261 Cho of other land was sold to 24,484 buyers for 2,473,181 Yen. Statistics recently secured from the office of the Seoul Press show that in 1924 the State owned 75,357 Cho of paddy fields and 41,270 Cho of dry land; and that the Oriental Development Company owned 54,397 Cho of paddy field, 19,797 Cho of dry land and 61,917 Cho of forest land. The above Statistics alone indicate that about one-tenth of the rice land and about one-quarter of other land under cultivation are owned by the State and the Oriental Developement Company. There are also other land companies which own large tracts of land and a considerable amount in addition to the above is owned by private Japanese of wh·   ⁷ ¹⁷¹ y··· ,¹· ¹,· ·¹ ·1 .¹   ·' ·, forestry and stock-raising at the end of 1924. Government statistics show that at the end of March 1923 there were Partnership, Limited Partnership, and Joint Stock Agricultural Companies with 53 Main Offices and 22 Branch Offices, and Forestry Companies with seven Main and three Branch Offices. Perhaps it is not too large an estimate to say that nearly two-fifths of the rice land and one-third to one-half of the dry land under cultivation has passed out of the ownership of Koreans.

It is in any case evident that the land situation is a very serious one for the Korean people and that nothing short of immediate and determined effort on their part can save them from complete economic disaster. Koreans in Japan say that in many parts of the country notices are posted offering farmers who will move to Chosen assistance to the amount of 200 Yen and even 400 Yen per household. The Seoul Press of Sept. 30th, 1925 stated that the Director of the Financial Bureau of Chosen was then in Tokyo asking permission to float a loan of one hundred and fifty million yen for the execution of public works and of obtaining from it a low interest loan of fifty million yen, including an item of two million yen for use as low interest loans to peasant proprietors for encouragement of agriculture, and that the authorities had in mind a plan of allowing two thousand yen per household to one thousand tenant proprietors and tenants. It is probable these loans are intended for Japanese farmers as the article stated that, "It is estimated that with 2,000 yen, an area of one chobu five tanbu of paddy fields and seven or eight tanbu of fields, can be purchased, cultivation of which will bring in an annual profit of 700 or 800 yen."

Much has been said in the public press during the past year regarding the necessity of supplementing Japan's food supply, especially of rice, one of the political parties stating that it would like to see an effort made to procure the right of developing the vast uncultivated areas of rich land in Manchuria and Siberia, working the same by Korean tenants and sending to Chosen ten million Japanese farmers to take the places these prospective tenants would vacate. We forbear comment on this frank suggestion more than to say that it ought to be published through the length and breath of the Korean Peninsula, and that if the knowledge of it is not sufficient to awaken Koreans to a sense of what they may have to face and to enable them to overcome their characteristic weakness for borrowing, the case is hopeless and they are doomed to serfdom at home and abroad. We know that many Japanese would not share the desire of the spokesman of the political party above referred to. Count M. Soejima's proposal in recent issues of the offiical Government organs of Chosen, that the Koreans should be given the hope of Home Rule ought also to be published in Korea in hope that it may encourage the Koreans to organize and hold what is still left of their birthright, success in which would mean as much to the future welfare of the Japanese nation as of the Korean people.

CHAPTER XXII

PROHIBITION FOR KOREA

Oh Keung Sun, M.D.

This subject has been considered by many leaders from the earliest times up to the present. Korean history tells us that in 51 B.C. one of the kings of Silla proclaimed a prohibition law at the time of famine in the country. Since that time it became a custom in Silana and Kokuryu, and under the Yi dynasty, that whenever a famine year came to the country, the king or even a governor, declared the prohibition law. Not only was such a law enacted or allowed during a famine but some kings prohibited the use of alcohol with a view to moral teaching. So we see that the people of long ago realized the harmful effects of alcohol both in economy and in morals.

There is some argument about the drink even now among Christians. Some say that drink is sin and some say it is not. I will not discuss the theological question but I want to say three things about the effects of alcohol.

1. From a medical standpoint alcohol is a powerful depressent or narcotic to the nervous system. It decreases or depresses the higher centers of *Will*, *Self-control*, *Reason* and *Judgment*. If you watch a drunkard, you will see it readily.

Habitual drinking of alcohol not only produces bad results on the individual but leads to hereditary abnorm as psychologists and neurologists prove by statistics, that insanity, idiocy and infantilism, are often due to alcohol and are diseases which destroy families and cause the fall of nations. The insane asylum is a splendid place to view the final results of alcohol in the subject or in his progeny.

2. From an economical standpoint. First let us examine the government statistics of consumption of liquors in the year 1923 all over Korea. (There are no later statistics).

a. From Japan proper or her territory:—

Sake	1,596,532 sho (sho=1588 quarts)	755,501
Sweet sake	50,89 sho	52,934
Beer	3,698,345 litre	712,353
Grape wine	124,779 ,,	184,297
Whisky and brandy	54,973 ,,	50,428
Spirits	232,325 ,,	51,010
Alcoholic Liq	487,411 ,,	106,435
	Total, Yen 7,912,961

b. From foreign countries:—

Spirits	30 litre	15,000
Wine	57 sho	63,000
Chinese wine	11,208 litre	4,906
Beer	1,191 ,,	1,429
Grape wine	27,379 ,,	19,277
Whisky and brandy	9,072 ,,	24,623
Alcoholic Liq.	3,094 ,,	7,113
	Total, Yen 135,348

c. From Korea herself:—

Spirits and wine 1,591,048 koku
(koku=39.7033 gallons or 4,0629 bushels)   45,376,983
                                  Grand Total Yen 49,347,470

In the second place, the statistics of Seoul City alone show a consumption in the year 1924 as follows·

·. Korea's products·

Cloudy wine (*Toak-ju*) 26,078 Koku cost Yen 573,730.96

> One koku of Toak-ju equals 3 Tu of rice and one Tu equals 3.9703 gallons.

Clear wine (*Chung-ju*) 14,161 koku cost Yen 778,955.52

> One koku of Chung-ju equals 4.5 Tu of rice.

b. Japanese and Chinese products:—

Spirit (*So-ju*) 774 koku   cost Yen 77,048.70

> One koku of So-ju equals one koku of rice.

Sake	3,492 koku	cost Yen 419,055.86
Spirit	67 „	5,378.96
Refined wine	18 „	7,404.25
Fruit wine (German)	18 „ .	6,527.75
Whang-ju (Chinese)	92 „	2,035.28

Total quantity of liquors	44,704 koku	
„ quantity of rice-wine	15,283 „	
„ value in money	Yen 1,870,326.78	

Now, let us see how much is consumed and also how much is spent per individual. The present population of Seoul city is 297,456 including Japanese and foreigners. That includes 154,106 males and 143,350 women. If we leave out the women, one man on the average drinks two Tu and nine and a half sho per year. At the same time, he spends Yen 12.13½ for liquor. At the same rate, if the seventeen million people of Korea spend Yen 12.13 per year per capita what an enormous total! In these days, people are talking about economic depression in Korea. Do they realize that they are spending money for nothing?

Let us see what the leading men of the United States say about the results of prohibition. Mr. Swift, president of the National Bank of Auburn, N. Y., says that the value of the city property is going up more and more. President Scott, of Reo Motor Car Co. of Mich., says that the sale of motor cars is increasing since the institution of prohibition. Dr. Fisk, of an insurance Company, says that prohibition is be̲i̲ ̲.̲ ̲ ̲t̲.̲ ̲w̲i̲t̲h̲ ̲.̲   ̲(̲   ̲ ̲.̲

I am glad and thankful that the W.C.T.U. in Korea is fighting this evil. In Proverbs, xxiii:21, we read "For the drunkard and the glutton shall come to poverty; and drowsiness will clothe a man with rags."

3. From the educational standpoint, the statistics of a number of primary schools and pupils in the city are as follows:—

a. Japanese primary schools..........   10
    Total number of pupils..........   10,484
    Total expenditure ....Yen 422,333

b. Korean primary schools......... ..   11
    Total number of pupils..........   12,827
    Total expenditure ....Yen 385,631
    Grand total ....Yen 807,964

What a difference in the amounts we are spending for education and for drink! It is a shame for the city of Seoul to spend double the amount of money for the drinking of liquors that it spends on education. People say that the want to educate their children but that there are no schools for them. If they want to have more schools for their children let people stop wasting their money on drink.

I noticed in the newspaper that the government is planning to increase rice production in Korea. That is well and good but I would suggest that the government teach the people to use the rice for food but not for liquors. All Korean wines and Japanese sake are made out of grains. What is the cause of starvation and poverty? I say that wine is the cause in Korea. In our fight against wrongs in Korea, we must not forget that the great enemy before us is *liquor*.

CHAPTER XXIII

WHAT KOREA HAS LOST

Rev. J. S. Gale, D.D.

The last quarter of a century has wrought more unexpected changes in Asia than the whole millennium preceding. Some say these changes are all for the good, some say for evil only. The changes are here, however, and are here to stay.

Let us examine for a little Korea's case and find if possible what these changes are and what they mean.

First, the great ideals which filled her soul for centuries are gone. No people were ever blessed with so mighty a moving picture as were the people of Korea in the history that they studied, learned off by heart, meditated on, talked over, dreamed of—a history stretching all the way from 3000 B.C. to 1000 A.D., four millennium of time in which the film reeled off great kings, great saints, great scholars, the ruling symbol ever being the Book not the Gun. Kings there were of unsullied character, one who brought in the Goldren Age; another who drained off the Noahic Deluge and saved the world; still another who offered himself a sacrifice and forgot even the cries of his little child in his zeal to uplife the state; kings like Moon and Moo, sages like Confucius who have lived for a thousand years in the imagination of this people, urging them on to good deeds and great. We see t · le

life · · · · · · · · · · · · · · · · · · · .50

A.D. He it was who invented the alphabet that we use today. He also worked with his father at moveable type years before Gutenberg; he it was who made arrangement for the orderly service of the hours on the water-clock. He it was who became Korea's master mind and saint, who made the deep things of religion his soul's delight, moving as he did among pictures of the saints on the walls of his palace and hearing the echoes of the Book of History ever in his heart. So true a king never lived. England's Alfred was good, but he was an unlettered peasant compared with Korea's highly trained, highly enlightened King Se-jong.

I might enlarge on this to the extent of a volume but I shall let it suffice to say that all these ideals are gone, for the world today cannot even spell out the books in which they are written much less meditate on their teachings. All these four thousand years, rich with earth's highest treasure are gone, good men and great wholly forgotten.

Second: Religion has departed from this people. The missionary, however, is here. Yes, and a powerful hold he had on the past generation, but that is gone likewise and his influence is diminishing. But truly, now, did Korea have a religion? She had indeed, if the definition of the Twentieth Century Dictionary is to be taken as true, "recognition of and allegiance in manner of life to a superhuman power to whom service is regarded as justly due." The East has had many great religious souls; Whang-je who left his throne 2300 B.C. to talk to the angels about the life that would lead to heaven; the Old Philosopher, the Buddha, how many on down through the ages, to the faithful priests, whose lives are recorded on the stones that stand by Korea's highway, to the saint Yool-gok, who lived in Queen Elizabeth's time and dared maintain that it was that God was God. Yool-gok said, "The really great man is anxious about Religion, and not about his accumulated treasures. Avoid filling your mind with the unclean manners of earth, fill it rather with the purities of heaven. Your call is to study carefully the Sacred Books, to hold the straight and honest way, with sincerity in all your actions. Let this be your dearest aim without ever for a moment thinking yourself good."

Outside the East Gate of Seoul is a great temple built in the year that Shakespeare was doing the Merry Wives of Windsor, built in honour of the God of War, a Chinaman of 300 A.D. What was this God of War noted for? Two things; first, he never told a lie, and, second, women were safe under his protecting hand. Though very fierce of face with his three pointed beard, yet he was a religious man, and one who served his day guided by a heavenly vision. Thus has he stood as a great model for a thousand years. But he too, has gone and Yool-gok's words are silent. Their very memory is blotted out and their names are never heard on the lips of this generation. Thus has religion receded from the active stage of life and today sees Korea's world without any standard of right doing, right speaking, right thinking. What desolations we behold!

Third: China once called Korea the "Land of Courtesy" (Ye-eui chi-pang) seeing she was governed in her life by those ceremonies that had come down through many centuries. The Five Relationships expressed it in a word: the courtier's devotion to the king; the son to the father; the wife to the husband; the brother to the brother, the friend to the friend. Hanging on these with the round of the year, the month, the day, came the ceremonies that governed life. In sweet accord therewith children bowed their goodnight to parents and made their respectful greeting in the morning. All stood as fathe .d ..thei .....d .. .. a

circle of reverence to parents dearly beloved. Such
was the children's world. When days of sacrifice
came they were all on hand. Long distances were
travelled to take part in the season's remembrances.
A son would strike off a finger to prove his devotion;
or bow before his mother's grave night and morning
for three long years. Men may smile today at such
crude methods of expressing the heart, but in the
true estimate of the ages it will be accounted beautiful. But whether it be accounted good or bad all
is gone today, and state ceremony, social ceremony,
religious ceremony, as known to Korea for two thousand years, have disappeared from the life of this
people as clean as you would wipe a dish.

Fourth: Music and Art are as though they had
never been. The present generation of Korea smiles
at the unseemly sounds its fathers called music, for-
getful, meanwhile, of their own attempts at foreign
imitation. Korea's music was based on the five notes
of the Oriental scale and to those who exercised patience enough to enter into its inner world, it was
full of a far-away charm that grew on one's heart
and ear. The music of the Confucian ceremony,
while odd to us, is one of the oldest expressions of
ancient religious ceremonial. But today the present
generation seems afraid of it, afraid to be caught
singing even a simple folk-song, though the charm
of the folk-song is infinitely superior to anything
found in the newer Western methods. The writer
can still hear the soft notes of the voice of twenty
years ago wafted along the evening twilight—delight-
ful, while the tender memory of it is buried now
beneath brass instruments blaring forth *Old Grimes*,
Marching Through Georgia, *Clementine* and whatnot.

Beautiful pictures were painted by her great
artists in days gone by, men and women, portraits,
too, such as the world has rarely seen. In fact the
oldest picture in Japan Proper today, prized beyond

rubies, is that in the temple of Pup-ryoong Sa near Nara, a painting by a Korea Crown Prince. A visit now to the annual exhibition of Art in Seoul is a sad journey indeed and impresses one with the fact that a land once matchless in touch and colour has indeed today lost it all.

Fifth: Korea has lost the greatest literature of the world. We have traces of profound Korean scholarship dating back to the Han Kingdom of China, or the beginning of the Christian Era. No books of that period remain, but on stones, on tiles, in tombs, and among the ancient literary remains of China are found samples of Korea's skill. The script in which she wrote is called *Wenli*, the Confucian style of the Sacred Books, the Book of History, the Book of Poetry, in fact the form in which all the great literature is found, that in which Korea's scholars were trained and equipped till 1894, that which has continued as a means of recording thought longer than any other written language, coming down from the dim days of 2000 B C. till the present time when my honoured friends Messrs. Yi, Cho, and Kim (men of the receding generation) write in the same classic style—a style accounted old even when Confucius and Mencius were born. It embraces all of the literature of the Chinese people as well as that of Korea, a literature covering a much longer period and of a much wider compass than that of any other part of the world. The Korean scholar could read it with ease, yes, sing it off with delight. Today all this has dropped out of his knowledge never to return. For example the father, a master of the old school, sits with the accumulated volumes of his work at his side, while his son, a graduate, it may be of the Imperial University, cannot read them to save his life. Such is Korea of today, a land once great in literature, stripped today with not a trace of it left. . . . .

attempts at poetry that we see, all give proof of how
great the loss has been.

Sixth: The woman's world has been turned up-
side down with law and order gone. The insidious
teachings of the West, present day tendencies, loose
novels and moving pictures have wrought their worst
on Asia. Especially is this seen in the relation of the
Asia. Especially is this seen in the relation of the
sexes. Women are out in the open as they please.
"Do not women of the West even so?" they ask.
When the wife of England's former Chancellor of
the Exchequer can write as though it were a noble
and inspiring thought: "Free as the wind, the
Socialist wife will be bound only by her natural love
for her husband and children" and that divorce
"will be made more easy of accomplishment." Also
that incompatibility of temperament will be a ground
for "complete dissolution of the contract with leave
to enter into another marriage," (The Woman Socialist 61,62) what need we expected of disordered
Asia?

Such teaching the young woman drinks in daily,
and the scandal of the movies she beholds night by
night so that, between the two, her innocent soul is
whirled along to do just what her fathers told her
was wrong; what Confucius warned against, and
what the Gospels hold up as darkest sin. The present generation has but few knights-errant out to
save womankind. The spirit of today would rather
say, Trap her, Lie in wait for her. Such is the so-
called civilization of the Twentieth Century as Korea,
beholds it. All the missionary effort in the world
cannot stay it any more than the children of the
village can with uplifted hands stay the tidal wave
that moves in from the Pacific. The womanhood
of Korea has no standards left and her only source
of literary entertainment is the Yun-ai So-sul, the
modern love story.

Seventh: Dress. Korean dress is a matter of interest. white from top to toe except the hat that crowns it. The while dress came, they say, with Keuija (1122 B.C.). Korea being located at the east compass point, as far as China is concerned, should really, according to Oriental philosophy, dress in blue or green, white being left to the West, Tibet or Tartary. Several attempts have been made to change from white to blue, but the answer has always been, "Keui-ja gave us white and white it shall be." It has remained white with, of course, extra tints for ceremony, for state occasion, for marriage, for office, etc. Nothing in the way of dress could show more variety of colour, or a greater perfection in the fineness of its fabric. The writer still remembers how wild and unkempt he felt when first ushered into the presence of a Provincial Governor, who, dressed in the proper fashion of his high office, looked like an inhabitant of some fairy sphere. The ancient dress that was expressive in every seam and fold of some thought deeply engraven on the life of the people is gone and instead of Keui-ja's hat we have the derby, the slouch felt, the stiff straw, or, like the last rose of summer, a remnant of the old horsehair. On the feet are some adaptation of the foreign shoe, in the case of school boys, always unblacked, often unlaced, with the tongue lolling out and the strings a tangle of confusion, where formerly, the Korean foot, shoe and sock, were the neatest combination in the world. Between hat and heel is the long roundabout (*turumaki*) still. A student of the Government University recently asked the writer what he thought of the *turumaki*. He said he thought it very becoming and also very useful. The young man smiled a sort of condescending smile and remarked, "I think it very folish. I will fight the *turumaki*" the confusion seen in the soul these days, its lack of all standards, its loss of everything that made its world one of the oldest, the best, the most highly to be honoured that civilization has yet wrought out of the varied tribes of earth.

It rests with the missionary today not to make Korea's world more confused than ever by introducing methods and manners unsuited to her but rather to pass on those quiet, unobtrusive, all conquering tenets of Christianity, not seen in outward show, but hidden deep in the heart. They alone are of value, they alone can offer hope in such a day as this where an ancient people has lost her ideals, her religion, her ceremonies, her music, her language, her woman's world and even her dress.

CHAPTER XXIV

WHAT THE KOREANS ARE READING

Rev. H. Namkung

Anyone who reads modern Korean literature will easily find that the papers and books are filled with the spirit of communism, socialism and Bolshevism, and anybody who understands clearly the situation and circumstances of the Korean people will not wonder very much at this. All these isms are not their own inventions, but have been imported from foreign countries. Geographically Korea is connected with Russia, the hot-bed of Bolshevism, politically she is under the autocratic government of Japan, and as a consequence the economic condition of the people gets worse and worse every day. A large part of the natural resources as well as an immense area of land are owned by Japanese. Thousands of poor farmers are driven out every month to the cold regions of Manchuria and Siberia. Socialism has indeed a very rich field in Korea especially in the south, where the severe distinction between poor and rich exists. It is only natural that these movements should be more marked south of Seoul than in the north. The living conditions of each class greatly different. In the north the economical situation is pretty much alike among the peoples but not in the south. In the south most of the lands are possessed by a few rich people, both Koreans and Japanese, and the great mass of poor farmers are workin maık to the missionaries who are working in the south that they should consider whether it is a wise policy to put emphasis on tho strict self-support policy which is being used In the north.

I find almost every article, whether it be prose, poetry, editorial, or story, full of complaints and murmurings which may be the natural expression of a people who live under such conditions.

In the first place I shall tell of some socialistic tendencies found in "Tong-A Ilpo," then I shall quote a few extracts from the Anti-Christian Movement which appeared ın November, 1925. Lastly I shall add some of the leading thoughts of Korean leaders concerning church matters.

"Tong-a Ilpo" of Feb. 9th, 1926, under the heading of "Mankilling Civilization," says "The aim of the capitalist is to get profit. It is a well-known fact that no business man would attempt to open any business if he had no hope of making profit out of it!

"The capitalist, in various ways does his best to make more money—he pays low wages to his laborers, he makes all the goods possible in a short space of time, and he sells them at as high prices as possible. Above all, it is also a fact, that ın order to put less money into his business, he does not pay much attention to the accommodations in his factory. Under such motive and spirit it is natural that he should not have any sympathy with humanıty, factory or anything else except profit. A modern factory, squeezing the labourers, ıs a slaughterhouse of mankind. It is not only so ın factories, but ıt ıs equally true in the mines of the mountains and the fisheries of the sea. Whenever profit can be obtaıned by the capıtalist, labourers are losing their precious lives. Oh you men who give your best efforts to maıntaıııı, the pıesent cıvilızatıon of capıtalism, what is the aim of your social ideal, especially your modern social ideal? Is it protecting human lives or slaughtering them?

"There are many so-called peace-lovers who neglect the fact of the killing of men in factories, and by machinery while they condemn the killing of men in warfare. Aren't they men who, by praising the one and condemning the other, approve these forms of killing the unfortunate?

"We are told that the number of fatalities in factories in the State of Pensylvania U.S.A. in 1924 far surpassed the number killed in the American-Spanish war, and that the number wounted in factories in that State in the same year was 174,000, a greater number by far than of those who were wounded at the great battle of Meldan.

"This is only an illustration of what happened in America, but it may be the same throughout the whole world wherever the so-called civilized nations, whose foundations are built on industry, exist. According to this view no one would deny that the civilization of capitalism is the civilization of man-killing!'"

The Korean Sunday School National Convention was held at Seoul for one week from October 22nd. last.   During that time also another interesting assembly was held in the same place.   That was the Anti-Christian Movement.   But curiously enough that movement was checked by the police power of the city. In a special number of "Kaibyuk" November, 1925, quite a number of articles concerning this are fround, of which I quote a few extracts from one as follows·

"The Christian says that the Christian religion is communistic and if the world follows the word of Jesus it will become a ocmmunistic society. If it is so, wl   5 to protecting this religion and forbidding the Anti-Christian Movement against it? This action calls for serious consideration. Now the evidence is clearly set forth. No orator can deny the fact. It is because religion takes the same stand as the modern police. In order to protect modern society both police and religion take the same step. The condition being such it is quite reasonable that the police should protect religion and that religion in turn, should receive the protection of the police!"

At the request of the editor of the Magazine concerning this movement, Mr. Hugh Shin, the general secretary of the Y.M.C.A. expresses his views as follows:

"I divide the movement into two. The recent movement is a movement of Anti-Christianity but not opposed to Christ. There may be objections to the Christian church as it is now but not against the personality and spirit of Christ Himself. There are in fact reasons to be urged against the church as it now exists, together with the men who constitute it. History up to the present proves the fact that the church itself is not transformed capitalism, yet it is a fact also that the church has been utilized and influenced by the rich people..... Under such circumstances that the Christian church should be attacked by socialists is rather natural. Whether there be an Anti-Christian Movement or not, the Christian church of today must be changed. It must be a church for the poor people—a church working for the welfare of the poor people!"

Under the caption of "New Christianity" in The Christian Messenger of December 30th. 1925, Rev. Chai Pil-Keun M.A. of Tokyo University, Professor in the Union Christian College of Pyengyang in suggestions made to missionaries said: "I hope missionaries will send many useful Korean young people to foreign countries to study Christianity there that they may perfectly digest the thought and make it their own. Then let them come back and do their own work. I think it is necessary that they should gradually turn the work over to the Koreans as soon as they find Koreans who are able to undertake the work." Then he turns his admonition toward Koreans. "We Koreans," he says "should not solely depend on foreigners, but whatever it may be, whether the propagation of religious doctrine, the establishment of educational work or whatsoever the movement may be, let it be tried by Koreans with their best effort; their full strength and ability...The recent China trouble is in the main the result of the awakening of the Oriental mind. Now if the western thought and the western system are not easternized by the people of the East, the inevitable result will folloN that there will be a terrible conflict and clash between the two. It may temporarily be painted and bandaged but it never can be delayed for long.....I call your attention to the fact that if Christianity be not Koreanized in Korea it can not Christianize the Korean people. We must make a new 'Christianity out of the old ...Let the Koreans possess their own Christian religion. Let them construct a Christian religion of their own. Christianity is the same and the Bible is the same book but it is our own business to make it our own, as a new and fresh religion."

"Under the caption of "Idol" Prof. Kangmai says," Idols are forbidden among Christians....We do not worship mountains, water, stone or anything of that kind yet we have another form of worshipping idols —more horrible and more dangerous than to worship mountains, water, stone or anything else." Then he sets forth how a simple faith was taught by Jesus— "repent, the kingdom of heaven is at hand. I am the way, the truth, and the life." He further describes how the Christian religion has been modified by many hand t t Greek. d Ar to Spee. "Tus

evangelism has been changed into ecclesiasticalism.
A Gospel of the free and spiritual life, such as redemption and new birth, is departed from, to be
taught through various forms of rites, doctrines and
systems of church government.   It seems that the
church takes the first seat and the Gospel a second.
Church is the higher and God the lower. Money by
which the church is to be organized comes first, and
the Gospel which is necessary to redemption and new
life comes next. Those who live a clean life and
have the indwelling of the Holy Spirit, honoured by
God, take the lowest seat in the church but those
who have a goodly appearance in the eyes of men
without regard to their spiritual bankruptcy, can
have the privilege of occupying the high seats in
the church, and of being placed in positions where
they can rule the believers. Not only does such a
man himself think it right, but the church recognizes
he himself thinks it right, but the church recognizes
its reasonableness because such men pay the church
expenses. This is, we are told, a fact of what has
recently occurred in the church of Great Britain and
America. Such a system and such an organization is
nothing more than an idol. Especially in Korea the
Gospel was introduced by American Sects. It seems
that it is suffering under that system and organization, and that the preaching of the truth of the Gospel,
—the doctrine of now spiritual life—is too much neglected. If we are under the bondage of an ecclesiastical system and organization, and neglect the truth of
God it is truly idolatry. Our faith must go back to the
original faith of the apostles, which was pure and
spotless. We must come out from all kinds of idolatry, visible and invisible, and turn to our pure and true
God. This is the very urgent step to be taken by
the modern Korean church. Oh, what will we do
with these idols?"

The following article is less important yet instructive to those who are interested in the educational work. This is a criticism of the instruction given by the president of one of the mission schools, found in "Kaihyuk," in the special New Year's number, 1926.

In his instruction to the students, the president, Mr. W., said: "The purpose to which we put this building is to train Christian leaders; therefore, if there is any one who is not willing to trust in Jesus let him leave school."

'Mr W., we do not ignore what you have said that the school, hospital, or whatever institution you may have is nothing more than the means through which you may win Christians. But isn't it too harsh and oppressive? Those who study science would not look upon Jesus as being so great and so divine as you do. The great crowds who are suffering from poverty would not believe the superstitous Bible and look for the second coming of Christ.... Modern education should be scientific. We Koreans need scientific education. We are not begging your mercy and grace."

This is only the cold criticism of the Anti-Christian spirit, but permit the writer of this article to say a few words with the purpose of helping our missionaries, especially those who are facing the difficult problems of educational work in Korea, as to the general attitude our missionary friends should take toward our young Koreans.

I assure you that Mr. W. spoke the truth. It is his duty to say that. It is, indeed, our purpose to educate our Christian children and train our Christian workers. It is not merely for the sake of national education. But I am sure that we Christians should not forget that whatsoever instrument we have, in the name ⸱. ⸱ ⸱   ;h which we may win some souls for Christ. We must not ignore that we are fishers of men. A fisherman ought to know how to use proper bait in order to catch fish. The success or failure of mission work in Korea today, I think, largely depends on how much he understands the psychology of the people. I honestly hope that our missionary friends will see the changing conditions of the people. It is time for the missionary to use his best trained psychology to be applied to his every day contact with Korean young people.

PART VII

OBITUARIES

Dr. Eugene Bell

On September 28, 1925 Rev. Eugene Bell, D.D. died at his home in Kwangju, Korea after several years of failing health. With the passing of this pioneer missionary the Southern Presbyterian Mission lost one of its members whose life was characterized by able leadership, wise statesmanship and depth of insight into Bible truths.

Dr. Bell was born at Scott's Station, Kentucky April 1, 1868. He was graduated from Central University of Kentucky in 1891, from Kentucky Theological Seminary in 1894, and in 1895 he sailed for Korea. During his early days in Korea Dr. Bell lived in Seoul and his itinerary included South Chulla Province, which at that time was six days distant from Seoul by pack pony. In 1899 he opened Mokpo Station in the South and six years later Kwangju Station.

During his thirty years of service Dr. Bell saw the Presbyterian Church of Korea grow from its infancy to a self-governing Assembly divided into twenty-one Presbyteries. He saw the local church which he established in Kwangju grow into four congregations of about a thousand attendants, and the girls' and boys' schools which he opened develop into institutions training hundreds of students. Moreover by his tireless itinerating he established many groups of Christians in the country districts.

In 1904 he lost his first wife, and the

Presbyterian Theological Seminary at Pyeng Yang and in 1914 he served as moderator of the General Assembly of the Korean church. Though active along many lines Dr. Bell also found time to do literary work, translating among other things the Church Book of Order and some excellent studies in Romans.

Dr. Bell is survived by his wife, three sons, Henry, Eugene and William and by his daughter, Mrs. W. A. Linton of Kunsan, Korea.

Mrs. Wm. P. Gilmer

Mrs. Katherine Newman Gilmer passed away very suddenly on March 27, 1926, at 2 p.m., in Mokpo, Korea.

In the summer of 1923, Miss Katherine Newman of Baldwyn, Mississippi, U.S.A., came to Mokpo as a teacher of missionaries' children. On June 1, 1924, she was married in Seoul, to Dr. William P. Gilmer who is in charge of the French Memorial Hospital in Mokpo, and became a regular member of the Southern Presbyterian Mission.

Mrs. Gilmer is survived by her husband and baby daughter, Kathryn Newman Gilmer. In the homeland, her mother and several brothers and sisters survive her.

Her sudden death was a sad shock to the entire Mission and especially to Mokpo Station where her spirit and her cordial hospitality in her home will be sorely missed.

From our human standpoint, it seems to us that her "sun went down while it was yet day," but we "know Whom we have believed" and we know that He makes no mistakes in His dealings with His children here.

Miss Pauline Glass Randle

The death of Pauline Glass Randle on May 19th, in Seoul, Korea, closed the earthly life of a young woman of rare attainments and usefulness, and a beloved missionary of the Womans' Missionary Council.

Miss Randle suffered from a sudden attack of appendicitis. At Severance Hospital, Seoul, she received every tender care and the best medical and surgical attention possible under modern science. The beautiful foreign cemetery overlooking the Han River has become a very sacred place to our Mission, and there, side by side with Ruby Kendrick and Mrs. J. P. Campbell, she rests.

Miss Randle was the daughter of Rev. and Mrs. Robert Randle of the Louisiana Conference. She was well prepared to render beautiful service: she was a granduate of Mansfield, Scarritt and Emory. She had a splendid business training and was gifte. in music and had artistic talents.

In August, 1918 Miss Randle came to Korea. She gave herself in her whole-hearted way to mastering the Korean language and made a marked success in it, giving evidence of ability in the language by the unusual ease with which she read the Chinese. Truly she was one of the best equipped workers Korea has ever had.

During her first term of service, Miss Randle's appointments were Songdo and Choo Chun in evangelistic work. On February 13, 1925 she returned from furlough, and had just started upon her new work in Chulwon when she was called up higher.

Miss Randle was quiet, reserved and did not make friends readily but when she did her friendship was beautiful and faithful to the end. There was no limit to her willingness to sacrifice herself; she g... ... ...

work. Her rules for herself were strict and hard— one of her Bible women said in speaking of her: "When she was in the country she seemed never to think of her body, she did not take time to cook or eat, and many times kept on the road when far stronger workers had fallen by the way.",

Mr. Stokes, in speaking of Miss Randle at her funeral, said that the one word which best described her was "dependable,"—when she once set herself a task to do, all might be well assured that it would be accomplished with perfection of detail. Nothing that was worth while doing at all was given less than her best effort.

She loved Korea and the Korean people, and was greatly beloved by them. They realized that she was glad to give them her very best and that she reserved no part of her time or strength. Her willingness to return to her station this fall alone, after her companion should return to America, is indicative of her character. She was not strong physically, and yet she did not consider even this, in her desire to do the thing that was best for the work.

The life of this splendidly gifted and well prepared woman seemed just begun. We cannot see how it was that she should have been taken just at this time when she was needed as never before. We believe that the life and death of the saints is in the Master's hands—He allowed it to be so, and it must be best. She is taken, and we are left. Why? As the seed of corn must fall into the ground and die, even so may the story of her life and sacrifice be the instrument under God, to bring light and inspiration to many young people in leading them into service for Him in this land. One of her helpers in Chulwon in speaking of her home-going said: "She did all that came to her hand so perfectly that God

called her to the Glory Land because He needed some
one up there to help Him in just her way."

Mrs. J. C. Thomas

The members of Pyengyang Station feel that
they have sustained a personal loss in the death of
Mrs. Thomas at Mansfield, Ohio on February 11th.
in the home of her daughter, Mrs. Mowry, a member
of the Station, and desire to express to Mr. and Mrs.
Mowry their sympathy in the sorrow that has come
to them.

We were looking forward to Mrs. Thomas' returning with them to Pyenyang after furlo to live
among us again. God, in his wisdom and love had
another plan for her. He has called her to the
Heavenly Home and we rejoice in the blessed hope
that we have of meeting her and other loved ones
in that better land where there will be no more
parting, neither sorrow nor dying.

During the seven years of her stay in Pyengyang,
Mrs. Thomas endeared herself to us all. Pure wo-
manliness combined with courage. of a high order
in meeting and overcoming the difficulties of a
strange environment, with failing physical strength
and a sympathetic and helpful interest that included
all in the community, from little children to people
near her own age, made her short sojourn among
us a blessing and a help. Her personal attractiveness
was a delight to us all. Her spirit was the spirit
of youth, never that of old age, and this was one of
her chief attractions and one of the secrets of her
influence with all classes of people.

Her influence with the boys and girls of the
Foreign School Dormitory during her years of residence there was always on the side that made for

the highest ideals in speech and conduct, and the
Foreign School will long remember and appreciate
the good service she rendered it for several years.

We will miss her in our community life and
individual lives. The Koreans and Japanese whose
lives she touched will feel that they too have lost
a friend. We all appreciate the privilege that has
been ours in having had the friendship of Mrs.
Thomas and would at this time assure Mr. and Mrs.
Mowry and their children, Mrs. Thomas' sister in
Chicago and other relatives, of our sincere sympathy
in their loss and sorrow and of our prayers that the
memory of this sweet and noble life may continue
to be a benediction to them.

Mrs. F. M. Stiles, Jr.

Louise Armisted was born in 1897 in Franklin,
Tennessee, where she spent her girlhood days. After
finishing her education at Ward-Belmont in Nashville,
Tennessee, she was married to Dr. Frank M. Stiles
Jr. in the fall of 1917. They left immediately for
Korea, where Dr. Stites took up work in Severance
Union Hospital in Seoul. From the beginning Mrs.
Stites took an active interest in her husband's work
and showed the true missionary spirit by cheerfully
remaining on the field in spite of the continued in-
validism of her mother, whose condition was a constant source of anxiety to her.

She felt the necessity of acquiring a working
knowledge of the language of the people among whom
she was to live, and completed the first year's course
at language school.

During the five years in Korea, two children
came to the home. Mrs. Stites was an ideal mother
and home-maker, and she considered the making of

a home a real part of missionary work. She radiated the spirit of true hospitality to all who came into her home.

Having served one term on the field, Dr. and Mrs. Stites returned to America on furlough in the spring of 1923. They had already engaged passage to return to Korea in the late summer of 1924, when it was thought best by the consulting physicians for Mrs. Stites not to return, due to her weakened condition following a serious illness.

She showed improvement during the winter months, but in March 1925 developed peritonitis, following an operation, and after a ten days' illness passed away on Sunday evening, March 29th, at Louisville, Kentucky. She was laid to rest in Franklin, Tennessee, and the love and high esteem in which she was held was attested by the beautiful floral offerings sent by hundreds of friends in Kentucky and Tennessee.

Mrs. Stites inspired all who knew her with the joy of living and yet there was underneath her buoyancy a deep spiritual nature which those who knew her best appreciated more the longer they knew her. In her letters to friends concerning their inability to return to Korea she spoke of having prayed for guidance, and expressed the confidence that they were doing the will of God. Although those of us who are left behind are saddened by the death of this dear friend and fellow missionary we feel that heaven has been made sweeter by her radiant presence.

Mrs. A. G. Welbon

In the calling away of Mrs. A. G. Welbon to higher service in July of this year the missionary body and

the missionary cause in Korea have lost a true friend
and sympathetic' fellow-worker.

Mrs. Welbon arrived in Korea in 1890 as Miss
Sadie Nourse. In 1901 she was married to the Rev.
A. G. Welbon of the Northern Presbyterian Mission.
The early years of her missionary life were spent in
Seoul; heie she rendered devoted service.   Later,
responding to a call for pioneer service in the newly
opened station of Andong in the South, she went
gladly with her husband and little children to the
new station where her hospitable home and efficient
efforts in the interests of the Koreans gave her a place
of large usefulness and influence.   The good accomplished by Mrs. Welbon's long itinerating trips into
the country, taking her small children with her, has
become a part of the history of the Kingdom of God
in the hearts and lives of the women of South Korea.

Mrs. Welbon lived also for several years in Pyengyang. Here too her home was open to all and her
stay though short was filled with acts of helpfulness.
In 1910 the family went to America on furlough, and
Mrs. Welbon did not return, her children's education
and her own failing health requiring a prolonged
stay in the homeland.   `

The call to her Heavenly Home came early and
now she is with the Saviour she loved and served so
devotedly.

To her husband, her two sons and two daughters,
we would express our sympthy in this their great
loss and pray that the God of all comfort may comfort and strengthen their hearts.

JAPAN AND KOREA

··········

APPENDICES

APPENDIX I

THE NATIONAL CHRISTIAN COUNCIL OF JAPAN

Office: 23 Kamitomizaka, Koishikawa-ku Tokyo

Bishop K. Uzaki .... Chairman
Rev. K. Matsuno .... ⎫
Rev. D. R. McKenzie, D.D..... ⎬ Treasurers
Rev. K. Miyazaki ....Japanese Secretary
Rev. W. Axling, D.D. .... Act. English Secretary

EXECUTIVE:

Rev. W. Axling, D.D.	Rev. A. K. Reischauer, D.D.
Rev. Y. Chiba, D.D.	Miss J. N. Scott
Rev. C. S. Gillett	Rev. D. B Schneder, D.D.
Rev. K. Ishikawa	Mr. C. Suzuki
Mr. K. Kakehi	Rev. C. Sakai
Rev. M. Kobayashi	Mr. D. Tagawa
Rev. H. Kozaki, D.D.	Bishop K. Uzaki
Mrs. O. Kubushiro	Rev. S. H. Wainright, D. D.
Rev. K. Matsuno	Mr. K. Uyesawa
Rev. S. Nukaga	Rev. Yorogi
Rev.	

APPENDIX I

CONSTITUTION OF THE FEDERATION OF CHRISTIAN MISSIONS IN JAPAN

ARTICLE I. NAME

The name of the organization shall be The Federation of Christian Missions in Japan.

ARTICLE II. PURPOSE

The purpose of the Federation shall be to promote fellowship, mutual understanding and the spirit of unity among the Missions comprising it; to provide an opportunity for gatherings of an inspirational and deducative character; and with due regard to the functions and purpose of the National Christian Council, to provide a channel for any cooperative work that may be necessary.

ARTICLE III. POWERS

The Federation may confer, investigate, give counsel, and take action regarding matters of common concern to the Missions represented in it—with due regard to the powers of the National Christian Council; it may also undertake such cooperative work as may be agreed upon by the constituent bodies; but no action may be taken affecting the independence of the Missions represented, or dealing with ecclesiastic principles, or questions of Christian doctrine.

ARTICLE IV. MEMBERSHIP

Membership in the Federation shall be open to all evangelical Christian Missions in Japan, which accept the Constitution and By-laws.   Application for membership may be made at any regular meeting of the Federation, and admission shall be by a two-thirds vote of the representatives present.

Note: The term, "evangelical," as used in this Article, includes by common consent those outstanding doctrines of the Christian faith that are held by the Churches, to which the bodies holding membership severally belong—the doctrines comprehended in St. Paul's words, found in Titus 2:13 (R.V.), "Our great God and Saviour Jesus Christ."

ARTICLE V. REPRESENTATION

1. The basis of representation in the Federation shall be as follows:

(a) Missions having from one to nine members shall be entitled to one representative.

(b) Missions having from ten to nineteen members shall be entitled to two representatives.

(c) Missions having from twenty to twenty-nine members shall be entitled to three representatives.

(d) Missions having from thirty to forty-nine members shall be entitled to four representatives.

(e) Missions having fifty members or more shall be entitled to five representatives.

(f) Two or more Missions, without regard to their size, may at their discretion combine to form a group. In such cases each group shall, so far as the purposes of the Federation are concerned, be counted as a Mission and shall be entitled to representation accordingly.

2. Representatives shall be appointed by the Missions or group of Missions for such terms as each Mission or group shall determine.

3. Each of the Bible Societies shall be entitled to representation in the Federation, irrespective of their representation on the field.

ARTICLE VI. WITHDRAWAL

A Mission may at any time withdraw from the Federation by notifying the Secretary in writing of its decision to do so, provided it shall have discharged its obligation to the Federation for the current year.

ARTICLE VII. OFFICERS

The officers of the Federation shall be a Chairman, a Vice-Chairman, a Secretary and a Treasurer, elected at each Annual Meeting. They shall assume office at the close of the meeting at which they are elected. Officers, when not official representatives of their Missions, shall be *ex officio* members of the Federation, but without voting power.

ARTICLE VIII. MEETINGS

1. Regular metings of the Federation shall be held annually at such time and place as the Federation shall determine. Special meetings may be held at the call of the Executive Committee.

2. A quorum for the transaction of business shall consist of representatives from at least two-thirds of the Mission or groups of Missions holding membership in the Federation.

ARTICLE IX. EXPENSES

1. The ordinary expenses of the Federation, including the cost of attendance of full members at its meeting,

constituent Missions of Yen 20 for each representative in the Federation, to which the Mission is entitled.*

* It is understood that traveling expenses to the meetings of the Federation shall be interpreted as including second-class railway fare with sleeper when necessary.   In the case of Committees, the Chairman, or other party, appointed to report for the committee, shall, if not a member of the Federation, be eligible to receive traveling expenses.

2. Extraordinary expenses shall be incurred only as special provision may be made by the Missions, or otherwise, for meeting them.

ARTICLE X.   AMENDMENTS

Amendments to the Constitution, if signed by three or more representatives, may be proposed at any Annual Meeting of the Federation. A majority vote shall determine whether such amendment will be considered. Final action shall not be taken till the Annual Meeting following, when a two-thirds vote of the total representation of the Federation shall be required to make the amendment effective.

BY-LAWS

1.   All meetings of the Federation shall be opened and closed with devotional exercises.

2.   All resolutions shall be submitted in writing.

3.   Questions of parliamentary procedure shall be decided in accordance with Roberts' Rules of Order.

4.   Previous to the Annual Meeting, the Executive Committee shall appoint a Minute Secretary to take the Minutes, a Business Committee of two to facilitate business procedure, and a Nominating Committee of Nine to nominate the officers and mem-

bers of the Standing Committees to be elected by the Federation at that meeting.

5. Standing Committees shall be constituted as below, and may include members of the constituent Missions other than the official representatives in the Federation. Vacancies occuring ad interim shall be filled by the Executive Committee on nomination by the Committee concerned. The coopting of additional members on ayn of the Committees shall be subject to the approval of the Executive. Typewritten reports shall be placed in the hands of the Secretary of the Federation at least one month previous to the Annual Meeting.

		members
(a)	Executive Committee	9
(b)	Committee on Christian Literature Society	12
(c)	Committee on The Japan Christian Quarterly	6
(d)	Committee on The Christian Movement	5
(e)	Committee of Examiners in Japanese Language	8
(f)	Committee on The Japanese Language School	6
(g)	Committee on Newspaper Evangelism	9
(h)	Committee on Necrology	1
(i)	Committee on American School in Japan	1
(j)	Committee on Canadian Academy	1

(N.B.—The Nominations Committee is instructed to proceed as follows in making nominations:

Executive: Officers *ex officio,* 3 members one year, 2 members two years.

Christian Movement: Editor-in-chief, 3 years; Assoc [

Japan Quarterly: 3 for one year, 3 for two years.

*Examiners Japanese Language: 3 for one year, 3 for two years.

Japanese Language School: 3 for one year, 3 for two years.

Newspaper Evangelism: 3 for one year, 3 for two years, 3 for three years.

Christian Literature Society: 4 for one year, 4 for two years, 4 for three years.

6. The Executive Committee shall be chosen with special reference to convenience of meeting ad interim. The Secretary of the Federation shall be Secretary of the Committee, and two-thirds of its members shall constitute a quorum for the transaction of business. The functions of the Executive Committee shall be (1) To transact the ordinary and ad interim business of the Federation; (2) To carry out such measures as may be referred to it by the Federation; (3) To authorize the disbursement of funds, call special meetings, arrange for the Annual Meeting, and submit a report of its transactions to that body.

7. A call for a special meeting of the Federation shall be issued at least one month in advance of the meeting, and except by the unanimous consent of those present, the business shall be limited to that stated in the call.

8. The Secretary shall furnish each member of the Federation with a copy of the proceedings of each meeting of the Federation.

9. The By-laws may be amended by a two-thirds vote of the members present at any regular meeting.

(*This Committee was not nominated by the Nominations Committee in Annual Meeting of 1925. Also, its number appears as 6 in one place and 8 in another. The Secretary can find no record of the abnegation of this Committee.

APPENDIX III

THE FEDERATION OF CHRISTIAN MISSIONS IN JAPAN

OFFICERS AND COMMITTEES FOR 1925-1926

OFFICERS:

Chairman—H. A. Stirewalt.
Vice-Chairman—(Miss) Jane Scott.
Secretary—Harvey Brokaw.
Treasurer—C. P. Garman.

EXECUTIVE COMMITTEE:

Term ending in 1926

W. K. Matthews.
P. S. C. Powles.
(Miss) O. I. Hodges.

Term ending in 1927

H. K. Miller.
Hilton Pedley.
JAPANESE LANGUAGE SCHOOL TRUSTEES:
H. S. V. Peeke (Convener).
W. H. Myers.
Wm. Axling.

JAPAN EVANGELIST BOARD:

Term ending in 1926

E. T. Iglehart.
W. H. Erskine.
(Miss) Mary Stowe.

Term ending in 1927

(Miss) K. Shepherd.
(Miss) B. E. Gillilan.
W. H. M. Walton (Ed.-in-Chief).

CHRISTIAN LITERATURE SOCIETY:

Term ending in 1926

(Miss) Evelyn Camp.
C. D. Kriete.
S. H. Wainright.
T. A. Young.

Term expiring in 1927

(Miss) J. N. Scott.
A. D. Berry.
W. F. Hereford.
E. T. Iglehart.
W. G. Seiple.

Term ending in 1928

D. H. Blake.
S. Heaslett.
G. M. Rowland.
A. J. Stirewalt.

NEWSPAPER EVANGELISM:

Term expiring in 1926

Harvey Brokaw.
F. W. Rowlands.
C. E. Norman.

Term ending in 1927

Rev. K. C. Hendricks.
C. H. Ross.
W. H. M. Walton.

Term ending in 1928

D. Norman.
R. J. Dosker.
R. S. Spencer.

CHRISTIAN MOVEMENT:

Term ending in 1926

A. Oltmans (Editor).
(Miss) E. Newlin.
F. W. Heckelman.

Term ending in 1927

C. B. Olds.
J. W. Hassell.

FRATERNAL DELEGATE TO KOREA:

B. F. Shively.

NECROLOGIST:

A. Oltmans.

REPRESENTATIVE TO AMERICAN SCHOOL:

(Mrs.) R. D. McCoy.

REPRESENTATIVE TO CANADIAN ACADEMY

(Mrs.) Sherwood F. Moran.

REPRESENTATIVES OF THE NATIONAL CHRISTIAN
COUNCIL:

A. J. Stirewalt.
(Miss) O. I. Hodges.

JAPAN AND FORMOSA
MISSIONARY DIRECTORY

· · · · · · · · ·

Compiled by J. W. HASSELL

LIST OF MISSION BOARDS AND CHURCHES

With names of Mission Secretaries and Statisticians on the field. (The initials used are the standard forms for America, India, China and Japan.)

1   ABCFM   American Board of Commissioners for Foreign Missions. Rev. H. Pedley.

2   ABF.   American Baptist Foreign Missionary Society. Rev. C. B. Tenny, Secretary; Miss Louise F. Jenkins, Statistician.

3.   AEPM.   Allgemeiner Evangelisch-Protestantischer Missions-verein. Rev. Emil Schiller.

4.   AFP   Foreign Missionary Association of Friends of Philadelphia. Mr. G. Burnham Braithwaite.

5.   AUBM.   Australian Board of Missions (Anglican). Rev. E. R. Harrison

6.   AG   Assembly of God Mrs. Gordon R. Bender, Secretary.

7   BS.   American Bible Society. Rev. K. E Aurell. British and Foreign Bible Society, and National Bible Society of Scotland Mr. Frederick Parrott

8.   CC.   Mission Board of the Christian Church (American Christian Convention). Miss Angie Crew.

9.   CG   Church of God Mr. Adam W. Miller.

10.   CLS.   Christian Literature Society Rev. S. H. Wainright.

11.   CMA.   Christian and Missionary Alliance. Rev. Arthur Petrie.

12.   CMS.   Church Missionary Society, Central Japan, Rev. John C. Mann; Kyushu, Rev. S. Painter; Hokkaido, Rev. G. J. Walsh.

13.   EC.   Evangelical Church of North America. Rev. A. A. Leininger.

14   FMAS.   General Mission Board of the Free Methodist Church of North America.

15.	IND.	Independent of Any Society.
16.	JEB.	Japan Evangelistic Band. Mr. J. Cuthbertson.
17.	JBTS.	Japan Book and Tract Society. Mr George Braithwaite.
18.	JRM.	Japan Rescue Mission; Secretary, Miss Bessie Butler; Statistician, Miss Mary Whiteman.
19.	KK.	Kumiai Kyokwai (Congregationalist). Rev. Kotaro Nishio, Nihon Kumiai Kyokwai Honbu, 57 Nakano Shima, 2 Chome, Kita Ku, Osaka.
20.	LCA.	Board of Foreign Missions of the United Lutheran Church in America · Rev. E T. Horn.
21.	LEF	The Lutheran Gospel Association of Finland. Rev. K. E. Salonen.
22.	MCC.	Methodist Church of Canada. Rev. D. R. McKenzie, Miss M. A. Robertson.
23.	MEFB.	Board of Foreign Missions of the Methodist Episcopal Church. Rev. E. T. Iglehart, Secretary; Miss O. M. Coe, Statistician.
		East Japan Woman's Conference, Miss N. M. Daniel.
		West Japan Conference, Miss Pauline Place, Secretary; Mrs. R. E. West, Statistician
24.	MES.	Board of Foreign Missions of the Methodist Episcopal Church South. Rev. J. B. Cobb, Secretary; Rev. J. W. Frank, Statistician.
25.	MP.	Board of Foreign Missions of the Methodist Protestant Church. Miss E. L. Hempstead, Secretary.
26.	MSCC.	Missionary Society of the Church of England in Canada. Rev J. G. Waller.
27.	NKK.	Nihon Kirisuto Kyokwai (Presbyterian and Reformed). Mr. Tomosaburo Inouye, Dendo Kyoku, 32 Fujimi Cho, 1 Chome, Kojimachi Ku, Tokyo.
28.	NMK.	Nihon Methodist Kyokwai (MCC, MEFB, MES). Rev. Denshiro Hatano, Dendo Kyoku, Care Kyo Bun Kwan, Tokyo.
29.	NSK.	Nippon Sei Ko Kai (CMS, MSCC, PE, SPG, and AuBM). Rev. J. G. Waller, Statistician.
30.	OMJ.	Omi Mission. I. Namikawa.
31.	OMS.	Oriental Missionary Society Mr Floyd Hitchcock

32	PB	Pentecostal Band. Mr. Leonard Coote
33.	PBW.	Pentecostal Bands of the World. Rev Fred Abel.
34	PE	Domestic and Foreign Missionary Society of the Protestant Episcopal Church in America.
		Tokyo District. Miss Ruth Burnside.
		Kyoto District: Miss L. S McGrath
35	PN.	Board of Foreign Missions of the Presbyterian Church of the United States of America Rev. Harvey Brokaw, Secretary; Rev E. M Clark, Statistician
36	PS.	Executive Committee of Foreign Missions of the Presbyterian Church 'n the United States. (Southern Presbyterian). Rev A. P Hassell, Secretary, Rev. S. M Erickson, Statistician.
37.	RCA.	Reformed Church in America. Rev D C. Ruigh, Secretary; Rev. A. Van Bronkhorst, Statistician.
38	RCUS.	Reformed Church in the United States. Rev E H Zaugg.
39	SA.	Salvation Army. Commissioner William Eadie
40	SAM	Scandinavian Alliance Mission. Rev Joel Anderson
41.	SBC	Southern Baptist Convention. Rev. C. Dozier.
42	SDA.	Seventh Day Adventists. Mr. H J Perkins.
43.	SPG.	Society for the Propagation of the Gospel in Foreign Parts.
		South Tokyo Diocese. Rev R. D. M. Shaw.
		Kobe Diocese: Rev. C Foxley.
44.	UB	Foreign Missionary Society of the United Brethren in Christ. Rev B F. Shively, Secretary.
45.	UCMS.	United Christian Missionary Society. R. D McCoy, Secretary.
46.	UGC.	Universalist General Convention. Mrs. H. M. Cary, Secretary.
47	WM.	Wesleyan Methodist Connection of America. Rev. M. A. Gibbs.
48	WU.	Woman's Union Missionary Society of America Miss Susan A. Pratt
49.	TM	Tokyo Mission. Mr. W. D. Cunningham.
50.	YMCA-A	Young Men's Christian Association (Ame-

F. Rusch, Secretary.

YMCA-T. Government School Teachers Affiliated with YMCA. Mr. P. F. Rusch.

51. YWCA. Young Women's Christian Association of the United States of America. Miss Jane N. Scott, Secretary

52. WSSA. World's Sunday School Association. Mr. Horace E Coleman, Secretary.

53. EPM. Foreign Missions of the Presbyterian Church of England. Rev. Edward Band, Secretary.

54. UCC. Board of Foreign Missions of the United Church of Canada. Mr. W. G. Coates, Secretary.

ALPHABETICAL LIST

The order is as follows: Name; Year of arrival in Japan or of joining the mission; initials of missionary society or board; address, postal transfer number and telephone number, (A) absent.

A

Abel, Rev. Fred. & W, 1913, PBW, (A), 101 Alton Ave., Salem Park, Indianapolis, Ind., U S A.

Acock, Miss Amy A., 1905, ABF, 50 Shimotera Machi, Himeji.

Acock, Miss Winifred M., 1922, ABF, 2 Nakajima Cho, Sendai.

Adair, Miss Lily, 1911, UCC, 79 Miyamae Cho, Taihoku, Formosa

Adams, Miss Alice Pettee, 1891, ABCFM, 95 Kadota Yashiki, Okayama

Ainsworth, Rev F. & W, 1915, MCC, 216 Sengoku Machi, Toyama. (F. C. Kanazawa 3324.)

Airo, Miss J, 1907, LEF, (A), Uusikaupunki, Korsaari, Finland.

Akard, Miss Martha B, 1913, LCA, Kyushu Jo Gakuin, Murozono, Kumamoto Shigai.

Alexander, Rev R P., & W., 1893, 1897, MEFB, 2 Aoyama Gakuin, Shibuya Machi, Tokyo Fu (Tel 2008)

Alexander, Miss Sallie, 1894, PN, 24 Kyarabashi En, Hamadera, Osaka Fu.

Alexander, Miss Virginia Elizabeth, 1903, MEFB, 12 Kita Ichijo, Higashi 6 Chome, Sapporo.

Allbrecht, Miss Helen R., 1921, MEFB, (A), 858 Park St. North, Columbus, O, U S A

Allen, Miss A. W, 1905, MCC, (A), 179 Davisville Ave., Toronto, Can

Allen, Miss Carolyn, 1919, YWCA, 2082 Minami Ota Machi, Yokohama

Allen, Miss Thomasine, 1915, ABF, 2 Nakajima Cho, Sendai.

Ambler, Miss Marietta, 1916, PE, (A), 281 Fourth Ave., N

Anderson, Pastor A. N., & W., 1913, SDA, 169-171 Amanuma, Suginami Machi, Tokyo.

Anderson, Rev Joel, (W. Absent), 1900, SAM, 920 Nakano, Tokyo Fu.

Anderson, Miss Myra P., 1922, MES, 35 Nakayamate Dori 4 Chome, Kobe.

Anderson, Miss Ruby L., 1917, ABF, 3131 Kanagawa Machi, Yokohama

Andrews, Rev. E. L, & W., 1922, PE, Hodono Naka Cho, Akita.

Andrews, Rev. R W, & W., 1899, PE, Irifune Cho, Tochigi Machi, Tochigi Ken

Andrews, Miss Sarah, 1919, Ind, 126 Oiwa, Ando Mura, Shizuoka Shigai.

Ankeney, Rev. Alfred, & W., 1914, 1923, RCUS, 112 Kita Niban Cho, Sendai.

Archer, Miss A. L, 1899, MSCC, Higashi Hibino Machi, Ichinomiya Shi

Armbruster, Miss Rose T., 1903, UCMS, (A), Care United Christian Missionary Society, St Louis, Mo, U.S A.

Armstrong, Miss Clare, 1923, YWCA, Yamamoto Dori, 4 Chome, Kobe.

Armstrong, Miss M E., 1903, MCC, Sogawa Cho, Toyama.

Armstrong, Rev R. C, Ph D., & W., 1903, MCC, (A), The United Church of Canada, Mission Rooms, Wesley Building, Toronto, Canada.

Armstrong, Pastor V T., & W., 1921, SDA, 169-171 Amanuma, Suginami Machi, Tokyo.

Asbury, Miss Jessie J, 1901, UCMS, (A), Care United Christian Missionary Society, St Louis, Mo, U S A

Ashbaugh, Miss Adella M, 1908, MEFB, (A), 149 E Blake St, Columbus, O., U.S A.

Atkinson, Miss Maria J., 1899, PS, Rokuban Cho, Takamatsu, Kagawa Ken

Auman, Rev J C., & W., 1921, MP, 43 Chokyuji Machi, Higashi Ku, Nagoya.

Aurell, Rev K E, & W., 1891, BS, 645 Kugahara, Ikegami, Tokyo Fu

Axling, Rev. Wm., D. D., & W., 1901, ABF, 10 Fujimi Cho, 6 Chome, Kojimachi, Tokyo

Aylard, Miss Gertrude D., 1920, FMA, 1260 Tennoji Cho, Sumiyoshi Ku, Osaka.

Ayres, Rev. J B D D., 1888, & W, 1913, PN, 739 Sumiyoshi M ... ... Ku, O k

B

Babcock, Miss Grace E., 1922, ABCFM, (A), 19 S. La Salle
St., Chicago, Ill., U.S.A.

Bach, Rev D G. M., & W., 1916, LCA, 1986 Maruyama
Machi, Shimonoseki.

Baggs, Miss M C., 1925, CMS, Bishop Poole Jo Gakko,
Tsuruhashi Cho, Osaka.

Bailey, Miss B M., 1919, MEFB, Aoyama Gakuin, Tokyo.

Baker, Mr. David D, 1924, & W., 1922, RCUS, (A), Care
Mis H W Otte, 722 Fisk St, Piqua, Ohio, USA.

Baker, Miss Effie, 1921, SBC, Seinen Gakuin, Nishijin
Machi, Fukuoka.

Baker, Miss Elsie M, 1924, CMS, Poole Jo Gakko, Tsuruhashi Cho, Osaka.

Ballard, Miss S, SPG, 3 Yarai Cho, Ushigome Ku, Tokyo.

Band, Rev. Edward, M. A., 1912, EPM, Presbyterian Middle
School, Tainan, Formosa.

Barber, Rev. W. A., & W., 1919, CMA, (A), 132 Pacific Ave,
Toronto, Can

Barclay, Rev. Thomas, D.D., 1874, EPM, (A), E P Mission,
Amoy, China.

Barnett, Miss Margaret, 1888, EPM, Shinro, Tainan,
Formosa.

Barns, Miss Helen V., 1921, MPW, (A), 500 Spruce St,
Morgantown, W Va., USA.

Barr, Capt Kenneth, 1921, SA, Care Salvation Army Headquarters, 5 Hitotsubashi Dori, Kanda Ku, Tokyo.

Barr, Miss L M, 1920, MCC, (A), Vinemount, Ont., Can.

Bartlett, Rev. Samuel C., & W., 1887, 1894, ABCFM, Nashinoki Cho, Imadegawa, Sagaru, Kyoto.

Barton, Miss Nellie, 1924, AG, Box 328, Sannomiva, Kobe.

Basil, The Rt Rev. Bishop, 1925, SPG, The Firs, Shino-
miya, Kobe.

Bassett, Miss Bernice C., 1919, MEFB, (A), 150 Fifth Ave,
New York, U.S.A

Batchelor, Ven. John, D.D., 1877, & W, 1883, CMS,
(Retired), 1 Kita Sanjo Nishi, 7 Chome, Sapporo.

Bates, Rev C J. L, DD, & W, 1902, MCC, Kwansei
Gakuin, Kobe. (Tel. Sannomiya 6308).

Bates, Miss E. L, 1921, MCC, 14 Saibansho Dori, Kanazawa.

Bauernfeind, Miss Susan M, 1900, EC, 84 Sasugaya Cho,
Koshikawa Ku, Tokyo (Tel Koishikawa 3546).

Bazley, Miss M, 1924, JEB, 1 of 15 Kurawa Machi, Ogaki,
Gifu Ken.

Beatty
Tc

Beers, Miss Susan E., 1920, OMS, (A), Greystone Park, N.J., U.S.A.

Bender, Mr. Gordon R., & W, 1925, AG, 320 Nishi Sugamo Machi, Tokyo Fu.

Bennett, Rev. Henry J, 1901, & W., 1903, ABCFM, (A), 5447 Morris St. Germantown, Pa., U.S.A.

Bennett, Miss Nellie, 1910, MES, Hatchobori Shirahata Shoji, Hiroshima.

Benninghoff, Rev. H B, D.D., & W., 1907, ABF, 551 Shimo Totsuka Mura, Tokyo Fu.

Benson, Mr. H. F, & W., 1906, SDA, 169-171 Amanuma, Suginami Machi, Tokyo.

Bergstrom, Rev. F. O., 1894, SAM, 123 Kashiwagi, Yodo-bashi, Tokyo Fu.

Berry, Rev. A. D, 1902, MLFB, 8 Aoyama Gakuin, Shibuya Machi, Tokyo Fu. (Tel. Aoyama 2008).

Best, Miss Blanche, 1919, YWCA, Demizu Agaru, Muro-machi Dori, Kyoto.

Bickel, Mrs. Luke W., 1898, ABF, (Retired), 3131 Kanagawa Machi, Yokohama.

Bickersteth, Mrs. Edward, 1893, SPG, (A), Guild of St. Paul Office, Church House, Westminster, London

Bielefeldt, Mr. Talbot, 1925, YMCA-T, Seinenkai, Nagoya.

Bigelow, Miss G. S., 1886, PN, Baiko Jo Gakko, 1850 Maru-yama Cho, Shimonoseki.

Bigwood, Staff-Capt E. W., & W, 1920, Care Salvation Army Headquarters, 5 Hitotsubashi Dori, Tokyo.

Binford, Mr. Gurney, & W., 1893, 1899, AFP, Shimotsuma, Makabe Gun, Ibaraki Ken.

Binsted, Rev. N. S., & W., 1915, PE, 10 Hinoki Cho, Akasaka, Tokyo.

Bishop, Miss A. B., 1922, MCC, Aiwa Jo Gakko, Kofu.

Bishop, Rev. Charles, & W., 1879, 1880, MEFB, (Retired), 140 Sangenjiya, Kami Umabikisawa, Tokyo Fu.

Bixby, Miss Alice C., 1914, ABF, 50 Shimotera Machi, Himeji.

Bixler, Mr. Orville D., & W., 1919, Ind., Shioda Mura, Naka Gun, Ibaraki Ken.

Black, Dr. D. M., 1925, UCC, 79 Miyamae Cho, Taihoku, Formosa.

Blackmore, Miss I. S., 1889, MCC, (A), Salem, Yarmouth Co., N.S.

Blakeney, Miss Bessie M., 1919, PS, Kinjo Jo Gakko, Nagoya

Boden, Miss M. K., 1924, JEB, 56 Kumano Cho, 1 Chome, Kobe.

Bolivar, Miss Anna A, 1921, CG, 1 Nishi Okubo, Tokyo Fu.

Bolliger, Miss Aurelia, 1922, RCUS, 168 Higashi Sanban Cho, Sendai.

Booth, Rev. Eugene S, D.D, & W., 1879, RCA, (Retired), 830 West 179th St., New York, U.S.A.

Bosanquet, Miss A. C, 1892, CMS, (A), Care CMS, Salisbury Square, London, E C., 4.

Bott, Rev G. E., & W., 1921, MCC, 23 Kamitomizaka Cho, Koishikawa, Tokyo.

Bouldin, Rev. G. W., D.D., & W, 1906, SBC, Seinen Gakuin, Nishijin Machi, Fukuoka.

Bowen, Miss Georgene, 1925, UGC, 50 Takata Oimatsu Cho, Koishikawa, Tokyo.

Bowles, Rev. Gilbert, 1901, & W., 1893, AFP, 30 Koun Cho, Mita, Shiba Ku, Tokyo. (Tel. Takanawa 2143).

Bowman, Miss N. F. J., 1907, MSCC, 5 Shirakabe Cho, 1 Chome, Nagoya.

Boyd, Miss Evelyn M., ABCFM, Kobe Jo Gakuin, Yamamoto Dori, 4 Chome, Kobe.

Boyd, Miss H., 1912, SPG, 3 Yarai Cho, Ushigome Ku, Tokyo.

Boyd, Miss Louisa H, 1902, PE, 26 Wakamea Cho, Ushigome, Tokyo.

Boydell, Miss K. M., 1919, CMS, 101 Takashi Cho, Kagoshima.

Brady, Rev. J. Harper, & W., 1917, PS, 602 Eikokuji Cho, Kochi.

Braithwaite, Mr. G Burnham, 1923, & W., 1922, AFP, 14 Mita Daimachi, 1 Chome, Shiba Ku, Tokyo.

Braithwaite, Mr. George, 1886, JBTS, 5 Hikawa Cho, Akasaka Ku, Tokyo.

Braithwaite, Mrs George, 1900, JEB, 5 Hikawa Cho, Akasaka Ku, Tokyo.

Branstad, Mr. K. E, 1924, PE, St. Paul's University, Ikebukuro, Tokyo.

Brokaw, Rev. H., D.D, & W., 1896, PN, Ichijo Dori, Muromachi Nishi, Ichijo, Kyoto.

Brown, Mr. F H., & W., 1913, YMCA-A, Seinenkai, Hakkeizaka, Omori, Tokyo Fu.

Brumbaugh, Rev. T. T., & W., 1924, MEFB, Hirosaki

Bruner, Mr G W., & W., 1920, MEFB, (A), 150 Fifth Ave., New York.

Buchanan, Rev. D C, & W. 1921, PN, (A), Hartford Theological Seminary, Hartford, Conn., U.S.A.

Buchanan, Miss Elizabeth O., 1914, PS, Mieji Cho, Gifu

Buchanan, Rev. Percy, & W., 1924, PS, 2189, Fukiai Cho, Kobe.

Bucha .. . .

Bucha . . .

Fukiai Cho, Kobe.

Buckland, Miss E Ruth, 1924, PS, Kinjo Jo Gakko, Nagoya.

Bull, Rev. E. R., & W., 1911, MEFB, (A), 150 Fifth Ave., New York, U.S.A.

Buncombe, Rev. W. P., & W., 1888, CMS, (Retired), 7 Sasugaya Cho, Koishikawa Ku, Tokyo.

Burnett, Miss Eleanor L, 1920, ABCFM, Kobe College, Yamamoto Dori, 4 Chome, Kobe.

Burnside, Miss Ruth, 1923, PE, 4 St. Paul s University, Ikebukuro, Tokyo.

Bushe, Miss S. L. K., 1921, CMS, Kure.

Buss, Miss Florence V., 1922, RCA, 178 Bluff, Yokohama.

Butler, Miss B., 1921, JRM, (A), "Sendai House," 16 Alexandra Road, Birkenhead, Cheshire, England.

Buzzell, Miss Annie S., 1892, ABF, Tono, Iwate Ken. (F.C., Sendai 3292).

C

Caldwell, Mr. H L, 1924, PE, St. Paul's University, Ikebukuro, Tokyo.

Callahan, Rev. W. J., & W., 1891, MES, 10 Ichiban Cho, Matsuyama.

Callbeck, Miss Louise, 1921, MCC, 12 Agata Cho, Nagano.

Camp, Miss Evelyn A., 1916, ABF, Joshi Shin Gakko, Imasato Machi, Higashi, Yodogawa Ku, Osaka.

Cannell, Miss Mona C., 1922, PE, (A), 281 Fourth Ave., New York, U S A.

Carlsen, Deaconess V. D., 1909, PE, Aoba Jo Gakuin, 69 Motoyanagi Cho, Sendai.

Carlson, Rev. C. E., & W., 1913, SAM, Ito, Izu.

Carpenter, Miss M. M., 1895, ABF, 72 Myogadani, Koishikawa Ku, Tokyo.

Cary, Miss Alice, 1915, ABCFM, Morigu, Taisha Mura, Muko Gun, Hyogo Ken.

Cary, Rev. Frank, & W., 1916, 1909, ABCFM, 5 Tomioka Cho, 3 Chome, Otaru.

Cary, Rev. Henry M., & W., 1924, UGC, 1752, Higashi Nakano, Tokyo Fu.

Case, Miss D, 1915, SPG, (A), SPG House, 15 Tufton St., Westminster, London.

Chaplin, Miss Louise, 1919, PN, (A), 4009 Harrington Ave., Oakland, Cal, U.S.A.

Chapman, Rev. E. N., & W., 1917, 1916, PN, Shingu, Wakayama Ken.

Chap[...] R[...] K [...] [...] he [...]

Chapman, Rev. J. J., & W., 1899, PE, Tsu, Ise.

Chappell, Miss Constance S., 1912, MCC, (A), London, England.

Chappell, Rev. James, & W., 1895, PE, 32 Kita Kuruwa Cho, Maebashi.

Chappell, Miss M. H., 1912, MEFB, 9 Aoyama Gakuin, Shibuya Machi, Tokyo Fu.

Chase, Miss Laura, 1915, MEFB, 4 Aoyama Gakuin, Tokyo

Cheal, Dr. Percival, M.R.C.S, L R C P, & W., 1919, EPM, Shinro Hospital, Tainan, Formosa.

Cheney, Miss Alice, 1915, MEFB, Iai Jo Gakko, Hakodate.

Chope, Miss D. M., 1917, SPG, 108 Zoshigaya, Koishikawa Ku, Tokyo.

Clark, Miss A., 1924, JEB, 5 Hikawa Cho, Akasaka Ku, Tokyo.

Clark, Rev. E. M., & W., 1920, PN, 738 Sumiyoshi Machi, Sumiyoshi Ku, Osaka.

Clark, Miss L. M., 1919, MCC, (A), 129 William St., N. Chatham, Ont., Canada.

Clark, Miss Rosamond H., 1924, ABCFM, 65 Kotojin Machi, Matsuyama.

Clarke, Miss Sara F., 1915, PN, 107 Kokutaiji Machi, 8 Chome, Hiroshima.

Clarke, Rev. W. H., & W., 1899, 1900, SBC, (A), 96 Gordon St., Atlanta, Ga., U.S.A.

Clawson, Miss Bertha F, 1898, UCMS, 354 Nakazato, Takinogawa, Tokyo Fu. (Tel. Koishikawa 523).

Clazie, Miss Mabel G., 1910, UCC, Tansui, Formosa.

Clench, Miss Marguerite, B.A., 1923, MSCC, Shinta Machi, Matsumoto.

Climpson, Staff-Capt. H. A., & W., 1920, SA, 5 Hitotsu-bashi Dori, Kanda Ku, Tokyo.

Coates, Miss Alice L., 1895, MPW, 10 Moto Shiro Cho, Hamamatsu.

Coates, Rev. H. H, D.D., & W., 1890, MCC, 105 Takamachi, Hamamatsu.

Coates, Rev. W. G., 1921, & W., 1922, UCC, Tansui, Formosa.

Cobb, Rev. E. S, & W., 1904, ABCFM, Ichijo Dori, Karasu-maru Nishi, Kyoto.

Cobb, Rev. J. B, & W., 1918, MES, 23 Kita Nagasa Dori, 4 Chome, Kobe.

Cockram, Miss H. S., 1893, CMS, Sasayama Cho, 3 Chome, Kurume.

Coe, Miss Estelle L, 1911, ABCFM, Higashi Machi, Tottori.

Coe, Miss Orpha M., 1923, MEFB, 6 Aoyama Gakuin, Shibuya Machi, Tokyo. (Tel. Aoyama 2008).

Colbo

Cole,   a.

Suginami Machi, Tokyo.

Coleman, Mr. H. E, & W., 1907, WSSA, 10 Hinoki Cho, Akasaka Ku, Tokyo. (Tel. Shiba 6934). Office address. National S.S Association, Nishiki Cho, Kanda Ku.

Coles, Miss A. M. M., 1910, JEB, 27 Okano Machi, Fukuchiyama, Kyoto Fu.

Collins, Mr. H. H, YMCA-T, Teppo Cho, Hiroshima Shi.

Connan, Miss J. M., 1925, EPM, Shoka, Formosa

Connell, Miss Hannah, 1905, UCC, Tansui, Formosa.

Conrad, Miss Florence, 1921, SBC, Seinan Gakuin, Nishijin Machi, Fukuoka.

Converse, Miss Clara A, 1890, ABF, 373 Aoki Cho, Yokohama.

Converse, Mr. G. C., 1915, & W., 1913, YMCA-A, Sumiyoshi, Hyogo Ken.

Cook, Miss M. M., 1904, MES, Lambuth Jo Gakuin, 5290 Ishigatsuji Cho, Tennoji, Minami Ku, Osaka.

Cooke, Miss M. S, 1909, MSCC, (A), 72 Greenville St, Toronto, Canada.

Coote, Mr. Leonard, W., & W., 1914, PB, 43 Funahashi Cho, Higashi Ku, Osaka.

Corey, Rev. H. H., & W., 1919, MSCC, Okaya, Suwa Gun, Nagano Ken.

Cornwall-Legh, Miss Mary H., 1916, PE, Jizo, Kusatsu, Gumma Ken.

Correll, Rev. I. H., D.D., & W., 1873, PE, 2 Kasumi Cho, Azabu, Tokyo.

Couch, Miss Helen, 1916, MEFB, Kwassui Jo Gakko, Nagasaki.

Couch, Miss Sarah M., 1892, RCA, (A), on furlough.

Courtice, Miss L. K, 1914, MEFB, Hirosaki Jo Gakko, Hirosaki.

Courtice, Miss Sybil R., 1910, MCC, Eiwa Jo Gakko, Shizuoka.

Cousar, Rev. J. E., & W., 1920, 1918, PS, (A), Bishopville, S.C.. U.S.A.

Covell, Mr J. Howard, & W, 1920, 1327 Minami Ota Machi, Yokohama.

Cowl, Rev. J, & W., 1916, CMS, 518 Haruyoshi, Fukuoka.

Cox, Miss A. M., 1900, CMS, Miya Machi, Amagasaki, Hyogo Ken.

Cozad, Miss Gertrude, 1888, ABCFM, (A), 140 W. 8th St., Claremont, Cal., U.S.A.

Cragg, Rev. W. J. M., & W., 1911, MCC, (A), The United Church of Canada, Mission Rooms, Wesley Building, Toronto, Ont., Canada.

Craig, Mr. E. B., & W., 1911, Ind., 468 Shimo Shibuya, Tokyo Fu.

Crawford, Miss Marian J., 1925, PE, Rikkyo Koto Jo Gakko, Kugayama, Takaido Mura, Tokyo Fu.

Crew, Miss Angie, 1923, CC, 41 Karahori Cho, Sendai.

Crewdson, Rev. Ira D., & W., 1922, UCMS, Kishi Hanematsu, Sumiyoshi, Nishinari Ku, Osaka

Cribb, Miss E R., Ind, 17 Kita Nichome, Denbo Machi Osaka.

Crosby, Miss Amy R., 1913, ABF, (A), Centerville, Mass. U.S.A.

Cull, Miss Hilda A, 1924, SPG, 4 of 60 Nakayamate Dori, 6 Chome, Kobe.

Cunningham, Rev W. D., & W, 1901, TM, 6 Naka Cho, Yotsuya Ku, Tokyo.

Currell, Miss Susan M, 1921, PS, (A), University of South Carolina, Columbia, S.C., U.S.A.

Curry, Miss Olive, 1926, MEFB, Aoyama Gakuin, Tokyo

Curtis, Miss Edith, 1912, ABCFM, Morigu, Taisha Mura, Muko Gun, Hyogo Ken.

Curtis, Rev. F. S., & W., 1888, PN, 1854 Maruyama Cho, Shimonoseki

Curtis, Miss G. P, 1918, PN, (A), 184 Fernwood Ave., Montclair, N.J, U.S.A.

Curtis, Rev. W. L, & W., 1890, 1908, ABCFM, Nashinoki Cho, Imadegawa, Sagaru, Kyoto.

Cuthbertson, Mr. J., & W., 1905, JEB, 102 Umemoto Cho, Kobe.

Cypert, Miss Lillie, 1917, Ind, 68 Zoshigaya, Tokyo Fu

D

Daniel, Miss N M., 1898, MEFB, 4 Aoyama Gakuin, Tokyo

Darrow, Miss Flora, 1922, RCA, 8 Oura Higashi Yamate, Nagasaki

Daugherty, Miss L G, 1915, PN, 102 Tsunohazu, Yodobashi, Tokyo Fu

Davidson, Miss F. E, 1914, PN, Hokusei Jo Gakko, Sapporo, Hokkaido.

Davidson, Mr Ronald, YMCA-T, Middle School, Odawara, Kanagawa Ken.

Davis, Mr. J. Merle, & W, YMCA-A, (A), 347 Madison Ave., New York, U.S.A.

Davis, Miss Lois L, 1924, MEFB, Kwassui Jo Gakko Nagasaki.

Dayton, Mr. Charles S., 1925, YMCA-T, Seinenkai, Nagoya.

DeChant, Miss Katherine B, 1924, RCUS, 61 Kozenji Dori, Sendai

DeFoi e,

Yamamoto Dori, 4 Chome, Kobe.

Demaree, Rev. T. W. B., D.D., & W., 1889, MES, 94 Niage Machi, Oita.

DeMiller, Miss Virginia, 1921, CMA, Kami Kubo Cho, Nara Shi.

Denton, Miss A. Grace, 1919, PE, Obama, Fukui Ken.

Denton, Miss Mary F., 1888, ABCFM, Doshisha Jo Gakko, Kyoto.

Derwacter, Rev F. M., & W., 1920, ABF, (A), Huntington, W. Va., U.S.A.

Dietrich, Mr George, & W., 1924, SDA, 46 Kagoike Dori, 7 Chome, Kobe.

Dievendorf, Mrs. D. K., 1924, CMA, Yanai Machi, Matsuyama Shi.

Disbrow, Miss Helen J., 1921, PE, Kamikyoku, Bishamon Cho, Kyoto.

Dithridge, Miss Hariet, AG, 3833 Sakoe Cho, Tachikawa Machi, Tokyo Fu.

Dorothy, Sister, 1922, Ind., Community of the Epiphany, 358 Sanko Cho, Shirokane, Shiba Ku, Tokyo.

Dosker, Rev. R. J., & W., 1916, PN, (A), 1213 First St., Louisville, Ky., U.S.A.

Douglas, Miss Bertha, 1920, UCMS, 4250 Daido Machi, 3 Chome, Tennoji, Minami Ku, Osaka.

Dowd, Miss Annie H., 1889, PS, 180 Takajo Machi, Kochi.

Downs, Rev. A. W., & W., 1920, ABCFM, Gakko Cho, Niigata.

Downs, Rev. Darley, & W., 1919, 1921, ABCFM, Karasumaru Dori, Imadegawa, Sagaru, Kyoto.

Dozier, Rev C. K., & W., 1906, SBC, Seinan Gakuin, Nishijin Machi, Fukuoka.

Drake, Miss K. I., 1909, MCC, 8 Toriizaka, Azabu Ku, Tokyo.

Draper, Rev. G. F., S.T.D., & W., 1880, MEFB, 222-B Bluff, Yokohama.

Draper, Miss Marion R., 1913, MEFB, (A), 150 Fifth Ave., New York, U.S.A.

Draper, Miss Winifred F., 1912, MEFB, (A), 150 Fifth Ave., New York, U.S.A.

Duncan, Miss Constance, 1922, YWCA, Demizu Agaru, Muromachi Dori, Kyoto.

Dunlop, Rev. J. G., D.D., & W., 1887, 1894, PN, 1236 Bezai Cho, Tsu, Mie Ken.

Durgin, Mr R. L., & W., 1919, YMCA-A, Seinenkai, Hakkeizaka, Omori, Tokyo Fu.

Durland, Miss Mabel I., ABCFM, Kobe Jo Gakuin, Yamamoto Dori 4 Chome, Kobe.

Dyer Mr. A. L. & W. (A), JIJB, Sair. M dzaru Ky so Fu.

Dykhuizen, Mr. Cornelius A., 1925, RCA, Meiji Gakuin, Shiba Ku, Tokyo.

E

Eadie, Commissioner William, & W., 1923, SA, 5 Hitotsu-bashi Dori, Kanda Ku, Tokyo.

Eaton, Miss A. G., 1918, PN, Hokuriku Jo Gakko, Kanazawa.

Edith Constance, Sister Superior, 1908, Ind., Home of the Epiphany, 358 Sanko Cho, Shirokane, Shiba Ku, Tokyo.

Eleanor Frances, Sister, 1922, Home of the Epiphany, 358 Sanko Cho, Shirokane, Shiba Ku, Tokyo.

Elliott, Miss Isabel, R N, 1912, UCC, (A), Care Rev. A. E Armstrong, 439 Confederation Chambers, Toronto, Can

Elliott, Dr Mabel E, 1925, PE, St. Luke's Hospital, Tsukiji, Tokyo.

Ellis, Mr Charles, & W, Ind., Takajo Machi, Kochi.

Erickson, Rev S. M., & W., 1905, PS, 127 Hamano Cho, Takamatsu

Eringa, Miss Dora, 1922, RCA, 178 Bluff, Yokohama.

Erskine, Rev. Wm. H., & W., 1904, UCMS, 1572 Kishimoto, Mikage, Hyogo Ken.

Essen, Miss M, 1926, SPG, 4 of 60 Nakayamate Dori, C Chome, Kobe.

Etheldreda, Sister 1924, Ind, Home of the Epiphany, 358 Sanko Cho, Shirokane, Shiba Ku, Tokyo.

Evans, Rev. Charles H, & W, 1894, PE, 536 Naka Machi, Mito.

Evans, Miss E M, 1911, PN, Hokusei Jo Gakko, Sapporo

F

Fairclo, Miss Nellie, 1923, MEFB, 5 Aoyama Gakuin, Shibuya Machi, Tokyo Fu (Tel Aoyama 2008).

Fanning, Miss Katherine F., 1914, ABCFM Karasumaru Dori, Imadegawa Sagaru, Kyoto.

Farnham, Miss Grace, 1925, TM 1766 Nakano, Tokyo.

Faucette, Mr Thomas, & W, YMCA-T, Fukuoka Koto Gakko, Fukuoka

Faust, Rev A K, Ph D., 1900, & W, 1903, RCUS, 162 Higashi Sanban Cho, Sendai.

Fehr, Miss Vera J., 1920, MEFB, Kwassui Jo Gakko, Nagasaki.

Ferguson, Mrs. Duncan, 1898, EPM, Shinro, Tainan, F- ---

Fesperman, Rev. F. L , & W., 1919, RCUS, (A), Concord, N.C., U S.A.

Field, Miss Sarah M , 1911, ABCFM, Kobe College, Yamamoto Dori, 4 Chome, Kobe.

Finch, Miss Mary, 1925, MES, 35 Nakayamate Dori, 4 Chome, Kobe.

Finlay, Miss Alice L , 1905, MEFB, 143 Kajiya Cho, Kagoshima.

Fisher, Mrs C. H. D , 1883, ABF, (Retired), 1327 Minami Ota Machi, Yokohama.

Fisher, Mr. Royal H., & W , 1914, ABF, 1327 Minami Ota Machi, Yokohama. (Furikae, Tokyo 32699).

Fisher, Mr Sterling, 1919, & W , 1920, MES, 10 Ichiban Cho, Matsuyama.   ,

Floyd, Mr. Arva C., & W , 1924, MES, Beppu, Oita Ken

Foote, Miss Edith L , 1923, PE, Karasumaru Dori, Shimotachi Uri, Kyoto.

Foote, Mr. E. W., 1923, PE, St Paul's University, Ikebukuro, Tokyo Fu

Foote, Rev. John A , & W , 1912, 1911, ABF, (A), 18 Howard St., Haverhill, Mass , U.S A.

Forsyth, Miss Pearl, 1925, YWCA, Yamamoto Dori, 4 Chome, Kobe.

Foxley, Rev C , & W , 1909, SPG, 5-A, Nakayamate Dori, 3 Chome, Kobe.

France, Rev. W. F., & W., 1909, SPG, (A), SPG House, 15 Tufton St., Westminster, London.

Francis, Miss R. M., 1910, CMA, Yanai Machi, Matsuyama

Francis, Rev. T. R , & W , 1913, CMA, Fukuyama Shi.

Frank, Rev. J W , & W , 1912, MES, 22 Sasa Machi, Uwajima, Ehime Ken. (Furikae, Osaka 56362).

Freeth, Miss F. M., 1895, CMS, Miyaji, Aso Gun, Kumamoto Ken.

Frehn, Mr. C., & W , 1926, CMA, Kaita Ichi Machi, Hiroshima Ken

Fry, Rev. E. C., & W., 1894, CC, 7 Nijo Machi, Utsunomiya, Tochigi Ken.

Fulghum, Miss S. E , 1918, SBC, 298 Jigyo, Higashi Machi, Fukuoka

Fullerton, Miss M., 1923, MCC, 8 Toriizaka, Azabu Ku, Tokyo.

Fulton, Rev. G W., D D., & W., 1889, PN, 740 Sumiyoshi Machi, Sumiyoshi Ku, Osaka

Fulton, Rev. S. P., D D., & W., 1888, PS, 45 Kamitsutsui Dori, 5 Chome, Kobe

Fuseller, Miss Emma, 1924, PB, Shichi Honmachi Dori, Saegy- M cl. D 1 1661 S s an Kuii, Osuka.

G

Gaines, Miss N. B., 1887, MES, Hiroshima Jo Gakko, Kami Nagarekawa Cho, Hiroshima.

Gaines, Miss Rachel, 1914, MES, (Associate), Hiroshima Jo Gakko, Kami Nagarekawa Cho, Hiroshima.

Gale, Mrs. Emma, 1925, PB, 43 Funabashi Cho, Higashi Ku, Osaka.

Gale, Rev. W. H., 1912, & W, 1918, (A), Rothsay, Ont., Canada.

Galt, Miss Jessie, 1922, EPM, Presbyterian Girls School, Tainan, Formosa.

Gameitsfelder, Miss Ina, 1924, EC, 84 Sasugaya Cho, Koishikawa Ku, Tokyo.

Gard, Miss Blance A, 1920, MEFB, Hirosaki Jo Gakko, Hirosaki.

Gardener, Miss F. E., 1907, CMS, (A), CMS, Salisbury Square, London, E C 4.

Gardiner, Miss Ernestine W, 1921, PE, 32 Dote Sanban Cho, Kojimachi Ku, Tokyo.

Gardner, Miss Emma Eve, 1921, PS, (A), Marietta, Ga., U S A.

Garman, Rev. C. P., & W., 1906, CC, 477 Naka Shibuya, Tokyo Fu

Garrard, Mr. M H., 1925, JEB, 200 Gembei Cho, Tokyo Fu.

Garst, Miss Gretchen, 1912, UCMS, 49 Shin Machi, Fukushima.

Garvin, Miss A. E, 1882, PN, (Retired), (A), 1824 H St. N.W, Washington, D C., U S A.

Gauld, Dr Flora, 1924, UCC, 79 Miyamae Cho, Taihoku, Formosa.

Gauld, Miss Greta, R N., 1924, UCC, 79 Miyamae Cho, Taihoku, Formosa

Gauld, Mrs. M A., 1892, UCC, 79 Miyamae Cho, Taihoku, Formosa.

Gealy, Rev. F. G, & W., 1923, MEFB, 2-A Aoyama Gakuin, Tokyo.

Geminill, Rev. Wm C., M A., 1893, SPG, 1833 Shimo Shibuya, Tokyo.

Gerhard, Miss Mary E., 1905, 28 Uwa Cho, Komegafukuro, Sendai.

Gerhard, Rev Paul L., & W., 1897, 1902, RCUS, (A), 129 E Vine St., Lancaster, Pa, U S.A.

Gibbs, Rev. Maurice A, & W, 1919, WM, (A).

Gibson, Miss Martha, 1924, UCMS, 4250 Daido Machi, 3 Chome, Tennoji, Minami Ku, Osaka.

Gifford, Miss Ella May, 1920, ABF, (A), 55 Eighteenth St., B

Gillespie, Miss Jean, 1926, MCC, 8 Toriizaka, Azabu Ku, Tokyo.

Gillespy, Miss J., 1902, JEB, 15 Kuruwa Machi, Ogaki.

Gillett, Rev. C S, & W., 1921, ABCFM, 6 Minami Rokken Cho, Sendai.

Gillett, Miss E. R., 1896, Ind., 123 Kashiwagi, Tokyo Fu.

Gillilan, Miss B E, 1923, PN, Hokusei Jo Gakko, Sapporo.

Gist, Miss Annette, 1915, MES, 55 Niage Machi, Oita.

Goodman, Miss Zora Eleanor, 1924, MEFB, Iai Jo Gakko, Hakodate.

Gorbold, Mrs. R. P., 1892, PN, 24 Kyarabashi En, Hamadera, Osaka Fu.

Gordon, Mrs Agnes D., 1872, ABCFM, (Retired), Kyoto.

Govenlock, Miss I., 1912, MCC, Eiwa Jo Gakko, Shizuoka.

Grant, Mr. J P, YMCA-T, Okura Higher Commercial School, Akasaka Ku, Tokyo.

Graves, Miss Stella M, 1922, ABCFM, Kobe College, Yamamoto Dori, 4 Chome, Kobe.

Gray, Miss Gladys V, 1920, PE, Aoba Jo Gakuin, 69 Moto Yanagi Cho, Sendai

Gray, Rev Louis G, & W, 1921, LCA, (A), Care First Lutheran Church, First and Wilkinson Sts, Dayton, Ohio, U.S A.

Green, Rev. C. P., & W, 1917, CMA, Imaichi Machi, Shimane Ken

Greenbank, Miss K, M., 1920, MCC, (A), Wawota, Sask., Canada.

Gressitt, Mr. J. Fullerton, & W., 1907, ABF, 2050 Tenth Ave, Oakland, Cal, U S.A.

Griswold, Miss Fanny E, 1889, ABCFM, Iwagami Cho, Maebashi.

Gubbins, Miss, Ind., 1925, 101 Takashi Cho, Kagoshima.

Guinther, Rev E H, & W, 1913, 1923, RCUS, (A), 4149 Congress St., Chicago, Ill., U.S.A.

Gulick, Miss Ethel, 1924, ABCFM, Morigu, Taisha Mura, Muko Gun, Hyogo Ken.

Gulick, Mr Leeds, & W, 1921, 1922, ABCFM, Niban Cho, Matsuyama.

Gundert, Prof Wilhelm, & W, 1906, AEPM, 804 Bizen Machi, Mito.

Gushue-Taylor, Dr. G., M.B.B S, F R C.S., & W., 1911, UCC, 79 Miyamae Cho, Taihoku, Formosa.

Gwinn, Miss Alice E, 1922, ABCFM, Doshisha Jo Gakko, Imadegawa, Kyoto.

H

Hackett, Mr. Harold W & W, 1920. ABCFM, 53 Yamamoto I.. ᵀ · · · ⸱ ᵗ I. ᵇⁱᵗ

Heden Rev. T. H., D.D., 1895, MES, Kwansei Gakuin,
    Kobe   (Tel. Sannomiya 3608).
Hager Miss Blanche D., 1919, MES, Lambuth Jo Gakuin,
    5290 Ishigatsuji Cho Tennoji, Minami Ku, Osaka
Hager, Rev S. E., D D., & W., 1893, MES, 33 Seido Mura,
    Uchide Harinoki (Ashiya), Muko Gun, Hyogo Ken.
Halg. Miss Mary T., 1920, UCC, (A), R.R 6, Cobourg, Ont,
    Canada.
Hail, Rev J. B. D D. & W., 1877, PN, (Retired),
    Wakayama.
Hailstone, Miss M., 1920, SPG, Koran Jo Gakko, Sanko
    Cho, Shiba Ku, Tokyo
Hall, Mr. M. E. & W., 1915, ABCFM, 132 Iwagami Cho,
    Maebashi
Halsey, Miss L S., 1904, PN, (A), Terra Ceia, Fla , U.S.A.
Hambly, Miss O P., 1920, MCC, Edo Shimo Cho, Fukui.
Hamilton, Miss F G., 1917, MCC, 8 Toriizaka, Azabu Ku,
    Tokyo.
Hamilton, Miss Florence, 1914, MSCC, (A), 604 Jarvis St.
    Toronto, Canada
Hamilton, Rt. Rev. H. J., 1892, & W, 1894, MSCC, (A),
    604 Jarvis St, Toronto, Canada
Hamilton, Miss K, 1924, CMS, Seishi Jo Gakuin, Ashiya,
    Hyogo Ken
Hammell, Miss Esther, 1924, EC, 93 Takehaya Cho,
    Koishikawa Ku, Tokyo.
Hannaford, Rev H D, & W., 1915, PN, Meiji Gakuin,
    Imazato Cho, Shiba Ku, Tokyo.
Hannah, Miss Lolita, 1925, SBC, Kami Tanaka Machi,
    Shimonoseki.
Hansen, Miss Kate I, 1907, RCUS, (A), Logan, Phillips
    County, Kansas, U S.A.
Harding, Miss Cecile, 1926, Ind., 99 Temma Bashi Suji,
    1 Chome, Kita Ku, Osaka
Harker, Miss Hazel, 1923, UCMS, (A), Frankfort, Ind,
    U S.A.
Harobin, Miss H. M., 1923, MSCC, Shinta Machi, Matsumoto
Harper, Miss Ruth, 1917, MCC, Marubori Cho, Ueda, Nagano
    Ken.
Harris, Mr. R. W, & W, 1910, JEB, (A), Care 55 Gower
    St, London, W.C.1.
Harrison, Rev E R., & W, 1916, AUBM, 1489 Samukawa,
    Chiba.
Hassell, Rev. A P., & W, 1909, PS, Hon Cho, Tokushima.
Hassell, Rev J W, & W., 1915 PS 439 Nakabu, Maru-
    game, Kagawa Ken. (Furikae Osaka 47295)
Hatha
    Ca

Haven, Miss Marguerite, 1916, ABF, 2 Nakajima Cho, Sendai.

Hawkins, Miss Frances, 1920, MSCC, 5 Shirakabe Cho, 1 Chome, Nagoya.

Hawkins, Miss Violet R , 1925, AFP, 30 Koun Cho, Mita, Shiba Ku, Tokyo.

Heaslett, Rt Rev S , D.D , & W., 1900, SPG, CMS, (A).

Heaton, Miss Carrie A., 1893, MEFB, 2 Higashi Sanban Cho, Sendai.

Heckelman, Rev. F. W., & W., 1906, MEFB, 5 Aoyama Gakuin, Shibuya Machi, Tokyo Fu. (Tel Aoyama 2008).

Heins, Rev F. W., & W., 1924, LCA, 175 Nakanohashi Koji, Saga.

Helmer, Miss Edith, 1924, YWCA, 75 Kobinatadai Machi, 1 Chome, Koshikawa Ku, Tokyo.

Hempstead, Miss Ethel L , 1921, MPW, 105 Tamanoi Cho, Minami Ku, Nagoya.

Hendricks, Rev. K C., & W , 1921, UCMS, 49 Shin Machi, Fukushima.

Hendrickson, Miss Reba M., 1921, LCA, (A), Rowenna, Pa., U.S.A.

Hennigar, Rev. E C., & W., 1905, MCC, (A), The United Church of Canada, Mission Rooms, Wesley Building, Toronto, Canada

Henty, Miss A M., 1905, CMS, Ashiya, Hyogo Ken.

Hepner, Rev. C. W., & W , 1912, LCA, 754 Saru Shinden, Ashiya, Hyogo Ken.

Hereford, Miss Grace, 1925, PN, Wilmina Jo Gakko, Tamatsukuri, Osaka.

Hereford, Rev. W. F., D.D , & W., 1902, PN, 189 Kokutaiji Machi, Hiroshima.

Hesketh, Miss E., 1924, JRM, 162 Yoban Cho, Sendai.

Hetherington, Miss Nellie, 1926, JRM, 162 Kita Yoban Cho, Sendai.

Hewlett, Rev. A. S , M A., 1914, SPG, Bluff Hotel, Yokohama.

Heywood, Miss C. Gertrude, 1904, PE, Rikkyo Koto Jo Gakko, Kugayama, Takaido Mura, Tokyo Fu.

Hilburn, Rev. S. M., & W., 1923, MES, 133 Kami Nobori Cho, Hiroshima.

Hilliard, Rev. F., & W., 1921, MCC, Kwansei Gakuin, Kobe.

Hind, Rev. J , 1890, & W., 1891, CMS, (Retired), Senbo Cho, Tobata Shi, Fukuoka Ken.

Hitchcock, Mr Floyd, & W., 1923, OMS, 391 Kashiwagi, Yodobashi Machi, Tokyo.

Hit   M   D   PE,   Yamaichi Cho,
H   l

Hoare, Miss D., 1919, JEB, 2 Koyama Machi, Hiratsuka
    Mura, Tokyo Fu.
Hodges, Miss Olive I., 1902, MPW, Eiwa Jo Gakko, 124
    Maita Machi, Yokohama. (Tel. Choja Machi 2405).
Hockje, Rev. Willis G, 1907, RCA, 13-A Higashi Yamate,
    Nagasaki.
Hoeksema, Mr. Martin, 1925, RCA, Tozan Gakuin, Nagasaki.
Hoffheins, Miss Mary V, 1923, RCUS, (A), 3115 Decatur
    St, N.W., Washington, D.C., U.S.A.
Holland, Miss C. G., 1915, MES, 35 Nakayamate Dori,
    4 Chome, Kobe.
Holland, Miss J. M., 1888, Ind C.E, (A), 1 Queens Road,
    Rock Ferry, Cheshire, England
Holmes, Rev. C. P, & W., MCC, 96 Hokoekami Cho,
    Fukui, Echizen.
Holmes, Rev. J. C, & W, 1913, ABCFM, (A), 14 Beacon
    St, Boston, Mass, U.S.A.
Holmes, Miss Mary, 1915, SPG, (A), SPG House, 15 Tufton
    St, Westminster, London.
Holtom, Rev. D. C, PhD., & W., 1910, ABF, (A), Care
    Mrs. Elmer Palmer, 1110 Fourth St, Jackson, Mich.,
    U S A.
Horn, Rev. E. T., & W, 1911, LCA, 388 Shinyashiki,
    Kumamoto.
Horne, Miss A C J, 1906, CMS, Azuma Cho, Nogata Machi,
    Kurate Gun, Fukuoka Ken.
Hotson, Miss Jennie L, 1918, PCC, 79 Miyamae Cho,
    Taihoku, Formosa.
Howard, Miss R D, 1891, CMS, (A), Care CMS, Salisbury
    Square, London, E C.
Howe, Miss Annie L, 1887, ABCFM, 22 Nakayamate Dori,
    6 Chome, Kobe
Howey, Miss Harriet M., 1916, MEFB, Fukuoka Jo Gakko,
    Fukuoka.
Hoyt, Miss Olive S., 1902, ABCFM, 65 Kotojin Machi,
    3 Chome, Matsuyama.
Huesing, Miss Edith H, 1924, RCUS, Miyagi Jo Gakko,
    Higashi Sanban Cho, Sendai.
Hughes, Miss A. M, 1897, CMS, 56 Saiwai Cho, Muroran
    Shi.
Humphreys, Miss Marian, 1915, PE, Hodono Naka Cho,
    Akita.
Hunter, Rev. J. B, & W., 1920, UCMS, (A), Care United
    Missionary Society, St Louis, Mo, U S A.
Hurd, Miss H. R, 1911, MCC, 8 Toriizaka, Azabu Ku,
    Tokyo.
Husted, Miss Edith E, 1917, ABCFM, 59 Nakayamate Dori,
    6

Hutchinson, Rev. A. C., 1909, W., 1912, CMS, 376 Shira-yama Cho, Kurume Shi.
Hutchinson, Rev E. G., 1916, CMS, Hojo, Boshu.

I

Iglehart, Rev. C W., & W., 1909, MEFB, Hirosaki.
Iglehart, Rev. E. T, D D., & W., 1904, MEFB, 6 Aoyama Gakuin, Shibuya Machi, Tokyo Fu.
Ihde, Rev W. A., & W, 1922, MEFB, 2 Naebo Cho, Sapporo.
Isaac, Miss Irene Louise, 1918, MSCC, San No Tsuji, Takata, Echigo.
Isaacson, Rev. R. W., & W, TM, 1766 Nakano, Tokyo.

J

Jackson, Miss Vera, 1925, PB, 43 Funahashi Cho, Higashi Ku, Osaka
Jenkins, Rev. C. Reese, & W., 1925, PS, Tokushima.
Jenkins, Mr. James Alan, 1924, ABCFM, Muromachi Dori, Imadegawa Agaru, Kyoto.
Jenkins, Miss Louise F., 1920, ABF, (A), 383 Ellsworth Ave., New Haven, Conn, U.S.A
Jesse Miss Mary D, 1911, ABF, (A), Ashland, Virginia, U S.A.
Johnson, Miss Katherine, 1922, MES, Hiroshima Girls School, Kami Nagarekawa Cho, Hiroshima
Johnson, Mr Theodore, 1925, PB, 43 Funahashi Cho, Higashi Ku, Osaka
Johnstone, Miss J M, 1905, PN, Baiko Jo Gakuin, 1850 Murayama Cho, Shimonoseki.
Jones, Rev H P, & W, 1908, MES, Kwansei Gakuin, Kobe. (Tel. Sannomiya 3608).
Jones, Mr Thomas E, 1917, & W, 1914, AFP, (A), 805 Franklin St, Wilmington, Del., U S.A
Jones, Mr. Tudor J, 1923, JEB, 2 of 3 Ishii Cho, 3 Chome, Kobe.
Jorgensen, Mr A, & W, 1912, YMCA-A, Care University of Nebraska, Lincoln, Neb, U.S.A.
Jost. Miss H J, 1898, MCC, 33 Kami Niban Cho, Koji-machi Ku, Tokyo.
Judson, Miss Cornelia, 1887, ABCFM, (A), W B.M., 14 Beacon St, Boston, Mass., U.S.A.
Juer͡ . . . . 1912, AG, ... no, . . .

Juergensen, Mr C. F., & W., 1913, AG, 320 Nishi Sugamo, Tokyo Fu.

Juergensen, Mr. J W., & W, 1919, AG, 736 Takinogawa Machi, Aza Takinogawa, Tokyo Fu.

Jyergensen, Miss Marie, 1913, AG, 320 Nishi Sugamo, Tokyo Fu.

K

Karen, Rev A, & W., 1922, LEF, Iida, Nagano Ken.

Kaufman, Miss Emma R., 1913, YWCA, 2 Sadowara Cho, 2 Chome, Ushigome, Tokyo

Kaufmann, Miss Irene, 1925, YWCA, 75 Kobinatadai Machi, 1 Chome, Koishikawa Ku, Tokyo.

Keagey, Miss M D., 1908, MCC, Hyakkoku Machi, Kofu.

Keen, Miss E. M, 1895, CMS, Seishi Jo Gakuin, Ashiya, Hyogo Ken.

Keizei, Miss Henrietta, 1926, RCA, Baiko Jo Gakuin, Shimonoseki.

Kellam, Miss Lucille C., 1923, PE, St. Luke's Hospital, Tsukiji, Tokyo.

Kennard, Rev. J. Spencer, Jr., & W., 1920, ABF, (A), 537 , W. 149 St., New York, U S A.

Kennion, Miss Olive, SPG, 56 Yuki no Gosho, Hirano, Kobe

Kent, Miss Bernice M., 1922, UGC, 50 Takata Oimatsu Cho, Koishikawa Ku, Tokyo.

Kerr, Mr. J. H. T., & W., 1925, JEB, 56 Kumano Cho, 1 Chome, Kobe.

Kerr, Rev. Wm. C., 1908, & W, 1912, PN, (A), Care Presbyterian Board of Foreign Missions, 156 Fifth Ave, New York, U.S.A.

Kettlewell, Rev. F, 1905, SPG, 5-A Nakayamate Dori, 3 Chome, Kobe.

Kilburn, Miss Elizabeth H, 1919, MEFB, 596 Kuhonji Oemura, Kumamoto.

Killam, Miss Ada, 1902, MCC, Fukui.

Kinney, Miss Janie, M., M.A, 1905, UCC, Tansui, Formosa.

Kirkaldy, Miss M, 1924, JRM, 162 Kita Yoban Cho, Sendai.

Kirtland, Miss Leila G, 1910, PS, Kinjo Jo Gakko, Nagoya.

Kludt, Miss Anna M, 1922, ABF, 101 Haramachi, Koishikawa Ku, Tokyo.

Knapp, Deaconess Susan T, 1918, PE, St. Paul's University, Ikebukuro, Tokyo.

Knipp, Rev. J. Edgar, & W., 1900, UB, (A), 4905 Ferndale Ave, Howard Park, Baltimore, Md., U S.A.

Knu

Koch, Mr. Alfred, & W., 1924, SDA, 3131 Kashimadani, Omachi, Tokyo Fu.

Kraft, Mr. E J., & W., 1921, SDA, 169-171 Amanuma, Suginami Machi, Tokyo.

Kramer, Miss Lois F., 1917, CE, 93 Takehaya Cho, Koishikawa Ku, Tokyo.

Krider, Rev. W. W., & W., 1920, MEFB, Nagasaki.

Kriete, Rev. C. D., & W., 1911, RCUS, 1016 Muika Machi, Yamagata   (F.C. Tokyo 29312).

Kuecklich, Miss Gertrude, 1922, EC, 93 Takehaya Cho, Koishikawa, Tokyo.

Kuyper, Rev. Hubert, & W., 1911, 1912, RCA, (A), Orange City, Ia., U S A.

L

Lackner, Miss E. A., 1917, MCC, 380 Sunahara, Yanagi Shima, Kameido, Tokyo Fu.

Lade, Miss Helen R., 1922, PE, St. Luke's Hospital, Tsukiji, Tokyo.

Lake, Rev. L C., & W., 1916, PN, 2 Kita Shichijo Nishi 6 Chome, Sapporo.

Lamott, Rev. Willis C, & W., 1919, PN, Imazato Cho, Shiba Ku, Tokyo.

Lancaster, Miss Cecile, 1920, SBC, Seinan Jo Gakuin, Itozu, Kokura Shigai.

Landsborough, Mr. David, 1895, & W., 1909, EPM, Shoka, Formosa.

Lane, Miss E A., 1912, CMS, (A), Care CMS, Salisbury Square, London, E.C. 4.

Lansing, Miss Hariet M., 1893, RCA, Seijo Gakuin, Kinuta Mura, Kitatama Gun, Tokyo Fu.

Laughton, Capt James F, & W., 1921, ABF, (A), 276 Fifth Ave., New York, U.S.A.

Lawrence, Miss F. H, 1919, CMS, 7 Nobori Cho, 2 Chome, Kure.

Layman, Rev H. L, D D., & W., 1895, MP, 20 Nami Yose Machi, Higashi Cho, Nagoya.

Lea, Rt. Rev. Arthur, D D., 1897, & W., 1900, CMS, Kami Haruyoshi, Fukuoka.

Learned, Rev. D W, & W., 1875, ABCFM, Imadegawa Dori, Teramachi Nishi, Kyoto

Leavitt, Miss Julia, 1881, PN, Tanabe, Wakayama Ken

Lediard, Miss Ella, 1916, MCC, 14 Saibansho Dori, Kanazawa.

Lee, Mi l...   ...   M '...   ... ...   ' ... ... Ave., N ' l' n (S A

Lee, Miss Mabel, 1903, MEFB. (A), 315 Insurance Exchange Building, Minneapolis, Minn, U.S.A

Lehman, Miss Lois, 1922, UCMS, 16 Naka Naga Machi, Akita.

Leininger, Rev. A. A., & W., 1922, 1921, EC, 500 Shimo Ochiai Machi, Tokyo Fu.

Lindgren, Rev. R., & W., 1917, LEF, (A), Ruokolahdenkatu 20, Helsinki, Finland.

Lindsay, Miss Olivia C., 1912, MCC, Woman's Christian College, Tokyo.

Lindsey, Miss Lydia A, 1907, RCUS, (A), 409 E. Third St., Cherryvale, Kan, U.S.A.

Lindstrom, Rev. H., & W., 1891, CMA, 18 Kitano Cho, 3 Chome, Kobe.

Linn, Rev. J A, & W., 1922, LCA, 2007-B Ryumon Machi, 2 Chome, Yamate, Moji.

Linn, Rev. J. K, & W, 1915, LCA, (A), Care United Lutheran Foreign Missions Board, 18 East Mt. Vernon Place, Baltimore, Md, U S A.

Lippard, Rev. C. K, D D., & W, 1900, LCA, 10 Hirabayashi, Nishiuma, Kobe.

Lippard, Miss Faith, 1925, LCA, 10 Hirabayashi Nishiuma, Kobe.

Livingston, Miss Anna A., 1913, EPM, Shinro, Shoka, Formosa.

Lloyd, Miss Jeannie, 1903, EPM, Presbyterian Girls School, Tainan, Formosa.

Lloyd, Rev. J. H, 1908, & W., 1914, PE, Wakayama.

Logan, Rev C A, D.D, & W, 1902, PS, 171 Terashima Machi, Tokushima.

Lombard, Rev. F. A., 1900, & W., 1911, ABCFM, (A), 138 Hancock St., Auburndale, Mass., U S A

London, Miss M H, 1907, PN, Joshi Gakuin, 33 Kami Niban Cho, Kojimachi Ku, Tokyo.

Loomis, Miss Clara D, 1901, WU, 212 Bluff, Yokohama.

Lorimer, Mr. Allen I., 1924, ABCFM, Doshisha Y.M.C.A., Karasumaru Dori, Imadegawa Sagaru, Kyoto.

Lory, Mr Frank B., & W., 1925, YMCA-T, Sapporo, Hokkaido.

Lumpkin, Miss Estelle, 1911, PS, Tokushima Hon Cho, Tokushima

Luthy, Rev. S. R., & W., 1922, MEFB, Higashi Sanban Cho, Sendai

Lynn, Mrs Hazel B, 1921, WU, 212 Bluff, Yokohama.

M

Macdonald, Miss A. C., 1904, Ind., 10 Sakae Cho, Shiba

]

MacKay, Mr. G W., & W., 1911, UCC, (A), 17 Kagoike
Dori, Kobe.

Mackenzie, Miss V. M., 1919, PN, Wilmina Jo Gakko,
Tamatsukuri, Osaka.

Mackintosh, Miss S. E., 1916, EPM, Presbyterian Girls
School, Tainan, Formosa.

MacLeod, Rev. Duncan, & W., 1907, UCC, Tainan, Formosa.

MacMillan, Rev. Hugh, & W., 1924, UCC, Tansui, Formosa.

Madden, Mr. M. B , & W., 1895, Ind., (A).

Maddux, Miss Lois, 1924, MES, 51 Kitazako Machi, Kure.

Madeley, Rev. W. F., 1898, PE, 9 Motokaji Cho, Sendai.

Makeham, Miss S. E , 1902, MSCC, Kitsune Ike, Nagano.

Mander, Miss, 1925, SPG, 3 Yanai Cho, Ushigome Ku, Tokyo.

Mann, Miss Irene P., 1896, PE, Shiken Cho, Nikko, Tochigi
Ken.

Mann, Rev. J. C., 1906, & W., 1908, CMS, Nishinomiya,
Hyogo Ken.

Marsh, Miss Carolyn, 1921, YWCA, 13 Nishiogi Machi,
Kita Ku, Osaka.

Marshall, Rev. D. F., 1923, UCC, Tansui, Formosa.

Martin, Rev. D. P., 1923, PN, Noda, Yamaguchi.

Martin, Prof. J. V., & W., 1900, 1914, MEFB, 10 Aoyama
Gakuin, Shibuya Machi, Tokyo Fu. (Tel Aoyama 2008).

Mary Katharine, Sister, 1919, Ind., Home of the Epiphany,
358 Sanko Cho, Shirokane, Shiba Ku, Tokyo.

Matthews, Rev. W. K., & W., 1902, MES, Kwansei Gakuin,
Kobe. (Tel. Sannomiya 3608).

Mauk, Miss Laura, 1915, EC, 84 Sasugaya Cho, Koishikawa Ku, Tokyo. (Tel. Koishikawa 3516).

Mayer, Rev. Paul S , & W., 1909, EC, 500 Shimo Ochiai
Machi, Tokyo Fu.

McAlpine, Rev. R E., D.D , & W , 1885, 1887, PS, Kwangju,
Korea.

McArthur, Miss Kathleen W., 1919, MCC, (A), Wesley
College, Winnipeg, Man.

McCaleb, Mr. J. M., & W., 1892, Ind , 68 Zoshigaya, Tokyo
Fu.

McCall, Rev. C. F , & W., 1908, UCMS, 8 Shima Honcho,
Tsukiji, Akita.

McCausland, Miss Isabelle, 1920, ABCFM, Kobe College,
Yamamoto Dori, 4 Chome, Kobe.

McCoy, Rev. R. D , & W , 1904, UCMS, 35 Nakano Cho,
Ichigaya, Ushigome Ku, Tokyo.

McCrory, Miss C. H., 1912, PN, (A), 6811 Sixth St , N.W.,
Takoma Park, Washington, D C., U.S.A.

McDonald, Miss M. D , 1911, PN, (A), 730 W. Main St.,
Cherokee, Ia., U.S.A.

McL... Rev. J. S., , & ... .. PS (A , .. St.

Nashville, Tenn., U.S.A.

McGill, Miss Mary B, Ind , C E., Hibarigaoka, Kawanishi Kyokunai, Hyogo Ken.

McGrath, Miss Etta S., 1917, PE, Karasumaru Dori, Shimo-tachi Uri, Kyoto.

McGregor, Miss Grace, 1920, YWCA, (A), 600 Lexington Ave., New York.

McIlwaine, Rev. W. A., & W., 1919, PS, 37 Aoi Cho, Higashi Ku, Nagoya.

McIlwaine, Rev W B, D.D , & W., 1889, PS, 221 Suido Cho, 3 Chome, Kochi.

McInnes, Miss B., 1924, JRM, 162 Yoban Cho, Sendai.

McKim, Rev. J. Cole, & W., 1914, PE, 20 Inari Machi, Kita Ku, Osaka.

McKechnie, Mr A R, 1920, W, 1924, PE, St Paul's University, Ikebukuro, Tokyo.

McKenzie, Rev A. P., & W., 1920, MCC, 6 Hisaya Cho, 5 Chome, Higashi Ku, Nagoya.

McKenzie, Rev. D. R, D.D., & W, 1888, MCC, 23 Kami Tomizaka Cho, Koishikawa Ku, Tokyo. (Tel. Koishi-kawa 638, F. C. Tokyo 24908)

McKim, Miss Bessie, 1904, PE, 32 Kita Kuruwa Cho, Maebashi.

McKim, Rev. J. Cole, & W., 1914, PE, 20 Inari Machi, Koriyama.

McKim, Rt. Rev John, D D, 1880, PE, 48 Minami Cho, 1 Chome, Aoyama, Tokyo.

McKim, Miss Nellie, 1915, PE, 48 Minami Cho, 1 Chome, Aoyama, Tokyo.

McKinnon, Miss Claire, 1921, YWCA, 75 Kobinatadai, 1 Chome, Koishikawa Ku, Tokyo.

McKnight, Rev. W Q, & W., 1920, CC, 41 Karahori Cho, Sendai.

McLachlan, Miss Annie May, 1924, MCC, Shizuoka.

McLean, Miss Annie L, 1923, MCC, Eiwa Jo Gakko, Kofu Shi.

McLeod, Miss A. O, 1910, MCC, 12 Agata Machi, Nagano.

McNaughton, Miss Margaret, 1923, YWCA, 2 Sadowara Cho, 3 Chome, Ushigome Ku, Tokyo.

McWilliams, Rev. W R, & W, 1916, MCC, 14 Nakatakajo Machi, Kanazawa.

Mead, Miss Bessie, 1904, PE, Kasumi Cho, Yamagata Shi.

Mead, Miss Lavinia, 1890, ABF, Joshi Shin Gakko, Imazato Cho, Higashi Yodogawa Ku, Osaka.

Megaffin, Miss B I, 1922, MCC, 8 Toriizaka, Azabu Ku, Tokyo.

Meline Miss Agnes S 1919 ABF (A) Colon. Neb U.S A.

Merri   .   . .   II,

3 Chome, Matsuyama.

Meyers, Rev J. T, D.D , 1893, MES, (A), Box 510, Nashville, Tenn., U.S.A.

Mickle, Mr. J. J., & W., 1921, MES, (A), Amarillo, Texas, U.S.A.

Miles, Miss Mary, 1921, PN, (A), Care Mrs. F. H. Dyer, Sweetwater, Monroe Co, Tenn, U.S.A.

Miller, Mr. Adam W., & W., 1922, CG, 2531 Miyanaka, Nishi Sugamo, Tokyo Fu.

Miller, Rev. H. K, D.D., 1892, & W., 1888, RCUS, 3 Dai Machi, Ichigaya, Ushigome Ku, Tokyo.

Miller, Rev. L. S. G., & W , 1907, LCA, 351 Zeho Oe Machi, Kumamoto.

Millican, Rev. Roy W., & W., 1911, FMA, 599 Harada Mura, Kobe.

Millman, Rev. R. M, & W., 1909, MSCC, (A), 604 Jarvis St, Toronto, Can.

Mills, Mr. E. O., 1908, & W., 1900, SBC, 1041 Narutaki Machi, Nagasaki.

Minkkinen, Rev .T., 1905, LEF, (A), Hameenlinna. Finland.

Minnis, Mr G. F., & W, YMCA-T, Yamaguchi Higher Commercial School, Yamaguchi.

Mintle, Miss Rosa, 1908, OMS, (A), Glenwood, Ia., U S A.

Mohler, Miss Anna M., 1923, PE, Rikkyo Koto Jo Gakko, Kugayama Takaido Mura, Tokyo Fu.

Monk, Miss A. M., 1904, PN, Hokusei Jo Gakko, Sapporo, Hokkaido.

Montgomery, Rev. W E, 1909, & W., 1910, EPM, Shimo, Tainan, Formosa.

Mooar, Miss Eva A , ABCFM, Morigu, Taisha Mura, Muko Gun, Hyogo Ken.

Moody, Rev. Campbell, N., 1895, & W., 1919, EPM, Shoka, Formosa.

Moon, Miss Mira B, 1911, MEFB, 9 Aoyama Gakuin, Shibuya Machi, Tokyo Fu. (Tel Aoyama 2008).

Moore, Rev Boude C, & W, 1924, RCA, 1423 Hanabatake, Kurume.

Moore, Rev. J. W, D.D., & W, 1890, 1893, PS, Hanazono Cho, Takamatsu, Kagawa Ken.

Moore, Rev. Lardner W., & W., 1924, PS, Yatsu Ume Cho, 1 Chome, Gifu Shi.

Morgan, Miss A. E , 1889, PN, Tono Machi, Matsuzaka, Ise.

Moran, Rev. S. F., & W., 1916, ABCFM, Morigu, Taisha Mura, Muko Gun, Hyogo Ken.

Morris, Rev. T. Kenneth, 1926, Karasumaru Dori, Shimotachi Uri, Kyoto.

Moss, Miss Adelaide F., 1918, MSCC, Naka Hatcho, Toyohashi.

Moule, Rev. G. H, 1903, & W., 1894, CMS, (A), Care CMS, Salisbury Square, London, E.C. 4.
Mumford, Dr R H., 1925, EPM, Shoka, Formosa.
Munroe, Mr. Alex, & W., 1920, AG, 869 Kohara Takinogawa, Tokyo Fu.
Munroe, Rev. H. H., & W, 1905, 1906, PS, Hamano Cho, Takamatsu, Kagawa Ken.
Murray, Miss Edna B, 1921, PE, Rikkyo Koto Jo Gakko, Kugayama Takaido Mura, Tokyo Fu.
Myers, Rev. H. W, D.D., & W., 1897, PS, 112 Yamamoto Dori, 4 Chome, Kobe.
Mylander, Miss Ruth, 1925, FMA, 1260 Tennoji Cho, Sumiyoshi Ku, Osaka.

N

Nace, Rev. I G, & W, 1920, RCUS, 12 Higashi Dote Machi, Kameno Cho, Akita.
Nash, Miss Elizabeth, 1891, CMS, Matsuye, Shimane Ken.
Neely, Miss Clara J, 1899, PE, Shin Tera Machi, Gojo, Kyoto.
Nelson, Mr. Andrew N., & W., 1917, SDA, (A), 1208 Shelby St, Seattle, Wash., U S.A.
Nettleton, Miss I. M., 1926, SPG, 4 of 60 Nakayamate Dori, 6 Chome, Kobe.
Newcomb, Miss Ethel, 1913, (A), St. Louis, Mo, U S A
Newbury, Miss Georgia M., 1921, ABF, 2 Nakajima Machi, Sendai.
Newell, Rev. H B, & W, 1887, ABCFM, 34 Onari Machi, Keijo, Korea
Newlin, Miss Edith, 1918, AFP, 30 Koun Cho, Mita, Shiba Ku, Tokyo.
Newman, Capt Herbert, & W., 1924, SA, 5 Hitotsubashi Dori, Kanda Ku, Tokyo.
Nichols, Rev. Shirley H., & W., 1911, PE, Yamachi Cho, Hirosaki
Nichols, Mr Stewart B, 1922, ABCFM, Muromachi Dori, Imadegawa Agaru, Kyoto.
Nichols, Rt. Rev. S H., & W, 1925, PE, Karasumaru Dori, Shimotachi Uri, Kyoto
Nicholson, Mr. Herbert V., & W., 1915, 1920, AFP, 816 Tokiwa Mura, Mito Shigai, Ibaraki Ken.
Nicodemus, Prof. F. B., & W., 1916, RCUS, 60 Kozenji Dori, Sendai.
Nielson, Rev. Andrew B., 1895, EPM, Shinro, Tainan, Formosa
Nielse

miya, Nogata Machi, Tokyo Fu.

Noordhoft, Miss Jeane M, 1911, RCA, Orange City, Ia., U S A.

Norman, Rev. C E, & W, 1917, LCA, 15 Gokurakuji Cho, Fukuoka.

Norman, Rev. Daniel, D.D., & W., 1897, MCC, 12 Agata Machi, Nagano.

Norman, Miss Lucy, 1913, MCC, Canadian Academy, Harada Mura, Kobe Shigai.

Norton, Miss E L. B., 1900, CMS, (A), Care CMS, Salisbury Square, London, E.C. 4.

Noss, Rev. Christopher, D.D, & W., 1895, 1910, RCUS, 31 Torii Machi, Aizu-Wakamatsu, Fukushima Ken.

Noss, Prof. George C., & W., 1921, RCUS, 61 Kozenji Dori, Sendai.

Nugent, Rev. W Carl, & W, 1920, RCUS, 28 Torii Machi Aizu-Wakamatsu, Fukushima Ken

Nunn, Mr. W. L., YMCA-T, (A), Buford, Ga, U S A

Nuno, Miss Christine, 1925, PE, St. Luke's Hospital, Tsukiji, Tokyo

O

Obee, Rev. E. I, & W., 1904, MP, 3 Hinoki Cho, Akasaka Ku, Tokyo.

Ogburn, Rev. N S, & W., 1912, MES, Kwansei Gakuin, Kobe. (Tel. Sannomiya 3608).

Olds, Rev C. B, & W., 1903, ABCFM, 195 Kadota Yashiki, Okayama.

Oltmans, Rev Albert, D.D., & W., 1886, RCA, (Retired), 5 Meiji Gakuin, Shirokane, Shiba Ku, Tokyo. (Tel Takanawa 820; F.C. Tokyo 29625).

Oltmans, Miss C. Janet, 1914, RCA, 178 Bluff, Yokohama

Oltmans, Miss F Evelyn, 1914, RCA, 5 Meiji Gakuin, Shirokane, Shiba Ku, Tokyo.

Ostrom, Rev H C., DD, & W., 1911, PS, 34 Yamamoto Dori, 5 Chome, Kobe.

Ott, Miss Fina Carol, 1924, ABCFM, Morigu, Taisha Mura, Muko Gun, Hyogo Ken.

Outerbridge, Rev H W., & W., 1910, MCC, (A), Methodist Mission Rooms, 299, Queen St., W, Toronto, Ont., Canada.

Owen, Miss Gertrude, 1924, YWCA, 104, Ota Machi, 6 Chome, Yokohama.

Oxford Mr J S. & W 1910 MES 23 Kitanagasa Dori, 4 Chome, Kobe

P

Page Miss Mary, 1912, YWCA, (A), 1043 Oxford St, Berkeley, Cal, USA

Paine, Miss Margaret R, 1922, PE, (A), 281 Fourth Ave, New York, USA.

Paine, Miss Mildred A, 1920, MEFB, (A), Albion, NY, USA.

Painter, Rev. S, 1896, & W, 1905, CMS, Nobeoka Machi, Miyazaki Ken.

Palmer, Miss H. M, 1921, PN, (A), Care Mr E S Palmer, Parkville, Mo, USA.

Palmer, Miss Jewel, 1918, UCMS, 354 Nakazato, Takinogawa, Tokyo Fu. (Tel. Koishikawa 523).

Palmore, Rev. P Lee,, & W, 1922, MES, 120 Goken Yashiki, Himeji.

Pamperrien, Miss Gertrude E, 1921, RCUS, (A), 3174 W 82 St, Cleveland, O, U.S.A.

Parker, Miss A, 1888 SPG, 56 Yuki no Gosho, Hirano, Kobe.

Parmelee, Miss H Frances, 1877, ABCFM, (Retired), Tsuchida, Omi-Hachiman.

Parrott, Mr F, 1899, & W, 1904 BS, 95 Yedo Machi, Kobe.

Patterson, Mr G S, & W., 1912, YMCA-A, (A), 347 Madison Ave, New York.

Patton Miss Annie V, 1900, PS, Asahi Machi, Toyohashi

Patton, Miss Florence D, 1895, PS, Okazaki.

Pawley, Miss Annabelle, 1915, ARF, 3131 Kanagawa Machi, Yokohama

Peavy, Miss Anne R, 1923, MES, 51 Kitazako Machi, Kure

Peckham, Miss Caroline S, 1915, MEFB, Kwassui Jo Gakko, Nagasaki

Pedley, Miss Florella F., 1922, ABCFM, Kobe College, Yamamoto Dori, 4 Chome, Kobe.

Pedley, Rev. Hilton, & W, 1889, 1887, ABCFM, Karasumaru Dori, Ichijo Sagaru, Kyoto

Peeke, Rev. H V. S, D D, & W, 1888, 1893, RCA, 2 Meiji Gakuin, Shirokane, Shiba Ku, Tokyo. (Tel. Takanawa 820, F.C. Tokyo 43352).

Peet, Miss Azalia E, 1916, MEFB, 38 Hamano Cho, Fukuoka.

Perkins, Mr H J., & W., 1920, SDA, 169-171 Amanuma, Suginami Machi, Tokyo.

Perkins, Miss M O, 1926, PN, Joshi Gakuin, 33 Kami Niban Cho, Kojimachi Ku, Tokyo.

Perry,
Cho

Peters, Miss Gertrude, PN, Wilmina Jo Gakko, Tama-tsukuri, Osaka

Peterson, Miss A J , 1891, SAM, Chiba Shi

Petrie, Rev. Arthur, & W , 1919, CMA, (A).

Phelps, Mr. G. S , & W., 1902, YMCA-A, 22 Fujimi Cho, 5 Chome, Kojimachi Ku, Tokyo.

Phillips, Miss G., 1901, SPG, 108 Zoshigaya, Koishikawa Ku, Tokyo.

Phillips, Rev. W. O., & W., 1921, MES, (A), Box 510, Nashville, Tenn , U.S.A.

Pickard-Cambridge, Rev. C O , 1906, & W., 1900, CMS, Nishi Cho, Yonago Machi, Tottori Ken.

Pickens, Miss Lillian O , 1918, FMA, 1260, Tennoji Cho. Sumiyoshi Ku, Osaka.

Pider, Miss M Z , 1911, MEFB, (A), 150 Fifth Ave , New York, U.S.A.

Pierson, Rev. G P., D D , & W., 1888, 1891, PN, Nokkeushi, Kitami, Hokkaido.

Pieters, Miss Jennie A , 1904, RCA, Baiko Jo Gakko, Shimonoseki. (Tel 1196).

Pifer, Miss B. Catherine, 1901, RCUS, 207 Kita Arai. Nagasaki Mura, Tokyo Fu.

Pinsent, Mrs A. M , 1905, MCC, (A), St Johns, New Foundland.

Place, Miss Paulina A , 1916, MEFB, Kwassui Jo Gakko, Nagasaki.

Pooley, Miss A , 1918, SPG, Shoin Jo Gakko, 4 of 60 Nakayamate Dori, 6 Chome, Kobe.

Porter, Miss C , 1925, MES, 35 Nakayamate Dori, 4 Chome, Kobe.

Porter, Miss F. E., 1882, PN, 541 Higashi Gojo Hashi, 6 Chome, Kyoto.

Post, Miss Vida, 1920, ABF, (A), 57 Edsall Boulevard, Palisades Park, N.J., U.S.A.

Potts, Miss Marion E , 1921, LCA, Kyushu Jo Gakuin, Murozono, Kumamoto Shigai.

Powell, Miss Cecilia R., 1922, PE, (A), 281 Fourth Ave., New York, U.S.A.

Powers, Mr. M E , & W., 1926, SDA, 169-171 Amanuma. Suginami Machi, Tokyo.

Powlas, Miss Annie, 1919, LCA, Yochien, Ogi Cho. Saga Ken.

Powlas, Miss Maude, 1918, LCA, Jiai En, Kumamoto Shigai.

Powlas, Rev. P. S C , & W , 1916, MSCC, Shi no Tsuji Dori, Takata.

Pratt ,Miss Susan A., 1893, WU, 212 Bluff, Yokohama

Preton Miss Evelyn D. 1908, CMS, (A), 9 Chalbert St., N J W London N W .

Price, Rev. P. G, & W, 1912, MCC, 23 Kami Tomizaka Cho, Koishikawa Ku, Tokyo. (Tel. Koishikawa 638)

Pugmire, Major E I, & W., 1919, SA, 5 Hitotsubashi Dori, Kanda Ku, Tokyo.

R

Ragan, Miss Ruth, 1914, YWCA, (A), 600 Lexington Ave, New York, U S A.

Ranck, Miss Elmina, 1906, EC, (A), 1016 N. Harvard Blvd, Los Angeles, Cal., U.S.A.

Ransom, Miss M H., 1901, PN, 11 Komatsubara Dori, 3 Chome, Wakayama

Ranson, Deaconess Anna L, 1904, PE, Shimizu Cho, Kawagoe.

Rawlings, Rev G W, & W, 1900, 1903, CMS, 82 Kita Batake, Sumiyoshi Ku, Osaka.

Ray, Rev. J. F., D D, & W., 1904, SBC, 456 Senda Machi, Hiroshima

Read, Di Rachel, Ind, 6 Reinanzaka, Akasaka Ku, Tokyo.

Reeves Miss Grace, ABCFM, Morigu, Taisha Mura, Muko Gun, Hyogo Ken.

Reifsnider, Rt. Rev. C. S., D D, & W., 1901, PE, St Paul's University, Ikebukuro, Tokyo Fu.

Reischauer, Rev. A. K., D D, & W., 1905, PN, Woman's Christian College, Iogi Mura, Tokyo Fu.

Reiser, Miss A I, 1920, PN, Hokuriku Jo Gakko, Kanazawa.

Revell, Miss Rachel, 1923, PE, Rikkyo Koto Jo Gakko, Kugayama Takaido Mura, Tokyo Fu.

Rhoads, Miss Esther, 1921, AFP, (A), New Hope, Bucks County, Pa., U S A

Rhodes, Mr E A, & W., Ind, Hitachi Omiya, Ibaraki Ken.

Richards, Rev W. A., & W., 1910, Ind. C.E, Tenge, Yamaguchi Machi

Richey, Miss Helen L, 1920, UCMS, (A), Care Christian Missionary Society, St Louis, Mo, U S A

Riddell, Miss H., 1890, Ind, C E, 436 Furu Shinyashiki, Kumamoto

Riker, Miss Jessie, 1904, PN, 17 Miyajiri Cho, Yamada, Ise.

Riker, Miss S. M, 1926, PN, 739 Sumiyoshi Machi, Sumiyoshi Ku, Osaka

Roberts, Miss A, 1897, CMS, 25 Iwata Machi, Ushigome Ku, Tokyo.

Robertson, Miss Eleanor, 1921, YWCA, 2 Sadowara Machi, 3 Chome, Ushigome Ku, Tokyo.

Robert
To

Robinson, Rev. Cuthbert C., & W, 1920, MSCC, (A), 604 Jarvis St , Toronto, Can.

Robinson, Rev C E., & W, 1907, UCMS, (A), Care United Christian Missionarv Society, St. Louis, Mo , U.S A.

Robinson, Miss Hilda M , Ind , C.E , Kyo Machi, 1 Chome, Gifu.

Robinson, Rev. J. Cooper, D D , 188, MSCC, (A), 604 Jarvis St., Toronto, Can.

Rogers, Miss Margaret S., 1921, WU, (A), Winter Park, Fla , U.S A.

Rolfe, Staff-Capt. Victor E , & W., 1925, SA, 5 Hitotsubashi Dori, Kanda Ku, Tokyo.

Rorke, Miss Luella, 1919, MCC, Shizuoka.

Ross, Rev C H., & W , 1910, ABF, 5 Nakajima Cho, Sendai.

Rowe, Mrs. Alice G., 1922, UGC, 50 Takata Oimatsu Cho, Koishikawa Ku, Tokyo.

Rowe, Rev. J. H , & W., 1906, 1915, SBC, Seinan Jo Gakuin, Itozu, Kokura Shigai.

Rowland, Rev. G. M , & W., 1886, ABCFM, 645 Togoshi, Hiratsuka Mura, Ebara Gun, Tokyo Fu.

Rowland, Miss M. E , 1923, MES, 51 Kitazako Mach, Kure.

Rowlands, Rev F W , & W , 1894, 1897, Ind. C E , 42 Yohano Cho, Fukuoka.

Ruigh, Rev. D C , 1901, & W., 1904, RCA, 16 Higashi Yamate, Nagasaki.

Rupert, Miss Nettie L , Ind , Care Methodist Mission House, 24 Gai Nakayamate Dori, 2 Chome, Kobe.

Rusch, Mr. Paul F, 1925, YMCA-A, 22 Fujimi Cho, 5 Chome, Kojimachi Ku, Tokyo

Russell, Miss Lucy K., 1921, ABF, Joshi Shin Gakko, Imasato Cho, Higashi Yodogawa Ku, Osaka.

Russell, Miss M. H , 1895, MEFB, (Retired), Hirosaki Jo Gakko, Hirosaki.

Ryan, Miss Esther L , 1913, MCC, (A), 81 Homewood Ave , Toronto, Can.

Ryan, Mr. W. S., & W , 1917, YMCA-A, Sumiyoshi, Hyogo Ken.

Ryder, Miss Gertrude E , 1908, ABF, 51 Temma Cho, 1 Chome, Yotsuya Ku, Tokyo.

Ryder, Rev. Stephen W , & W , 1913, RCA, 143 Akamatsu Machi, Nishi Hirobata, Saga   (F.C. Fukuoka 7771)

S

Salor r r   K , & W   1   J PS 1683 M   na, J   ki T   t

Sandberg. Miss Minnie V. 1918, ABF, (A), 614 E. St., N.W., Washington, D.C, USA.

Saville, Miss Rose, 1925, IRM, 162 Kita Yoban Cho, Sendai.

Sivalainen, Rev V., & W. 1907, LEF, (A) Hameenlinna, Finland.

Sawyer, Miss Esther, 1926, CMA, Yanai Machi, Matsuyama.

Schaeffer, Miss Mabel R, 1921, PE, Rikkyo Koto Jo Gakko, Kugayama Takaido Mura, Tokyo Fu.

Schell, Miss Naomi, 1921, SBC, Seinan Jo Gakuin, Itozu, Kokura Shigai

Schereschewsky, Miss Caroline E, 1910, PE. Tenma, Nara.

Schiller, Supt. Emil, DD., & W., 1895, AEPM, (A), Care Pastor Wendt, Netzen bei, Lehnin, Brandenburg, Germany.

Schillinger, Rev. George W, & W, 1920, LCA, 351 Zeho Oe Machi, Kumamoto.

Schirmer, Miss Kathryn, 1917, EC, 14 Yojo Dori, 2 Chome, Nishi Ku, Osaka.

Schneder, Rev. D. B. DD, LLD, & W., 1887, RCUS, 164 Higashi Sanban Cho, Sendai.

Schneder. Miss Mary E, 1918, RCUS, 164 Higashi Sanban Cho, Sendai.

Schroer, Rev G W. & W, 1922, RCUS, 71 Osawa Kawarakoji, Morioka.

Schweitzer, Miss Edna M., 1912, EC, 84 Sasugaya Cho, Koishikawa Ku, Tokyo. (Tel Koishikawa 3546).

Scott, Miss Ada C, 1916 UCMS, (A) Care United Christian Missionary Society, St Louis, Mo, USA.

Scott, Rev. F. N, DD, & W, 1903, MEFB, 9 Aoyama Gakuin, Tokyo.

Scott, Rev. J. H, & W., 1892, 1910, ABF, 228 Koyashiki, Ashiya, Hyogo Ken.

Scott, Rev. J. J, & W, 1910, CMS, Suketo Machi, Tokushima

Scott, Miss Jane N 1920, YWCA, 75 Kobinatadai Machi, 1 Chome, Koishikawa Ku, Tokyo.

Scott, Miss Leona O, 1920, YWCA, (A), 600 Lexington Ave, New York, USA

Scott. Miss Mary, 1911, MCC, Marubari Cho, Ueda, Nagano Ken

Scott, Miss M D A, 1921, EPM, (A), Westminster College, Cambridge, Eng

Scruton, Miss Fern, 1926, MCC, 8 Toriizaka, Azabu Ku, Tokyo.

Searcy, Miss Mary G., 1923, MES, (A), Box 510 Nashville, Tenn, USA

Searle, Miss Susan 1883 ABCFM, Kobe College, Yamamot. Dor

Seeds, Miss L. M., 1890, MEFB, 150 Fifth Ave , New York, U S.A

Seiple. Rev. W. G., Ph.D., & W., 1905, RCUS, 125 Tsuchidoi, Saruhiki Cho, Sendai

Sells, Miss E. A. P , 1893, CMS, Nagaike Machi, Oita.

Senior, Miss Annie R N , 1924, UCC, 79 Miyamae Cho, Taihoku, Formosa.

Shacklock, Rev. F W , & W., 1920, MEFB, (A), 150 Fifth Ave., New York, U S.A.

Shafer, Miss Bessie J , 1925, RCA, 8 Oura Higashi Yamate, Nagasaki.

Shafer, Rev. Luman J , & W , 1912, RCA, 178 Bluff, Yokohama.

Shannon, Miss Ida L , 1904, MES, Hiroshima Jo Gakko, Kami Nagare Kawa Cho, Hiroshima.

Shannon, Miss Katherine, 1908, MES, Hiroshima Jo Gakko, Kami Nagare Kawa Cho, Hiroshima.

Sharpe, Rev A. L , 1903, SPG, Zushi, Kanagawa Ken.

Sharpless, Miss Edith F., 1910, AFP, 888 Tenno Cho, Mito, Ibaraki Ken.

Shaver, Rev. I L., & W., 1919, MES, Morino Cho, Kanaya, Nakatsu, Oita Ken.

Shaw, Miss L. L., CMS, Poole Jo Gakko, Tsuruhashi Cho, Osaka

Shaw, Rev. Mark R., & W., 1922, MEFB, 3 Aoyama Gakuin, Shibuya Machi, Tokyo Fu　(Tel Aoyama 2008).

Shaw, Rev. R. D. M., & W , 1907, SPG, Hamadake, Hiratsuka, Kanagawa Ken.

Shepherd, Miss K , 1910, SPG, Nishi no Jo, Numazu Shi.

Shirk, Miss Helen, LCA, 337 Haruyoshi, 3 Chome, Fukuoka.

Shively, Rev. B. F., D.D., & W , 1907, UB, 216 Muromachi, Kyoto　(F C Osaka 34076).

Sholty, Rev. Alva H., & W., 1922, UB, 1912 Shimo Shibuya, Tokyo Fu　(Tel Shiba 5429).

Shore, Miss Gertrude, 1921, MSCC, (A), 604 Jarvis St., Toronto, Can.

Simeon, Miss R., 1919, SPG, (A), SPG House, 15 Tufton St , Westminster, W M.I , London.

Simpson, Miss M. E., 1920, MCC, Hyakkoku Machi, Kofu.

Sinclair, Mr. Gregg M , YMCA-T, Hikone, Shiga Ken.

Singleton, Mr. Leslie, 1921, & W., 1922, EPM, Shinro, Tainan, Formosa.

Singley, Rev. D. F., & W., 1918, RCUS, (A), 127 Grand View Road, Ardmore, Pa., U.S.A.

Skiles, Miss Helen, 1922, PE, (A), 281 Fourth Ave., New York, U.S.A.

Slate, Miss Anna B., 1902, MEFB, (A), 361 Mulberry St., Williamsport Pa , U S A.

Smith, Prof A. D., & W., 1919, 1921, RCUS, (A), 311 Orient
    Way, Rutherford, N.J., U S A.

Smith, Miss E. D., 1926, SPG, 5 Nakayamate Dori, 3 Chome,
    Kobe

Smith, Miss Frederica, 1922, PE, Muro Machi, Shimo'achi
    Uri Sagaru, Kyoto

Smith, Rev F H, D D, & W, 1905, MEFB, Seoul, Chosen.

Smith, Mr Herbert, & W., 1925, PB, Shichi Hon Machi
    Dori, Sasaya Machi Dori, 1001 Sue no Kuchi Machi,
    Osaka

Smith, Miss I. W., 1917, JEB, Daimon Dori, Shin Maizuru,
    Kyoto Fu

Smith, Rev P. A., & W, 1903, PE, Hikone, Shiga Ken

Smith, Mr. Roy, & W, 1903, MES, 29 Kitano Cho, 1 Chome,
    Kobe.

Smith, Miss S. C., 1880, PN, (Retired), 2 Kita Shichijo,
    Nishi 6 Chome, Sapporo.

Smyser, Rev. M. M., & W, 1903, Ind., Yokote, Akita Ken.
    (F C Sendai 5183)

Smyth, Staff-Capt. Annie, 1906, SA, 5 Hitotsubashi Dori,
    Kanda Ku, Tokyo

Smythe, Rev. L. C M., D.D, 1913, & W, 1916, PS, 11
    Shirakabe Cho, 1 Chome, Nagoya.

Snevd, Mr. H. S., & W, 1913, YMCA-A, Seinen Kai,
    Hakkeizaka, Omori, Tokyo Fu.

Soal, Miss A, 1916, JEB, Daimon Dori, Shin Maizuru,
    Kyoto Fu.

Somervell, Miss M, 1919, SPG, (A).

Southard, Mr. Paul, CMA, Matsuyama.

Southworth, Dr J. D., & W., 1923, PE, 5 of 371 Saruko
    Sumiyoshi Cho, Sumiyoshi Ku, Osaka.

Sowers, Mr G M., & W, 1925, LCA, 65 Miyashit Cho,
    Koishikawa Ku, Tokyo.

Spackman, Rev. H. C, & W, PE, St. Paul's University,
    Ikebukuro, Tokyo Fu.

Spencer, Rev. D S, D D., & W., 1883, MEFB, 435 Furu
    Shin Yashiki, Kumamoto.

Spencer, Miss Gladys, 1921, PE, Ura Machi, Aomori

Spencer, Rev. R S. & W., 1917, MEFB, 878 Kigo, Fukuoka.

Spencer, Rev V C, 1913, MSCC, 43 Higashi Kataha Machi,
    Nagoya.

Sprowles, Miss A B, 1906, MEFB, 4 Aoyama Gakuin,
    Tokyo.

Stacy, Miss Martha, 1919, CC, 41 Karahori Cho, Sendai.

Staples, Miss Marie M., 1915, MCC, Edo Shimo Cho, Fukui.

Starkey, Miss Bertha, 1910, MEFB, Seoul, Korea.

Steadman, Rev. F W., & W, 1902, ABF, (A), Granville, O,
    U.

Stegeman, Rev. H. V. E., & W., 1917, RCA, Meiji Gakuin, Tokyo.

Stetson, Rev. Clifford R., & W, 1922, UGC, 33 Higashi-kusabuka Cho, 2 Chome, Shizuoka.

Stevens, Miss C. B., 1920, MES, Hiroshima Jo Gakko, Kami Nagarekawa Cho, Hiroshima

Stewart, Rev. S. A., & W, 1906, MES, Hiroshima Girls School, Kami Nagarekawa Cho, Hiroshima

Stirewalt, Rev. A. J., & W., 1905, LCA, 303 Hyakunin Cho, Okubo, Tokyo Shigai.

St John, Mrs Alice C., 1918, PE, St. Luke's Hospital, Tsukiji, Tokyo

Stokes, Miss K., 1922, SPG, 56 Yuki no Gosho, Hirano, Kobe

Stoudt, Mr O M., & W., 1917, RCUS, 15 Naga Cho, Sendai

Stowe, Miss Grace H, 1908, ABCFM, Kobe College, Yama-moto Dori, 4 Chome, Kobe.

Stowe, Miss Mary E, 1908 ABCFM, Kobe College, Yama-moto Dori, 4 Chome, Kobe

Straub, Miss Mae, 1921, AG, Box 328, Sannomiya, Kobe.

Strong, Rev. Eustace M, Ind C E. (A).

Strothard, Miss A. O, 1915, MCC, Eiwa Jo Gakko, Kofu

Sturtevant, Miss Abby L, 1921, MEFB, 12 Kita Ichijo Higashi 6 Chome, Sapporo.

Suess, Miss Elizabeth, RCUS, 1925 168 Higashi, Sanban Cho, Sendai

Swan, Mr. G D, & W, 1913, YMCA-A, (A), 347 Madison Ave, New York, U S A

T

Tait, Miss S. O, 1916 MCC 14 Saibansho Dori, Kanazawa.

Tammio, Rev K, & W., 1913, LEF, (A), Tampere, Finland.

Tannei, Miss K, SPG, (A)

Tapson, Miss M. A, Ind, 1888, Garden Home, Nogata Mura, Tokyo Shigai.

Teague, Miss Carolyn, 1912, MEFB, 586 Kuhonji, Oe Mura, Kumamoto.

Teets, Miss Edith V., 1921, RCA, (A), 5 Sawyer St., Hornell, N Y.

Tench, Rev. G. R., & W, 1920, MCC, Canadian Academy, Kwansei Gakuin, Kobe.

Tenny, Rev. Chas. B, 1900, & W., 1913, ABF, 29 Sanai Cho, Ushigome Ku, Tokyo.

Ter Borg, Rev. John, & W, 1922, RCA, 45 Shimo Tatsuo Cho Kagoshima

Tetl   ,   va.

Teusler, Dr. R. D., & W., 1899, PE, St. Luke's Hospital, Tsukiji, Tokyo

Tharp, Miss Elmer R., 1918, ABF, 72 Myogidani, Koishikawa Ku, Tokyo.

Thede, Rev. Harvey, & W., 1920, EC. 14 Yojo-dori Nichome Minato-ku, Osaka.

Thompson, Mrs. David, 1873, PN, (Retired), 22 Fujimi Cho, 5 Chome, Koishikawa Ku, Tokyo.

Thompson, Miss F. L., 1905, CMS, (A), Care CMS, Salisbury Square, London, E C 4.

Thompson, Rev. R A., D.D., 1888, & W., 1889, ABF, 39 Kitano Cho, 2 Chome, Kobe.

Thoren, Miss Amy, 1925, LCA, 65 Miyashita Cho, Koishikawa Ku, Tokyo.

Thorlaksson, Rev S. O., & W., 1916, LCA, 131 Kyo Machi, 4 Chome, Kurume.

Thornton, Mr. Harrison, & W., 1926, JRM, 162 Kita Yoban Cho, Sendai.

Thornton, Rev J. B., & W., 1908, JEB, (A), 809 Schaff Building, Philadelphia, Pa., U S.A.

Thurston, Miss E. V., 1920, MEFB, (A), 150 Fifth Ave., New York, U.S.A.

Topping, Miss Helen, 1918, YWCA, (A), 600 Lexington Ave., New York, U.S.A.

Topping, Rev. Henry, & W., 1895, ABF, (A), Care ABFMS, 276 Fifth Ave., New York, U.S.A.

Topping, Mr. Willard F., & W., YMCA-T, 1327 Kanoe Kochi, Minami Ota Machi, Yokohama.

Towson, Miss Mamie, 1917, MES, (A), Box 510 Nashville, Tenn., U.S.A.

Towson, Rev. W. L., & W., 1890, MES, (A), Box 510 Nashville, Tenn., U.S.A.

Tracy, Miss Mary E., 1903, WU, (A), 67 Bible House, New York, U.S.A.

Tremain, Mr. Martel A., & W., YMCA-T, 63 Nishiyama Cho, 2 Chome, Hashida Ku, Kobe.

Trent, Miss E. M., 1894, MSCC, 8 Kita Takajo Machi 2 Chome, Nagoya.

Tristram, Miss K. A. S., 1888, CMS, Poole Jo Gakko, Tsuruhashi Cho, Osaka.

Trott, Miss, 1925, SPG, 8 Sakae Cho, Shiba Ku, Tokyo.

Trout, Miss Jessie M., 1921, UCMS, 16 Naka Naga Machi, Akita.

Trueman, Mr. G E., & W., 1910, YMCA-A, (A), 347 Madison Ave., New York, U S.A.

Tundin, Miss Mozelle, 1923, MES, 55 Niage Machi, Oita.

Twee' ''
T '

U

Umbreit, Rev. S. J , D.D., & W., 1905, EC, (A), Naperville, Ill., U.S.A.

Upton, Miss Eliabeth F., 1916, PE, Omiya, Saitama Ken

Uusitalo, Miss S., 1903, LEF, (A), Fredrikink. 42, Helsinki, Finland.

V

VanAken, Miss H. E., 1925, PN, Hokuriku Jo Gakko, Kanazawa

Van Bronkhorst, Rev. Alexander, & W , 1916, RCA, 429 Minami Shinchi, Oita.

VanDyke, Rev. P. S , & W., 1921, PS, Kabuto Yama, Okazaki.

Van Kirk, Miss Anna S , PE, 281 Fourth Ave., New York, U S A.

Veazey, Miss M. A., 1926, MCC, Kameido, Tokyo.

Verry, Miss Hazel, 1918, YWCA, 2082 Minami Ota Machi, Yokohama.

Vories, Mrs. Julia E., 1914, OMJ, Omi Hachiman, Shiga Ken.

Vories, Mr. W. M , & W., 1905, OMJ, Omi Hachiman, Shiga Ken.

Voules, Miss Jessie E , 1913, SPG, (A), SPG House, 15 Tufton St., Westminster, London.

W

Wagner, Miss Dora, 1913, MEFB, Tokyo Joshi Dai Gakko, Iogi Mura, Nishi Ogikubo, Tokyo Fu.

Wagner, Rev. H. H , & W., 1918, FMA, Baba Cho, Sumoto Machi, Awaji.

Wainright, Rev S H , D.D., & W., 1888, MES, 33 Onden Cho, Aoyama, Tokyo.

Walker, Mr. F. B., & W , 1903, 1906, SPG, (A), SPG House, 15 Tufton St., Westminster, London.

Waller, Rev. J. G , & W., 1890, MSCC, Nishi Nagano Machi, Nagano.

Walne, Rev E. N , D D., & W., 1892, SBC, Kami Tanaka Machi, Shimonoseki.

Walne, Miss Florence, 1919, SBC, Kami Tanaka Machi, Shimonoseki.

Walser Rev T D. & W 1916, I N 1 or 3 Tsuno Machi, Meiji, Shiba Ku, Tokyo.

Walsh, Rev. G. J., & W., 1913, CMS, 5 Jo Dori, 10 Chome,
 Asahigawa, Hokkaido.
Walters, Miss Mary, 1923, SBC, Kami Tanaka Machi,
 Shimonoseki.
Walton, Rev. W. H. M, & W., 1915, CMS, 25 Iwato Machi,
 Ushigome Ku, Tokyo.
Walvoord, Miss Florence, 1922, RCA, Baiko Jo Gakuin,
 Shimonoseki.
Ward, Miss Ruth C., 1919, (A), 1725 Garfield Ave.,
 Pasadena, Cal, U.S.A.
Warner, Rev. Paul F., 1924, MP, 43 Chokyuji Machi,
 Nagoya.
Warren, Rev. Charles M., & W., 1899, ABCFM, Kami Beppu,
 Miyazaki Ken.
Warren, Rev. F. F., & W., 1925, FMA, 1260 Tennoji Cho,
 Sumiyoshi Ku, Osaka.
Waters, Rev. George L., 1922, MES, Kwansei Gakuin, Kobe.
Waters, Rev. Harris, & W., 1925, MES, Niomon Dori,
 Hiromichi Nishi, Kyoto.
Weakley, Rev. W. R., & W., 1895, MES, Hon Cho, Toku-
 yama, Yamaguchi Ken.
Webber, Mr. P A., & W., 1926, SDA, 169-171 Amanuma,
 Suginami Machi, Tokyo.
Weed, Miss Helen I., 1921, RCUS, 33 Uwa Cho, Komega-
 fukuro, Sendai.
Welda, Mr. F. Wharton, 1925, RCUS, 125 Tsuchidoi,
 Suruhiki Cho, Sendai.
Weidinger, Dr. Karl, & W., 1926, AEPM, 39 Kamitomizaka
 Cho, Koishikawa Ku, Tokyo.
Weiss, Miss Ruth, 1920, MEFB, (A), Denison, Ia., U.S.A.
Welbourn, Rev. J. A., 1899, & W., 1915, PE, Karasumaru
 Dori, Imadegawa Sagaru, Kyoto.
Welch, Bishop Herbert, & W, 1916, MEFB, Seoul, Korea.
Wells, Miss L A, 1900, PN, 12 Noda, Yamaguchi.
Welte, Miss Jane M., 1923, PE, Kamikyoku, Bishamon
 Cho, Kyoto
Wengler, Miss Jessie, 1919, AG, 33 Oiwake Cho, Hachioji
 Shi, Tokyo Fu.
West, Rev R. E, & W., 1922, MEFB, Higashi Yamate,
 Nagasaki.
Weston, Rev. F., & W., 1916, SPG, (A), SPG House, 15
 Tufton St., Westminster, London.
Whent, Miss Ruth M, 1923, PE, (A), 281 Fourth Ave,
 New York, U.S.A.
White, Miss Anna Laura, 1911, MEFB, Kwassui Jo Gakko,
 Nagasaki.
Whitehead, Miss Mabel 1917 MES Lambuth Jo Gakuin,
 5:

Whiteman, Miss Mary, 1920, JRM, 162 Kita Yoban Cho, Sendai.

Whiting, Rev. M. M., & W., 1912, MCC, Kwansei Gakuin, Kobe (Tel. Sannomiya 6308).

Whitney, Mrs. Mary C., 1886, Ind., 5 Hikawa Cho Akasaka Ku, Tokyo.

Wilbur, Mr. H. A., & W., 1925, YMCA-A, 22 Fujimi Cho, 5 Chome, Kojimachi Ku, Tokyo.

Wilcox, Miss Edith F., 1904, ABF, 50 Shimotera Machi, Himeji.

Wilkes, Mr. A. Paget, & W., 1899, JEB, 55 Gower St., London, W.C. 1, England.

Wilkinson, Rev. A. T., & W., 1905, MCC, Nishi Kusabuka Cho, Shizuoka.

Wilkinson, Mr. C. S., & W., 1912, JEB, 27 Okano Machi, Fukuchiyama, Kyoto Fu.

Wilkinson, Miss Jessie M. G., 1919, ABF, (A), 5 Ardmore Road, West Roxbury, Boston, Mass., U.S.A.

Williams, Miss A. B., 1910, MES, (A), Box 510, Nashville, Tenn., U.S.A.

Williams, Miss A. S., 1915, CMS, Poole Jo Gakko, Tsuru-hashi Cho, Osaka.

Williams, Miss Hallie R., 1916, PE, (A), 281 Fourth Ave., New York, U.S.A.

Williams, Miss Mary E., 1897, MP, 105 Tamanoi Cho, Atsuta, Nagoya.

Williams, Miss T., 1913, SPG, Koran Jo Gakko, Sanko Cho, Shiba Ku, Tokyo.

Williamson, Rev. E., & W., 1924, EC, Koriyama, Fukushima Ken.

Williamson, Miss Jeanie, 1926, JRM, 162 Kita Yoban Cho, Sendai.

Williamson, Rev. N. F., & W., 1918, 1919, SBC, 135 Kyo Machi, 2 Chome, Kumamoto.

Wilson, Miss Eleanor, ABCFM, Morigu, Taisha Mura, Muko Gun, Hyogo Ken.

Wilson, Rev. Jesse R., & W., 1921, ABF, 201 Imasato Cho, Higashi Yodogawa Ku, Osaka.

Wilson, Brigadier T. W., & W., 1906, SA, 5 Hitotsubashi Dori, Kanda Ku, Tokyo.

Wilson, Rev. W. A., & W., 1890, MES, 113 Kunitomi, Okayama.

Winn, Rev. M. C., & W., 1916, PN, 34 Tobiume Cho, Kodatsuno, Kanazawa.

Winn, Miss M. L., 1881, Ind., Rokuban Cho, Takamatsu, Kagawa Ken.

Wiser

Wolfe, Miss Evelyn M, 1920, MP, Eiwa Jo Gakko, 124 Maita Machi, Yokohama. (Tel. Chojamachi 2405).

Woodard, Rev W. P., & W, 1921, ABCFM, 10 Kita Ichijo, Higashi 6 Chome, Sapporo.

Woodbridge, Mr. W. F, 1914, Ind., Kaibara, Hikami Gun, Hyogo Ken.

Woodsworth, Rev. H F., & W., 1911, MCC, (A), The United Church of Canada, Mission Rooms, Wesley Building, Toronto, Can.

Woodworth, Rev. A. D., & W, 1892, CC, 26 Kasumi Cho, Azabu Ku, Tokyo.

Woolley, Miss Alice, 1925, PB, 43 Funahashi Cho, Higashi Ku, Osaka.

Woolley, Miss K., 1915, SPG, Koran Jo Gakko, Sanko Cho, Shiba Ku, Tokyo.

Wordsworth, Miss, SPG, Juji Machi, Odawara Machi, Kanagawa Ken.

Worth, Miss Ida M., 1895, MES, Ashiya, Hyogo Ken.

Worthington, Miss H. J., 1899, CMS, 7 Nobori Cho, 2 Chome, Kure.

Wright, Miss Ada H., 1897, Ind., C.E., 436 Furu Shin-yashiki, Kumamoto.

Wylie, Miss M. L., 1905, CMA, Futami Gun, Kisa Machi, Hiroshima Ken.

Wynd, Rev. Wm. O., 1891, & W., 1894, ABF, 257 Nakazato, Takinogawa, Tokyo Fu.

Wythe, Miss K. Grace, 1909, MEFB, 38 Hamano Cho, Fukuoka.

Y

Yarnell, Dr D E, & W, 1921, YMCA-A, (A), 347 Madison Ave., New York, U.S.A.

Young, Miss Mariana, 1897, MEFB, 11 Oura, Nagasaki.

Young, Rev T. A., 1912, & W., 1905, UCMS, (A), Care United Christian Missionary Society, St. Louis, Mo., U.S.A.

Z

Zaugg, Rev. E. H, Ph D, & W, 1903, RCUS, 69 Kata Hira Machi, Sendai.

Ziemann, Rev. P P W, 1920, & W, 1921, ABF, 6 Naka Cho, Yotsuya Ku, Tokyo.

LIST BY TOWNS

Akita Shi, Akita Ken.

Andrews, Rev. E. L., & W., PE.
Humphreys, Miss Marian, PE.
Lehman, Miss Lois, UCMS
McCall, Rev. C. F., & W, UCMS.
Nace, Rev. I G, & W, RCUS.
Trout, Miss Jessie M., UCMS.

Amagasaki, Hyogo Ken.

Cox, Miss A. M., CMS.

Aomori Shi, Aomori Ken

Spencer, Miss Gladys, PE.

Asahigawa Shi, Hokkaido.

Walsh, Rev J. G., & W., CMS.

Ashiya, Hyogo Ken.

Hamilton, Miss K., CMS.
Henty, Miss A. M., CMS.
Hepner, Rev C. W., & W., LCA.
Keen, Miss E. M., CMS.
Scott, Rev. J. H., & W., ABF.
Worth, Miss Ida M., MES.

Beppu, Oita Ken.

Floyd Rev Arva C & W M .r

Chiba, Chiba Ken.

Harrison, Rev. E R, & W., AUBM.
Peterson, Miss A. J., SAM.

Fukui Shi, Fukui Ken.

Holmes, Rev. C. P, & W., MCC.
Killam, Miss Ada, MCC
Staples, Miss M. M., MCC.

Fukuoka Shi, Fukuoka Ken.

Baker, Miss Effie, SBC.
Bouldin, Rev. O. W., & W., SBC.
Conrad, Miss Florence, SBC.
Cowl, Rev. J, & W., CMS.
Dozier, Rev. C. K., & W SBC.
Faucette, Mr. Thomas W, & W., YMCA-T.
Fulghum, Miss S. F., SBC.
Howey, Miss Harriet M, MEFB.
Lea, Bishop Arthur, & W., CMS.
Norman, Rev. C E., & W., LCA.
Peet, Miss A. L., MEFB.
Rowlands, Rev. F. W., & W., Ind
Shirk, Miss Helen, LCA.
Spencer, Rev. R. S., & W., MEFB

Fukushima Shi, Fukushima Ken.

Hendricks, Rev. K. C., & W., UCMS.

Fukuyama Shi, Hiroshima Ken.

Francis, Mr. T. R., & W., CMA.

Gifu Shi, Gifu Ken.

Buchanan, Miss E O , PS.
Buchanan, Rev. Wm. C., PS.
Moore, Rev. L. W., & W., PS.
Robinson, Miss H. M., Ind.

Kawagoe.

Ranson, Deaconess Anna L., PE.

Omi-Hachiman, Shiga Ken.

Parmelee, Miss H. F., ABCFM, (Retired).
Vories, Mrs Julia E., OMJ.
Vories, Mr. W. M , & W , OMJ.

Hakodate Shi, Hokkaido.

Cheney, Miss Alice, MEFB.
Goodman, Miss Z. E., MEFB.

Hamamatsu Shi, Shizuoka Ken.

Coates, Miss A. L., MP.
Coates, Rev. H. H., MCC.

Hibarigaoka, Hyogo Ken.

McGill, Miss M. B., Ind.

Hikone, Shiga Ken

Sh.. , Rev P. A & W., PE.

Sinclair, Mr. G M , YMCA-T.

Himeji Shi, Hyogo Ken.

Acock, Miss A A , ABF
Bixby, Miss A. C., ABF
Palmore, Rev P. Lee, & W., MES.
Wilcox, Miss E F., ABF.

Hiratsuka, Kanagawa Ken.

Shaw, Rev. R. D. M., & W,. SPG

Hirosaki Shi, Aomori Ken.

Brumbaugh, Rev. T. T , & W., MEFB.
Courtice, Miss L. K, MEFB.
Gard, Miss B. A., MEFB
Hittle, Miss Dorothy, PE.
Iglehart, Rev. C. W., & W., MEFB.
Russell, Miss M. H., MEFB.

Hiroshima Shi, Hiroshima Ken.

Bennett, Miss Nellie, MES
Clarke, Miss S F., PN.
Collins, Mr. H. H., YMCA-T
Farrar, Miss Virginia, MES.
Gaines, Miss N. B., MES.
Gaines, Miss Rachel, MES.
Hereford, Rev. W. F., & W , PN.
Hilburn, Rev. S. M., & W., MES.
Johnson, Miss Katherine, MES.
Ray, Rev. J. F., & W., SBC.
Shannon Miss I L. MES.
S.. .. o. Miss .. .. ine, MES.

Stevens, Miss C. B., MES.
Stewart, Rev. S. A., & W.,
MES.

Hitachi Omiya, Ibaraki Ken

Rhodes, Mr E. A., & W.,
Ind.

Hojo Boshu, Chiba Ken.

Hutchinson, Rev E. G., &
W., CMS.
Colborne, Mrs. W W., Ind

**Ichinomiya Owari, Aichi
Ken.**

Archer, Miss A. L., MSCC

Iida Machi, Nagano Ken.

Karen, Rev. A., & W.,
LEF.
Minkkinen, Rev. T., LEF

Imaichi Machi, Shimane Ken

Green Rev C P, & W
CMA.

Ito, Izu

Carlson, Rev C E, & W,
SAM

**Kagoshima Shi, Kagoshima
Ken**

Boydell, Miss K M CMS
Finley, Miss A MEFB.
Gubbins, Miss, Ind.
Lance, Miss D D CMS
TerPorg, Rev J., & W.,
RCA

Kaibara, Hyogo Ken

Metcalfe, Rev. D F Ind
Woodbridge, Mr W F
Ind

**Kaita Ichi Machi, Hiroshima
Ken**

Fre-

**Kanazawa Shi, Ishikawa
Ken.**

Bates, Miss E. L, MCC.
Eaton, Miss A G, PN.
Lediard, Miss Ella, MCC.
McWilliams, Rev W. R,
& W., MCC.
Reiser, Miss A. I, PN
Tait, Miss S. O, MCC.
Tetlow, Miss Helen, L, PE.
Van Aken, Miss H. E, PN.
Winn, Rev. M. C, & W.,
PN.

Kisa Machi, Hiroshima Ken.

Wylie, Miss M. L., CMA.

Kobe Shi, Hyogo Ken.

Anderson, Miss Myra P,
MES.
Armstrong, Miss Clare,
YWCA.
Barton, Miss Nellie, AG
Basil, The Rt Rev, SPG
Bates, Rev C J L, & W,
MCC
Boden, Miss M K, JEB.
Boyd, Miss Evelyn M,
ABCFM
Buchanan, Rev W McS,
& W., PS.
Buchanan Rev Percy, &
W. PS.
Purnett, Miss E L,
ABCFM
Cobb, Rev J W, & W,
MES
Cull, Miss Hilda A, SPG
Cuthbertson Mr J, & W,
JEB
DeForest Miss C B,
ABCFM
Dietrich, Mr G, & W,
SDA.
Durland Miss Mabel I,
ABCFM
Esson Miss M SPG

I

Finch, Miss Mary, MES
Forsyth, Miss Pearl, YWCA.
Foxley, Rev. C., & W., SPG.
Fulton, Rev. S. P , & W , PS.
Graves, Miss S. M , ABCFM.
Hackett, Mr H. W., & W , ABCFM.
Haden, Rev. T H., MES
Hilliard, Mr. Foster, & W., MCC.
Holland, Miss C. G , MES
Howe, Miss A L , ABCFM.
Husted, Miss E E , ABCFM.
Jones, Rev H. P , & W , MES.
Jones, Mr. T M , JEB.
Kennion, Miss O., SPG.
Kerr, Mr. J T. H., & W , JEB.
Kettlewell, Rev. F., SPG.
Lindstrom, Rev. H , & W., CMA.
Lippard, Rev C. K , & W., LCA.
Lippard, Miss Faith, LCA
Matthews, Rev. W. K., & W., MES.
McCausland, Miss Elizabeth, ABCFM.
Millican, Rev. R. W., & W., FMA.
Myers, Rev H. W., & W., PS.
Nettleton, Miss I M., SPG.
Norman, Miss Lucy, MCC.
Ogburn, Rev. N S , & W., MES.
Ostrom, Rev. H. C., & W , PS.
Oxford, Mr. J. S., & W , MES.
Parrott, Mr F., & W BS
Pooley, Miss A., SPG

Porter, Miss C , MES.
Rupert, Miss Nettie L., Ind.
Searle, Miss S. A., ABCFM.
Smith, Miss E B., SPG
Smith, Mr. Roy W., & W., MES.
Stokes, Miss K., SPG.
Stowe, Miss G. H., ABCFM.
Stowe, Miss M. E., ABCFM.
Tench, Rev G. R., & W., MCC.
Thede, Rev H., & W., EC.
Thomson, Rev R A , & W , ABF.
Tremain, Mr M A., & W., YMCA-T.
Waters, Rev Geo. L., MES.
Whiting, Rev. M. M., & W., MCC.

Kochi Shi, Kochi Ken.

Brady, Rev J H , & W., PS.
Dowd, Miss Annie H., PS.
Ellis, Mr C., & W., Ind
McIlwaine, Rev. Wm. B , & W., PS.

Kofu Shi, Yamanashi Ken.

Bishop, Miss A. B., MCC.
Keagey, Miss M D., MCC.
McLean, Miss Annie E., MCC.
Simpson, Miss M. E., MCC.
Strothard, Miss A O , MCC.

Kokura Shi, Fukuoka Ken.

Lancaster, Miss Cecile, SBC
Rowe, Rev. J. H., & W., SBC.
Sneil, Miss Naomi SBC.

Koriyama, Fukushima Ken.

McKim, Rev. J. C., & W.,
PE.

Schweitzer, Miss Kathryn,
EC.

Williamson, Rev. E., & W.,
EC.

Kumamoto Shi, Kumamoto
Ken.

Akard, Miss M. B., LCA.

Horn, Rev. E. T., & W.,
LCA.

Kilburn, Miss Elizabeth,
MEFB.

Miller, Rev. L. S. G., &
W., LCA.

Potts, Miss Marion, LCA.

Powlas, Miss Maude, LCA.

Riddell, Miss H., Ind.

Schillinger, Rev. G. W., &
W., LCA.

Spencer, Rev. D. S., & W.,
MEFB.

Teague, Miss Carolyn M.,
MEFB.

Williamson, Rev. N. F., &
W., SBC.

Wright, Miss A. D., Ind.

Kure Shi, Hiroshima Ken.

Bushe, Miss S. L. K., CMS.

Lawrence, Miss F. H.,
CMS.

Maddux, Miss Lois, MES.

Peavey, Miss Annie, MES.

Rowland, Miss M. B., MES.

Worthington, Miss H. J.,
CMS.

Kurume, Fukuoka Ken.

Cockram, Miss H. S.,
CMS.

Hutchinson, Rev. A. C., &
W., CMS.

Moore, Rev. Boude C., &
W. R. \

Thorlaksson, Rev. S. O., &
W., LCA.

Kusatsu, Gumma Ken.

Cornwall-Legh, Miss Mary
H., PE.

Kyoto Shi, Kyoto Fu.

Bartlett, Rev. S. C., & W.,
ABCFM.

Best, Miss Blanche,
YWCA.

Brokaw, Rev. H., & W.,
PN.

Cobb, Rev. E. S., & W.,
ABCFM.

Coles, Miss A. M. M., JEB.

Curtis, Rev. W. L., & W.,
ABCFM.

Denton, Miss M. F.,
ABCFM.

Disbrow, Miss H. J., PE.

Downs, Rev. Darley, & W.,
ABCFM.

Duncan, Miss C., YWCA.

Dyer, Mr. A. L., & W.,
JEB.

Fanning, Miss K. F.,
ABCFM.

Foote, Miss E. L., PE.

Gordon, Mrs. Agnes D.,
ABCFM. (Retired).

Gwinn, Miss A. E.,
ABCFM.

Jenkins, Mr. J. A.,
ABCFM.

Learned, Rev. D. W., &
W., ABCFM.

Lorimer, Mr. A. I.,
ABCFM.

McGrath, Miss E. S., PE.

Morris, Rev. T. K., & W.,
PE.

Neely, Miss C. J., PE.

Nichols, Rt. Rev. S. H., &
W., PE.

Nixon, Miss E., Ind.

P . . . . PE.

Pedley, Rev. H., & W.,
ABCFM
Porter, Miss F. E, PN.
Shively, Rev B F., & W.,
UB.
Smith, Miss Frederica, PE.
Smith, Miss I, JEB.
Soal, Miss A, JEB.
Waters, Rev. Harris, &
W., MES
Welbourn, Rev. J. A., &
W, PE
Welte, Miss Jane M, PE
Wilkinson, Mr. C S, &
W., JEB.
Wiser, Miss Edna, YWCA.

Maebashi Shi, Gumma Ken.

Chappell, Rev. James, &
W, PE.
Griswold. Miss F. E.,
ABCFM
Hall, Rev. M. E, & W,
ABCFM
McKim, Miss Bessie, PE

Marugame Shi, Kagawa Ken.

Hassell, Rev J W, & W,
PS

Matsumoto Shi, Nagano Ken

Clench, Miss M., MSCC
Harobin, Miss H M,
MSCC.

Matsuyama Shi, Ehime Ken

Callahan, Rev W. J., &
W., MES
Clark, Miss Rosamond H.,
ABCFM.
Dievendorf, Mrs., CMA
Fisher, Mr S., & W, MES.
Francis, Miss R M, CMA.
Gulick, Mr. Leeds, & W.,
ABCFM
Hoyt, Miss O S, ABCFM
Merrill Miss Katherine
A

Sawyer, Miss Esther, CMA.

Matsuye Shi, Shimane Ken

Nash, Miss Elizabeth,
CMS

Matsuzaka Shi, Mie Ken

Morgan, Miss A E, PN.

Mito Shi, Ibaraki Ken.

Evans, Rev. C. H, &W.,
PE
Gundert, Prof. W., AEPM.
Nicholson, H. V, & W,
AFP.
Sharpless, Miss E. F,
AFP

Miyaji, Kumamoto Ken.

Freeth, Miss F. M, CMS

Miyazaki, Miyazaki Ken.

Clark, Rev C A, ABCFM.
Warren, Rev. C M, & W,
ABCFM

Moji Shi, Fukuoka Ken

Lynn, Rev. J. A., & W.,
LCA

**Morigu, Taisha Mura, Muko
Gun, Hyogo Ken.**

Curtis, Miss Edith,
ABCFM.
Mooar, Miss Eva A.,
ABCFM.
Reeves, Miss Grace,
ABCFM.
Wilson, Miss Eleanor,
ABCFM.

Morioka Shi.

Schroer, Rev. G. W., & W.,
RCUS

Muroran Shi, Hokkaido.

..., ..., MS.

Nagano Shi, Nagano Ken.

Callbeck, Miss Louise, MCC
Makeham, Miss S. E.,
MSCC.
McLeod, Miss Annie O.,
MCC
Norman, Rev. Daniel, D D.,
& W, MCC.
Waller, Rev. J G., & W.,
MSCC.

Nagasaki Shi, Nagasaki Ken

Couch, Miss Helen, MEFB.
Darrow, Miss F, RCA.
Davis, Miss L L, MEFB
Fehr, Miss V J, MEFB
Hoekje, Rev Willis G., &
W, RCA.
Hoeksema, Mr. Martin,
RCA.
Krider, Rev. W. W., & W,
MEFB.
Mills, Mr. E O, & W.,
SBC
Peckham, Miss C. S.,
MEFB
Place, Miss P A., MEFB.
Ruigh, Rev D C, & W.,
RCA.
Shafer, Miss Bessie Jane,
RCA
West, Rev R E, & W,
MEFB.
White, Miss Anna Laura,
MEFB
Young, Miss Mariana,
MEFB.

Nagoya Shi, Aichi Ken.

Auman, Rev. J. C., & W.,
MP.
Biclefeldt, Mr Talbot,
YMCA-T.
Blakeney, Miss Bessie, PS.
Bowman, Miss N. F. J.,
M

Buckland, Miss E Ruth,
PS.
Dayton, Mr. Charles S,
YMCA-T.
Hawkins, Miss Frances,
MSCC.
Hempstead, Miss E L,
MP.
Kirtland, Miss Leila G,
PS.
Knudten, Rev, A C., & W,
LCA.
Layman, Rev H L, & W.,
MP.
McIlwaine, Rev. W A, &
W., PS.
McKenzie, Rev. A. P, &
W., MCC
Ohee, Rev E I & W, MP
Smythe, Rev. L. C. M., &
W, PS
Spencer, Rev. V C., MSCC.
Tient, Miss E. M, MSCC
Warner, Rev Paul F, MP.
Williams, Miss Mary E,
MP.

Nakatsu Machi, Oita Ken.

Shaver, Rev. I. L, & W,
MES.

Nara Shi.

DeMiller, Miss V., CMA.
Schereschewsky, Miss
Caroline, PE.

Niigata Shi, Niigata Ken.

Downs, Rev. A. W., & W.,
ABCFM.

Nikko, Tochigi Ken.

Mann, Miss Irene P., PE.

Nishinomiya, Hyogo Ken.

Mann, Rev. J C., & W.,

Nobeoka, Miyazaki Ken.

Painter, Rev. S , & W.,
CMS.

Nogata Machi, Fukuoka Ken.

Horne, Miss A. C. J , CMS

Nokkeushi, Hokkaido.

Pierson, Rev. G. P., & W.,
PN.

Numazu Shi, Shizuoka Ken.

Shepherd, Miss K , SPG.

Obama, Fukui Ken.

Denton, Miss A Grace, PE.

Odawara, Kanagawa Ken.

Davidson, Mr. Ronald,
YMCA-T.
Woodsworth, Miss, SPG

Ogaki Shi, Gifu Ken.

Bazley, Miss M., JEB.
Gillespy, Miss J , JEB.

Ogi, Saga Ken.

Powlas, Miss Annie, LCA.

Oita Shi, Oita Ken.

Demaree, Rev. T. W. B ,
& W., MES.
Gist, Miss Annette, MES.
Sells, Miss E A. P , CMS.
Tumlin, Miss Mozelle,
MES.
Van Bronkhorst, Rev.
Alexander, & W., RCA.

Okaya, Suwa Gun, Nagano
Ken.

Corey, Rev. H. H , & W.,
MSCC.

Okayama Shi, Okayama Ken.

Adams, Miss Alice P.,
ABCFM

Olds, Rev. C. B., & W.,
ABCFM.
Wilson, Rev. W. A., & W.,
MES.

Okazaki Shi, Aichi Ken.

Patton, Miss Florence D.,
PS.
Van Dyke, Rev. P. S., &
W., PS.

Omiya, Saitama Ken.

Upton, Miss E. F , PE.

Osaka Shi and Osaka Fu

Alexander, Miss Sallie, PN.
Aylard, Miss Gertrude D.,
FMA.
Ayres, Rev. J. B., & W.,
PN.
Baggs, Miss M. C , CMS.
Baker, Miss E. M., CMS.
Camp, Miss E A., ABF.
Cary, Miss A. E., ABCFM
Clark, Rev. E M , & W.,
PN.
Clark, Miss R. H., ABCFM.
Cook, Miss M., MES.
Coote, Mr. Leonard W., &
W., PB.
Cox, Miss A. M., Ind.
Crewdson, Rev Ira D., &
W , UCMS.
Cribb, Miss E R., Ind.
Douglas, Miss Bertha,
UCMS.
Erskine, Rev. W. H., &
W., UCMS
Fulton, Rev. G. W., & W.,
PN
Fuselier, Miss Emma, PB.
Gale, Mrs Emma, PB.
Gibson, Miss Martha,
UCMS.
Gorbold, Mrs. R P., PN.
Gulick, Miss Ethel,
ABCFM.

Hager, Miss B. D., MES.
Harding, Miss Cecile, Ind
Hereford, Miss Grace, PN.
Holland, Miss J. M., Ind
Jackson, Miss Mona, PB
Jackson, Miss Vera, PB.
Johnson, Mr. Theodore, PB.
Mackenzie, Miss V. M, PN.
Marsh, Miss Carolyn, YWCA.
McIntosh, Miss E., YWCA
Mead, Miss L., ABF.
Moran, Rev. S F., & W, ABCFM.
Mylander, Miss Ruth, FMA.
Ott, Miss F. C., ABCFM.
Peters, Miss Gertrude, PN
Pickens, Miss Lillian O, FMA
Rawlings, Rev G W., & W., CMS.
Riker, Miss S M, PN
Russell, Miss L K., ABF.
Schirmer, Miss Kathryn, EC.
Shaw, Miss L. L., CMS.
Smith, Mr. Herbert, & W., PB
Southworth, Dr. J D., & W, PE.
Straub Miss Mae, AG.
Tristram, Miss K A S, CMS.
Warren, Rev. F F, & W, FMA.
Whitehead, Miss Mabel, MES
Williams, Miss A. C, CMS.
Wilson, Rev. J R., & W, ABF.
Woolley, Miss Alice, PB.

O'aru Shi, Hokkaido.

Cary
AI

Saga Shi, Saga Ken.

Heins, Rev. F. W., & W., LCA.
Ryder, Rev S. W., & W., RCA.

Sapporo Shi, Hokkaido.

Alexander, Miss V. E, MEFB.
Batchelor, Ven J, & W, CMS. (Retired).
Davidson, Miss F. E., PN.
Evans, Miss E. M, PN.
Gillilan, Miss B. E., PN.
Ihde, Rev. W A., & W., MEFB.
Lake, Rev. L. C., & W., PN.
Lory, Mr. Frank B., & W., YMCA-T.
Monk, Miss A. M., PN.
Smith, Miss S. C, PN, (Retired).
Sturtevant, Miss A. L. MEFB.
Woodard, Rev W P., & W., ABCFM.

Sendai Shi, Miyagi Ken.

Acock, Miss W. M., ABF.
Allen, Miss Thomasine, ABF.
Ankeney, Rev. Alfred, & W, RCUS.
Bolliger, Miss Aurelia, RCUS.
Carlsen, Deaconess V. D, PE.
Coates, Miss Mary V., PE.
Crew, Miss Angie, CC
DeChant, Miss Katherine B, RCUS.
Faust, Rev A K, RCUS
Gerhard, Miss Mary E, RCUS.

Gray, Miss G. V., PE.

Haven, Miss Marguerite, ABF.

Heaton, Miss C. A., MEFB.

Hesketh, Miss E, JRM.

Hetherington, Miss N., JRM.

Huesing, Miss Edith H., RCUS.

Kirkaldy, Miss M., JRM

Luthy, Rev. R S., & W., MEFB.

Madeley, Rev. W. F, PE

McInnes, Miss E, JRM.

McKnight, Rev. W Q, & W., CC.

Newbury, Miss G M., ABF.

Nicodemus, Prof F. B, & W, RCUS.

Noss, Prof G S, & W., RCUS.

Perry, Miss H L, MEFB

Ross, Rev. C. H, & W., ABF.

Saville, Miss Rose, JRM

Schneder, Rev D B., & W., RCUS.

Schneder, Miss M. E, RCUS.

Seiple, Rev W G, & W., RCUS.

Stacy, Miss M. R., CC.

Stoudt, Mr O. M., & W. RCUS

Suess, Miss Elizabeth, RCUS.

Thornton, Mr. H, & W., JRM

Weed, Miss H I, RCUS

Weida, Mr F Wharton, RCUS.

Whiteman, Miss Mary, JRM.

Williamson, Miss J., JRM.

Zaue, H, H & W, RCUS

Seoul, Korea.

Smith, Rev. F. H., & W., MEFB.

Starkey, Miss Bertha, MEFB.

Welch, Bishop Herbert, MEFB.

Newell, Rev. H. B, & W., ABCFM.

Shimonoseki Shi, Yamaguchi Ken.

Bach, Rev. D G. M, & W., LCA.

Bigelow, Miss G. S., PN.

Curtis, Rev. F. S, & W., PN.

Hannah, Miss Lolita, SBC.

Johnstone, Miss J M., PN.

Keizer, Miss Henrietta, RCA.

Pieters, Miss J A, RCA.

Walne, Rev. E. N., & W., SBC.

Walne, Miss Florence, SBC

Walvoord, Miss Florence C, RCA.

Walters, Miss Mary, SBC.

Shimotsuma, Ibaraki Ken

Binford, Mr. G., & W., AFP

Shingu, Wakayama Ken.

Chapman, Rev. E. N., & W., PN.

Shioda Mura, Ibaraki Ken.

Bixler, Mr. O. D., & W, Ind.

Shizuoka Shi, Shizuoka Ken

Andrews, Miss Sarah, Ind.

Courtice, Miss S R, MCC.

Govenlock, Miss I., MCC.

... J, Burd, Miss A M., MCC

Rorke, Miss M. L, MCC.
Stetson, Rev. C. R., & W,
UGC.
Wilkinson, Rev. A. T., &
W., MCC.

Shoka, Formosa.

Connan, Miss J M, EPM.
Landsborough, Dr D., &
W., EPM.
Livingston, Miss A. A.,
EPM.
Moody, Rev. Campbell N,
& W., EPM.
Mumford, Dr R H, EPM.

Sumiyoshi, Hyogo Ken.

Converse, Mr. Guy C, &
W, YMCA-A.
Ryan, Mr. W. S., & W.,
YMCA-A.

Sumoto, Awaji.

Wagner, Rev H. H, & W.,
FMA.

Taihoku, Formosa.

Adair, Miss Lily, UCC.
Black, Dr. D M., UCC.
Elliott, Miss Isabelle, UCC
Gauld, Dr Flora, UCC.
Gauld, Miss Greta, UCC.
Gauld, Mrs. M. A, UCC
Gushue-Taylor, Dr. G., &
W, UCC.
Haig, Miss M. T., UCC
Hotson, Miss J. L., UCC.
McKay, Mr. G. W., & W.,
UCC.
Senior, Miss Annie, UCC

Tainan, Formosa.

Band, Rev. Edward, EPM
Barnett, Miss Margaret,
EPM.
Che

Ferguson, Mrs. Duncan,
EPM.
Galt, Miss Jessie W., EPM.
Lloyd, Miss Jeannie, EPM.
Mackintosh, Miss S. E,
EPM.
MacLeod, Rev. Duncan &
W., UCC.
Montgomery, Rev. W. E.,
& W., EPM.
Nielson, Rev. A B., EPM.
Singleton, Mr L, & W.,
EPM.

**Takamatsu Shi, Kagawa
Ken.**

Atkinson, Miss M. J, PS
Erickson, Rev. S. M., &
W., PS.
Moore, Rev. J. W., & W,
PS.
Moore, Mr., Wallace,
YMCA-T.
Munroe, Rev H H., & W.,
PS.
Winn, Miss M. L, Ind

Takata Shi, Niigata Ken

Isaac, Miss Irene Louise,
MSCC.
Powles, Rev P S C, &
W., MSCC.

Tansui, Formosa.

Clazie, Miss M G, UCC
Coates, Rev. W. G., & W,
UCC.
Connell, Miss Hannah,
UCC.
Kinney, Miss J. M, UCC
MacMillan, Rev. Hugh, &
W., UCC.
Marshall, Rev. D. F., UCC.

Tobata Shi, Fukuoka Ken

Hind, Rev. J., & W.

Tochigi Machi, Tochigi Ken.

Andrews, Rev. R. W., PE.

Tokushima Shi, Tokushima Ken.

Hassell, Rev. A. P., & W., PS.

Jenkins, Rev. C. R., & W., PS.

Logan, Rev. C. A., & W., PS.

Lumpkin, Miss Estelle, PS.

Scott, Rev. J. J, & W. CMS.

Tokuyama Machi, Yamaguchi Ken.

Weakley, Rev. W. R., & W., MES

Tokyo Shi, and Tokyo Fu

Alexander, Rev. R. P., & W., MEFB.

Anderson, Pastor, A. N., & W., SDA.

Anderson, Rev. Joel, SAM.

Armstrong, Pastor V. T., & W., SDA.

Aurell, Rev. K. E., & W, BS

Axling, Rev. William, & W, ABFM.

Bailey, Miss B M, MEFB.

Ballard, Miss S, SPG.

Barr, Capt. K., & W, SA.

Bauernfeind, Miss S. M., EC.

Beatty, Rev. H. E, & W, TM.

Bender, Mi G R., & W., AG.

Benninghoff, Rev. H. B., & W., ABF.

Benson, Mr. H. F, & W, SDA.

Berg⸳ ⸳⸳ (⸳⸳ SAM.

Berry, Rev. A D, MEFB.

Bigwood, Staff-Capt. E. W., & W., SA.

Binsted, Rev. N. S., & W., PE.

Bishop, Rev. Charles, & W., MEFB, (Retired).

Bolitho, Miss A. A., CG.

Bott, Rev. G. E, & W., MCC.

Bowen, Miss Georgene, UGC

Bowles, Gilbert & W, AFP.

Boyd, Miss H, SPG.

Boyd, Miss L H., PE

Braithwaite, Mr. George, JBTS.

Braithwaite, Mrs. George, JEB.

Braithwaite, Mr. G. B., & W., AFP

Branstad, Mr. K E, PE.

Brown, Mr. F. H., & W., YMCA-A.

Buncombe, Rev. W. P, & W., CMS, (Retired).

Burnside, Miss Ruth, PE.

Caldwell, Mr H L, PE.

Carpenter, Miss M. M, ABF.

Cary, Rev. Henry M., & W., UGC.

Cate, Mrs. E. S, Ind

Chappell, Miss M. H., MEFB.

Chase, Miss Laura, MEFB

Chope, Miss B M, SPG.

Clark, Miss A, JEB.

Clawson, Miss Bertha F., UCMS.

Climpson, Staff-Capt. H. A, & W, SA.

Coe, Miss O M., MEFB.

Cole, Mr. A. B., & W., SDA.

(⸳⸳ ⸳⸳ ⸳⸳ ⸳⸳ & W. WSSA

Correll, Rev. I H., & W.,
PE.
Craig, Mr. E. B., & W.,
Ind.
Crawford, Miss Marian J,
PE.
Cunningham, Rev. W. D.,
& W., TM.
Curry, Miss Olive, MEFB
Cypert, Miss L., Ind.
Daniel, Miss N M., MEFB
Daugherty, Miss L. G., PN.
Dithridge, Miss Harriet,
AG.
Dorothy, Sister, C. E.
Drake, Miss K. I., MCC.
Durgin, Mr. R L., & W.,
YMCA-A.
Dykhuizen, Mr Cornelius
A., RCA.
Eadie, Comm. W., & W.,
SA.
Edith Constance, Sister,
Ind., C.E.
Eleanor Frances, Sister,
C. E.
Elliott, Dr. Mabel E., PE.
Etheldreda, Sister, Ind.
Fairclo, Miss Nellie,
MEFB
Farnham, Miss Grace, TM
Foote, Mr L W., PE.
Fullerton, Miss M., MCC.
Gamertsfelder, Miss Ina,
EC.
Gardiner, Miss Ernestine
W, PE.
Garman, Rev. C. P., & W
CC.
Garrard, Capt. M., JEB.
Gealy, Rev F. G., & W,
MEFB.
Gemmill, Rev. Wm. C.,
SPG.
Gillespie, Miss Jean, MCC
Gillett, Miss E R, Ind
Grant, Mr I D, YMCA-T
Hal

Hamilton, Miss F. G,
MCC.
Hammel, Miss Esther, EC
Hannaford, Rev. H. S., &
W., PN.
Hawkins, Miss Violet R,
AFP.
Heckelman, Rev. F. W., &
W., MEFB.
Helmer, Miss Edith,
YWCA.
Heywood, Miss C. G., PE.
Hitchcock, Mr. F., & W,
OMS.
Hoare, Miss D., JEB.
Hurd, Miss Helen R., MCC.
Hutchinson, Rev. L G.,
CMS.
Iglehart, Rev. E. T., & W.,
MEFB.
Isaacson, Rev. R. W., &
W., TM.
Jackson, Mr. Ivor, YMCA-
A.
Jost, Miss H. J., MCC
Juergensen, Miss Agnes,
AG.
Juergensen, Mr. C. F., &
W., AG.
Juergensen, Mr. J. W., &
W, AG.
Juergensen, Miss Marie,
AG.
Kaufman, Miss Emma R.,
YWCA.
Kaufman, Miss Irene,
YWCA.
Kellam, Miss L C., PE.
Kent, Miss B. M, UGC.
Kludt, Miss A M., ABF.
Knapp, Deaconess, S. T,
PE.
Koch, Mr. A., & W, SDA.
Kraft, Mr. E. J, & W,
SDA.
Kramer, Miss L F., EC.

Lade, Miss H. R , PE.

Lamott, Rev. W. C., & W., PN.

Lansing, Miss Harriet M , RCA.

Leininger, Rev. A. A., & W., EC.

Lindsay, Miss O. C., MCC.

London, Miss M. H , PN.

Macdonald, Miss A. C., Ind

Mander, Miss, SPG.

Martin, Prof. J. V, & W., MEFB.

Mary Katherine ,Sister, C E , Ind.

Mauk, Miss Laura, EC.

Maver, Rev. Paul S., & W,. EC.

McCaleb, Mr. J. M., & W., Ind.

McCoy, Rev. R. D., & W., UCMS.

McKechnie, Mr. A. R., & W., PE.

McKenzie, Rev D. R., & W., MCC.

McKim, Bishop John, PE

McKim, Miss Nellie, PE.

McKinnon, Miss Claire, YWCA.

McLachlin, Miss Annie May, MCC.

McNaughton, Miss Margaret, YWCA.

Megaflin, Miss B. I , MCC.

Miller, Miss Alice, Ind

Miller, Rev. A. W., & W.. CG.

Miller, Rev. H. K., & W., RCUS.

Mohler, Miss A. M., PE.

Moon, Miss M. B., MEFB.

Munroe, Mr. Alex, & W., AG.

Mu.. , M. T. D. PE.

Newin Miss Emma at P.

Newman, Capt. Herbert, & W , SA.

Nielsen, Rev. J. P., & W., LCA.

Nuno, Miss Christine M., PE.

Obee, Rev. E. I., & W., MP.

Oltmans, Rev. A., & W., RCA, (Retired).

Oltmans, Miss F. Evelyn, RCA.

Palmer, Miss Jewel, UCMS.

Peeke, Rev. H. V. S., & W , RCA.

Perkins, Mr. H. J., & W., SDA.

Perkins, Miss M. O , PN.

Phelps, Mr G. S., & W., YMCA-A.

Philipps, Miss G., SPG.

Pifer, Miss B. C., RCUS.

Powers, Mr. M. L , & W., SDA.

Price, Rev. P. G., & W., MCC.

Pugmire, Maj E. I. & W., SA.

Read, Dr. Rachel, Ind

Reifsnider, Bishop C S , & W , PE.

Reischauer, Rev. A. K., & W , PN

Revell, Miss Rachel, PE.

Roberts, Miss A., CMS.

Robertson, Miss E ,YWCA.

Robertson, Miss M. A , MCC.

Rolfe, Mr. Victor E , & W , SA.

Rowe, Mrs Alice G., UGC.

Rowland, Rev. G. M., & W., ABCFM.

Rusch, Mr. Paul F., YMCA-A.

Ryder, Mi G . F.

Salonen, Rev K., & W., LEF.

Schaeffer, Miss M. R., PE

Scott, Rev. F. N., & W., MEFB.

Scott, Miss Jane N., YWCA.

Scruton, Miss Fern, MCC.

Shaw, Rev. M. R., & W., MEFB.

Sholty, Rev. A H., & W., UB.

Smyth, Staff-Capt Annie, SA.

Sneyd, Mr H. S., & W., YMCA-A.

Sowers, Mr. G. M., & W., LCA.

Spackman, Rev. H. C., & W., PE.

Sprowles, Miss A. B., MEFB.

Stegeman, Rev. V. E., & W., RCA.

Stirewalt, Rev. A. J., & W., LCA.

St John, Mrs. Alice C., PE

Tapson, Miss A. M, Ind.

Tenny, Rev C. B, & W., ABF.

Teusler, Dr. R. B., & W., PE.

Tharp, Miss E R., ABF.

Thompson, Mrs. David, PN, (Retired).

Thoren, Miss Amy, LCA

Trott, Miss, SPG.

Umbreit, Rev. S J, & W., EC.

Veazey, Miss M. A, MCC.

Wagner, Miss Dora, MEFB.

Wainright, Rev. S. H., & W., MES.

Wa
P

Walton, Rev. W. H. M., & W., CMS.

Webber, Mr. M. E., & W., SDA.

Weidinger, Dr. Karl, & W, AEPM.

Wengler, Miss Jessie, AG.

Whitney, Mrs M C, Ind

Wilbur, Mr. H. A, & W., YMCA-A.

Williams, Miss T., SPG.

Wilson, Brig. T. W., & W., SA.

Woodworth, Rev. A. D., & W., CC.

Woolley, Miss K., SPG.

Wynd, Rev. W. O., & W, ABF

Ziemann, Rev P. P. W., & W., ABF.

Tono, Iwate Ken.

Buzzell, Miss A. S, ABF.

Tottori Shi, Tottori Ken.

Cue, Miss E L, ABCFM.

Toyama Shi, Toyama Ken

Ainsworth, Rev F., & W, MCC.

Armstrong, Miss M E, MCC.

Tweedie, Miss E Gertrude, MCC.

Toyohashi Shi, Aichi Ken

Moss, Miss A. Frances, MSCC.

Patton, Miss A. V., PS

Tsu Shi, Mie Ken.

Chapman, Rev J. J., & W., PE.

Buxton Rev J G & W.,

Ueda Shi, Nagano Ken.

Harper, Miss Ruth, MCC.
Scott, Miss Mary C., MCC.

Utsunomiya, Tochigi Ken.

Fry, Rev F. C., & W., CC.

Uwajima Shi, Ehime Ken.

Frank, Rev. J. W, & W, MES.

Wakamatsu Shi, Fukushima Ken.

Noss, Rev. C., RCUS.
Nugent, Rev. C. W, & W., RCUS.

Wakayama Shi, Wakayama Ken.

Hail, Rev. J B., & W., PN, (Retired).
Lloyd, Rev. J. H., & W, PE.
Ransom, Miss M. H, PN.

Yamada, Mie Ken.

Riker, Miss Jessie, PN.

Yamagata Shi, Yamagata Ken.

Kriete, Rev C. D, & W, RCUS.
Mead, Miss Bessie, PE.

Yamaguchi Shi, Yamaguchi Ken.

Martin, Rev. D. P., PN.
Minnis, Mr G F., & W., YMCA-T.
Richards, Rev. W. A., & W, Ind.
Wells, Miss L A, PN.

Yokohama Shi.

Allen, M. YWCA.

Anderson, Miss R L, ABF.
Bickel, Mrs. L W., ABF, (Retired).
Buss, Miss Florence V., RCA.
Converse, Miss C. A., ABF.
Covell, Mr. J. H., & W., ABF.
Draper, Rev. G. F., & W., MEFB.
Eringa, Miss D, RCA.
Fisher, Mrs C. H D., ABF, (Retired).
Fisher, Mr Royal H, & W., ABF.
Hewlett, Rev. A. S., SPG
Hodges, Miss Olive I, MP.
Loomis, Miss Clara D., WU.
Lynn, Mrs. Hazel B., WU.
Oltmans, Miss C. Janet, RCA.
Owen, Miss Gertrude, YWCA.
Pawley, Miss Annabelle, ABF.
Pratt, Miss Susan A., WU.
Shafer, Rev. Luman J, & W, RCA
Topping, Mr. W. F., & W, YMCA-T
Verry, Miss Hazel, YWCA.
Wolfe, Miss E M., MP.

Yokote, Akita Ken.

Smyser, Rev. M. M., & W., Ind.

Yonago Machi, Tottori Ken

Pickard-Cambridge, Rev. C. O, & W., CMA.

Zushi, Kanagawa Ken.

Stone, Rev A. L, & W., SPG.

LIST BY MISSIONS

1. American Board of Commissioners for Foreign Missions.

Adams, Miss Alice P., Okayama.
Babcock, Miss Grace E., (A).
Bartlett, Rev. S. C. & W., Kyoto.
Bennett, Rev. H. J, & W., (A).
Boyd, Miss Evelyn M., Kobe.
Burnett, Miss E L, Kobe.
Cary, Miss Alice, Osaka.
Cary, Rev. Frank, & W., Otaru
Clark, Miss R H., Matsuyama
Cobb, Rev. E. S, & W., Kyoto.
Coe, Miss E L, Tottori.
Cozad, Miss Gertrude, Kobe
Curtis, Miss Edith, Morigu.
Curtis, Rev W. L, & W., Kyoto.
DeForest, Miss C. B, Kobe.
Denton, Miss M F, Kyoto
Downs, Rev. A W. & W., Niigata
Downs, Rev. Darley, & W., Kyoto
Durland, Miss Mabel I, Kobe.
Fanning, Miss K. F, Kyoto
Field, Miss S M, Kobe.
Gillett, Rev S C., & W., Sendai.
Gordon, Miss Agnes D Kyot

Graves, Miss S M, Kobe.
Griswold, Miss F. E., Maebashi.
Gulick, Mr. L, & W., Matsuyama
Gulick, Miss Ethel, Osaka Fu.
Gwinn, Miss A E., Kyoto.
Hackett, Mr. H. W., & W., Kobe.
Hall, Mr. M E, & W., Maebashi.
Holmes, Rev. J. C., & W., (A).
Howe, Miss A L, Kobe.
Hoyt, Miss O S, Matsuyama.
Husted, Miss E E, Kobe
Jenkins, Mr. J. A., Kyoto.
Judson, Miss Cornelia, (A).
Lombard, Rev. F. A, (A).
Learned, Rev D W, & W., Kyoto.
Lorimer, Mr. A I, Kyoto.
McCausland, Miss I., Kobe.
Merrill, Miss Katherine, Matsuyama
Mooar, Miss Eva A., Morigu.
Moran, Rev. S. F., & W, Osaka.
Newell, Rev. H B, & W, Seoul.
Olds, Rev. C B., & W, Okayama.
Ott, Miss F. C, Osaka Fu.
Pedley, Rev. H., & W., Kyoto

Rowland, Rev. G. M., & W.,
Tokyo Fu
Searle, Miss S A, Kobe.
Stanford, Mrs. J P, (Retired).
Stowe, Miss G H, Kobe.
Stowe, Miss G. E., Kobe.
Warren, Rev. C. M., & W,
Miyazaki.
Wilson, Miss Eleanor, Morigu.
Woodard, Rev W. P, & W.,
Sapporo.

2. American Baptist Foreign Missionary Society.

Acock, Miss A A., Himeji.
Acock, Miss W. M., Sendai
Allen, Miss Thomasine,
Sendai.
Anderson, Miss R. L, Yokohama.
Axling, Rev William, Tokyo
Benninghoff, Rev. H. B, &
W., Tokyo.
Bickel, Mrs. L W., Yokohama.
Bixby, Miss A. C., Himeji.
Buzzell, Miss A. S, Tono
Camp, Miss E. A., Osaka.
Carpenter, Miss M M,
Tokyo.
Converse, Miss C. A, Yokohama.
Covell, Mr. J. H, & W,
Yokohama
Crosby, Miss A. R., (A)
Derwacter, Rev. F M, & W.,
(A).
Fisher, Mrs. C. H D., Yokohama, (Retired).
Fisher, Mr. Royal H., & W.,
Yokohama.
Foote, Rev J. A., & W.,
(A).
Gifford, Miss E. M., (A).
Gre... M ... L & W.
(A).

Haven, Miss Marguerite,
Sendai.
Holtom, Rev. D. C, & W.,
(A).
Jenkins, Miss L F, (A).
Jesse, Miss Mary D, (A)
Kennard, Rev. J S., & W.,
(A).
Kludt, Miss A M., Tokyo.
Laughton, Capt. J F., & W,
(A).
Mead, Miss Lavinia, Osaka.
Meline, Miss Agnes S, (A).
Newbury, Miss G. M, Sendai.
Pawley, Miss A, Yokohama.
Post, Miss Vida, (A).
Ross, Rev. C. H., & W.,
Sendai.
Russell, Miss L K., Osaka.
Ryder, Miss G. E Tokyo.
Sandberg, Miss M. V., (A).
Steadman, Rev. F. W., & W.,
(A).
Tenny, Rev. C. B., & W,
Tokyo.
Tharp, Miss E. R., Tokyo.
Thomson, Rev R. A., & W.,
Kobe.
Topping, Rev. H., & W.,
(A).
Ward, Miss Ruth C, (A).
Wilcox, Miss E. F, Himeji
Wilkinson, Miss J. M. G.,
(A).
Wilson, Rev. J. R., & W.,
Osaka.
Wynd, Rev. W. O., & W.,
Tokyo.

3. Allgemeiner Evangelisch-Protestantischer Missions-verein (General Evangelical Protestant Missionary Society).

Gundert, Prof. W., Mito.
Smith S ap L & W.,
(A).

Weidinger, Dr. Karl, & W.,
Tokyo.

4. Foreign Missionary Association of Friends, Philadelphia.

Binford, Mr G., & W.,
Shimotsuma, Ibaraki Ken.
Bowles, Mr. G., & W., Tokyo.
Braithwaite, Mr. G B., &
W., Tokyo
Hawkins, Miss Violet R.,
Tokyo.
Newlin, Miss Edith, Tokyo
Nicholson, Mr. H. V., & W.,
Mito.
Rhoads. Miss Esther, (A).
Sharpless, Miss Edith F.,
Mito.

5. Australian Board of Missions (Anglican).

Harrison, Rev E. R., &
W., Chiba.

6. Assembly of God.

Barton, Miss Nellie, Kobe.
Bender, Mr. Gordon R., &
W., Tokyo.
Dithridge, Miss Harriet,
Tokyo Fu.
Juergensen, Miss Agnes,
Tokyo Fu.
Juergensen, Mr. C. F., & W.,
Tokyo Fu.
Juergensen, Mr J. W., &
W., Tokyo.
Juergensen, Miss Marie
Tokyo Fu
Munroe, Mr. Alex, & W.,
Tokyo.
Straub, Miss Mae, Kobe.
Wengler, Miss Jessie, Tokyo

7. Bible Societies.

Aurell, Rev. K E., & W.,
T(

Parrott, Mr. F., & W., Kobe.

8. Mission Board of The Christian Church (American Christian Convention).

Crew, Miss A., Sendai.
Fry, Rev. E. C., & W.,
Utsunomiya.
Garman, Rev. C. P., & W.,
Tokyo.
McKnight, Rev. W Q., &
W., Sendai.
Stacy, Miss M. R, Sendai
Woodworth, Rev. A D., &
W., Tokyo.

9. Church of God Mission.

Bolitho, Miss A. A., Tokyo.
Miller, Mr. A. W., & W,
Tokyo.

10. Christian Literature Society.

Wainright, Rev. S H.,
Tokyo.

11. Christian and Missionary Alliance.

Barber, Rev. W. A., & W.
(A).
DeMiller, Miss V., Nara.
Dievendorf, Mrs., Matsuyama.
Francis, Miss R. M., Matsuyama.
Francis, Mr. T. R., & W.,
Fukuyama.
Frehn, Mr. C., & W., Kaita
Ichi Machi, Hiroshima
Ken.
Green, Rev. C P., & W., Ima
Ichi Machi, Shimane Ken.
Lindstrom, Rev H., & W.,
Kobe.
A).

Sawyer, Miss Esther, Matsu-
yama.
Southard, Mr. Paul, Matsu-
yama.
Wylie, Miss M. L, Kisa
Machi, Hiroshima Ken.

12. Church Missionary Society.

Baker, Miss E M., Osaka.
Batchelor, Archdeacon J., &
W, Sapporo, (Retired).
Bosanquet, Miss A. C.,
Tokyo.
Boydell, Miss K. M, Osaka.
Buncombe, Rev. W. P., &
W, Tokyo, (Retired).
Bushe, Miss S. L K, Kure.
Cockram, Miss H. S,
Kurume.
Cowl, Rev. J., & W., Kanoya
Machi, Kagoshima Ken
Cox, Miss A M, Amagasaki.
Freeth, Miss S M., Miyaji,
Kumamoto Ken.
Galgey, Miss L. A, (A).
Gardener, Miss F. E., (A).
Hamilton, Miss K., Kure.
Heaslett, Bishop W., & W,
Tokyo.
Henty, Miss A. M, (A)
Hind, Rev. J, & W, Tobata.
Horne, Miss A. C. J, Nogata
Machi, Fukuoka Ken.
Howard, Miss R. D, Osaka.
Hughes, Miss A. M., Muro-
ran Shi.
Hutchinson, Rev. A C, &
W., Kurume.
Hutchinson, Rev. E. G,
Tokyo.
Keen, Miss E M., Ashiya,
Hyogo Ken
Lane, Miss E. A, Ashiya,
Hyogo Ken.
Lawrence, Miss F. H., Kure.
Lea, Bishop Arthur, & W.,
Fuk...

Mann, Rev. J C., & W.,
Nishinomiya.
Moule, Rev. G H, & W,
Tokyo.
Nash, Miss Elizabeth, Aka-
yama, Matsuye.
Norton, Miss E. L B, (A).
Painter, Rev. S., & W.,
Nobeoka.
Pickard-Cambridge, Rev. O.
C., & W., Yonago Machi,
Tottori Ken.
Preston, Miss E. D., (A).
Rawlings, Rev. G. W., & W,
Osaka.
Roberts, Miss A, (A).
Scott, Rev. J J., Tokushima.
Sells, Miss E A P., Oita.
Shaw, Miss L. L, Osaka.
Thompson, Miss F. L., Kago-
shima.
Tristram, Miss K. A. S.,
Osaka
Walsh, Rev. G. J, & W,
Asahigawa
Walton, Rev. W. H M., &
W, Tokyo
Williams, Miss A. C., Osaka.
Worthington, Miss H. J,
(A)

13 Evangelical Church of North America.

Bauernfeind, Miss S M,
Tokyo.
Gamertsfelder, Miss Ina,
Tokyo.
Hammel, Miss Esther,
Tokyo.
Kramer, Miss L F, Tokyo.
Kuecklich, Miss Gertrude,
Tokyo
Leininger, Rev. A. A., & W,
Tokyo
Mauk, Miss Laura, Tokyo.
Mayer, Rev. Paul S., & W,
Tokyo.
Rine, Miss Elinir, (A).

Schirmer, Miss Kathryn, Osaka.

Schweitzer, Miss E. M., Tokyo.

Thede, Rev. H., & W., Kobe.

Umbreit, Rev. S. J., & W., (A).

Williamson, Rev. E., & W., Koriyama, Fukushima Ken.

14. General Missionary Board of the Free Methodist Church in North America.

Aylard, Miss Gertrude D., Osaka.

Millican, Rev. R. W., & W., Kobe.

Mylander, Miss Ruth, Osaka.

Pickens, Miss Lillian, Osaka.

Wagner, Rev. H. H., & W., Sumoto.

Warren, Rev. F. F., & W., Osaka.

15. Independent Workers.

Andrews, Miss Sarah, Shizuoka.

Bixler, Mr. O. D., & W., Shioda Mura.

Craig, Mr. E. B., & W., Tokyo.

Cribb, Miss E. R., Osaka.

Cypert, Miss L., Tokyo.

Ellis, Mr. Charles, & W., Kochi.

Gillett, Miss E. R., Tokyo.

Harding, Miss Cecile, Osaka.

Macdonald, Miss A. C., Tokyo.

Madden, Mr. M. B., & W., (A).

McCaleb, Mr. J. M., & W., Tokyo.

Read, Dr. Rachel, Tokyo.

Rhodes

Hitachi, Omiya.

Rupert, Miss Nettie L., Kobe.

Smyser, Rev. M. M., & W., Yokote, Akita Ken.

Tapson, Miss A. M., Tokyo.

Whitney, Mrs. Mary C., Tokyo.

Winn, Miss M. L., Takamatsu.

Woodbridge, Mr. W. F., Kaibara.

16. Anglican.

Coleborne, Mrs. S. E., Hojo, Boshu.

Holland, Miss J. M., (A).

McGill, Miss M. B., Hibarigaoka.

Richards, Rev. W. A., & W., Yamaguchi.

Riddell, Miss H., Kumamoto.

Robinson, Miss H. M., Gifu.

Rowlands, Rev. F. W., & W., Fukuoka.

Strong, Rev. E. M., (A).

Wright, Miss A. H., Kumamoto.

Dorothy, Sister, Tokyo.

Eleanor Frances, Sister, Tokyo.

Edith Constance, Sister, Tokyo.

Etheldreda, Sister, Tokyo.

Mary Katharine, Sister, Tokyo.

17. Japan Evangelistic Band.

Bazley, Miss M., Ogaki.

Boden, Miss M. K., Kobe.

Braithwaite, Mrs. G., Tokyo.

Clark, Miss A., Tokyo.

Coles, Miss A. M. M., Kyoto.

Cuthbertson, Mr. J., & W., Kobe.

Dyer, Mr. A. L., & W.,

Garrard, Capt. M., Tokyo.
Gillespy, Miss J., Ogaki
Harris, Mr R. W , & W.,
(A)
Hoare, Miss D Tokyo
Jones, Mr T J , Kobe.
Kerr Mr. J. T. II , & W.,
Kobe.
Smith, Miss I W., Kyoto.
Soal, Miss A , Kyoto.
Thornton, Rev. J B , & W.,
(A).
Wilkes, Mr A P., & W , (A)
Wilkinson, Mr C. S., & W.,
Kyoto.

18. Japan Book and Tract Society.

Braithwaite, Mr. George,
Tokyo.

19. Japan Rescue Mission.

Butler, Miss B , (A).
Hesketh, Miss E. Sendai
Hetherington, Miss Nellie,
Sendai.
Kirkaldy, Miss M., Sendai
McInnes, Miss B., Sendai.
Saville, Miss Rose, Sendai
Thornton, Mr Harrison, &
W , Sendai
Whiteman, Miss Mary, Sen-
dai.
Williamson, Miss Jeanie,
Sendai.

21. United Lutheran Church in America.

Akard, Miss M. B., Kuma-
moto.
Bach, Rev. D G. M , & W..
Shimonoseki
Gray, Rev L G , & W., (A).
Heins, Rev F W , & W.,
Saga.
Hepner, Mr R. M.,
(A).

Hepner, Rev. C. W , Ashiya,
Hyogo Ken
Horn, Rev E T., & W.,
Kumamoto
Knudten, Rev A. C , & W ,
Nagoya.
Linn, Rev. J A , & W , Moji
Linn, Rev J K , & W., (A).
Lippard, Rev. C. K., & W ,
Kobe.
Lippard, Miss Faith, Kobe.
Miller, Rev. L S. G , & W ,
Kumamoto
Nielsen, Rev. J. P , & W.,
Tokyo
Norman, Rev. C E , & W ,
Fukuoka
Potts, Miss M E , Kuma-
moto.
Powlas, Miss Annie, Ogi
Saga Ken.
Powlas, Miss Maude, Kuma-
moto.
Schillinger, Rev. G W , &
W , Kumamoto
Shirk, Miss Helen. Fukuoka.
Sowers, Mr. G M , & W ,
Tokyo.
Stirewalt, Rev A. J , & W.,
Tokyo.
Thoren, Miss Amy, Tokyo.
Thorlaksson, Rev S. O., &
W , Kurume.

22. Lutheran Gospel Association of Finland.

Airo, Miss J , (A)
Karen, Rev A , & W , Iida.
Lindgren, Rev. R., & W ,
(A)
Minkkinen, Rev. T., & W.,
(A)
Salonen, Rev. K., & W ,
Tokyo.
Savolainen, Rev. V , & W ,
(A).
Tö... Rev K , & W , (A).
T... l , Miss S , (A)).

23. Methodist Church of Canada.

(a) General Board of Missions.

Ainsworth, Rev. F, & W, Toyama.

Armstrong, Rev. R. C., & W, (A).

Bates, Rev. C. J. L., & W., Kobe.

Bott, Rev. G E., & W., Tokyo.

Coates, Rev H H, & W., Hamamatsu

Cragg, Rev. W. J. M, & W., (A)

Hennigar, Rev E C, & W., (A).

Hilliard, Rev. F., & W., Kobe.

Holmes, Rev. C. P, & W., Fukui.

McKenzie, Rev. A. P, & W., Nagoya.

McKenzie, Rev. D. R., & W., Tokyo

McWilliams, Rev. W. R., & W., Kanazawa

Norman, Rev. D., & W., Nagano.

Norman, Miss L, Kobe.

Outerbridge, Rev. H W., & W., (A)

Price, Rev. P. G., & W., Tokyo

Tench, Rev G. R, & W., Kobe.

Whiting, Rev. M. M, & W., Kobe.

Wilkinson, Rev A T, & W, Shizuoka.

Woodsworth, Rev. H. F, & W, (A).

(b) Woman's Missionary Society.

Allen

Armstrong, Miss M. E., Toyama.

Barr, Miss L. M., (A).

Bates, Miss E. L., Kanazawa.

Blackmore, Miss I S, (A).

Bishop, Miss A B., Kofu

Callbeck, Miss L, Nagano.

Chappell, Miss C., (A).

Clark, Miss Lola M., (A).

Courtice, Miss S. R, Shizuoka.

Drake, Miss K I, Tokyo

Fullerton, Miss M., Tokyo.

Gillespie, Miss Jean, Tokyo

Govenlock, Miss I, Shizuoka.

Greenbank, Miss K. M., (A)

Hamilton, Miss F. G., Tokyo

Harper, Miss Ruth, Ueda.

Hurd, Miss H. R., Tokyo

Jost, Miss H. J., Tokyo.

Keagey, Miss M. D., Kofu

Killam, Miss Ada, Fukui.

Lackner, Miss E A, Tokyo

Lediard, Miss Ella, Kanazawa.

Lindsay, Miss O C., Tokyo.

McArthur, Miss K W, (A)

McLachlin, Miss Annie May Shizuoka.

McLean, Miss Annie E., Kofu.

McLeod, Miss Annie O, Nagano.

Megaffin, Miss B. I., Tokyo.

Pinsent, Mrs A. M., (A).

Robertson, Miss M A., Tokyo

Rorke, Miss L., Shizuoka.

Ryan, Miss D. L., (A).

Scott, Miss M. C., Ueda, Nagano Ken.

Scruton, Miss Fern, Tokyo

Simpson, Miss M. E, Kofu.

Staples, Miss M. M., Fukui.

Strothard, Miss A O, Kofu.

Tweedle, Miss E. G.,
Toyama.

Veazey, Miss M A., Tokyo.

24. Methodist Episcopal Church.

(a) Japan Mission Council.

Alexander, Rev. R P., & W.,
Tokyo.

Berry, Rev. A. D , Tokyo

Bishop, Rev. C., & W.,
(Retired)

Brumbaugh, Rev. T T., &
W., Hirosaki.

Bruner, Mr. G W., & W ,
(A).

Bull, Rev. E. R , & W., (A).

Coe, Miss Orpha, Tokyo

Draper, Rev. G. F. & W ,
Yokohama.

Fairclo, Miss Nellie, Tokyo.

Gealy, Rev. F G, & W , (A).

Heckelman, Rev. F. W., &
W., Tokyo

Iglehart, Rev. C. W., & W ,
Hirosaki.

Iglehart, Rev. E. T., & W ,
Tokyo.

Ihde, Rev. W. A., & W.,
Sapporo.

Krider, Rev. W. W., & W.,
Nagasaki.

Luthy, Rev. S. R., & W.,
Sendai.

Martin, Prof. J V., & W.,
Tokyo.

Moon, Miss Mira B., Tokyo

Scott, Rev. F. N., & W ,
Tokyo.

Shacklock, Rev F. W., & W.,
(A).

Shaw, Rev. M. R., & W ,
Tokyo.

Smith, Rev. F. H., & W.,
Seoul

Spencer Rev D S & W ,
Kun. ʊtʊ

Spencer, Rev. R. S , & W.,
Fukuoka.

Welch, Bishop Herbert &
W , Seoul.

West, Rev. R. E, & W.,
Nagasaki.

(b) East Japan Woman's Conference.

Alexander, Miss V. E, Sapporo.

Bailey, Miss B. M , Tokyo

Bassett, Miss B. C., (A).

Chappell, Miss M. H ,
Tokyo.

Chase, Miss L., Tokyo

Cheney, Miss Alice, Hakodate.

Couch, Miss H., Nagasaki.

Courtice, Miss L K , Hirosaki.

Curry, Miss O . Tokyo

Daniel, Miss N. M , Tokyo.

Draper, Miss M , (A)

Draper, Miss W., (A).

Gard, Miss B A., Hirosaki

Goodman, Miss Z. E., Hakodate.

Heaton, Miss C. A., Sendai.

Perry, Miss H L , Sendai.

Pider, Miss M. Z., (A).

Russell, Miss M. H , Hirosaki.

Seeds, Miss L. M., (A).

Sprowles, Miss A. B , Tokyo.

Sturtevant, Miss A , Sapporo.

Thurston, Miss E V., (A).

Wagner, Miss Dora, Tokyo

Weiss, Miss R , (A).

(c) West Japan Woman's Conference.

Allbrecht, Miss H. R , (A).

Ashbaugh, Miss A. M , (A).

Davis, Miss L L , Nagasaki.

Fehr, Miss V., Nagasaki.

Finlay, Miss A. L, Kago-
shima .

Howey, Miss H. M., Fuku-
oka.
Kilburn, Miss E. H., Kuma-
moto.
Lee, Miss E. M., (A).
Lee, Miss M., (A).
Paine, Miss M. A., (A).
Peckham, Miss C. S., Naga-
saki.
Peet, Miss A. E., Fukuoka.
Place, Miss P. A., Nagasaki.
Starkey, Miss B., Seoul.
Teague, Miss C. M., Kuma-
moto.
White, Miss A. L., Nagasaki.
Wythe, Miss K. G., Fukuoka.
Young, Miss M., Nagasaki.

25. Methodist Episcopal Church, South.

Anderson, Miss M. P., Kobe.
Bennet, Miss N., Hiroshima.
Callahan, Rev. W. J., & W.,
Matsuyama.
Cobb, Rev. J. B., & W.,
Kobe.
Cook, Miss M. M., Osaka.
Demaree, Rev. T. W. B., &
W., Oita.
Finch, Miss M., Kobe.
Fisher, Mr. Sterling, & W.,
Matsuyama.
Floyd, Rev. A. C., & W.,
Beppu.
Frank, Rev. J. W., & W.,
Uwajima.
Gaines, Miss N. B., Hiro-
shima.
Gaines, Miss R., Hiroshima.
Gist, Miss Annette, Oita.
Haden, Rev. T. H., Kobe.
Hager, Miss B. D., Osaka.
Hager, Rev. S. E., & W.,
Ashiya.
Hilburn, Rev. S. M., & W.,
Hiroshima.
Hollan

Johnson, Miss Katherine,
Hiroshima.
Jones, Rev. H. P., & W.,
Kobe.
Maddux, Miss L., Kure.
Matthews, Rev. W. K., &
W., Kobe.
Meyers, Rev. J. T., (A).
Mickle, Mr. J. J., & W., (A).
Newcomb, Miss E., (A).
Ogburn, Rev. N. S., & W.,
Kobe.
Oxford, Mr. J. S., & W.,
Kobe.
Palmore, Rev. P. L., & W.,
Himeji.
Peavy, Miss A., Kure.
Phillips, Rev. W. O., & W.,
(A).
Porter, Miss C., Kobe.
Rowland, Miss M. E., Kure.
Searcy, Miss Mary G., (A).
Shannon, Miss I. L., Hiro-
shima.
Shannon, Miss K., Hiro-
shima.
Shaver, Rev. I. L., & W.,
Nakatsu.
Smith, Mr. Roy & W., Kobe.
Stevens, Miss C. B., Hiro-
shima.
Stewart, Rev. S. A., & W.,
Hiroshima.
Towson, Miss M., (A).
Towson, Rev. W. E., & W.,
(A).
Tumlin, Miss M., Oita.
Wainright, Rev. S. H., & W.,
Tokyo.
Waters, Rev. G. L., Kobe.
Waters, Rev. H. & W.,
Kyoto.
Weakley, Rev. W. R., & W.,
Tokuyama Machi, Yama-
guchi Ken.
Whitehead, Miss M., Osaka.
Williams, Miss A. B., (A).

Okayama.

Worth, Miss I. M , Ashiya, Hyogo Ken.

26. Methodist Protestant Church.

Auman, Rev. J. C., & W., Nagoya.
Barnes, Miss H. V , (A).
Coates, Miss A. L , Hamamatsu.
Hempstead, Miss E. L., Nagoya.
Hodges, Miss O. I., Yokohama.
Layman, Rev. H. L, & W., Nagoya.
Obee, Rev. E. I, & W , Tokyo.
Warner, Rev. P. F , Nagoya.
Williams, Miss M. E, Nagoya.
Wolfe, Miss E M., Yokohama.

27. Missionary Society of the Church of England in Canada.

Archer, Miss A. L , Ichinomiya, Owari.
Bowman, Miss N. F J, Nagoya.
Clench, Miss M., Matsumoto.
Cooke, Miss M S , (A)
Corey, Rev. H H , & W , Okaya, Nagano Ken.
Hamilton, Miss F., (A).
Hamilton, Bishop H J., & W., (A).
Hawkins, Miss F , Nagoya
Harobin, Miss H M , Matsumoto.
Isaac Miss I. L , Takata.,
Makeham, Miss S E, Nagano.
Millman, Rev. R M , & W., (A)
Moss Mi ·

Powles, Rev P S C., & W., Takata.
Robinson, Rev C C , & W., (A).
Robinson, Rev. J. C , (A).
Shore, Miss G , (A).
Spencer, Rev. B. C., Nagoya.
Trent, Miss E. M., Nagoya.
Waller, Rev. J. G., & W., Nagano

30 Omi Mission.

Vories, Mrs Julia E , Omi-Hachiman, Shiga Ken
Vories, Mr. W M., & W., Omi-Hachiman.

31. The Oriental Missionary Society.

Beers, Miss Susan E , (A).
Hitchcock, Mr F, & W., Tokyo
Mintle, Miss Rosa, (A).

32. Pentecostal Band.

Coote, Mr Leonard W , & W., Osaka.
Fuselier, Miss Emma, Osaka.
Gale, Mrs. Emma, Osaka.
Jackson, Miss Mona, Osaka
Jackson, Miss Vera, Osaka
Johnson, Mr. Theodore, Osaka
Smith, Mr. Herbert, & W., Osaka
Woolley, Miss Alice, Osaka.

33. Pentecostal Bands of the World.

Abel, Rev Fred, & W , (A)

34. Domestic and Foreign Missionary Society of the Protestant Episcopal C   the United   of America

(a) Missionary District of Kyoto.

Ambler, Miss Marietta, (A).

Cannell, Miss M C, (A).

Chapman, Rev. J. J , & W, Tsu.

Correll, Rev. I H, & W., Tokyo.

Denton, Miss A G., Obama.

Disbrow, Miss H. J , Kyoto.

Foote, Miss F L., Kyoto.

Lloyd, Rev J. H, & W, Wakayama.

McGrath, Miss E S, Kyoto.

Morris, Rev. T. K, & W., Kyoto

Neely, Miss C J, Kyoto.

Nichols, Rt. Rev S. H, & W., Kyoto.

Paine, Miss M. R, Kyoto.

Powell, Miss C. R., (A).

Schereschewsky, Miss C, Nara.

Skiles, Miss H, (A)

Smith, Miss F., Kyoto.

Smith, Rev. P. A., & W., Hikone.

Southworth, Dr. J. D., & W., Osaka.

Tetlow, Miss H. L, Kanazawa.

Van Kirk, Miss A. S, (A).

Welbourn, Rev. J. A, & W., Kyoto.

Welte, Miss Jane M, Kyoto.

Whent, Miss R. M., (A).

Williams, Miss H. R., (A).

(b) Missionary District of Tokyo.

Andrews, Rev. E L, & W., Akita.

Andrews, Rev. R W, & W, Tochigi Machi.

Binsted, Rev. N. S, & W, Tokyo.

Boyd, Miss L H, Tokyo.

Branstad, Mr. K. L., Tokyo.

Burns

Caldwell, Rev. H. L., Tokyo.

Carlsen, Deaconess V. D., Sendai.

Chappell, Rev. James & W., Maebashi.

Cornwall-Legh, Miss M. H, Kusatsu.

Crawford, Miss M. J , Tokyo.

Elliott, Dr. M. E, Tokyo

Evans, Rev. C. H., & W, Mito.

Foote, Mr. E. W, Tokyo.

Gardiner, Miss E. W, Tokyo.

Gray, Miss G V., Sendai.

Heywood, Miss C. G, Tokyo.

Hittle, Miss D, Hirosaki.

Humphreys, Miss M., Akita.

Kellam, Mrs L. C, Tokyo.

Knapp, Deaconess S. T., Tokyo

Lade, Miss H R, Tokyo.

Madeley, Rev. W. F, Sendai.

Mann, Miss I. P., Nikko

McKechnie, Mr A R., & W., Tokyo.

McKim, Miss Bessie, Maebashi.

McKim, Rev. J. C, & W., Koriyama.

McKim, Bishop John, & W., Tokyo.

McKim, Miss Nellie, Tokyo

Mohler, Miss A M, Tokyo.

Murray, Miss D B., Tokyo.

Nuno, Miss C. M, Tokyo.

Ranson, Deaconess A. L, Kawagoe.

Reifsnider, Bishop C. S., & W, Tokyo.

Revell, Miss R., Tokyo.

Schaeffer, Miss M. R, Tokyo.

Spackman, Rev. H. C., & W., Tokyo.

Spencer, Miss G., Aomori.

St. John, Mrs A. C., Tokyo.

Teusler, Dr. R. B, & W,

Upton, Miss E. F., Omiya.

35. Board of Foreign Missions of the Presbyterian Church in the United States of America.

Alexander, Miss Sallie, Osaka Fu.

Ayres, Rev. J. B., & W., Osaka.

Bigelow, Miss G. S., Shimonoseki.

Brokaw, Rev. H.. & W., Kyoto.

Buchanan, Rev. D. C., & W., (A).

Chapin, Miss L., (A).

Chapman, Rev. E. N., & W, Shingu.

Chapman, Rev. G. K., & W., (A).

Clark, Rev E M, & W., Osaka.

Clarke, Miss S. F, Hiroshima.

Curtis, Rev. F. S.. & W., Shimonoseki.

Curtis, Miss G P., (A).

Daugherty, Miss L G., Tokyo.

Davidson, Miss F. E., Sapporo.

Dosker, Rev. R. J., & W., (A).

Dunlop, Rev. J. G., & W., Tsu.

Eaton, Miss A. G., Kanazawa.

Evans, Miss E. M., Sapporo.

Fulton, Rev. G. W., & W, Osaka.

Gillilan, Miss B E, Sapporo.

Gorbold, Mrs. R. P., Osaka.

Hail, Rev J B, & W., Wakayama, (Retired).

Halsey, Miss L. S, (A).

Hannaford, Rev. H. D.. & W Tokyo.

Hereford, Rev. W F, & W, Hiroshima.

Johnstone, Miss J. M, Shimonoseki.

Kerr, Rev. W. C, & W, (A).

Lake, Rev. L. C., & W., Sapporo.

Lamott, Rev. W. C., & W., Tokyo.

Leavitt, Miss J, Tanabe.

London, Miss M. H, Tokyo.

Mackenzie, Miss V. M, Osaka.

Martin, Rev. D. P., Yamaguchi.

McCrory, Miss C. H., (A).

McDonald, Miss M. D., (A).

Miles, Miss Mary, (A).

Monk, Miss A. M, Sapporo.

Morgan, Miss A. E, Matsuzaka, Mie Ken.

Palmer, Miss H. M, (A).

Perkins, Miss M. O, Tokyo.

Peters, Miss G., Osaka.

Pierson, Rev. G P., & W, Nokkeushi.

Porter, Miss F E, Kyoto.

Ransom, Miss M. H., Wakayama.

Reischauer, Rev. A. K, & W., Tokyo.

Reiser, Miss A. I., Kanazawa.

Riker, Miss Jessie, Yamada.

Riker, Miss S. M., Osaka.

Smith, Miss S. C., (Retired), Sapporo.

Thompson, Mrs. David, (Retired), Tokyo.

Van Aken, Miss H. E., Kanazawa.

Walser, Rev. T. D., & W, Tokyo.

Wells, Miss L. A., Yamaguchi.

Winn, Rev. M. C., & W., Kanazawa.

36. Executive Committee of Foreign Missions of the Presbyterian Church in the United States

(Southern Presbyterian).

Atkinson, Miss M. J, Takamatsu.
Blakeney, Miss B M, Nagoya.
Brady, Rev. J H., & W, Kochi.
Buckland, Miss E R, Nagoya.
Buchanan, Miss E. O, Gifu
Buchanan, Rev. W. C, Gifu.
Buchanan, Rev. W M., & W., Kobe.
Buchanan, Rev Percy, & W., Kobe.
Cousar, Rev J E, & W., (A).
Curnell, Miss S. M, (A)
Dowd, Miss A. H., Kochi
Erickson, Rev. S. M., & W., Takamatsu.
Fulton, Rev. S. P, & W, Kobe.
Gardner, Miss E E, (A).
Hassell, Rev. A P, & W., Tokushima.
Hassell, Rev. J W, & W., Marugame.
Jenkins, Rev C R, & W., Tokushima.
Kirtland, Miss L G, Nagoya.
Logan, Rev. C A., & W., Tokushima.
Lumpkin, Miss E, Tokushima.
McAlpine, Rev R E, & W., Kwangju, Korea
McElroy, Rev. I S., & W., (A).
McIlwaine, Rev. W. A., & W, Nagoya
McIl·

W., Kochi.
Moore, Rev. J. W., & W., Takamatsu.
Moore, Rev. L. W., & W., Gifu
Munroe, Rev. H H., & W, Takamatsu.
Myers, Rev. H. W, & W, Kobe
Ostrom, Rev H C, & W, Kobe.
Patton, Miss A. V., Toyohashi.
Patton, Miss F. D., Okazaki.
Smythe, Rev. L C. M., & W, Nagoya.
Van Dyke, Rev. P. S., & W, Okazaki.

37. Reformed Church in America.

Buss Miss F V., Yokohama
Couch, Miss S M., (A)
Darrow, Miss F, Nagasaki.
Dykhuizen, Mr Cornelius A, Tokyo.
Eringa, Miss D; Yokohama
Hoekje, Rev. W. G., & W, Nagasaki.
Hoeksema, Mr. M, Nagasaki.
Keizer, Miss H, Shimonoseki.
Kuyper, Rev. H, & W. (A).
Lansing, Miss H M., Tokyo.
Moore, Rev. B. C, & W, Kurume.
Nordhoff, Miss J M, (A)
Oltmans, Rev. A., & W, Tokyo, (Retired).
Oltmans, Miss C J., Yokohama.
Oltmans, Miss F. E, Tokyo
Peeke, Rev. H. V. S., & W., Tokyo.
Pieters, Miss Jennie A, Shimonoseki.

V.,

Nagasaki.

Ryder, Rev. S. W., & W., Saga.

Shafer, Miss B. J., Nagasaki.

Shafer, Rev. L. ,J , & W., Yokohama.

Stegeman, Rev. H. V. E , & W., Tokyo.

Teets, Miss E V , (A).

TerBorg, Rev. J , & W., Kagoshima

Van Bronkhorst, Rev. A., & W , Oita.

Walvoord, Miss F , Shimonoseki.

38. Reformed Church in the United States.

Ankeney, Rev. A., & W., Sendai.

Baker, Mr. D D., & W., (A).

Bolliger, Miss A., Sendai.

DeChant, Miss K B., Sendai.

Faust, Rev. A. K , & W., Sendai

Fesperman, Rev F. L , & W., (A).

Gerhard, Miss M. E , Sendai.

Gerhard, Rev. P. L., & W., (A).

Guinther, Rev. E. H., & W., (A).

Hansen, Miss K. I., (A).

Hoffheins, Miss M. V., (A)

Huesing, Miss E. H., Sendai.

Kriete, Rev. C. D., & W., Yamagata.

Lindsey, Miss L. A.. (A).

Miller, Rev. H. K., & W., Tokyo

Nace, Rev. I. G , & W , Akita.

Nicodemus, Prof F. B., & W , Sendai

Noss, Rev. C., & W , Aizu-Wakamatsu.

Noss Frd. G. S. & W.,

Sendai.

Nugent, Rev. W. C., & W, Aizu-Wakamatsu.

Pamperrien, Miss G E , (A).

Pifer. Miss B. C , Tokyo.

Schneder, Rev. D. B , & W., Sendai

Schneder, Miss Mary E., Sendai.

Schroer, Rev. G. W., & W., Morioka.

Seiple, Rev. W. G., & W., Sendai

Smith, Prof. A. D., & W., W , (A).

Stoudt, Prof. O. M., & W.. Sendai.

Suess, Miss E., Sendai.

Weed, Miss H. I , Sendai.

Weida, Mr. F. W., Sendai.

Zaugg, Rev. E. H., & W , Sendai.

39. Salvation Army.

Barr, Capt. Kenneth, Tokyo.

Bigwood, Staff-Capt E. W., & W., Tokyo.

Climpson, Staff-Capt H. A., & W., Tokyo.

Eadie, Commander William, & W.. Tokyo.

Newman, Capt. Herbert, & W., Tokyo.

Pugmire, Maj. E I, & W., Tokyo.

Smyth, Staff-Capt. Annie. Tokyo.

Rolfe, Staff-Capt. Victor E , & W., Tokyo.

Wilson, Brig. T. W., & W., Tokyo.

40. Scandinavian Alliance Mission.

Anderson, Rev. Joel. Tokyo.

Bergstrom, Rev. F. O , Tokyo.

Carlson, Rev. C E, & W., Ito, Izu.

Peterson, Miss A. J., Chiba Shi.

41. Southern Baptist Convention.

Baker, Miss E, Fukuoka.

Bouldin, Rev. G. W., & W., Fukuoka.

Clarke, Rev. W H., & W., (A).

Conrad, Miss F., Fukuoka.

Dozier, Rev C. K. & W, Fukuoka

Fulghum, Miss S E, Fukuoka.

Hannah, Miss L, Shimonoseki.

Lancaster, Miss C., Kokura.

Mills, Mr. E. O., & W., Nagasaki

Ray, Rev. J. F., & W, Hiroshima.

Rowe, Rev. J. H, & W., Kokura

Schell, Miss N, Kokura

Walne, Rev E. N., & W., Shimonoseki.

Walne, Miss F., Shimonoseki

Walters, Miss M., Shimonoseki.

Williamson, Rev. N. F., & W, Kumamoto.

42. Seventh Day Adventists.

Anderson, Pastor A. N, & W., Tokyo.

Armstrong, Pastor V T, & W., Tokyo.

Benson, Mr. H. F, & W., Tokyo.

Cole, Mr A B, & W. Tokyo.

Dietrich, Mr. G, & W., Kobe.

Koch, Mr A. & W., Kyoto

Kraft, Mr E. J, & W, Tokyo.

Nelson, Mr. A N, & W. (A).

Powers, Mr M. E, & W, Tokyo.

Perkins, Mr H J., & W, Tokyo.

Webber, Mr P A, & W, Tokyo.

43. Society for the Propagation of the Gospel in Foreign Parts.

(a) Osaka Diocese.

Basil, The Rt. Rev. Bishop, Kobe.

Case, Miss D, (A).

Chope, Miss D M, Tokyo

Cull, Miss H. A, Kobe.

Essen, Miss M, Kobe.

Foxley, Rev. C, & W, Kobe.

Holmes, Miss Mary, (A).

Kennion, Miss O, Kobe

Kettlewell, Rev F Kobe.

Nettleton, Miss I M, Kobe.

Parker, Miss A, Kobe.

Pooley, Miss A, Kobe

Stokes, Miss K., Kobe

Smith, Miss E B, Kobe

Voules, Miss J. E, (A)

Walker, Mr. F. B, & W., (A).

Weston, Rev. Frank, & W., (A).

(b) South Tokyo Diocese.

Ballard, Miss S, Tokyo.

Bickersteth, Mrs. E, (A).

Boyd, Miss H, Tokyo.

France, Rev. W. F, & W, (A).

Gemmill, Rev. W C, Tokyo.

Hallstone, Miss M, Tokyo.

Heaslett, Bishop S, & W., (A).

Hewlett. Rev. A. S., Yokohama.
Mander, Miss, Tokyo.
Phillips, Miss G., Tokyo.
Sharpe, Rev A. L, Zushi.
Shaw, Rev. R D. M., & W.,
Hiratsuka, Kanagawa Ken
Shepherd, Miss K, Numazu.
Simeon, Miss R, (A).
Smith, Miss E M, Kobe.
Somervell, Miss M, (A)
Tanner, Miss K., (A).
Trott. Miss, Tokyo.
Williams, Miss T., Tokyo.
Woolley, Miss K. Tokyo
Wordsworth, Miss, Odawara,
Kanagawa Ken

44. Church of the United Brethren in Christ.

Knipp, Rev. J. E., & W.,
(A).
Shively, Rev B F, & W,
Kyoto.
Sholty, Rev A. H., & W,
Tokyo.

45. United Christian Missionary Society.

Armbruster, Miss R T., (A)
Asbury, Miss J J., (A).
Clawson, Miss B. F., Tokyo.
Crewdson, Rev. I. D., & W.,
Osaka.
Douglas, Miss B, Osaka.
Erskine, Rev. W. H, & W.,
Mikage, Hyogo Ken
Gibson, Miss M., Osaka.
Harker, Miss H, (A).
Hendricks, Rev. K. C, &
W., Fukushima
Hunter, Rev. J. B, & W.,
(A).
Lehman, Miss L.. Akita
McC-ll Rev C F & W
Ak.' t.

McCoy, Rev. R. D., & W,
Tokyo.
Palmer, Miss J., Tokyo.
Richey, Miss H. L., (A).
Robinson, Rev. C. E., & W.,
(A)
Scott, Miss A C, (A)
Trout, Miss J. M., Akita.
Young, Rev. T. A., & W,
(A).

46. Universalist General Convention.

Cary, Rev H, & W., Tokyo.
Bowen, Miss G, Tokyo.
Hathaway, Miss M. A, (A).
Kent. Miss B M., Tokyo.
Rowe, Mrs A. G., Tokyo.
Stetson, Rev. C. R., & W.,
Shizuoka.

47. Wesleyen Methodist Connection of America.

Gibbs, Rev M A, & W,
(A).

48. Woman's Union Missionary Society of America.

Loomis, Miss C D., Yokohama.
Lynn, Mrs H B, Yokohama.
Pratt, Miss S A., Yokohama.
Rogers, Miss M S., (A).
Tracy, Miss M. E., (A).

49. Tokyo Mission.

Beatty, Rev. H. E., & W,
Tokyo.
Cunningham, Rev. W. D., &
W, Tokyo
Farnham, Miss G., Tokyo.
I   Rev R W & W,
T k o.

50. Young Men's Christian Association

(a) American International Committee.

Brown, Mr F. H., & W., Tokyo.

Converse, Mr. Guy C., & W., Sumiyoshi, Hyogo Ken

Davis, Mr. J. M, & W, (A).

Durgin, Mr. R. L, & W, (A).

Jorgensen, Mr. A, & W., (A).

Patterson, Mr. G S., & W, (A).

Phelps, Mr G. S, & W., Tokyo.

Rusch, Mr. P F., Tokyo,

Ryan, Mr. W S, & W., Sumiyoshi, Hyogo Ken.

Sneyd, Mr H S, & W., Tokyo.

Swan, Mr G. D, & W., (A).

Trueman, Mr G. E, & W., (A).

Wilbur, Mr. H. A., & W., Tokyo.

Yarnell, Mr. D E, & W., (A).

(b) YMCA Teachers Affiliated.

Bielefeldt, Mr Talbot, Nagoya

Collins, Mr H H, Hiroshima.

Davidson, Mr. Ronald, Odawara.

Dayton, Mr. C S., Nagoya.

Faucette, Mr Thomas, & W, Fukuoka.

Grant, Mr J P, Tokyo.

Lory, Mr. F. B, & W., Sapporo.

Minnis, Mr. G F., & W., Yamaguchi.

Nunn, : s, G. A

Sinclair, Mr. G. M., Hikone.

Topping, Mr. W. F., & W, Yokohama.

Tremain, Mr. M. A., & W, Kobe

51. Young Women's Christian Association.

Allen, Miss Carolyn, Yokohama.

Armstrong, Miss Clare, Kobe

Best, Miss B, Kyoto

Duncan, Miss C, Kyoto

Eddy, Mrs K. W, Tokyo.

Forsyth, Miss P, Kobe

Helmer, Miss E, Tokyo.

Kaufman, Miss E. R, Tokyo

Kaufmann, Miss Irene, Tokyo

Marsh, Miss C., Osaka.

McGregor, Miss G, (A).

McIntosh, Miss E, Osaka

McKinnon, Miss C., Tokyo.

McNaughton, Miss M, Tokyo

Owen, Miss G, Yokohama.

Page, Miss M, (A).

Ragan, Miss R, (A).

Robertson, Miss E., Tokyo.

Scott, Miss J N, Tokyo

Scott, Miss L. O, (A).

Verry, Miss H, Yokohama.

Wiser, Miss E, Kyoto.

52. World's Sunday School Association.

Coleman, Mr. H. L., & W., Tokyo.

FORMOSA

53. Foreign Mission's Committee of the Presbyterian Church of England.

Band, Rev. E, Tainan

Barnett, Miss M., Tainan.

Cheal, Dr. P., & W., Tainan.

Connan, Miss J. M., Shoka.

Ferguson, Mrs. C. M V., Tainan.

Galt, Miss J., Tainan.

Landsborough, Mr. D., & W, Shoka.

Livingston, Miss A. A., Shoka.

Lloyd, Miss J, Tainan.

Mackintosh, Miss S. E., Tainan.

Montgomery, Rev W. E., & W., Tainan.

Moody, Rev. C. N., & W., Shoka.

Mumford, Dr. R. H., Shoka.

Nielson, Rev. A. B, Tainan.

Scott, Miss M. D. A., (A).

Singleton, Mr. L., & W., Tainan.

54. Board of Foreign Missions of the United Church of Canada.

Adair, Miss L, Taihoku.

Black, Dr. D. M., Taihoku

Clazie, Miss M. G., Tansui.

Coates, Rev. W. G., & W., Tansui.

Connell, Miss H, Tansui.

Elliott, Miss I., (A)

Gauld, Dr. F., Taihoku.

Gauld, Miss G, Taihoku.

Gauld, Miss M. A., Taihoku.

Gushue-Taylor, Dr. G., & W, Taihoku.

Haig, Miss M. T., (A).

Hotson, Miss J L., Taihoku.

Kinney, Miss J M, Tansui.

MacKay, Mr. G. W, & W, (A).

MacMillan, Rev. H, & W, Tansui

Marshall, Rev D. F., Tansui.

Senior, Miss A, Taihoku.

KOREA

MISSIONARY DIRECTORY

· · · · · · · · · ·

Compiled by G. BONWICK

KOREA MISSIONARY LIST

LIST OF MISSIONS AND KINDRED SOCIETIES.

WITH NAMES OF SECRETARIES OR TREASURERS ON THE FIELD

Au P —Presbyterian Church of Victoria, Australia — Rev. J. N. Mackenzie, Fusanchin.

B F B S —British & Foreign Bible Society —Mr. Hugh Miller, Seoul.

C L S —Christian Literature Society of Korea.—Mr Gerald Bonwick.

U C C. —United Church of Canada —Mr. J G McCaul, Wonsan.

E C M. —English Church Mission (S P.G.)—Rev. H J Drake, Suwon

M.E.F.B—Methodist Episcopal Church.—Rev J. Z. Moore, D D, Pyengyang.

M E S —Methodist Episcopal Church, South.—Rev J. W. Hitch, Seoul

O.M S —Oriental Missionary Society — Rev H F. Woods Seoul.

P N —Presbyterian Church in U S A —Mr J F Genso, Seoul.

P S. —Presbyterian Church in U S.—Mr M L. Swine-hart, Kwangju

R C. —Roman Catholic.—Rev. M P B Villemot, Seoul

R O C. —Russian Orthodox.—Rev. Father Feodosi, Seoul

S A. —Salvation Army —Lieut -Colonel W. Twilley Seoul

S D A. —Seventh Day Adventist.—Mr. L I Bowers, Seoul

Y M C A —Young Men's Christian Association.—Mr. F. M

ALPHABETICAL LIST

The order is as follows.—Name; year of arrival in Korea, initials of Missionary Society, Address in Korean and Japanese; A—Absent.

A

Adams, Rev B N. & W, 1923, PN., Taiku, Taikyu

Adams, Rev. Edward & W, 1921, PN., Taiku, Taikyu.

Ainsworth, Rev. Bishop W N., D.D., & W, 1926, M E S, Seoul, Keijo.

Akerholm, Mrs Adjutant M K, 1914, SA., Kosan, Kosan

Alexander, Miss M. L., 1911, AuP, Fusanchin, Fusanchin.

Allen, Rev A. W, 1913, AuP., Chinju Shinshu

Amendt, Rev. C C & W, 1919, MEFB., Kongju, Koshu

Anderson, A G, M.D & W., 1911, MEFB, of Pyengyang Heijo.

Anderson, E. W., M.D. & W, 1914, MES, Wonsan, Gensan

Anderson, Rev. G. & W, 1922, AuP, Fusanchin, Fusanchin

Anderson, Rev L P. & W, 1914, MES, Choonchun Shunsen.

Anderson, Miss N., 1911, MEFB, Pyengyang, Heijo

Anderson, Rev. W. J. & W., 1917, PN., Seoul, Keijo

Appenzeller, Miss A. R, 1915, MEFB, Seoul, Keijo

Appenzeller, Rev. H. D. & W., 1917, MEFB., Seoul, Keijo

Armstrong, Miss L., 1925, UCC, Yongjung, Ryusei.

Arndt, Captain G. S, 1924, SA., Kosan.

Arnold, Rev E. II, 1915, ECM., Seoul, Keijo

Ashe, Mrs. A S, 1922, PN., Pyengyang, Heijo.

Auer, Bro. G, RC., Wonsan, Gensan

Austin, Miss L, 1912, PS, Chinju, Shinshu   (A)

Avison, Douglas B, M D. & W, 1920, PN, Seoul, Keijo. (A)

Avis   v   a "   ʼ ʼ(ʼ k   u   , k   ʼu

Avis   ʼ ʼ ʼ ʼ(ʼ   ʼ   W   ʼ ʼ, PN, S((l Iʼ ʼ(o.

B

Bahr, Mr. E & W., 1925, SDA, Seoul, Keijo

Bain, Miss Mary, 1921, PS, Mokpo, Mokpo   (A)

Bainger, Rev. M, RC, Phalji, Hatdoku

Bah, Miss B. R, 1913, MEFB, Seoul, Keijo.

Baird, Rev. R H & W., 1923, PN, Kangkei, Kokai.

Baird, Rev W. M, D D. & W, 1890, PN, Pyengyang, Heijo. (A)

Baird, Rev W. M, Jr., 1923, PN., Chairyung, Sainei.

Barbara. Lay-sister, 1911, ECM., Suwon, Suigen.

Barlow, Miss Jane, 1912, MEFB, Haiju, Kaishu.

Barnhart, Mr. B P & W, 1916, YMCA., Pyengyang, Heijo

Bass, Mr. H. J. & W., SDA, Kyengsan, Keizan

Battersby, Adjutant (Miss) 1920, SA, Hongsung, Kojo

Bauer, Bro C., RC, Seoul, Keijo.

Becker, Rev. A L., Ph.D. & W, 1903, MEFB, Seoul, Keijo. (A)

Bell, Mrs E., PS., Kwangju, Kwoshu

Bercovitz, Z., M.D, Ph.D & W., 1924, PN., Andong, Anto.

Bergman, Miss A L, 1921, PN, Pyengyang, Heijo. (A)

Bergman, Miss G. O, 1915, PN., Taiku, Taikyu

Bermond, Pere J. M, RC, Masanpo, Masanpo.

Bernheisel, Rev. C. F., D.D. & W, 1900, PN, Pyengyang, Heijo.

Bernsten, Staff-Captain A. & W, SA, Chunju, Zenshu

Best, Miss M., 1897, PN, Pyengyang, Heijo.

Biggar, Miss M. L., 1910, PS, Soonchun, Junten

Bigger, J D, M D. & W., 1911, PN, Pyengyang, Heijo.

Billings, Rev. B. W., D.D. & W., 1908, MEFB, Seoul, Keijo.

Black, Miss E M, 1919, CMS, Seoul, Keijo.

Black, Miss N, 1924, MES, Wonsan, Gensan

Blair, Rev H. E & W, 1904, PN, Taiku, Taikyu.

Blair, Rev W N., D.D. & W., 1901, PN., Pyengyang, Heijo.

Boggs, L K, M D & W., 1925, PS, Chunju, Zenshu.

Bonwick, Mr. G & W., 1908, CLS, Seoul, Keijo.

Booth, Rev William, 1925, RC., Yengju, Yeiju.

Boots, J. L, D.D S. & W., 1921, PN, Seoul, Keijo. (A)

Bording, Miss M. P. 1922, MEFB, Kongju, Koshu

Borrow, Dr. Nancy, ECM., Yoju, Yoshu

Bouillon, Pere C, RC, Eumchook, Inchitku.

Bowers, Mr. L I. & W., 1917, SDA, Seoul, Keijo.

Boyer, Rev. E. T, 1921, PS., Chunju, Zenshu.

Bradshaw, Miss M., 1925, UCC., Yongjung, Ryusei.

Brand, B L C, M D. & W., 1925, PS, Kunsan, Kunsan.

Brannan Rev. L C. & W., 1910, MES, Choonchun, Shunsen,
Breher,

Brockman, Mr. F. M & W., 1905, YMCA , Seoul, Keijo.
Brownlee, Miss C , 1913, MEFB , Seoul, Keijo (A)
Bruen, Rev H. M. & W, 1899, PN , Taiku, Taikyu
Buckland, Miss S , 1908, PS., Chunju, Zenshu.
Buie, Miss H , 1909, MES., Seoul, Keijo
Bull Rev W. F. & W , 1899, PS., Kunsan, Kunsan.
Bunker, Rev. D A. & W , 1886, MEFB , Seoul, Keijo
Burbidge, Rev W. A. & W , 1925, UCC., Wonsan, Gensan.
Burdick, Rev. G. M , 1903, MEFB , Seoul, Keijo
Butts, Miss A. M., 1907, PN., Pyengyang, Heijo. (A)
Butts, Miss E., 1921, MEFB , Pyengyang. Heijo.
Byram, R. M., M D. & W., 1921, PN., Kangkei, Kokai. (A)
Byrne, Very Rev. P. J , 1923, RC., Sinmiju, Shingishu

C

Cable, Rev E M , D D. & W., 1899, MEFB , Seoul, Keijo.
Cadars, Pere J F., RC.. Kangkyeng, Kokei.
Campbell, Rev. A. & W., 1916, PN., Kangkei, Kokai
Campbell, Mr. F L & W , 1913, PN , Syenchun, Sensen.
Cardwell, Miss V.. 1923, UCC., Hamheung, Kanko.
Carlson, Rev C F & W., 1923, MEFB., Wonju, Genshu.
Cass, Miss G. L., 1916, UCC , Yongjung, Ryusei.
Cassidy, Rev J H., 1924, Wiju, Gishu
Cate, W. R , M.D & W , 1921, MES , Seoul, Keijo. (A)
Chabot, Pere J. F. G , RC., Yongsan, Ryuzan.
Chaffin, Mrs A. B , 1913, MEFB., Seoul, Keijo. (A)
Chamness, Rev. O. V. & W , 1925, PN , Taiku, Taikyu.
Chisholm, Rev D. V., 1925, RC., Yengyu, Yeiju.
Chisholm, W H , M D & W , 1923, PN , Syenchun, Sensen.
Chizallet, Pere, P., RC , Wonju, Genshu.
Church, Miss M , 1915, MEFB , Seoul, Keijo (A)
Clark, Rev. C. A , D D. & W., 1902, PN., Pyengyang, Heijo
Clark, Rev. W M , D D , 1909, PS., Seoul, Keijo.
Cleary, Rev. P. H., 1923, RC., Pyengyang, Heijo.
Clerke, Miss A L , 1910, AuP., Chinju, Shinshu.
Coen, Rev. R. C. & W., 1913, PN., Seoul, Keijo.
Coit, Rev. R T. & W., 1909, PS., Soonchun, Junten.
Colton, Miss S. A , 1911, PS., Chunju, Zenshu.
Conrow, Miss M. L , 1922, MEFB., Seoul, Keijo.
Cook, Rev. W. T. & W., 1908, PN., Hingking, Kokei.
Cooper, Rev. A. C., 1908, ECM., Pyengyang, Heijo.
Cooper, Adjutant H. & W.. 1921, SA., Haiju, Kaishu.
Cooper, Miss K , 1908, MES., Wonsan, Gensan
Covington, Miss H , 1917, PN., Syenchun, Sensen.
Craig Rev H   RC., Yen   n, Y   t
Craig M   T   P3, Ch   n, Zen n

Crane, Rev. J. C. & W, 1913, PS., Soonchun, Junten (A)
Crothers, Rev. J Y. & W, 1909, PN., Andong, Anto. (A)
Cumming, Rev. D. J, 1918, PS, Mokpo, Mokpo.
Cunningham, Rev. F W. & W., 1913, AuP., Chinju, Shinshu (A)
Curller, Pere, J. J. L., RC., Anak, Angaku.
Cutler, Miss M M., M.D., 1893, MEFB, Pyengyang, Heijo
Currie, Miss C, 1921, UCC., Hamheung, Kanko.

D

D'Avernas, Rev. Count I., RC, Seoul, Keijo.
D'Avernas, Rev K., RC., Wonsen, Gensan.
Davies, Miss E. J, M.B., 1918, AuP, Chinju, Shinshu.
Davies, Miss M. S., 1911, AuP., Fusanchin, Fusanchin. (A)
Davis, Miss M. V., 1921, PS., Soonchun, Junten.
Deal, Mr. C. H. & W, 1915, MES, Songdo, Kaijo.
Dean, Miss M. L, 1916, PN., Chungju, Seishu.
DeCamp, Rev. A F. & W., 1910, PN., Seoul, Keijo.
DeHass, Miss M, 1921, PS, Kwangju, Kwoshu
Delmarter, Miss Jean, 1920, PN, Seoul, Keijo.
Demange, Rt Rev Bishop F, RC., Taiku, Taikyu.
Deming, Rev. C. S, S T D. & W., 1905, MEFB, Seoul, Keijo (A)
Deneux, Pere, S. A. J, RC., Chemulpo, Jinsen.
Deslandes, Pere, K, RC., Fusan, Fusan.
Dicken, Miss L. H, 1920, MEFB., Pyengyang, Heijo. (A)
Dillingham, Miss G L, 1911, MEFB, Pyengyang, Heijo
Dixon, Miss E. V., 1913, AuP., Kuchang, Kyosho.
Dodson, Miss M. L, 1912, PS, Kwangju, Kwoshu. (A)
Dodson, Rev. S K, 1912, PS, Kwangju, Kwoshu (A)
Donahue, Rev Bro. J. L, 1925, RC, Sinwiju, Shingishu
Doriss, Miss A. S., 1908, PN., Pyengyang, Heijo.
Drake, Rev. H J., 1897, ECM., Chemulpo, Jinsen.
Duffy, Rev. P. J, 1924, RC, Chinnampo, Chinnampo
Dunn, Miss E., 1923, AuP., Tongyeng, Toei. '
Dupuy, Miss L, 1912, PS, Kunsan, Kunsan

E

Ebert, Rev. P. H., RC., Seoul, Keijo
Eckhardt, Rev. A., RC., Seoul, Keijo.
Edith, Helena, Sister, 1907, ECM, Seoul, Keijo.
Edwards Miss L, 1909, MES., Seoul, Keijo.
Ellis, Miss Clare, AuP, 1925, Tongyeng, Toei.
Emmer,

Engel, Rev. G., D D. & W., 1900, AuP , Pyengyang, Heijo.
English, Miss M., 1922, MEFB., Pyengyang, Heijo.
Erdman, Rev W. C & W., 1906, PN., Pyengyang, Heijo.
(A)
Eriksson, Adjutant (Miss) I., 1914, SA., Seoul, Keijo
Erwin, Miss C., 1905, MES., Chulwon, Tesuen
Esteb, Miss K M , 1915, PN., Chungju, Seishu
Eurelle, Major J & W., SA , Seoul, Keijo.
Eversole, Rev. F M. & W., 1912, PS., Chunju, Zenshu. (A)

F

Fangauer, Bro. P. B , RC., Wonsan, Gensan
Fenwick, Rev. M. C , & W , Wonsan, Gensan.
Ferrand, Pere, P C., RC., Taiku, Taikyu.
Feodosi, Rev. Father, ROC , Seoul, Keijo
Field, Miss H , 1921, PN , Taiku, Taikyu. (A)
Fisher, Mr. J E. & W., 1919, MES., Seoul, Keijo (A)
Fletcher, A. G , M D & W , 1909, PN., Taiku, Taikyu. (A)
Flotzinger, Bro. I , RC , Wonsan, Gensan.
Fontaine, Miss L , 1923, PS , Chunju, Zenshu.
Foote, Miss J. N., 1922, PN , Pyengyang, Heijo
Foote, Rev W. R , D D & W., 1898, UCC , Pyengyang, Heijo
Found, Norman, M.D. & W., 1922, MEFB., Kongju, Koshu
Francis, Miss A., 1924, AuP., Kyumasan, Kyumasan.
Fraser, Rev. E. J. C. & W., 1914, UCC., Yongjung, Ryusei
French, Rev. O. W. & W , 1925, OMS , Seoul, Keijo.
Furry, Miss A , 1921, MES , Choonchun, Shunsen. (A)

G

Gale, Rev J. S., D D & W., 1888, PN., Seoul, Keijo.
Gamble. Rev F. K. & W., 1908, MES., Seoul, Keijo
Garvin, Miss A E , 1923, PN , Seoul, Keijo.
Gay, Staff-Captain H. J. & W , 1910, SA., Hongsung, Kojo
Gaylord, Miss E F , 1924, MEFB., Pyengyang, Heijo
Genso, Mr J. F. & W., 1908, PN., Seoul, Keijo.
Gerdine, Rev J. L & W., 1902, MES , Songdo, Kaijo
Gernet, Bro , P , RC , Seoul, Keijo.
Gibson, Miss N , 1924, PN., Pyengyang, Heijo.
Giles, Rev. E , 1925, ECM., Chinchun, Chinsen.
Gilmer, Wm. P , M D & W., 1923, PS , Mokpo, Mokpo
Gombert, Pere A , RC , Ansung, Anjo.
Gombert Pere. J. M E . RC . Lonsan, Ronzan
Good
Good

Graham, Miss Agnes, 1923, MES., Songdo, Kaijo.
Graham, Miss E. I., 1907, PS, Kwangju, Kwoshu   (A)
Grahamer, Bro J, RC., Seoul, Keijo.
Gray, Miss A. L, 1921, PS, Kunsan, Kunsan
Greene, Miss W. B., 1919, PS., Kunsan, Kunsan.
Greer, Miss A. I, 1912, PS, Soonchun, Junten.
Gregg, Mr. G. A, 1906, YMCA., Seoul, Keijo.
Grierson, Rev R, M D & W, 1898, UCC., Sungjin, Joshin
   (A)
Grimes, Miss E. B, 1919, PN, Taiku, Taikyu.
Grosjean, Miss V. C., 1907, ECM, Pyengyang, Heijo.
Guinand, Pere, P. J, RC., Yongsan, Ryuzan

H

Hafner, Rev. P A, RC, Seoul, Keijo.
Haines, Rev. P. & W, 1920, OMS, Seoul, Keijo.
Hall, Miss A B, 1921, MEFB, Seoul, Keijo   (A)
Hall, Mrs. R S, M D, 1890, MEFB, Seoul, Keijo.
Hall, Sherwood, M D & W., 1926, MEFB, Haiju, Kaishu
Hamilton, Rev. F E & W, 1919, PN, Pyengyang, Heijo.
Hankins, Miss I, 1911, MES., Songdo, Kaijo
Hanson, Miss M L, PN., 1918, Andong, Anto
Hardie, Rev. R A, M D & W, 1898, MES, Seoul, Keijo. (A)
Harrison, Rev W B & W, 1896, PS, Kunsan, Kunsan.
Hartness, Miss M, 1916, PN., Seoul, Keijo.
Hartmann, Bro. G., RC, Seoul, Keijo
Harvey, Mrs A S, 1917, PN, Chairyung, Sainel
Hatch, Miss H, 1920, MEFB, Kongju, Koshu.   (A)
Hauser, Bro. B, RC, Seoul, Keijo.
Hauser, Miss B, 1923, MES, Wonsan, Gensan
Hayes, Miss L B, 1922, PN, Pyengyang, Heijo.
Haynes, Miss E. I, 1906, MEFB, Pyengyang, Heijo.   (A)
Haysmer, C A, M D. & W, SDA, Soonan, Junan.
Hedberg, Miss C, 1923, PN, Taiku, Taikyu.
Helen, Constance, Sister, 1920, ECM., Seoul, Keijo.
Helstrom, Miss H., 1909, PN, Kangkei, Kokai
Henderson, Rev. H. H. & W., 1918, PN, Taiku, Taikyu.
Henderson, Miss L E, 1923, PN, Seoul, Heijo.
Henderson, Rev. L P. & W., 1920, PN., Hingking, Kokei.
   (A)
Hess, Miss M. I, 1923, MEFB, Chemulpo, Jinsen.   (A)
Hewlett, Rev. G E, 1909, ECM, Eumsung, Injo.
Hewson, Miss G., 1920, PS, Kwangju, Kwoshu
Hiemer, Rev. C, RC, Seoul, Keijo.
Hill, Major A. W. & W., 1910, SA, Seoul, Keijo.
Hill, R   M J & W 1917 PN P   Heijo

Hill, P. L., M.D. & W., 1917, MES., Choonchun, Shunsen
Hillman, Miss M. R, 1900, MEFB, Seoul, Keijo.
Hirst, J. W., M.D. & W., 1904, PN, Seoul, Keijo.
Hitch, Rev. J. W. & W., 1907, MES, Seoul, Keijo.
Hobbs, Mr. T. & W., 1910, BFBS., Seoul, Keijo
Hocking, Miss D., 1916, AuP., Fusanchin, Fusanchin.
Hoftman, Rev. C. S. & W., 1910, PN., Syenchun, Sensen.
Hoiss, Bro. H, RC., Yongjung, Ryusei.
Holdcroft, Rev J. G., D D. & W, 1909, PN, Seoul, Keijo.
Hopper, Rev. Joseph & W., 1920, Mokpo, Mokpo.
Hopper, Miss M., 1924, PS., Mokpo, Mokpo.
Howard, Miss Clara, 1923, MES., Songdo, Kaijo.
Hoyt, H. S., M D. & W., 1923, PN., Taiku, Taikyu.
Hughes, Miss F., 1924, PS., Soonchun, Junten. (A)
Hulbert, Miss E., 1924, MEFB, Seoul, Keijo.
Hulbert, Miss J. C., 1914, MEFB., Seoul, Keijo.
Hunt, Rev. C, 1915, ECM., Seoul, Keijo. (A)
Hunt, Rev. J. A., 1925, RC., Antung, Manchuria.
Hunt, Rev W. B. & W., 1897, PN., Chairyung, Sainei

I

Ingerson, Miss V. F., 1916, PN, Syenchun, Sensen.
Irwin, Captain (Miss) A, 1926, S A, Seoul, Keijo.

J

Jackson, Miss C U., 1911, MES., Choochun, Shunsen.
Jaquett, Miss E., 1925, PN, Pyengyang, Heijo.
Jaugey, Pere, J. M. A., RC, Seoul, Keijo.
Jessie Faith, Sister, 1920, ECM., Suwon, Suigen.
Johnson, Miss O. C., 1921, PN., Chungju, Seishu. (A)
Jones, Miss K., 1922, OMS., Taiku, Taikyu.

K

Kerr, Rev. W. C. & W., 1908, PN., Seoul, Keijo. (A)
Keir, Miss E, 1921, AuP., Kyumasan, Kyumasan. (A)
Kestler, Miss E. E, 1905, PS, Chunju, Zenshu
Kinsler, Miss H C., 1923, PN., Taiku, Taikyu.
Kinsler, Miss M., 1922, PN., Seoul, Keijo.
Knox, Rev. R, D.D. & W., 1907, Kwangju, Kwoshu.
Koons, Rev. E W. & W., 1903, PN., Seoul, Keijo
Kostrup, Miss B. A., 1922, MEFB., Chemulpo, Jinsen
Kre   :r I .   . J. .. RC, ... Keijo.
Kug.,.en. R . C RC, Phuji, Heidoku.

L

Lacy, Rev. J. V. & W., 1919, MEFB., Chemulpo, Jinsen. (A)
Lacroute, Pere M., RC., Taiku, Taikyu.
Laing, Miss C. J., 1913, AuP., Chinju, Shinshu.
Laird, Miss E., 1926, MEFB., Seoul, Keijo.
Lampe, Rev. H. W., D D. & W., 1908, PN., Syenchun, Sensen.
Larribeau, Pere A. J., RC., Seoul, Keijo.
Lathrop, Miss L O., 1912, PS., Kunsan, Kunsan.
Lassen, Rev. L., OMS., Seoul, Keijo.
Lawrence, Miss E. M., 1920, PN., Seoul, Keijo. (A)
Laws, A. F., M D. & W., 1897, ECM., Chinchun, Chinsen.
Leary, Captain (Miss) N., 1921, SA., Yongdong.
Lee, Rev. A., 1921, ECM., Chungju, Seishu.
Lee, Pastor C W & W., 1922, SDA., Kyengsan, Keizan.
Lee, Pastor H. M & W., SDA., Soonan, Junan.
Lee, Miss Ruby, 1922, MES., Seoul, Keijo
Le Gendre, Pere L. G., RC., Seoul, Keijo
Le Merre, Pere L B., RC., Suwon, Suigen.
Lenz, Rev. P., RC., Kukchakga, Kyokukoka
Levie, J K., D D S. & W., 1924, PS., Kwangju, Kwoshu
Lewis, Miss M. L., 1910, PN., Seoul, Keijo. (A)
Lingquist, Adjutant (Miss) E., 1914, SA., Seoul, Keijo.
Linton, Mr. W. A & W., 1912, PS., Kunsan, Kunsan.
Livesay, Rev. J. B & W., 1923, PN., Chairyung, Sainei.
Lord, Staff-Capt. H. A & W., 1910, SA., Seoul, Keijo.
Lowder, Miss R., 1916, MES., Songdo, Kaijo.
Lucas, Pere, F., RC., Chinnampo, Chinnampo.
Lucas, Pere, L. M. B., RC., Chunju, Seishu.
Ludlow, A. I., M.D & W., 1911, PN., Seoul, Keijo.
Lund, Miss Pearl, 1922, MEFB., Haiji, Kaishu.
Lutz, Mr. D. N. & W., 1920, Pyengyang, Heijo. (A)
Lyon, Mr. Wm B. & W., 1923, PN., Taiku, Taikyu.

M

Macdonald, Rev. D. A. & W., 1912, UCC., Wonsan, Gensan.
MacEachern, Rev. J. & W., 1912, PS., Kunsan, Kunsan. (A)
Mackenzie, Rev. J. N & W., 1910, AuP., Fusanchin, Fusanchin.
Macomber, Miss T., 1923, PN., Taiku, Taikyu.
Macrae, Rev. F. J. L. & W., 1910, AuP., Kyumasan, Kyumasan.
Marker, Miss J. B., 1905, MEFB., Seoul, Keijo
Martin, S. H., M.D. & W., UCC., 1915, Yongjung, Ryusei.
Mart'

Martin, Miss M., 1921, PS., Kwangju, Kwoshu.   (A)
Mary Clare, Sister, ECM., Seoul, Keijo.
Matthews, Miss E, 1916, PS., Chunju, Zenshu.
Mauk, Miss M. V., 1921, MES, Songdo, Kaijo.
Maynor, Mrs. V. H, 1921, MES., Seoul, Keijo.
McAnlis, J. A., D.D S. & W, 1921, PN, Seoul, Keijo.
McCague, Miss J. E., 1918, AuP., Kuchang, Kyosho.
McCallie, Rev. H. D. & W, 1907, PS, Mokpo, Mokpo.
McCaul, Mr. J. G & W., 1920, UCC, Wonsan, Gensan.
McCully, Miss E. A., 1909, UCC., Wonsan, Gensan.
McCully, Miss L. H., 1900, UCC, Wonsan, Gensan.
McCune, Miss K., 1908, PN., Chanyung, Sainei.   (A)
McCutchen, Rev. L O. & W., 1902, PS., Chunju, Zenshu.
McDonald, Rev. R. T., 1922, ECM, Paikchun, Hakusen.
McEachein, Miss E., 1913, UCC, Hamheung, Kanko.
McFarland, Rev. E. F., 1904, PN., Taiku, Taikyu.
McKee, Miss A. M., 1909, PN., Chanyung, Sainei.   (A)
McKenzie, Miss R J., 1920, PN., Andong, Anto.
McLaren, Rev. C. I., M.D. & W, 1911, AuP, Seoul, Keijo.
McLellan, Miss E. A., 1913, UCC, Hoiryung, Kainei.
McMakin, Miss A., 1923, MES, Songdo, Kaijo.
McManis, S E, M D. & W., 1924, MEFB., Wonju, Gensan.
McMullin, Rev. R. M. & W., 1920, UCC., Hoiryung, Kainei
McMurphy, Miss A., 1912, PS., Mokpo, Mokpo
McMurtrie, Mr. R., 1907, PN., Pyengyang, Heijo.
McPhee, Miss I, 1911, AuP, Kyumasan, Kyumasan.
McQueen, Miss A., 1909, PS., Kwangju, Kwoshu.
McQueen, Miss F., 1924, PS., Kwangju, Kwoshu.
McQuie, Miss Ada, 1922, MEFB, Yengbyen, Neiben
McRae, Rev. D. M. & W, 1898, UCC, Hamheung, Kanko.
Meltzan, Pere, P. M. D., RC., Sosun, Zuizan.
Metzger, Bro. M., RC., Seoul, Keijo
Mialon, Pere J L., RC., Kimjei, Kintei.
Miller, Miss E., 1918, MEFB., Yengbyen, Neihen.
Miller, Rev. E. H. & W, 1901, PN, Seoul, Keijo.   (A)
Miller, Rev. F. S. & W., 1892, PN., Chungju, Seishu.
Miller, Mr. H. & W., 1899, BFBS, Seoul, Keijo
Miller, Miss Lisette, 1920, PN., Kangkei, Kokai.
Miller, Miss Louise, 1920, PS, Soonchun, Junten   (A)
Miller, Miss Lula A., 1901, MEFB., Chemulpo, Jinsen.
Miller, Miss Ruth, 1925, PS., Kwangju, Kwoshu
Moffett, Rev. S. A, D.D. & W, 1889, PN., Pyengyang.
    Heijo.
Moore, Rev. J. Z., D.D. & W., 1903, MEFB., Pyengyang
    Heijo.
Moore, Miss S. M. 1924, MES., Wonsan, Gensan.
Morley, Rev. G. H. 1921, L.M., Taiku, Taikyu.

Morris, Rev. C D. & W., 1900, MEFB, Wonju, Genshu.
Morris, Miss H P, 1921, MEFB, Pyengyang, Heijo. (A)
Morris, Rev. J. E., 1923, RC., Yongyu, Yeiju
Morse, Rev W P, 1922, ECM, S S J E, Paikchun, Hakusen.
Mousset, Pere J F. G, RC, Taiku, Taikyu
Mowry, Rev. E M. & W., 1909, PN., Pyengyang, Heijo.
Murphy, Rev. Thos. D & W, 1921, PS., Mokpo, Mokpo
Murray, Miss F J. M.D, 1921, UCC, Hamheung, Kanko.
Mutel, Rt Rev Bishop G C., RC., Seoul, Keijo
Myers, Miss M D., 1906, MES, Choonchun, Junten.

N

Napier, Miss G, 1912, AuP., Chinju, Shinshu.
Nash, Mr W L & W, 1921, YMCA, Seoul, Keijo
Newell, Rev. H. B., D D & W., 1887. (A.B C F M) Congregational, Seoul, Keijo
Newland, Rev L. T. & W, 1911, PS., Kwangju, Kwoshu
Nichols, Miss L. E., 1906, MES, Songdo, Kaijo.
Nisbet, Rev J. S., D.D. & W., 1907, PS., Mokpo, Mokpo
Noble, Mr Alden & W, 1925, MEFB, Seoul, Keijo.
Noble, Rev. W. A., Ph.D. & W., 1892, MEFB., Seoul, Keijo

O

Oberg, Pastor H. A & W, 1910, SDA, Seoul, Keijo (A)
Oldfather, Miss J, 1924, MEFB., Chemulpo, Jinsen
Oliver, Miss B, 1912, MES, Wonsan, Gensan (A)
Olsson, Staff-Captain (Miss) V., 1911, S.A., Yungdong, Yeido
Orr, Miss E B, 1924, MEFB, Seoul, Keijo.
Ostermeier, Bro. E., RC., Seoul, Keijo.
Overman, Miss B., 1917, MEFB, Haiju, Kaishu
Owens, Mr. H. T. & W., 1918, PN, Seoul, Keijo.

P

Paisley, Rev J I & W, 1921, PS, Kwangju, Kwoshu
Palethorpe, Miss E M., 1916, UC, Yongjung, Ryusei.
Parker, Mr. W P. & W, 1912, PS, Pyengyang, Heijo
Parks, Miss A. M, OMS, Seoul, Keijo. (A)
Parthenay, Pere T, RC, Chunju, Zenshu.
Peloquin, Rev. Leo, 1925, RC, Yengyu, Yeiju.
Pethpren, Rev R, 1925, RC, Yenkyu, Yeiju.
Perrin, Pere, P. F. L, RC, Tangtjin, Doshin.
Peschel, Pere P F G RC, Chingenn, Seivu

Peynet, Pere J. C., RC., Taiku, Taikyu.
Phillips, Rev. C. L. & W., 1910, PN., Pyengyang, Heijo.
Pichon, Pere L, RC, Ichun, Risen
Pieters, Rev. A. A. & W., 1895, PN., Syenchun, Sensen.
Pollard, Miss H E, 1911, PN., Taiku, Taikyu.   (A)
Polly, Pere D.J.B.M., RC., Wonju, Genshu.
Posphichal, Rev. H., 1925, RC., Yengyu, Yeiju.
Poyand, Pere G. C., RC., Seoul, Keijo.
Preston, Rev. J. F. & W., 1903, PS , Soonchun, Junten.
Proctor, Rev. S. J. & W., 1913, UCC., Sungjin, Joshin.
Pudewell, Mr. W. J. & W., SDA., Seoul, Keijo.

R

Rehrer, Miss M , 1917, PN., Kangkei, Kokai.
Reid, W. T., M D. & W., 1907, MES , Songdo, Kaijo.
Reiner, Mr. R O. & W., 1908, PN., Pyengyang, Heijo.
Reynolds, Mr. J. B. & W , 1918, PS , Kwangju, Kwoshu.
Reynolds, Miss Ella, 1925, PS , Soonchun, Junten.
Reynolds, Rev. W. D , D.D & W., 1892, PS., Pyengyang
    Heijo.
Rhodes, Rev. H A., D D. & W., 1908, PN , Seoul, Keijo
Riffel, Mr. J. E. & W., 1920, SDA., Soonan, Junan
Robb, Rev. A. F. & W., 1901, UCC., Hoiryung, Kwainei.
Robb, Miss J. B , 1903, UCC., Hamheung, Kanko.   (A)
Robbins, Miss H. P., 1902, MEFB., Pyengyang, Heijo.
Roberts, Miss F., 1917, MEFB , Pyengyang, Heijo.
Roberts, Rev. S. L., D.D. & W., 1907, PN., Pyengyang, Heijo
Rogers, J. McL., M. D & W., 1917, PS., Soonchun, Junten
Rogers, Miss M. M., 1909, UCC., Sungjin, Joshin.
Romer, Rev. A., RC., Seoul, Keijo.
Rose, Miss A., 1921, UCC., Sungjin, Joshin.
Rosenberger, Miss E. T., 1921, MEFB., Seoul, Keijo.   (A)
Ross, Rev. A. R. & W., 1907, UCC., Yongjing, Ryusei.
Ross, Rev. Cyril, Ph D. & W., 1897, PN., Syenchun, Sensen
Ross, J. B., M.D. & W., 1901, MES., Wonsan, Gensan.
Resser, Miss H., 1924, MES., Songdo, Kaijo.
Rouvelet, Pere H. P., RC., Tachun, Talden.

S

Salisbury, Staff-Capt. H. J. & W., 1913, SA., Taiku, Taikyu.
Salling, Adjutant (Miss) M , 1914, SA., Seoul, Keijo.
Samuel, Miss J., 1902, PN., Syenchun, Sensen.
Sauer, Rt Rev Bishop B., RC , Seoul, Keijo.
Sauer, M., C. A. & W , 1921, MEFB., Yengbyen, Neinen.

Scharpff, Miss H., 1911, MEFB., Yechun, Reisen. (A)
Schmid, Rev. S., RC., Wonsan, Gensan.
Schnell, Rev. S, RC., Wonsan, Gensan.
Schrodtter, Rev. S, RC., Seoul, Keijo.
Scott, Miss H. M, 1908, SDA., Soonan, Junan.
Scott, Miss S. M, 1916, AuP., Kuchang, Kyosho.
Scott, Rev. W. & W, 1914, UCC., Hamheung, Kanko.
Scruton, Miss E. J., 1922, UCC., Hoiryung, Kwainel.
Sharp, Mrs. Alice, 1900, MEFB, Kongju, Koshu.
Shaw, Rev. W. E. & W., 1921, MEFB., Pyengyang, Heijo.
Shearouse, Rev. C. F. & W., 1921, MES., Choonchun, Shunsen. (A)
Shepping, Miss E. J., 1912, PS, Kwangju, Kwoshu.
Shields, Miss E. L, 1897, PN., Seoul, Keijo.
Shipp, Mr. E. T. & W., 1925, YMCA., Syenchun, Sensen.
Skinner, Miss A. G. M., 1914, AuP., Tongyeng, Toei.
Sloan, Miss Jeanne G., 1925, PN, Pyengyang, Heijo.
Smith, Miss Bertha A., 1910, MES., Songdo, Kaijo.
Smith, Miss E, 1925, MES., Songdo, Kaijo.
Smith, Miss Olive L., 1925, MES., Choonchun, Shunsen
Smith, Captain (Miss) R, SA., Seoul, Keijo.
Smith, Ensign W. H., & W, 1926, SA., Seoul, Keijo.
Smith, Pastor W. R. & W., 1905, SDA, Seoul, Keijo (A)
Smith, R. K, M.D. & W, 1911, PN., Chairyung, Sainei.
Snavely, Miss G, 1906, MEFB, Seoul, Keijo.
Snook, Miss V. L., 1900, PN., Pyengyang, Heijo.
Snyder, Mr. L. H & W., 1907, MES, Songdo, Kaijo.
Soltau, Mr. D. L. & W., 1921, PN., Pyengyang, Heijo. (A)
Soltau, Rev. T. S. & W, 1914, PN, Chungju, Seishu.
Southwell, Ensign (Miss) L, SA., Kosan, Kosan.
Standen, Miss E. V., 1925, Seoul, Keijo.
Starkey, Miss Bertha, 1925, MEFB, Pyengyang, Heijo.
Stevens, Miss B. I., 1911, PN, Syenchun, Sensen.
Stewart, Mrs. M. S., M.D., 1911, MEFB., Seoul, Keijo
Stokes, Rev. M. B. & W., 1907, MES., Seoul, Keijo.
Stover, Miss M., 1925, MEFB., Seoul, Keijo.
Swallen, Rev. W. L, D D. & W., 1892, PN., Pyengyang, Heijo.
Swallen, Miss O. R, 1922, PN., Syenchun, Sensen.
Swicord, Rev. D. A, 1921, PS, Chunju, Zenshu.
Swinchart, Mr. M L & W., 1911, PS, Kwangju, Kwoshu.
Switzer, Miss M, 1911, PN, Taiku, Taikyu.
Sweeney, Rev J A., 1924, RC., Pihyen, Hiken.
Sylvester, Staff-Capt. C. & W., 1910, SA., Seoul, Keijo.

T

Tait,

Talmage, Rev J. V. N. & W., 1910, PS., Kwangju, Kwoshu
Taquet, Pere E. J., RC., Taiku, Taikyu.
Tate, Miss Ida, 1921, OMS., Seoul, Keijo.
Tate, Miss M. S., 1892, PS., Chunju, Zenshu.
Taylor, Rev. W., L.R C.P. & S. & W., 1913, AuP., Chinju, Shinshu.
Thomas, Miss M., 1916, UCC., Sungjin, Joshin.
Tinsley, Miss H, 1911, MES, Seoul, Keijo.
Tipton, S. F, M.D. & W., 1914, PN., Syenchun, Sensen.
Toft, Lieut.-Commissioner, J. & W., 1926, SA, Seoul, Keijo
Tourneux, Pere V. L., RC., Chilkok, Silukoku.
Trollope, Rt. Rev. Bishop M. N., D D., 1891, ECM, Seoul, Keijo. (A)
Treischman, Miss H. F., 1925, MEFB., Seoul, Keijo.
Trissel, Miss M. V., 1914, MEFB., Wonju, Genshu.
Troxel, Miss M, 1925, MEFB., Seoul, Keijo.
Trudinger, Rev. M. & W., 1923, AuP., Kyumasan, Kyumasan.
Turner, Rev. V. R. & W., 1912, MES, Wonsan, Gensan. (A)
Twilley, Lieut.-Colonel W. E. & W., 1910, SA, Seoul, Keijo

U

Underwood, Mr. H. H, Ph.D. & W., 1912, PN, Seoul, Keijo (A)
Unger, Rev. J. K. & W., 1921, PS., Soonchun, Junten
Urquhart, Pastor E J & W., 1910, SDA., Seoul, Keijo.

V

Van Buskirk, Rev. J. D., M D. & W., 1908, MEFB, Seoul, Keijo.
Van Fleet, Miss E. M, 1918, MEFB, Seoul, Keijo.
Vermorel, Pere J., RC., Taiku, Taikyu.
Vesey, Rev. F. G. & W., 1908, UCC., Sungjin, Joshin (A)
Vierhaus, Rev C., RC., Seoul, Keijo.
Villemot, Pere M. P. P, RC, Seoul, Keijo.

W

Wachs, Rev. V. H. & W., 1911, MEFB, Haiju, Kaishu.
Wagner, Miss D, 1904, MES, Wonsan, Gensan.
Walford, Miss C., 1925, ECM, Yoju, Reishu.
Walter, Miss A J, 1911, MEFB, Pyengyang, Heijo.
Wambold, Miss Katherine E 1896 PN Seoul Keijo
Wang

Ward, Field-Major Edith, 1908, SA , Seoul, Keijo
Wasson, Rev. A. W. & W., 1905, MES., Seoul, Keijo (A)
Watson, Rev R. D & W., 1910, AuP., Tongyeng, Toei.
Weber, Rev. L, RC , Yongjung, Ryusei.
Weems, Rev C. N. & W., 1909, MES., Songdo, Kaijo.
Weinberger, Rev. M , RC., Kukchakga, Kyokukoka.
Welbon, Rev A G , 1900, PN., Andong, Anto.
Welbourn, Captain B & W , 1921, SA , Songdo, Kaijo.
Welch, Rev Bishop H , D D , LL D & W., 1916, Seoul, Keijo
Whitelaw, Miss Jessie G. D , 1919, UCC , Hoiryung, Kainen.
Williams, Rev. F. E C. & W., 1906, MEFB , Kongju, Koshu
Wilson, R M , M D. & W., 1908, PS , Kwangju, Kwoshu.
Winn, Miss E. A , 1912, PS., Chunju, Zenshu.
Winn, Rev. G. H. & W , 1908, PN , Seoul, Keijo
Winn, Mrs R L., 1909, PN., Pyengyang, Heijo (A)
Winn, Rev. S D, 1912, PS., Chunju, Zenshu
Withers, Miss M , 1918, AuP., Fusanchin, Fusanchin
Woods, Rev. H. F. & W., OMS., 1918, Seoul, Keijo
Woods, Rev. H F & W , OMS., 1918, Seoul, Keijo.
Wright, Rev A. C & W , 1912, AuP., Fusanchin, Fusan-
    chin (A)

Y

Young, Rev L L & W , 1906, UCC., Hamheung, Kanko.
    (A)
Young, Miss M B , 1920, UCC., Seoul, Keijo.
Young, Miss M. E , 1920, MEFB., Seoul, Keijo.

Z

Zelles, Rev V , RC., Yongjung, Ryusei

STATISTICS FOR 1925

JAPAN AND KOREA

JAPAN CHRISTIAN STATISTICS 1925

Compiled by DAVID S. SPENCER, Kumamoto.

NOTE·—The numbering of Missions and Churches in the following lists is the same as that used in the list of Mission Boards and Churches.

References in the statistics following should be understood as under:

(1) All reported under No 22.

(2) No report received by the Statistician

(3) No report received, but figures for 1924 substituted.

(4) Reported under No. 33.

(5) Composed of such work as Hospitals for Lepers, evangelization of the same and in training social workers in some lines Evangelistic work is carried on from the Resurrection of Hope Hospital, Kumamoto in four or five distinct sections, and treatments of private patients accompanies. Reports on these lines lack definiteness.

(6) Have no Church Organization

(7) No report received for the men's side of the work: 1924 figures used.

(8) Ordained Japanese, if employed by Missions or Schools, are included under No 32.

(9) Repeated requests for statistics though accompanied with paid reply brought no answer of any form.

(10) Foreign Staff and Mission Employees reported under Nos. 25, 26, & 27.

(11) Includes work carried on by Nos 5, 12, 29, 37 & 48

(12) Corrected by figures from 1924

(13) Affilated with No. 26 in theological work at Aoyama Gakuin, Tokyo

(1·

(15) Affiliated with Meiji Gakuin, Tokyo, in educational work.
(16) Co-operate with No. 22 at the Doshisha.
(17) Co-operate in the work of the Woman's Christian College, Tokyo.
      There is therefore Co-operation in Educational work at
      Meiji Gakuin, Tokyo, between Nos. 38 & 40.
      Baiko Jo Gakko, Shimonoseki, between No. 38 & 40.
      Woman's Christian College, Tokyo, between Nos 2, 25, 26, 38, 41, & 51.
      Kwansei Gakuin, Kobe, between Nos. 25 & 27.
      Aoyama Gakuin, Tokyo, between Nos. 8, 14, 25, 26, & 51.
      Doshisha, Kyoto, between Nos. 1, 22 & 50.
(18) American Bible Society.
(19) British & Foreign Bible Society.
(20) Scripture Union Productions.
(21) Estimated production for year prior to union with No. 10.

NOTE:—No answer to request for statistics was received from Woman's Christian College, Tokyo, but there are 6 foreign teachers, 35 native teachers, and 300 pupils in attendance, in addition to other figures given under Education.

JAPAN CHRISTIAN STATISTICS—1925

1. PERSONNEL

1 Total Foreign Staff
2. Ordained men.
3. Unordained men.
4 Wives
5. Foreign Unmarried Women
6. Physicians, men.
7. Physicians, women.
8. Nurses.

9 Foreign short term workers (in medical lines)
10. Total Native Staff.
11 Ordained men.
12 Unordained men.
13. Women workers.
14. Professing Christians.

	A. FOREIGN STAFF									B. NATIVE STAFF				
	1	2	3	4	5	6	7	8	9	10	11	12	13	14
ABCFM (1). 1896														
ABF ... 1872	60	16	4	20	29	0	0	0	0	273	25	121	127	182
AEPM .. .1886	4	2	0	2	0	0	0	0	0	7	4	0	3	7
AFP ... 1885	12	0	4	4	4	0	0	0	0	7	0	5	2	7
AG (2).. ..1908														
BS 1876	4	1	1	2	0	0	0	0	0	58	0	31	6	37
CC ... .1887	10	4	0	4	2	0	0	0	0	14	12	0	2	14
CG .... .1910	3	1	0	1	1	0	0	0	0	0	0	0	0	0
CLS	6	1	1	2	2	0	0	0	0	9	0	6	3	9
11. CMA (3) . 1895	15	5	1	5	4	0	0	0	0	28	4	16	8	23

12.	CMS (4) 1869	22	5	0	5	12	0	0	62	28	16	18	34
14.	EC 1876	9	3	0	3	3	0	0	26	14	6	6	12
15.	FMA 1903	2	0	0	0	2	0	0	0	1	0	0	1
16.	HFMA 1901	16	0	5	4	7	0	0	48	6	26	16	47
17.	Ind (5) 1892	26	1	8	4	8	0	0	29	4	21	4	29
18.	JEB (6) 1900	2	0	1	1	0	0	0	2	0	2	0	2
19.	JBTS 1874	6	0	0	0	6	0	0	6	1	1	4	5
21.	JRM (3- 1892	69	17	4	18	30	0	0	135	85	39	11	135
22.	KK 1869	40	16	0	16	8	0	0	77	17	42	18	49
23.	LCA 1893	14	6	0	6	2	0	0	9	4	3	2	9
24.	LEF 1900	79	20	0	20	39	0	0	191	0	0	45	
25.	MCC (7)... 1873	92	18	4	20	50	0	0	372	0	135	231	366
26.	MEFB (8) .. 1873	70	22	4	23	21	0	0	81	0	44	37	81
27.	MES (8) 1886	13	4	0	3	6	0	0	118	8	64	46	72
28.	MP 1880												
30.	NC (9) 1908												
31.	NKK (9) (3)								337	192	145	0	337
32.	NMK (10).. 1873	216	48	12	51	105	1	0	360	133	129	98	360
33.	NSK (11).. 1859	3	0	1	1	1	0	2	306	186	62	58	306
34.	OMJ 1905	4	1	1	2	0	0	0	48	1	27	20	44
35.	OMS 1901	4	1	1	2	0	0	0	109	32	68	9	109
36.	PBW (3).... 1913	2	1	0	1	0	0	0	4	1	2	1	4

	Year														
38. PN (9) (3)	.1859	71	21	0	21	29	0	0	0	0	248	17	129	102	201
39. PS	1885	57	23	0	23	11	0	0	0	0	87	48	23	16	9
RCA	.1859	39	11	2	11	15	0	0	0	0	107	9	73	22	62
RCUS	.1879	52	15	5	20	12	0	0	0	0	214	34	114	66	186
RC (9)	.1844														
ROC (9)	.1877	14	7	0	6	1	0	0	0	0	258	127	0	131	131
SA (3)	.1895	5	3	0	1	1	0	0	0	0	8	5	3	0	0
SAM	.1891	29	10	0	10	9	0	0	0	0	88	13	75	0	70
SBC	.1886	22	5	6	11	0	0	0	0	0	20	4	15	1	16
SDA	.1896	6	3	0	3	0	0	0	0	0	37	14	4	19	23
UB	.1895	27	7	1	8	11	0	0	0	0	104	20	70	14	62
UCMS	.1883	7	2	0	2	3	0	0	0	0	17	5	1	11	12
UGC	.1890	2	1	0	1	0	0	0	0	0	2	0	2	0	2
WM (3)	.1919	5	0	0	0	5	0	0	0	0	31	4	3	24	20
WU	.1871	19	2	17	9	0	0	0	0	0	64	64	0	0	64
YMJ (3)	.1901	12	0	0	2	0	0	0	0	0	53	0	0	0	0
YMCA	.1889	20	0	0	0	0	0	0	0	0	39	0	0	0	39
YWCA (3)	.1904	2	0	1	1	0	0	0	0	0	6	6	3	3	6
WSAA	.1915	2	0	1	1	0	1	0	0	1	6	6	3	3	6
EPM	.1865	25	5	5	7	8	4	0	1	0	132	13	88	31	119
PCC	.1872	25	4	3	7	11	2	1	4	0	102	10	63	29	97
Totals		1250	311	91	364	458	7	1	1	0	4333	1145	1679	1244	3405

C. EVANGELISTIC

15. Organized Churches.
16. Self-sup. Churches.
17. Kogisho, not in 15.
18. Communicants added in Yr.
19. Total Columns 20 & 21.
20. Communicants.
21. Baptized Non-communicants.
22. Sunday Schools.
23. S.S. Teachers.
24. Teachers & Pupils
25. Contributions to Church Work.

	15	16	17	18	19	20	21	22	23	24	25
2. ABF	37	12	50	390	4438	4438	0	122	400	8691	50796
3. AEPM	4	1	1	13	392	582	10	5	5	183	4129
4. AFP	8	0	0	0	700	700	0	8	50	600	3500
8. CC	18	0	10	124	1848	651	1197	26	80	2205	6473
9. CG	3	0	1	0	120	120	0	5	20	325	0
11. CMA (3)	7	2	8	68	309	309	0	14	38	760	4120
14. EC	13	1	18	281	1752	1739	13	57	165	4047	1555
15. FMA	11	1	5	80	905	578	327	30	108	1459	12688
16. HFM (12)	5	0	1	5	20	20	0	7	1	800	400
18. JEB	5	0	0	0	170	170	0	18	31	834	2233
22. KK	160	81	79	2066	25491	25491	0	236	1455	22368	373069
23. LCA	13	1	14	156	2045	1500	545	34	80	3158	10636
24. LEF	7	0	10	88	769	701	68	14	20	541	1376
28. MP	19	2	35	741	2950	2539	411	62	189	4234	16876
31. NKK (9, 3)	230	99	81	3440	38344	38344	0	451	1480	20475	505103

32. NMK	219	67	136	2388	28789	28789	0	554	1892	42570	335161
33. NSK	241	36	0	1567	30315	20453	9862	343	700	19873	155329
OMJ	0	0	7	11	0	0	0	12	12	420	0
OMS	116	30	0	890	3123	3123	0	116	307	9253	109018
PBW (3)	3	0	1	7	110	40	70	9	5	405	1102
PN (9, 3)	42	0	98	519	4562	4562	0	124	0	7893	43871
PS	97	11	87	163	1267	1149	118	87	129	3313	12106
RCA	18	0	18	107	927	799	128	43	67	1385	5300
RCUS	57	7	27	454	4852	4571	281	97	316	7517	34772
SA (3)	110	15	0	0	0	0	0	96	157	6214	40075
SAM	9	1	10	58	596	596	0	19	41	874	0
SBC	17	6	8	238	1978	1978	0	34	200	2242	13460
SDA	10	0	5	60	480	480	0	12	34	512	25000
UB	19	2	1	134	1712	1604	108	30	134	2276	18687
UCMS	22	5	15	95	1656	1656	0	30	129	2113	15459
UGC	4	0	2	30	348	326	22	6	35	435	1500
WMI (3)	2	0	1	29	62	62	0	3	18	240	962
WU	2	2	4	25	90	65	25	44	40	1990	
YMJ (3)	6	1	15	108	343	343	0	21	36	1150	3126
EPM	111	20	0	345	13145	6402	6743	68	605	5010	50884
PCC	47	9	6	209	3075	2677	398	40	260	2322	24580
Totals	1692	412	754	14889	177683	157558	20326	2877	9239	188687	1886546

D. EDUCATIONAL WORK

26. Kindergartens.
27. No. Pupils
28. Primary Schools.
29. No. Pupils.
30. Middle Schools, Men.
31. Enrollment.
32. Middle Schools, Women.
33. Enrollment.
34. Theological Schools, Men.
35. Enrollment.
36. Bible Training Schools, Women.
37. Enrollment.

	26	27	28	29	30	31	32	33	34	35	36	37
ABCFM (1)												
ABF	21	1193	0	0	1	440	3	834	1	6	1	25
AEPM	1	44	0	0	0	0	0	0	0	0	0	0
AEP	3	150	0	0	0	0	1	200	0	0	0	0
CC (13)	6	270	0	0	0	0	0	0	0	0	0	0
CMA (2)												
CC (13)	12	642	0	0	0	0	0	0	0	0	1	45
FMA	0	0	0	0	0	0	0	0	1	15	0	0
JEB	0	0	0	0	0	0	0	0	2	26	0	0
KK	25	1257	1	53	1	940	7	2538	3	51	1	22
LCA	5	206	0	0	1	670	1	69	1	12	0	0
LEF	1	45	0	0	0	0	0	0	1	10	0	0

25.	MCC (3, 14)	32	1433	3	448	0	0	3	638	0	0	0	0
26.	MEFB	14	903	0	0	3	1922	5	2183	1	116	1	23
	MES	30	1284	1	263	1	834	1	386	1	54	1	14
	MP	6	413	1	120	1	1142	1	306	0	0	0	0
	NSK (3)	49	1871	1	50	2	1256	5	1949	2	49	2	41
	OMJ	1	39	0	0	0	0	0	0	0	0	0	0
	OMS	0	0	0	0	0	0	0	0	1	24	1	22
	PN (15, 3)	11	590	0	0	1	780	5	1563	1	20	0	0
	PS	9	395	0	0	0	0	1	323	1	35	0	0
	RCA (15)	0	0	0	0	1	864	1	627	0	0	0	25
	RCUS	10	307	0	0	1	558	1	225	1	30	1	25
	SBC	6	223	0	0	1	498	1	291	1	15	0	0
	SDA	0	0	0	0	1	20	1	15	0	0	0	0
	UB (16)												
	UCMS	6	316	1	50	1	200	1	277	1	7	1	1
	UGC	3	168	0	110	0	0	0	0	0	0	0	0
	WU	0	0	0	0	0	0	1	115	0	0	1	21
	YMJ (3)	1	50	0	0	0	0	0	0	0	0	0	0
	FPM	0	0	0	0	1	228	1	203	1	22	1	53
	PCC	2	105	0	0	1	220	1	80	1	16	1	35
	Totals	254	11904	9	1094	18	10572	41	12822	21	508	13	327

38. Colleges, Men.
39. Enrollment.
40. Colleges, Women.
41. Enrollment.
42. Indust. Schools.
43. Enrollment
44. Night Schools.
45. Enrollment.

46. Normal Training Schools.
47. Enrollment.
48. Medical Schools.
49. Enrollment.
50. Nurses Schools.
51. Enrollment.
52. Educational Fees, Yen.

	38	39	40	41	42	43	44	45	46	47	48	49	50	51	52
1. ABCFM (1)															
2. ABF	1	10	2	98	0	0	10	467	1	21	0	0	0	0	83188
3. AEPM	0	0	0	0	0	0	1	43	0	0	0	0	0	0	900
4. AEP	0	0	0	0	0	0	1	55	0	0	0	0	0	0	12000
x. CC	0	0	0	0	0	0	0	0	0	0	0	0	0	0	0
11. CMA (2).......	0	0	0	0	0	0	0	0	0	0	0	0	0	0	0
14. EC	0	0	0	0	0	0	3	285	0	0	0	0	0	0	2520
15. FMA	0	0	0	0	0	0	0	0	0	0	0	0	0	0	0
18. JEB (2)															
22. KK	4	1602	5	889	0	0	5	575	1	31	0	0	0	0	0
23...LCA	0	0	0	0	0	0	1	36	0	0	0	0	0	0	4000

24.	LEF (2)	0	0	0	0	0	0	0	0	0	0	0	0	0	0
25.	MCC (3, 7, 17)	1	768	1	0	0	0	0	0	0	32	0	0	0	0	27649
	MEFB	2	942	1	300	0	0	1	30	1	0	0	0	0	0	273218
	MES	0	0	0	92	0	0	2	1374	1	39	0	0	0	0	207216
	MP	0	693	0	0	0	0	0	0	0	0	0	0	0	0	74640
	NSK	1	0	1	135	2	178	6	301	3	55	0	1	0	23	0
	OMJ	0	0	0	0	0	0	2	57	0	0	0	0	0	0	350
	OMS (2)	0	0	0	0	0	0	0	0	0	0	0	0	0	0	
	PN (15, 3)	0	0	1	0	0	0	0	0	0	0	0	0	0	0	79005
	PS	0	0	1	72	1	67	0	0	0	0	0	0	0	0	0
	RCA (15)	1	130	0	0	0	0	0	0	0	0	0	0	0	0	94009
	RCUS	1	267	1	200	0	0	0	0	0	0	0	0	0	0	64595
	SBC	1	220	0	0	0	0	1	360	0	0	0	0	0	0	51507
	SDA (2)	0	0	0	0	0	0	0	0	0	0	0	0	0	0	
	UB (16)	0	0	0	0	0	0	0	0	0	0	0	0	0	0	6338
	UCMS	0	0	0	0	0	0	2	1496	0	0	0	0	0	0	47187
	UGC	0	0	0	0	0	0	1	200	0	0	0	0	0	0	2500
	WU	0	0	0	0	0	0	0	0	0	0	0	0	0	0	5580
	YMJ (2)	0	0	0	0	0	0	0	0	0	0	0	0	0	0	
	EPM	0	0	0	0	0	0	0	0	0	0	0	0	1	0	42746
	PCC	0	0	0	0	0	0	0	0	0	0	0	0	0	9	11000
	Totals	12	4632	12	1786	3	245	-36	5279	7	178	0	0	2	32	1040317

E. MEDICAL WORK

53. Native Physicians, Men.
54. Native Physicians, Women.
55. Trained Assistants, Men.
56. Trained Assistants, Women.
57. No. Hospitals & Sanitoriums.
58. Total No. Beds therein.
59. No. Inpatients treated.
60. No. Dispensaries.
61. No. Dispensary Treatments.
62. No. Outside Visits.
63. No. Major Operations.
64. No. Minor Operations.
65. Total No. Patients.
66. Total No. Treatments.
67. Medical Fees rec'd, Yen.

	53	54	55	56	57	58	59	60	61	62	63	64	65	66	67
2. ABF	0	3	0	2	0	0	0	2	19842	0	0	0	0	0	359
17. Ind.	3	0	0	3	7	70	70	2	2128	2198	0	50	170	300	38014
18. JEB	2	3	1	6	1	30	171	1	730	149	0	76	901	5969	5752
22. KK (2)															
25. MCC (3)	1	0	0	4	0	0	0	1	2000	250	0	0	2250	0	1255
33. NSK	2	1	1	3	1	6	33	1	1172	140	0	6	1195	1576	10027
34. OMJ	3	0	1	0	1	50	129	0	0	0	0	0	556	0	2158
44. SA (2)															
51. UCMS	0	0	0	0	0	0	0	1	3925	0	0	0	0	0	224
59. EPM	1	0	1	0	1	145	2873	0	0	0	977	373	3637	2711	15810
60. PCC	1	0	5	1	1	80	531	1	9282	150	85	383	3411	0	0
Totals	13	6	9	19	12	381	3807	9	39079	2887	1062	888	12120	10556	73629

F. PHILANTHROPIC WORK

68. No. Orphanages.
69. Total Inmates.
70. No. Leper Asylums.
71. Total Inmates.
72. Christians in Column 71.
73. No. Institutions for the Blind.
74. Total Inmates.
75. No. Rescue Homes.
76. Total Inmates.
77. No. Industrial Homes.
78. Total Inmates.

	68	69	70	71	72	73	74	75	76	77	78
EC	1	30	0	0	0	1	50	0	0	0	0
Ind.	0	0	2	382	275	0	0	0	0	0	0
KK (3)	3	280	0	0	0	5	180	4	180	6	0
LCA (3)	1	15	0	0	0	0	0	4	107	0	0
MCC	3	53	0	0	0	0	0	0	0	3	118
MEFB	0	0	0	0	0	1	21	0	0	0	0
NSK (3)	3	160	0	0	0	1	64	0	0	1	6
Totals	11	538	2	382	275	8	315	8	287	10	124

G. LITERATURE PRODUCTION

79. No. Christian Books Published this year.
80. Total No. Books Sold this year.
81. No. Portions or Tracts published this year.
82. Total No. Sold this year.
83. Amt. in Yen received for Sales this year.

	79	80	81	82	83
?. BS (18)	989662	896867	60000	0	106,027
?. BS (19)	263970	263088	195681	195779	0
16. CLS	104500	0	1000700	0	31,180
19. JBTS	43000	48137	176925	485612	55,561
19. JBTS (20)	0	0	186100	0	2,146
26. MEPB (21)	60000	55000	0	0	300,000
34. OMJ	0	1208	20000	8720	6,323
35. OMS	25000	9600	105000	19500	5,671
47. SDA	0	0	0	0	41,283
50. UB	0	0	15600	0	0
53. EPM	3000	7713	49970	17688	7,303
Totals	1489132	7281613	1809976	727299	555,495

PROTESTANT CHRISTIAN PROGRESS AS SHOWN BY STATISTICS.

Compiled by DAVID S. SPENCER.

1. Missionaries, Wives Included.
2. Church Members,—all baptized persons.
3. Ordained Japanese Ministers.
4. Unordained Japanese Helpers, men.
5. Bible
6. Organized Churches.
7. Churches Wholly Self-supporting.
8. Sunday Schools.
9. Enrollment.
10. Total Contributions to Evangelistic work, Yen.
11. No Christian Schools.
12. Enrollment.

Year	1	2	3	4	5	6	7	8	9	10	11	12
72	28	10	0	0	0	(2)1	0	0	0	0	0	0
73	87	59	0	0	0	2	0	0	0	0	0	0
82	231	5092	56	81	14	95	14	49	4060	9722	40	1277
85	284	9536	72	170	27	115	18	73	6853	32843	49	1900
88	434	23026	106	223	66	206	68	267	16820	54996	101	8405
91	583	31361	121	391	94	297	69	353	20886	59894	129	8065
94	646	35534	202	509	158	351	77	575	28142	63303	157	9377
97	676	36207	264	555	332	375	70	791	34440	87132	176	11502
00	723	37068	306	518	289	416	71	864	33039	107459	147	8069
1905	889	60862	463	562	354	529	102	857	64910	181996	165	11462

1910	958	78875	547	601	484	586	173	1659	97760	300367	217	16598
1915	1050	123595	712	1823	(1)	1056	255	2485	148833	585512	332	28190
1920	1305	164497	814	1639	469	1505	390	3042	182563	1590030	346	36297
19..	1250	177683	1145	1679	1244	1692	412	2877	188687	1886546	464	54658

(1) No. 4 Includes Bible Women for that year.

(2) The first Protestant Church was organized, Yokohama, Mar. 10, 1872, by James Ballagh, and 9 Japanese men. The first recorded baptism was by Jas. Ballagh, Nov. 1864, man named Yano, at Yokohama. This man died within a few weeks later. The second recorded baptism was by Dr. G. F. Verbeck, May 20, 1866, at Nagasaki, 2 men, of whom Wakasa was one.

GROWTH OF MISSION SCHOOLS AS SHOWN BY STATISTICS.

Compiled by David S. Spencer.

26. No. Kindergartens & Day Schools.
27. Enrollment of same.
28. Primary Schools, Night and Day.
29. Total Enrollment.
30. Middle Schools, Men.
31. Enrollment.
32. Middle Schools, Women.
33. Total Enrollment.
34. No. Theological & Bible Training Schools, Men.
35. Total Enrollment.
36. No. Bible Training Schools, Women.

Column key (37–52):

- 37. Total Enrollment.
- 38. No. Colleges, Men.
- 39. Total Enrollment.
- 40. No. Colleges, Women.
- 41. Total Enrolment.
- 42. No. Industrial Schools.
- 43. Total Enrollment.
- 44. No. Night Schools.
- 45. Total Enrollment.
- 46. No. Normal & Training Schools.
- 47. Total Enrollment.
- 50. No. Nurses' Training Schools.
- 51. Total Enrollment.
- 52. Educational Fees Received. Yen.

26	27	28	29	30	31	32	33	34	35	36	37	38	39	40	41	42	43	44	45	46	47	50	51
19	749	0	0	0	5	290	7	291	6	47	0	0	0	0	0	0	0	0	0	0	0	0	0
22	755	0	0	0	7	529	13	604	6	32	0	0	0	0	0	0	0	0	0	0	0	0	0
39	2813	0	0	0	14	2072	56	3237	12	233	0	0	0	0	0	0	0	0	0	0	0	0	0
51	5225	0	0	0	17	1399	45	2625	13	316	0	0	0	0	0	0	0	0	0	0	0	0	0
72	4664	0	0	0	15	1630	52	2886	15	247	0	0	0	0	0	0	0	0	0	0	0	0	0
96	6727	0	0	0	16	1585	47	3026	17	164	0	0	0	0	0	0	0	0	0	0	0	0	0
74	5111	0	0	0	15	1898	41	2962	14	98	0	0	0	0	0	0	0	0	0	0	0	0	0
82	4149	0	0	0	11	2125	41	4290	16	282	16	216	0	0	0	0	0	0	0	0	0	0	0
95	7319	0	0	0	14	3853	51	4786	21	401	35	231	0	0	0	0	0	0	0	0	0	0	0
130	6962	89	9874	46	9205	(1)		34	747	(1)	(1)	10	1029	0	0	5	164	0	0	5	209	0	0
192	9211	47	5932	18	7934	37	8343	29	534	(1)	(1)	10	2976	0	0	7	1222	0	0	6	90	0	0
254	11904	45	6573	18	10572	41	12322	21	505	13	327	12	4682	12	1786	3	265	36	5279	7	17	4	32

*—The reported contributions of Japanese, in 1925, as school fees are Yen 1,040,314, but this sum is known to be much short of the total received.

) The Statistician reported under same head the schools for men and women, and did the same as to enrollment But there were 21,166 under Christian instruction that year.

INDEX

大正十五年七月二十五日印刷
大正十五年八月三日發行

不許複製

定價　金參圓

編輯者　エー、オルトマンス

印刷所　東京市麹町區内幸町一丁目五番地
　　　　ジヤパン・タイムス社印刷部

印刷者　東京市麹町區内幸町一丁目五番地
　　　　北村東一

發行所　東京市京橋區銀座四丁目一番地
　　　　教文館

THE JAPAN TIMES

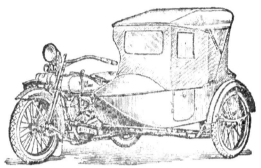